Linux Shell Scripting Cookbook

Third Edition

Over 110 incredibly effective recipes to solve real-world
problems, automate tedious tasks, and take advantage of
Linux's newest features

Clif Flynt
Sarath Lakshman
Shantanu Tushar

D1452159

BIRMINGHAM - MUMBAI

Linux Shell Scripting Cookbook

Third Edition

First published: January 2011
Second edition: May 2013
Third edition: May 2017

Production reference: 1250517

Published by Packt Publishing Ltd.
Livery Place
35 Livery Street
Birmingham
B3 2PB, UK.

ISBN 978-1-78588-198-5

www.packtpub.com

Credits

Authors
Clif Flynt
Sarath Lakshman
Shantanu Tushar

Reviewer
John Kennedy

Commissioning Editor
Kartikey Pandey

Acquisition Editor
Larissa Pinto

Content Development Editor
Radhika Atitkar

Technical Editor
Nidhisha Shetty

Copy Editor
Tom Jacob

Project Coordinator
Judie Jose

Proofreader
Safis Editing

Indexer
Tejal Daruwale Soni

Graphics
Kirk D'Penha

Production Coordinator
Nilesh Mohite

About the Authors

Clif Flynt has been programming computers since 1970, administering Linux/Unix systems since 1985, and writing since he was 9 years old.

He's active in the Tcl/Tk and Linux user communities. He speaks frequently at technical conferences and user groups.

He owns and runs Noumena Corporation, where he develops custom software and delivers training sessions. His applications have been used by organizations ranging from one man startups to the US Navy. These applications range from distributed simulation systems to tools to help fiction authors write better (Editomat). He has trained programmers on four continents.

When not working with computers, Clif plays guitar, writes fiction experiments with new technologies, and plays with his wife's cats.

He's the author of *Tcl/Tk: A Developer's Guide* by *Morgan Kauffman*, 2012, as well as several papers, and magazine articles. His poetry and fiction have been published in small journals, including *Write to Meow* by *Grey Wolfe Press*, 2015.
http://www.noucorp.com
https://www.linkedin.com/in/clifflynt/

I'd like to thank my wife for putting up with me during my writing marathons, and my editors at Packt Publishing, Sanjeet Rao, Radhika Atitkar, and Nidhisha Shetty for their support and assistance.

Sarath Lakshman is a 27 year old who was bitten by the Linux bug during his teenage years. He is a software engineer working in ZCloud engineering group at Zynga, India. He is a life hacker who loves to explore innovations. He is a GNU/Linux enthusiast and hactivist of free and open source software. He spends most of his time hacking with computers and having fun with his great friends. Sarath is well known as the developer of SLYNUX (2005)—a user friendly GNU/Linux distribution for Linux newbies. The free and open source software projects he has contributed to are PiTiVi Video editor, SLYNUX GNU/Linux distro, Swathantra Malayalam Computing, School-Admin, Istanbul, and the Pardus Project. He has authored many articles for the Linux For You magazine on various domains of FOSS technologies. He had made a contribution to several different open source projects during his multiple Google Summer of Code projects. Currently, he is exploring his passion about scalable distributed systems in his spare time. Sarath can be reached via his website http://www.sarathlakshman.com.

I would like to thank my friends and family for the great support and encouragement they have given me for all my endeavors. I would like to thank my friends Anu Mahadevan and Neenu Jacob for the tireless enthusiasm and patience to read through the chapter developments and providing comments during development. I would also like to thank Mr. Atanu Datta for helping me come up with the chapter titles. I extend my gratitude to the team at Packt Publishing who helped me in making this book happen.

Shantanu Tushar is an advanced GNU/Linux user since his college days. He works as an application developer and contributes to the software in the KDE projects. Shantanu has been fascinated by computers since he was a child, and spent most of his high school time writing C code to perform daily activities. Since he started using GNU/Linux, he has been using shell scripts to make the computer do all the hard work for him. He also takes time to visit students at various colleges to introduce them to the power of Free Software, including its various tools. Shantanu is a well-known contributor in the KDE community and works on Calligra, Gluon and the Plasma subprojects. He looks after maintaining Calligra Active – KDE's offie document viewer for tablets, Plasma Media Center, and the Gluon Player. One day, he believes, programming will be so easy that everybody will love to write programs for their computers. Shantanu can be reached by e-mail on shantanu@kde.org, shantanutushar on   Identi.ca/Twitter, or his website http://www.shantanutushar.com.

About the Reviewer

John Kennedy has been a UNIX and Linux system administrator since 1997. He started on Solaris and has worked exclusively with Linux since 2005. He started scripting in 1999, when he realized that scripts could do much of his work for him, using the "a lazy sysadmin is a great sysadmin" philosophy. John currently works for Daon, a biometric security company, as a DevOps engineer.

John started tech editing in 2001 and also worked on the first edition of this book.

John has been married to Michele since 1994 and has a daughter, Denise, and a son, Kieran.

First, I'd like to thank my family for all their support. I also thank my dogs for their patience while I worked away on this book. Thanks also to my employers, Daon, Inc, who are awesome to work for.
Finally, I would like to thank Judie Jose for her patience on those occasions when life got in the way of my editing. Your exceptional support was greatly appreciated.

www.PacktPub.com

For support files and downloads related to your book, please visit www.PacktPub.com.

Did you know that Packt offers eBook versions of every book published, with PDF and ePub files available? You can upgrade to the eBook version at www.PacktPub.com and as a print book customer, you are entitled to a discount on the eBook copy. Get in touch with us at service@packtpub.com for more details.

At www.PacktPub.com, you can also read a collection of free technical articles, sign up for a range of free newsletters and receive exclusive discounts and offers on Packt books and eBooks.

https://www.packtpub.com/mapt

Get the most in-demand software skills with Mapt. Mapt gives you full access to all Packt books and video courses, as well as industry-leading tools to help you plan your personal development and advance your career.

Why subscribe?

- Fully searchable across every book published by Packt
- Copy and paste, print, and bookmark content
- On demand and accessible via a web browser

Customer Feedback

Thanks for purchasing this Packt book. At Packt, quality is at the heart of our editorial process. To help us improve, please leave us an honest review on this book's Amazon page at https://www.amazon.com/dp/1785881981.

If you'd like to join our team of regular reviewers, you can e-mail us at customerreviews@packtpub.com. We award our regular reviewers with free eBooks and videos in exchange for their valuable feedback. Help us be relentless in improving our products!

Table of Contents

Chapter 2: Have a Good Command

Chapter 4: Texting and Driving 169

Preface

This book will show you how to get the most from your Linux computer. It describes how to perform common tasks such as finding and searching files, explains complex system administration activities such as monitoring and tuning a system, and discusses networks, security, distribution, and how to use the cloud.

Casual users will enjoy recipes for reformatting their photos, downloading videos and sound files from the Internet, and archiving their files.

Advanced users will find the recipes and explanations that solve complex issues, such as backups, revision control, and packet sniffing, useful.

Systems administrators and cluster managers will find recipes for using containers, virtual machines, and the cloud to make their job easier.

What this book covers

Chapter 1, *Shell Something Out*, explains how to use a command line, write and debug bash scripts, and use pipes and shell configuration.

Chapter 2, *Have a Good Command*, introduces common Linux commands that can be used from the command line or in bash scripts. It also explains how to read data from files; find files by name, type, or date; and compare files.

Chapter 3, *File In, File Out*, explains how to work with files, including finding and comparing files, searching for text, navigating directory hierarchy, and manipulating image and video files.

Chapter 4, *Texting and Driving*, explains how to use regular expressions with awk, sed, and grep.

Chapter 5, *Tangled Web? Not At All!*, explains web interactions without a browser! It also explains how to script to check your website for broken links and download and parse HTML data.

Chapter 6, *Repository Management*, introduces revision control with Git or Fossil. Keep track of the changes and maintain history.

Chapter 7, *The Backup Plan*, discusses traditional and modern Linux backup tools. The bigger the disk, the more you need backups.

Chapter 8, *The Old-Boy Network*, explains how to configure and debug network issues, share a network, and create a VPN.

Chapter 9, *Putting on the Monitor's Cap*, helps us know what your system is doing. It also explains how to track disk and memory usage, track logins, and examine log files.

Chapter 10, *Administration Calls*, explains how to manage tasks, send messages to users, schedule automated tasks, document your work, and use terminals effectively.

Chapter 11, *Tracing the Clues*, explains how to snoop your network to find network issues and track problems in libraries and system calls.

Chapter 12, *Tuning a Linux System*, helps us understand how to make your system perform better and use memory, disk, I/O, and CPU efficiently.

Chapter 13, *Containers, Virtual Machines, and the Cloud*, explains when and how to use containers, virtual machines, and the cloud to distribute applications and share data.

What you need for this book

The recipes in this book run on any Linux-based computer—from a Raspberry Pi to IBM Big Iron.

Who this book is for

Everyone, from novice users to experienced admins, will find useful information in this book. It introduces and explains both the basic tools and advanced concepts, as well as the tricks of the trade.

Sections

In this book, you will find several headings that appear frequently (*Getting ready, How to do it..., How it works..., There's more...,* and *See also*).

To give clear instructions on how to complete a recipe, we use these sections as follows:

Getting ready

This section tells you what to expect in the recipe, and it describes how to set up any software or any preliminary settings required for the recipe.

How to do it...

This section contains the steps required to follow the recipe.

How it works...

This section usually consists of a detailed explanation of what happened in the previous section.

There's more...

This section consists of additional information about the recipe in order to make the reader more knowledgeable about the recipe.

See also

This section provides helpful links to other useful information for the recipe.

Conventions

In this book, you will find a number of styles of text that distinguish between different kinds of information. Here are some examples of these styles, and an explanation of their meaning.

Code words in text, database table names, folder names, filenames, file extensions, path names, dummy URLs, user input, and Twitter handles are shown as follows: "Shebang is a line on which #! is prefixed to the interpreter path."

A block of code is set as follows:

```
$> env
PWD=/home/clif/ShellCookBook
HOME=/home/clif
SHELL=/bin/bash
# ... And many more lines
```

When we wish to draw your attention to a particular part of a code block, the relevant lines or items are set in bold:

```
$> env
PWD=/home/clif/ShellCookBook
HOME=/home/clif
SHELL=/bin/bash
# ... And many more lines
```

Any command-line input or output is written as follows:

```
$ chmod a+x sample.sh
```

New terms and **important words** are shown in bold. Words that you see on the screen, for example, in menus or dialog boxes, appear in the text like this: "Select **System info** from the **Administration** panel."

Warnings or important notes appear in a box like this.

Tips and tricks appear like this.

Reader feedback

Feedback from our readers is always welcome. Let us know what you think about this book—what you liked or disliked. Reader feedback is important for us as it helps us develop titles that you will really get the most out of.

To send us general feedback, simply e-mail feedback@packtpub.com, and mention the book's title in the subject of your message.

If there is a topic that you have expertise in and you are interested in either writing or contributing to a book, see our author guide at www.packtpub.com/authors.

Customer support

Now that you are the proud owner of a Packt book, we have a number of things to help you to get the most from your purchase.

Downloading the example code

You can download the example code files for this book from your account at http://www.p acktpub.com. If you purchased this book elsewhere, you can visit http://www.packtpub.c om/support and register to have the files e-mailed directly to you.

You can download the code files by following these steps:

1. Log in or register to our website using your e-mail address and password.
2. Hover the mouse pointer on the **SUPPORT** tab at the top.
3. Click on **Code Downloads & Errata**.
4. Enter the name of the book in the **Search** box.
5. Select the book for which you're looking to download the code files.
6. Choose from the drop-down menu where you purchased this book from.
7. Click on **Code Download**.

You can also download the code files by clicking on the **Code Files** button on the book's webpage at the Packt Publishing website. This page can be accessed by entering the book's name in the **Search** box. Please note that you need to be logged in to your Packt account.

Once the file is downloaded, please make sure that you unzip or extract the folder using the latest version of:

- WinRAR / 7-Zip for Windows
- Zipeg / iZip / UnRarX for Mac
- 7-Zip / PeaZip for Linux

The code bundle for the book is also hosted on GitHub at

https://github.com/PacktPublishing/Linux-Shell-Scripting-Cookbook-Third-Edition.

We also have other code bundles from our rich catalog of books and videos available at

https://github.com/PacktPublishing/. Check them out!

Downloading the color images of this book

We also provide you with a PDF file that has color images of the screenshots/diagrams used in this book. The color images will help you better understand the changes in the output. You can download this file from the following link:

`https://www.packtpub.com/sites/default/files/downloads/LinuxShellScriptingCookbookThirdEdition_ColorImages.pdf`

Errata

Although we have taken every care to ensure the accuracy of our content, mistakes do happen. If you find a mistake in one of our books—maybe a mistake in the text or the code—we would be grateful if you could report this to us. By doing so, you can save other readers from frustration and help us improve subsequent versions of this book. If you find any errata, please report them by visiting `http://www.packtpub.com/submit-errata`, selecting your book, clicking on the **Errata Submission Form** link, and entering the details of your errata. Once your errata are verified, your submission will be accepted and the errata will be uploaded to our website or added to any list of existing errata under the Errata section of that title.

To view the previously submitted errata, go to `https://www.packtpub.com/books/content/support` and enter the name of the book in the search field. The required information will appear under the **Errata** section.

Piracy

Piracy of copyrighted material on the Internet is an ongoing problem across all media. At Packt, we take the protection of our copyright and licenses very seriously. If you come across any illegal copies of our works in any form on the Internet, please provide us with the location address or website name immediately so that we can pursue a remedy.

Please contact us at `copyright@packtpub.com` with a link to the suspected pirated material.

We appreciate your help in protecting our authors and our ability to bring you valuable content.

Questions

If you have a problem with any aspect of this book, you can contact us at `questions@packtpub.com`, and we will do our best to address the problem.

1
Shell Something Out

In this chapter, we will cover the following recipes:

- Displaying output in a terminal
- Using variables and environment variables
- Function to prepend to environment variables
- Math with the shell
- Playing with file descriptors and redirection
- Arrays and associative arrays
- Visiting aliases
- Grabbing information about the terminal
- Getting and setting dates and delays
- Debugging the script
- Functions and arguments
- Sending output from one command to another
- Reading n characters without pressing the return key
- Running a command until it succeeds
- Field separators and iterators
- Comparisons and tests
- Customizing bash with configuration files

Introduction

In the beginning, computers read a program from cards or tape and generated a single report. There was no operating system, no graphics monitors, not even an interactive prompt.

By the 1960s, computers supported interactive terminals (frequently a teletype or glorified typewriter) to invoke commands.

When Bell Labs created an interactive user interface for the brand new Unix operating system, it had a unique feature. It could read and evaluate the same commands from a text file (called a shell script), as it accepted being typed on a terminal.

This facility was a huge leap forward in productivity. Instead of typing several commands to perform a set of operations, programmers could save the commands in a file and run them later with just a few keystrokes. Not only does a shell script save time, it also documents what you did.

Initially, Unix supported one interactive shell, written by Stephen Bourne, and named it the **Bourne Shell (sh)**.

In 1989, Brian Fox of the GNU Project took features from many user interfaces and created a new shell—the **Bourne Again Shell (bash)**. The bash shell understands all of the Bourne shell constructs and adds features from csh, ksh, and others.

As Linux has become the most popular implementation of Unix like operating systems, the bash shell has become the de-facto standard shell on Unix and Linux.

This book focuses on Linux and bash. Even so, most of these scripts will run on both Linux and Unix, using bash, sh, ash, dash, ksh, or other sh style shells.

This chapter will give readers an insight into the shell environment and demonstrate some basic shell features.

Displaying output in a terminal

Users interact with the shell environment via a terminal session. If you are running a GUI-based system, this will be a terminal window. If you are running with no GUI, (a production server or ssh session), you will see the shell prompt as soon as you log in.

Displaying text in the terminal is a task most scripts and utilities need to perform regularly. The shell supports several methods and different formats for displaying text.

Getting ready

Commands are typed and executed in a terminal session. When a terminal is opened, a prompt is displayed. The prompt can be configured in many ways, but frequently resembles this:

```
username@hostname$
```

Alternatively, it can also be configured as `root@hostname` # or simply as $ or #.

The $ character represents regular users and # represents the administrative user root. Root is the most privileged user in a Linux system.

 It is a bad idea to directly use the shell as the root user (administrator) to perform tasks. Typing errors have the potential to do more damage when your shell has more privileges. It is recommended that you log in as a regular user (your shell may denote this as $ in the prompt), and use tools such as `sudo` to run privileged commands. Running a command as `sudo` `<command>` `<arguments>` will run it as root.

A shell script typically begins with a shebang:

```
#!/bin/bash
```

Shebang is a line on which `#!` is prefixed to the interpreter path. `/bin/bash` is the interpreter command path for Bash. A line starting with a # symbol is treated by the bash interpreter as a comment. Only the first line of a script can have a shebang to define the interpreter to be used to evaluate the script.

A script can be executed in two ways:

1. Pass the name of the script as a command-line argument:

   ```
   bash myScript.sh
   ```

2. Set the execution permission on a script file to make it executable:

   ```
   chmod 755 myScript.sh
   ./myScript.sh.
   ```

If a script is run as a command-line argument for `bash`, the shebang is not required. The shebang facilitates running the script on its own. Executable scripts use the interpreter path that follows the shebang to interpret a script.

Scripts are made executable with the `chmod` command:

```
$ chmod a+x sample.sh
```

This command makes a script executable by all users. The script can be executed as follows:

```
$ ./sample.sh #./ represents the current directory
```

Alternatively, the script can be executed like this:

```
$ /home/path/sample.sh # Full path of the script is used
```

The kernel will read the first line and see that the shebang is `#!/bin/bash`. It will identify `/bin/bash` and execute the script as follows:

```
$ /bin/bash sample.sh
```

When an interactive shell starts, it executes a set of commands to initialize settings, such as the prompt text, colors, and so on. These commands are read from a shell script at `~/.bashrc` (or `~/.bash_profile` for login shells), located in the home directory of the user. The Bash shell maintains a history of commands run by the user in the `~/.bash_history` file.

The ~ symbol denotes your home directory, which is usually `/home/user`, where user is your username or `/root` for the root user. A login shell is created when you log in to a machine. However, terminal sessions you create while logged in to a graphical environment (such as GNOME, KDE, and so on), are not login shells. Logging in with a display manager such as GDM or KDM may not read a `.profile` or `.bash_profile` (most don't), but logging in to a remote system with ssh will read the `.profile`. The shell delimits each command or command sequence with a semicolon or a new line. Consider this example: `$ cmd1 ; cmd2`
This is equivalent to these:
`$ cmd1`
`$ cmd2`

A comment starts with # and proceeds up to the end of the line. The comment lines are most often used to describe the code, or to disable execution of a line of code during debugging:

```
# sample.sh - echoes "hello world"
echo "hello world"
```

Now let's move on to the basic recipes in this chapter.

How to do it...

The echo command is the simplest command for printing in the terminal.

By default, echo adds a newline at the end of every echo invocation:

```
$ echo "Welcome to Bash"
Welcome to Bash
```

Simply, using double-quoted text with the echo command prints the text in the terminal. Similarly, text without double quotes also gives the same output:

```
$ echo Welcome to Bash
Welcome to Bash
```

Another way to do the same task is with single quotes:

```
$ echo 'text in quotes'
```

These methods appear similar, but each has a specific purpose and side effects. Double quotes allow the shell to interpret special characters within the string. Single quotes disable this interpretation.

Consider the following command:

```
$ echo "cannot include exclamation - ! within double quotes"
```

This returns the following output:

```
bash: !: event not found error
```

If you need to print special characters such as !, you must either not use any quotes, use single quotes, or escape the special characters with a backslash (\):

```
$ echo Hello world !
```

Alternatively, use this:

```
$ echo 'Hello world !'
```

Alternatively, it can be used like this:

```
$ echo "Hello World\!" #Escape character \ prefixed.
```

When using `echo` without quotes, we cannot use a semicolon, as a semicolon is the delimiter between commands in the Bash shell:

```
echo hello; hello
```

From the preceding line, Bash takes `echo hello` as one command and the second `hello` as the second command.

Variable substitution, which is discussed in the next recipe, will not work within single quotes.

Another command for printing in the terminal is `printf`. It uses the same arguments as the C library `printf` function. Consider this example:

```
$ printf "Hello world"
```

The `printf` command takes quoted text or arguments delimited by spaces. It supports formatted strings. The format string specifies string width, left or right alignment, and so on. By default, `printf` does not append a newline. We have to specify a newline when required, as shown in the following script:

```
#!/bin/bash
#Filename: printf.sh

printf  "%-5s %-10s %-4s\n" No Name  Mark
printf  "%-5s %-10s %-4.2f\n" 1 Sarath 80.3456
printf  "%-5s %-10s %-4.2f\n" 2 James 90.9989
printf  "%-5s %-10s %-4.2f\n" 3 Jeff 77.564
```

We will receive the following formatted output:

```
No    Name       Mark
1     Sarath     80.35
2     James      91.00
3     Jeff       77.56
```

How it works...

The %s, %c, %d, and %f characters are format substitution characters, which define how the following argument will be printed. The %-5s string defines a string substitution with left alignment (– represents left alignment) and a 5 character width. If – was not specified, the string would have been aligned to the right. The width specifies the number of characters reserved for the string. For Name, the width reserved is 10. Hence, any name will reside within the 10-character width reserved for it and the rest of the line will be filled with spaces up to 10 characters total.

For floating point numbers, we can pass additional parameters to round off the decimal places.

For the Mark section, we have formatted the string as %-4.2f, where .2 specifies rounding off to two decimal places. Note that for every line of the format string, a newline (\n) is issued.

There's more...

While using flags for echo and printf, place the flags before any strings in the command, otherwise Bash will consider the flags as another string.

Escaping newline in echo

By default, echo appends a newline to the end of its output text. Disable the newline with the -n flag. The echo command accepts escape sequences in double-quoted strings as an argument. When using escape sequences, use echo as echo -e "string containing escape sequences". Consider the following example:

```
echo -e "1\t2\t3"
1   2   3
```

Printing a colored output

A script can use escape sequences to produce colored text on the terminal.

Colors for text are represented by color codes, including, reset = 0, black = 30, red = 31, green = 32, yellow = 33, blue = 34, magenta = 35, cyan = 36, and white = 37.

To print colored text, enter the following command:

```
echo -e "\e[1;31m This is red text \e[0m"
```

Here, \e[1;31m is the escape string to set the color to red and \e[0m resets the color back. Replace 31 with the required color code.

For a colored background, reset = 0, black = 40, red = 41, green = 42, yellow = 43, blue = 44, magenta = 45, cyan = 46, and white=47, are the commonly used color codes.

To print a colored background, enter the following command:

```
echo -e "\e[1;42m Green Background \e[0m"
```

These examples cover a subset of escape sequences. The documentation can be viewed with man console_codes.

Using variables and environment variables

All programming languages use variables to retain data for later use or modification. Unlike compiled languages, most scripting languages do not require a type declaration before a variable is created. The type is determined by usage. The value of a variable is accessed by preceding the variable name with a dollar sign. The shell defines several variables it uses for configuration and information like available printers, search paths, and so on. These are called **environment variables**.

Getting ready

Variables are named as a sequence of letters, numbers, and underscores with no whitespace. Common conventions are to use UPPER_CASE for environment variables and camelCase or lower_case for variables used within a script.

All applications and scripts can access the environment variables. To view all the environment variables defined in your current shell, issue the env or printenv command:

```
$> env
PWD=/home/clif/ShellCookBook
HOME=/home/clif
SHELL=/bin/bash
# ... And many more lines
```

To view the environment of other processes, use the following command:

```
cat /proc/$PID/environ
```

Set `PID` with a process ID of the process (`PID` is an integer value).

Assume an application called `gedit` is running. We obtain the process ID of `gedit` with the `pgrep` command:

```
$ pgrep gedit
12501
```

We view the environment variables associated with the process by executing the following command:

```
$ cat /proc/12501/environ
GDM_KEYBOARD_LAYOUT=usGNOME_KEYRING_PID=1560USER=slynuxHOME=/home/slynux
```

Note that the previous output has many lines stripped for convenience. The actual output contains more variables.

The `/proc/PID/environ` special file contains a list of environment variables and their values. Each variable is represented as a name=value pair, separated by a null character (`\0`). This is not easily human readable.

To make a human-friendly report, pipe the output of the `cat` command to `tr`, to substitute the `\0` character with `\n`:

```
$ cat /proc/12501/environ  | tr '\0' '\n'
```

How to do it...

Assign a value to a variable with the equal sign operator:

```
varName=value
```

The name of the variable is `varName` and `value` is the value to be assigned to it. If `value` does not contain any space character (such as space), it need not be enclosed in quotes, otherwise it must be enclosed in single or double quotes.

Note that `var = value` and `var=value` are different. It is a usual mistake to write `var = value` instead of `var=value`. An equal sign without spaces is an assignment operation, whereas using spaces creates an equality test.

Access the contents of a variable by prefixing the variable name with a dollar sign ($).

```
var="value" #Assign "value" to var
echo $var
```

You may also use it like this:

```
echo ${var}
```

This output will be displayed:

```
value
```

Variable values within double quotes can be used with printf, echo, and other shell commands:

```
#!/bin/bash
#Filename :variables.sh
fruit=apple
count=5
echo "We have $count ${fruit}(s)"
```

The output will be as follows:

```
We have 5 apple(s)
```

Because the shell uses a space to delimit words, we need to add curly braces to let the shell know that the variable name is fruit, not fruit(s).

Environment variables are inherited from the parent processes. For example, HTTP_PROXY is an environment variable that defines which proxy server to use for an Internet connection.

Usually, it is set as follows:

```
HTTP_PROXY=192.168.1.23:3128
export HTTP_PROXY
```

The export command declares one or more variables that will be inherited by child tasks. After variables are exported, any application executed from the current shell script, receives this variable. There are many standard environment variables created and used by the shell, and we can export our own variables.

For example, the PATH variable lists the folders, which the shell will search for an application. A typical PATH variable will contain the following:

```
$ echo $PATH
/home/slynux/bin:/usr/local/sbin:/usr/local/bin:/usr/sbin:/usr/bin:/sbin:/b
in:/usr/games
```

Directory paths are delimited by the : character. Usually, $PATH is defined in /etc/environment, /etc/profile or ~/.bashrc.

To add a new path to the PATH environment, use the following command:

```
export PATH="$PATH:/home/user/bin"
```

Alternatively, use these commands:

```
$ PATH="$PATH:/home/user/bin"
$ export PATH
$ echo $PATH
/home/slynux/bin:/usr/local/sbin:/usr/local/bin:/usr/sbin:/usr/bin:/sbin:/b
in:/usr/games:/home/user/bin
```

Here we have added /home/user/bin to PATH.

Some of the well-known environment variables are HOME, PWD, USER, UID, and SHELL.

When using single quotes, variables will not be expanded and will be displayed as it is. This means, $ echo '$var' will display $var.

Whereas, $ echo "$var" will display the value of the $var variable if it is defined, or nothing if it is not defined.

There's more...

The shell has many more built-in features. Here are a few more:

Finding the length of a string

Get the length of a variable's value with the following command:

```
length=${#var}
```

Consider this example:

```
$ var=12345678901234567890$
echo ${#var}
20
```

The `length` parameter is the number of characters in the string.

Identifying the current shell

To identify the shell which is currently being used, use the SHELL environment variable.

```
echo $SHELL
```

Alternatively, use this command:

```
echo $0
```

Consider this example:

```
$ echo $SHELL
/bin/bash
```

Also, by executing the `echo $0` command, we will get the same output:

```
$ echo $0
/bin/bash
```

Checking for super user

The UID environment variable holds the User ID. Use this value to check whether the current script is being run as a root user or regular user. Consider this example:

```
If [ $UID -ne 0 ]; then
  echo Non root user. Please run as root.
else
  echo Root user
fi
```

Note that `[` is actually a command and must be separated from the rest of the string with spaces. We can also write the preceding script as follows:

```
if test $UID -ne 0:1
  then
    echo Non root user. Please run as root
  else
```

```
        echo Root User
fi
```

The `UID` value for the root user is 0.

Modifying the Bash prompt string (username@hostname:~$)

When we open a terminal or run a shell, we see a prompt such as `user@hostname:/home/$`. Different GNU/Linux distributions have different prompts and different colors. The `PS1` environment variable defines the primary prompt. The default prompt is defined by a line in the `~/.bashrc` file.

- View the line used to set the `PS1` variable:

  ```
  $ cat ~/.bashrc | grep PS1
  PS1='${debian_chroot:+($debian_chroot)}\u@\h:\w\$ '
  ```

- To modify the prompt, enter the following command:

  ```
  slynux@localhost: ~$ PS1="PROMPT> " # Prompt string changed
  PROMPT> Type commands here.
  ```

- We can use colored text using the special escape sequences such as `\e[1;31` (refer to the *Displaying output in a terminal* recipe of this chapter).

Certain special characters expand to system parameters. For example, `\u` expands to username, `\h` expands to hostname, and `\w` expands to the current working directory.

Function to prepend to environment variables

Environment variables are often used to store a list of paths of where to search for executables, libraries, and so on. Examples are `$PATH` and `$LD_LIBRARY_PATH`, which will typically resemble this:

```
PATH=/usr/bin;/bin
LD_LIBRARY_PATH=/usr/lib;/lib
```

This means that whenever the shell has to execute an application (binary or script), it will first look in `/usr/bin` and then search `/bin`.

When building and installing a program from source, we often need to add custom paths for the new executable and libraries. For example, we might install `myapp` in `/opt/myapp`, with binaries in a `/opt/myapp/bin` folder and libraries in `/opt/myapp/lib`.

How to do it...

This example shows how to add new paths to the beginning of an environment variable. The first example shows how to do this with what's been covered so far, the second demonstrates creating a function to simplify modifying the variable. Functions are covered later in this chapter.

```
export PATH=/opt/myapp/bin:$PATH
export LD_LIBRARY_PATH=/opt/myapp/lib;$LD_LIBRARY_PATH
```

The `PATH` and `LD_LIBRARY_PATH` variables should now look something like this:

```
PATH=/opt/myapp/bin:/usr/bin:/bin
LD_LIBRARY_PATH=/opt/myapp/lib:/usr/lib;/lib
```

We can make adding a new path easier by defining a prepend function in the `.bashrc` file.

```
prepend() { [ -d "$2" ] && eval $1=\"$2':'\$$1\" && export $1; }
```

This can be used in the following way:

```
prepend PATH /opt/myapp/bin
prepend LD_LIBRARY_PATH /opt/myapp/lib
```

How it works...

The `prepend()` function first confirms that the directory specified by the second parameter to the function exists. If it does, the `eval` expression sets the variable, with the name in the first parameter equal to the second parameter string, followed by : (the path separator), and then the original value for the variable.

If the variable is empty when we try to prepend, there will be a trailing : at the end. To fix this, modify the function to this:

```
prepend() { [ -d "$2" ] && eval $1=\"$2\$\{$1:+':'\$$1\}\" && export $1 ; }
```

In this form of the function, we introduce a shell parameter expansion of the form:
`${parameter:+expression}`
This expands to expression if parameter is set and is not null.
With this change, we take care to try to append : and the old value if, and only if, the old value existed when trying to prepend.

Math with the shell

The Bash shell performs basic arithmetic operations using the `let`, `(( ))`, and `[]` commands. The `expr` and `bc` utilities are used to perform advanced operations.

How to do it...

1. A numeric value is assigned to a variable the same way strings are assigned. The value will be treated as a number by the methods that access it:

   ```
   #!/bin/bash
   no1=4;
   no2=5;
   ```

2. The `let` command is used to perform basic operations directly. Within a `let` command, we use variable names without the `$` prefix. Consider this example:

   ```
   let result=no1+no2
   echo $result
   ```

   Other uses of `let` command are as follows:

   - Use this for increment:

     ```
     $ let no1++
     ```

   - For decrement, use this:

     ```
     $ let no1--
     ```

- Use these for shorthands:

```
let no+=6
let no-=6
```

These are equal to `let no=no+6` and `let no=no-6`, respectively.

- Alternate methods are as follows:

The `[]` operator is used in the same way as the `let` command:

```
result=$[ no1 + no2 ]
```

Using the $ prefix inside the [] operator is legal; consider this example:

```
result=$[ $no1 + 5 ]
```

The `(( ))` operator can also be used. The prefix variable names with a $ within the `(( ))` operator:

```
result=$(( no1 + 50 ))
```

The `expr` expression can be used for basic operations:

```
result=`expr 3 + 4`
result=$(expr $no1 + 5)
```

The preceding methods do not support floating point numbers, and operate on integers only.

3. The `bc` application, the precision calculator, is an advanced utility for mathematical operations. It has a wide range of options. We can perform floating point arithmetic and use advanced functions:

```
echo "4 * 0.56" | bc
2.24
no=54;
result=`echo "$no * 1.5" | bc`
echo $result
81.0
```

The `bc` application accepts prefixes to control the operation. These are separated from each other with a semicolon.

- **Decimal places scale with bc**: In the following example, the `scale=2` parameter sets the number of decimal places to 2. Hence, the output of `bc` will contain a number with two decimal places:

  ```
  echo "scale=2;22/7" | bc
  3.14
  ```

- **Base conversion with bc**: We can convert from one base number system to another one. This code converts numbers from decimal to binary and binary to decimal:

  ```
  #!/bin/bash
  Desc: Number conversion
  no=100
  echo "obase=2;$no" | bc
  1100100
  no=1100100
  echo "obase=10;ibase=2;$no" | bc
  100
  ```

- The following examples demonstrate calculating squares and square roots:

  ```
  echo "sqrt(100)" | bc #Square root
  echo "10^10" | bc #Square
  ```

Playing with file descriptors and redirection

File descriptors are integers associated with the input and output streams. The best-known file descriptors are `stdin`, `stdout`, and `stderr`. The contents of one stream can be redirected to another. This recipe shows examples on how to manipulate and redirect with file descriptors.

Getting ready

Shell scripts frequently use standard input (`stdin`), standard output (`stdout`), and standard error (`stderr`). A script can redirect output to a file with the greater-than symbol. Text generated by a command may be normal output or an error message. By default, both normal output (`stdout`) and error messages (`stderr`) are sent to the display. The two streams can be separated by specifying a specific descriptor for each stream.

File descriptors are integers associated with an opened file or data stream. File descriptors 0, 1, and 2 are reserved, as given here:

- 0: `stdin`
- 1: `stdout`
- 2: `stderr`

How to do it...

1. Use the greater-than symbol to append text to a file:

   ```
   $ echo "This is a sample text 1" > temp.txt
   ```

   This stores the echoed text in `temp.txt`. If `temp.txt` already exists, the single greater-than sign will delete any previous contents.

2. Use double-greater-than to append text to a file:

   ```
   $ echo "This is sample text 2" >> temp.txt
   ```

3. Use `cat` to view the contents of the file:

   ```
   $ cat temp.txt
   This is sample text 1
   This is sample text 2
   ```

The next recipes demonstrate redirecting `stderr`. A message is printed to the `stderr` stream when a command generates an error message. Consider the following example:

```
$ ls +
ls: cannot access +: No such file or directory
```

Here + is an invalid argument and hence an error is returned.

Successful and unsuccessful commands
When a command exits because of an error, it returns a nonzero exit status. The command returns zero when it terminates after successful completion. The return status is available in the special variable $? (run echo $? immediately after the command execution statement to print the exit status).

The following command prints the stderr text to the screen rather than to a file (and because there is no stdout output, out.txt will be empty):

```
$ ls + > out.txt
ls: cannot access +: No such file or directory
```

In the following command, we redirect stderr to out.txt with 2> (two greater-than):

```
$ ls + 2> out.txt # works
```

You can redirect stderr to one file and stdout to another file.

```
$ cmd 2>stderr.txt 1>stdout.txt
```

It is also possible to redirect stderr and stdout to a single file by converting stderr to stdout using this preferred method:

```
$ cmd 2>&1 allOutput.txt
```

This can be done even using an alternate approach:

```
$ cmd &> output.txt
```

If you don't want to see or save any error messages, you can redirect the stderr output to /dev/null, which removes it completely. For example, consider that we have three files a1, a2, and a3. However, a1 does not have the read-write-execute permission for the user. To print the contents of all files starting with the letter a, we use the cat command. Set up the test files as follows:

```
$ echo A1 > a1
$ echo A2 > a2
$ echo A3 > a3
$ chmod 000 a1  #Deny all permissions
```

Displaying the contents of the files using wildcards (a*), will generate an error message for the a1 file because that file does not have the proper read permission:

```
$ cat a*
cat: a1: Permission denied
A2
A3
```

Here, `cat: a1: Permission denied` belongs to the `stderr` data. We can redirect the `stderr` data into a file, while sending `stdout` to the terminal.

```
$ cat a* 2> err.txt #stderr is redirected to err.txt
A2
A3

$ cat err.txt
cat: a1: Permission denied
```

Some commands generate output that we want to process and also save for future reference or other processing. The `stdout` stream is a single stream that we can redirect to a file or pipe to another program. You might think there is no way for us to have our cake and eat it too.

However, there is a way to redirect data to a file, while providing a copy of redirected data as `stdin` to the next command in a pipe. The `tee` command reads from `stdin` and redirects the input data to `stdout` and one or more files.

```
command | tee FILE1 FILE2 | otherCommand
```

In the following code, the `stdin` data is received by the `tee` command. It writes a copy of `stdout` to the `out.txt` file and sends another copy as `stdin` for the next command. The `cat -n` command puts a line number for each line received from `stdin` and writes it into `stdout`:

```
$ cat a* | tee out.txt | cat -n
cat: a1: Permission denied
     1  A2
     2  A3
```

Use cat to examine the contents of out.txt:

```
$ cat out.txt
A2
A3
```

 Observe that cat: a1: Permission denied does not appear, because it was sent to stderr. The tee command reads only from stdin.

By default, the tee command overwrites the file. Including the -a option will force it to append the new data.

```
$ cat a* | tee -a out.txt | cat -n
```

Commands with arguments follow the format: command FILE1 FILE2 ... or simply command FILE.

To send two copies of the input to stdout, use - for the filename argument:

```
$ cmd1 | cmd2 | cmd -
```

Consider this example:

```
$ echo who is this | tee -
who is this
who is this
```

Alternately, we can use /dev/stdin as the output filename to use stdin. Similarly, use /dev/stderr for standard error and /dev/stdout for standard output. These are special device files that correspond to stdin, stderr, and stdout.

How it works...

The redirection operators (> and >>) send output to a file instead of the terminal. The > and >> operators behave slightly differently. Both redirect output to a file, but the single greater-than symbol (>) empties the file and then writes to it, whereas the double greater-than symbol (>>) adds the output to the end of the existing file.

By default, the redirection operates on standard output. To explicitly take a specific file descriptor, you must prefix the descriptor number to the operator.

The > operator is equivalent to 1> and similarly it applies for >> (equivalent to 1>>).

When working with errors, the `stderr` output is dumped to the `/dev/null` file. The `./dev/null` file is a special device file where any data received by the file is discarded. The null device is often known as a **black hole**, as all the data that goes into it is lost forever.

There's more...

Commands that read input from `stdin` can receive data in multiple ways. It is possible to specify file descriptors of our own, using `cat` and pipes. Consider this example:

```
$ cat file | cmd
$ cmd1 | cmd2
```

Redirection from a file to a command

We can read data from a file as `stdin` with the less-than symbol (<):

```
$ cmd < file
```

Redirecting from a text block enclosed within a script

Text can be redirected from a script into a file. To add a warning to the top of an automatically generated file, use the following code:

```
#!/bin/bash
cat<<EOF>log.txt
This is a generated file. Do not edit. Changes will be overwritten.
EOF
```

The lines that appear between `cat <<EOF >log.txt` and the next `EOF` line will appear as the `stdin` data. The contents of `log.txt` are shown here:

```
$ cat log.txt
This is a generated file. Do not edit. Changes will be overwritten.
```

Custom file descriptors

A file descriptor is an abstract indicator for accessing a file. Each file access is associated with a special number called a file descriptor. 0, 1, and 2 are reserved descriptor numbers for `stdin`, `stdout`, and `stderr`.

The `exec` command can create new file descriptors. If you are familiar with file access in other programming languages, you may be familiar with the modes for opening files. These three modes are commonly used:

- Read mode
- Write with append mode
- Write with truncate mode

The < operator reads from the file to `stdin`. The > operator writes to a file with truncation (data is written to the target file after truncating the contents). The >> operator writes to a file by appending (data is appended to the existing file contents and the contents of the target file will not be lost). File descriptors are created with one of the three modes.

Create a file descriptor for reading a file:

```
$ exec 3<input.txt # open for reading with descriptor number 3
```

We can use it in the following way:

```
$ echo this is a test line > input.txt
$ exec 3<input.txt
```

Now you can use file descriptor 3 with commands. For example, we will use `cat<&3`:

```
$ cat<&3
this is a test line
```

If a second read is required, we cannot reuse the file descriptor 3. We must create a new file descriptor (perhaps 4) with `exec` to read from another file or re-read from the first file.

Create a file descriptor for writing (truncate mode):

```
$ exec 4>output.txt # open for writing
```

Consider this example:

```
$ exec 4>output.txt
$ echo newline >&4
$ cat output.txt
newline
```

Now create a file descriptor for writing (append mode):

```
$ exec 5>>input.txt
```

Consider the following example:

```
$ exec 5>>input.txt
$ echo appended line >&5
$ cat input.txt
newline
appended line
```

Arrays and associative arrays

Arrays allow a script to store a collection of data as separate entities using indices. Bash supports both regular arrays that use integers as the array index, and associative arrays, which use a string as the array index. Regular arrays should be used when the data is organized numerically, for example, a set of successive iterations. Associative arrays can be used when the data is organized by a string, for example, host names. In this recipe, we will see how to use both of these.

Getting ready

To use associate arrays, you must have Bash Version 4 or higher.

How to do it...

Arrays can be defined using different techniques:

1. Define an array using a list of values in a single line:

   ```
   array_var=(test1 test2 test3 test4)
   #Values will be stored in consecutive locations starting
   from index 0.
   ```

   Alternately, define an array as a set of index-value pairs:

   ```
   array_var[0]="test1"
   array_var[1]="test2"
   array_var[2]="test3"
   array_var[3]="test4"
   array_var[4]="test5"
   array_var[5]="test6"
   ```

2. Print the contents of an array at a given index using the following commands:

```
echo ${array_var[0]}
test1
index=5
echo ${array_var[$index]}
test6
```

3. Print all of the values in an array as a list, using the following commands:

```
$ echo ${array_var[*]}
test1 test2 test3 test4 test5 test6
```

Alternately, you can use the following command:

```
$ echo ${array_var[@]}
test1 test2 test3 test4 test5 test6
```

4. Print the length of an array (the number of elements in an array):

```
$ echo ${#array_var[*]}6
```

There's more...

Associative arrays have been introduced to Bash from Version 4.0. When the indices are a string (site names, user names, nonsequential numbers, and so on), an associative array is easier to work with than a numerically indexed array.

Defining associative arrays

An associative array can use any text data as an array index. A declaration statement is required to define a variable name as an associative array:

```
$ declare -A ass_array
```

After the declaration, elements are added to the associative array using either of these two methods:

- Inline index-value list method:

```
$ ass_array=([index1]=val1 [index2]=val2)
```

- Separate index-value assignments:

```
$ ass_array[index1]=val1
$ ass_array'index2]=val2
```

For example, consider the assignment of prices for fruits, using an associative array:

```
$ declare -A fruits_value
$ fruits_value=([apple]='100 dollars' [orange]='150 dollars')
```

Display the contents of an array:

```
$ echo "Apple costs ${fruits_value[apple]}"
Apple costs 100 dollars
```

Listing of array indexes

Arrays have indexes for indexing each of the elements. Ordinary and associative arrays differ in terms of index type.

Obtain the list of indexes in an array.

```
$ echo ${!array_var[*]}
```

Alternatively, we can also use the following command:

```
$ echo ${!array_var[@]}
```

In the previous `fruits_value` array example, consider the following command:

```
$ echo ${!fruits_value[*]}
orange apple
```

This will work for ordinary arrays too.

Visiting aliases

An **alias** is a shortcut to replace typing a long-command sequence. In this recipe, we will see how to create aliases using the `alias` command.

How to do it...

These are the operations you can perform on aliases:

1. Create an alias:

```
$ alias new_command='command sequence'
```

This example creates a shortcut for the `apt-get install` command:

```
$ alias install='sudo apt-get install'
```

Once the alias is defined, we can type `install` instead of `sudo apt-get install`.

2. The `alias` command is temporary: aliases exist until we close the current terminal. To make an alias available to all shells, add this statement to the `~/.bashrc` file. Commands in `~/.bashrc` are always executed when a new interactive shell process is spawned:

```
$ echo 'alias cmd="command seq"' >> ~/.bashrc
```

3. To remove an alias, remove its entry from `~/.bashrc` (if any) or use the `unalias` command. Alternatively, `alias example=` should unset the alias named `example`.

4. This example creates an alias for `rm` that will delete the original and keep a copy in a backup directory:

```
alias rm='cp $@ ~/backup && rm $@'
```

 When you create an alias, if the item being aliased already exists, it will be replaced by this newly aliased command for that user.

There's more...

When running as a privileged user, aliases can be a security breach. To avoid compromising your system, you should escape commands.

Escaping aliases

Given how easy it is to create an alias to masquerade as a native command, you should not run aliased commands as a privileged user. We can ignore any aliases currently defined, by escaping the command we want to run. Consider this example:

```
$ \command
```

The \ character escapes the command, running it without any aliased changes. When running privileged commands on an untrusted environment, it is always a good security practice to ignore aliases by prefixing the command with \. The attacker might have aliased the privileged command with his/her own custom command, to steal critical information that is provided by the user to the command.

Listing aliases

The `alias` command lists the currently defined aliases:

```
$ aliasalias lc='ls -color=auto'
alias ll='ls -l'
alias vi='vim'
```

Grabbing information about the terminal

While writing command-line shell scripts, we often need to manipulate information about the current terminal, such as the number of columns, rows, cursor positions, masked password fields, and so on. This recipe helps in collecting and manipulating terminal settings.

Getting ready

The `tput` and `stty` commands are utilities used for terminal manipulations.

How to do it...

Here are some capabilities of the `tput` command:

- Return the number of columns and rows in a terminal:

  ```
  tput cols
  tput lines
  ```

- Return the current terminal name:

  ```
  tput longname
  ```

- Move the cursor to a 100,100 position:

  ```
  tput cup 100 100
  ```

- Set the terminal background color:

  ```
  tput setb n
  ```

  The value of `n` can be a value in the range of 0 to 7

- Set the terminal foreground color:

  ```
  tput setf n
  ```

  The value of `n` can be a value in the range of 0 to 7

  Some commands including the common `color ls` may reset the foreground and background color.

- Make text bold, using this command:

  ```
  tput bold
  ```

- Perform start and end underlining:

  ```
  tput smul
  tput rmul
  ```

- To delete from the cursor to the end of the line, use the following command:

  ```
  tput ed
  ```

- A script should not display the characters while entering a password. The following example demonstrates disabling character echo with the `stty` command:

```sh
#!/bin/sh
#Filename: password.sh
echo -e "Enter password: "
# disable echo before reading password
stty -echo
read password
# re-enable echo
stty echo
echo
echo Password read.
```

The `-echo` option in the preceding command disables the output to the terminal, whereas `echo` enables output.

Getting and setting dates and delays

A time delay is used to wait a set amount of time(such as 1 second) during the program execution, or to monitor a task every few seconds (or every few months). Working with times and dates requires an understanding of how time and date are represented and manipulated. This recipe will show you how to work with dates and time delays.

Getting ready

Dates can be printed in a variety of formats. Internally, dates are stored as an integer number of seconds since 00:00:00 1970-01-01. This is called **epoch** or **Unix time**.

The system's date can be set from the command line. The next recipes demonstrate how to read and set dates.

How to do it...

It is possible to read the dates in different formats and also to set the date.

1. Read the date:

```
$ date
Thu May 20 23:09:04 IST 2010
```

2. Print the epoch time:

```
$ date +%s
1290047248
```

The date command can convert many formatted date strings into the epoch time.
This lets you use dates in multiple date formats as input. Usually, you don't need
to bother about the date string format you use if you are collecting the date from a
system log or any standard application generated output.
Convert the date string into epoch:

```
$ date --date "Wed mar 15 08:09:16 EDT 2017" +%s
1489579718
```

The `--date` option defines a date string as input. We can use any date formatting
options to print the output. The date command can be used to find the day of the
week given a date string:

```
$ date --date "Jan 20 2001" +%A
Saturday
```

The date format strings are listed in the table mentioned in the *How it works...*
section

3. Use a combination of format strings prefixed with + as an argument for the `date`
command, to print the date in the format of your choice. Consider this example:

```
$ date "+%d %B %Y"
20 May 2010
```

4. Set the date and time:

```
# date -s "Formatted date string"
# date -s "21 June 2009 11:01:22"
```

 On a system connected to a network, you'll want to use `ntpdate` to set the date and time:
`/usr/sbin/ntpdate -s time-b.nist.gov`

5. The rule for optimizing your code is to measure first. The date command can be used to time how long it takes a set of commands to execute:

```
#!/bin/bash
#Filename: time_take.sh
start=$(date +%s)
commands;
statements;
end=$(date +%s)
difference=$(( end - start))
echo Time taken to execute commands is $difference seconds.
```

 The date command's minimum resolution is one second. A better method for timing commands is the `time` command:
`time commandOrScriptName.`

How it works...

The Unix epoch is defined as the number of seconds that have elapsed since midnight proleptic **Coordinated Universal Time (UTC)** of January 1, 1970, not counting leap seconds. Epoch time is useful when you need to calculate the difference between two dates or times. Convert the two date strings to epoch and take the difference between the epoch values. This recipe calculates the number of seconds between two dates:

```
secs1=`date -d "Jan 2 1970"
secs2=`date -d "Jan 3 1970"
echo "There are `expr $secs2 - $secs1` seconds between Jan 2 and Jan 3"
There are 86400 seconds between Jan 2 and Jan 3
```

Displaying a time in seconds since midnight of January 1, 1970, is not easily read by humans. The date command supports output in human readable formats.

The following table lists the format options that the date command supports.

Date component	Format
Weekday	%a (for example, Sat) %A (for example, Saturday)
Month	%b (for example, Nov) %B (for example, November)
Day	%d (for example, 31)
Date in format (mm/dd/yy)	%D (for example, 10/18/10)
Year	%y (for example, 10) %Y (for example, 2010)
Hour	%I or %H (For example, 08)
Minute	%M (for example, 33)
Second	%S (for example, 10)
Nano second	%N (for example, 695208515)
Epoch Unix time in seconds	%s (for example, 1290049486)

There's more...

Producing time intervals is essential when writing monitoring scripts that execute in a loop. The following examples show how to generate time delays.

Producing delays in a script

The sleep command will delay a script's execution period of time given in `seconds`. The following script counts from 0 to 40 seconds using `tput` and `sleep`:

```
#!/bin/bash
#Filename: sleep.sh
echo Count:
tput sc

# Loop for 40 seconds
for count in `seq 0 40`
do
   tput rc
   tput ed
   echo -n $count
   sleep 1
done
```

In the preceding example, a variable steps through the list of numbers generated by the `seq` command. We use `tput  sc` to store the cursor position. On every loop execution, we write the new count in the terminal by restoring the cursor position using `tput  rc`, and then clearing to the end of the line with `tputs  ed`. After the line is cleared, the script echoes the new value. The sleep command causes the script to delay for 1 second between each iteration of the loop.

Debugging the script

Debugging frequently takes longer than writing code. A feature every programming language should implement is to produce trace information when something unexpected happens. Debugging information can be read to understand what caused the program to behave in an unexpected fashion. Bash provides debugging options every developer should know. This recipe shows how to use these options.

How to do it...

We can either use Bash's inbuilt debugging tools or write our scripts in such a manner that they become easy to debug; here's how:

1. Add the -x option to enable debug tracing of a shell script.

    ```
    $ bash -x script.sh
    ```

    Running the script with the -x flag will print each source line with the current status.

     You can also use sh -x script.

2. Debug only portions of the script using set -x and set +x. Consider this example:

    ```
    #!/bin/bash
    #Filename: debug.sh
    for i in {1..6};
    do
        set -x
        echo $i
        set +x
    done
    echo "Script executed"
    ```

    In the preceding script, the debug information for echo $i will only be printed, as debugging is restricted to that section using -x and +x.
    The script uses the {start..end} construct to iterate from a start to end value, instead of the seq command used in the previous example. This construct is slightly faster than invoking the seq command.

3. The aforementioned debugging methods are provided by Bash built-ins. They produce debugging information in a fixed format. In many cases, we need debugging information in our own format. We can define a _DEBUG environment variable to enable and disable debugging and generate messages in our own debugging style.

Look at the following example code:

```
#!/bin/bash
function DEBUG()
{
    [ "$_DEBUG" == "on" ] && $@ || :
}
for i in {1..10}
do
  DEBUG echo "I is $i"
done
```

Run the preceding script with debugging set to "on":

```
$ _DEBUG=on ./script.sh
```

We prefix DEBUG before every statement where debug information is to be printed. If _DEBUG=on is not passed to the script, debug information will not be printed. In Bash, the command : tells the shell to do nothing.

How it works...

The -x flag outputs every line of script as it is executed. However, we may require only some portions of the source lines to be observed. Bash uses a set builtin to enable and disable debug printing within the script:

- set -x: This displays arguments and commands upon their execution
- set +x: This disables debugging
- set -v: This displays input when they are read
- set +v: This disables printing input

There's more...

We can also use other convenient ways to debug scripts. We can make use of shebang in a trickier way to debug scripts.

Shebang hack

The shebang can be changed from `#!/bin/bash` to `#!/bin/bash -xv` to enable debugging without any additional flags (-xv flags themselves).

It can be hard to track execution flow in the default output when each line is preceded by +. Set the PS4 environment variable to `'$LINENO: '` to display actual line numbers:

```
PS4='$LINENO: '
```

The debugging output may be long. When using −x or set −x, the debugging output is sent to `stderr`. It can be redirected to a file with the following command:

```
sh -x testScript.sh 2> debugout.txt
```

Bash 4.0 and later support using a numbered stream for debugging output:

```
exec 6> /tmp/debugout.txt
BASH_XTRACEFD=6
```

Functions and arguments

Functions and aliases appear similar at a casual glance, but behave slightly differently. The big difference is that function arguments can be used anywhere within the body of the function, while an alias simply appends arguments to the end of the command.

How to do it...

A function is defined with the function command, a function name, open/close parentheses, and a function body enclosed in curly brackets:

1. A function is defined as follows:

```
function fname()
{
    statements;
}
```

   Alternatively, it can be defined as:

```
fname()
{
    statements;
}
```

   It can even be defined as follows (for simple functions):

```
fname() { statement; }
```

2. A function is invoked using its name:

```
$ fname ; # executes function
```

3. Arguments passed to functions are accessed positionally, $1 is the first argument, $2 is the second, and so on:

```
fname arg1 arg2 ; # passing args
```

   The following is the definition of the function fname. In the fname function, we have included various ways of accessing the function arguments.

```
fname()
{
    echo $1, $2; #Accessing arg1 and arg2
    echo "$@"; # Printing all arguments as list at once
    echo "$*"; # Similar to $@, but arguments taken as single
    entity
    return 0; # Return value
}
```

Arguments passed to scripts can be accessed as $0 (the name of the script):

- $1 is the first argument
- $2 is the second argument
- $n is the *n*th argument
- "$@" expands as "$1" "$2" "$3" and so on
- "$*" expands as "$1c$2c$3", where c is the first character of IFS
- "$@" is used more often than $*, since the former provides all arguments as a single string

- **Compare alias to function**
- Here's an alias to display a subset of files by piping ls output to grep. The argument is attached to the end of the command, so lsg txt is expanded to ls | grep txt:

```
$> alias lsg='ls | grep'
$> lsg txt
 file1.txt
 file2.txt
 file3.txt
```

- If we wanted to expand that to get the IP address for a device in /sbin/ifconfig, we might try the following:

```
$> alias wontWork='/sbin/ifconfig | grep'
$> wontWork eth0
eth0   Link   encap:Ethernet   HWaddr 00:11::22::33::44:55
```

- The grep command found the eth0 string, not the IP address. If we use a function instead of an alias, we can pass the argument to the ifconfig, instead of appending it to the grep:

```
$> function getIP() { /sbin/ifconfig $1 | grep 'inet ';  }
$> getIP eth0
inet addr:192.168.1.2 Bcast:192.168.255.255 Mask:255.255.0.0
```

There's more...

Let's explore more tips on Bash functions.

The recursive function

Functions in Bash also support recursion (the function can call itself). For example, `F () { echo $1; F hello; sleep 1; }`.

Fork bomb

A recursive function is a function that calls itself: recursive functions must have an exit condition, or they will spawn until the system exhausts a resource and crashes.

This function: `: () { :|:& };:` spawns processes forever and ends up in a denial-of-service attack.

The `&` character is postfixed with the function call to bring the subprocess into the background. This dangerous code forks processes forever and is called a fork bomb.

You may find it difficult to interpret the preceding code. Refer to the Wikipedia page `http://en.wikipedia.org/wiki/Fork_bomb` for more details and interpretation of the fork bomb.
Prevent this attack by restricting the maximum number of processes that can be spawned by defining the `nproc` value in `/etc/security/limits.conf`.

This line will limit all users to 100 processes:

```
hard nproc 100
```

Exporting functions

Functions can be exported, just like environment variables, using the `export` command. Exporting extends the scope of the function to subprocesses:

```
export -f fname
$> function getIP() { /sbin/ifconfig $1 | grep 'inet '; }
$> echo "getIP eth0" >test.sh
$> sh test.sh
  sh: getIP: No such file or directory
$> export -f getIP
$> sh test.sh
  inet addr: 192.168.1.2 Bcast: 192.168.255.255 Mask:255.255.0.0
```

Reading the return value (status) of a command

The return value of a command is stored in the $? variable.

```
cmd;
echo $?;
```

The return value is called **exit status**. This value can be used to determine whether a command completed successfully or unsuccessfully. If the command exits successfully, the exit status will be zero, otherwise it will be a nonzero value.

The following script reports the success/failure status of a command:

```
#!/bin/bash
#Filename: success_test.sh
# Evaluate the arguments on the command line - ie success_test.sh 'ls |
grep txt'
eval $@
if [ $? -eq 0 ];
then
    echo "$CMD executed successfully"
else
    echo "$CMD terminated unsuccessfully"
fi
```

Passing arguments to commands

Most applications accept arguments in different formats. Suppose -p and -v are the options available, and -k N is another option that takes a number. Also, the command requires a filename as argument. This application can be executed in multiple ways:

- $ command -p -v -k 1 file
- $ command -pv -k 1 file
- $ command -vpk 1 file
- $ command file -pvk 1

Within a script, the command-line arguments can be accessed by their position in the command line. The first argument will be $1, the second $2, and so on.
This script will display the first three command line arguments:

```
echo $1 $2 $3
```

It's more common to iterate through the command arguments one at a time. The `shift` command shifts eachh argument one space to the left, to let a script access each argument as `$1`. The following code displays all the command-line values:

```
$ cat showArgs.sh
for i in `seq 1 $#`
do
echo $i is $1
shift
done
$ sh showArgs.sh a b c
1 is a
2 is b
3 is c
```

Sending output from one command to another

One of the best features of the Unix shells is the ease of combining many commands to produce a report. The output of one command can appear as the input to another, which passes its output to another command, and so on. The output of this sequence can be assigned to a variable. This recipe illustrates how to combine multiple commands and how the output can be read.

Getting ready

The input is usually fed into a command through `stdin` or arguments. The output is sent to `stdout` or `stderr`. When we combine multiple commands, we usually supply input via `stdin` and generate output to `stdout`.

In this context, the commands are called **filters**. We connect each filter using pipes, sympolized by the piping operator (|), like this:

```
$ cmd1 | cmd2 | cmd3
```

Here, we combine three commands. The output of cmd1 goes to cmd2, the output of cmd2 goes to cmd3, and the final output (which comes out of cmd3) will be displayed on the monitor, or directed to a file.

How to do it...

Pipes can be used with the subshell method for combining outputs of multiple commands.

1. Let's start with combining two commands:

   ```
   $ ls | cat -n > out.txt
   ```

   The output of `ls` (the listing of the current directory) is passed to `cat -n`, which in turn prepends line numbers to the input received through `stdin`. The output is redirected to `out.txt`.

2. Assign the output of a sequence of commands to a variable:

   ```
   cmd_output=$(COMMANDS)
   ```

   This is called the **subshell method**. Consider this example:

   ```
   cmd_output=$(ls | cat -n)
   echo $cmd_output
   ```

   Another method, called **back quotes** (some people also refer to it as **back tick**) can also be used to store the command output:

   ```
   cmd_output=`COMMANDS`
   ```

   Consider this example:

   ```
   cmd_output=`ls | cat -n`
   echo $cmd_output
   ```

Back quote is different from the single-quote character. It is the character on the ~ button on the keyboard.

There's more...

There are multiple ways of grouping commands.

Spawning a separate process with subshell

Subshells are separate processes. A subshell is defined using the ( ) operators:

- The pwd command prints the path of the working directory
- The cd command changes the current directory to the given directory path:

```
$> pwd
/
$> (cd /bin; ls)
awk bash cat...
$> pwd
/
```

When commands are executed in a subshell, none of the changes occur in the current shell; changes are restricted to the subshell. For example, when the current directory in a subshell is changed using the cd command, the directory change is not reflected in the main shell environment.

Subshell quoting to preserve spacing and the newline character

Suppose we are assigning the output of a command to a variable using a subshell or the back quotes method, we must use double quotes to preserve the spacing and the newline character ($\backslash$n). Consider this example:

```
$ cat text.txt
1
2
3

$ out=$(cat text.txt)
$ echo $out
1 2 3 # Lost \n spacing in 1,2,3

$ out="$(cat text.txt)"
$ echo $out
1
2
3
```

Reading n characters without pressing the return key

The bash command `read` inputs text from the keyboard or standard input. We can use `read` to acquire input from the user interactively, but `read` is capable of more. Most input libraries in any programming language read the input from the keyboard and terminate the string when return is pressed. There are certain situations when return cannot be pressed and string termination is done based on a number of characters received (perhaps a single character). For example, in an interactive game, a ball is moved upward when + is pressed. Pressing + and then pressing *return* to acknowledge the + press is not efficient.

This recipe uses the `read` command to accomplish this task without having to press *return*.

How to do it...

You can use various options of the `read` command to obtain different results, as shown in the following steps:

1. The following statement will read *n* characters from input into the `variable_name` variable:

   ```
   read -n number_of_chars variable_name
   ```

   Consider this example:

   ```
   $ read -n 2 var
   $ echo $var
   ```

2. Read a password in the non-echoed mode:

   ```
   read -s var
   ```

3. Display a message with `read` using the following command:

   ```
   read -p "Enter input:"  var
   ```

4. Read the input after a timeout:

```
read -t timeout var
```

Consider the following example:

```
$ read -t 2 var
# Read the string that is typed within 2 seconds into
variable var.
```

5. Use a delimiter character to end the input line:

```
read -d delim_char var
```

Consider this example:

```
$ read -d ":" var
hello:#var is set to hello
```

Running a command until it succeeds

Sometimes a command can only succeed when certain conditions are met. For example, you can only download a file after the file is created. In such cases, one might want to run a command repeatedly until it succeeds.

How to do it...

Define a function in the following way:

```
repeat()
{
  while true
  do
    $@ && return
  done
}
```

Alternatively, add this to your shell's rc file for ease of use:

```
repeat() { while true; do $@ && return; done }
```

How it works...

This repeat function has an infinite `while` loop, which attempts to run the command passed as a parameter (accessed by `$@`) to the function. It returns if the command was successful, thereby exiting the loop.

There's more...

We saw a basic way to run commands until they succeed. Let's make things more efficient.

A faster approach

On most modern systems, true is implemented as a binary in `/bin`. This means that each time the aforementioned `while` loop runs, the shell has to spawn a process. To avoid this, we can use the shell built-in `:` command, which always returns an exit code 0:

```
repeat() { while :; do $@ && return; done }
```

Though not as readable, this is faster than the first approach.

Adding a delay

Let's say you are using `repeat()` to download a file from the Internet which is not available right now, but will be after some time. An example would be as follows:

```
repeat wget -c http://www.example.com/software-0.1.tar.gz
```

This script will send too much traffic to the web server at `www.example.com`, which causes problems for the server (and maybe for you, if the server blacklists your IP as an attacker). To solve this, we modify the function and add a delay, as follows:

```
repeat() { while :; do $@ && return; sleep 30; done }
```

This will cause the command to run every 30 seconds.

Field separators and iterators

The **internal field separator** (**IFS**) is an important concept in shell scripting. It is useful for manipulating text data.

An IFS is a delimiter for a special purpose. It is an environment variable that stores delimiting characters. It is the default delimiter string used by a running shell environment.

Consider the case where we need to iterate through words in a string or **comma separated values** (**CSV**). In the first case, we will use IFS=" " and in the second, IFS=", ".

Getting ready

Consider the case of CSV data:

```
data="name,gender,rollno,location"
To read each of the item in a variable, we can use IFS.
oldIFS=$IFS
IFS=, # IFS is now a ,
for item in $data;
do
    echo Item: $item
done

IFS=$oldIFS
```

This generates the following output:

```
Item: name
Item: gender
Item: rollno
Item: location
```

The default value of IFS is a white-space (newline, tab, or a space character).

When IFS is set as , the shell interprets the comma as a delimiter character, therefore, the $item variable takes substrings separated by a comma as its value during the iteration.

If IFS is not set as , then it will print the entire data as a single string.

How to do it...

Let's go through another example usage of IFS to parse the `/etc/passwd` file. In the `/etc/passwd` file, every line contains items delimited by `:`. Each line in the file corresponds to an attribute related to a user.

Consider the input: `root:x:0:0:root:/root:/bin/bash`. The last entry on each line specifies the default shell for the user.

Print users and their default shells using the IFS hack:

```
#!/bin/bash
#Desc: Illustration of IFS
line="root:x:0:0:root:/root:/bin/bash"
oldIFS=$IFS;
IFS=":"
count=0
for item in $line;
do

    [ $count -eq 0 ]   && user=$item;
    [ $count -eq 6 ]   && shell=$item;
    let count++
done;
IFS=$oldIFS
echo $user's shell is $shell;
```

The output will be as follows:

root's shell is /bin/bash

Loops are very useful in iterating through a sequence of values. Bash provides many types of loops.

- **List-oriented** for **loop**:

```
for var in list;
do
    commands; # use $var
done
```

A list can be a string or a sequence of values.

We can generate sequences with the `echo` command:

```
echo {1..50} ;# Generate a list of numbers from 1 to 50.
echo {a..z} {A..Z} ;# List of lower and upper case letters.
```

We can combine these to concatenate data.
In the following code, in each iteration, the variable i will hold a character in the a to z range:

```
for i in {a..z}; do actions; done;
```

- **Iterate through a range of numbers**:

```
for((i=0;i<10;i++))
{
    commands; # Use $i
}
```

- **Loop until a condition is met**:

The while loop continues while a condition is true, the until loop runs until a condition is true:

```
while condition
do
    commands;
done
```

For an infinite loop, use `true` as the condition:

- **Use a** `until` **loop**:

A special loop called `until` is available with Bash. This executes the loop until the given condition becomes true. Consider this example:

```
x=0;
until [ $x -eq 9 ]; # [ $x -eq 9 ] is the condition
do
    let x++; echo $x;
done
```

Comparisons and tests

Flow control in a program is handled by comparison and test statements. Bash comes with several options to perform tests. We can use `if`, `if else`, and logical operators to perform tests and comparison operators to compare data items. There is also a command called `test`, which performs tests.

How to do it...

Here are some methods used for comparisons and performing tests:

- Use an `if` condition:

```
if condition;
then
    commands;
fi
```

- Use `else if` and `else`:

```
if condition;
then
    commands;
else if condition; then
    commands;
else
    commands;
fi
```

Nesting is possible with if and else. The if conditions can be lengthy; to make them shorter we can use logical operators:

```
[ condition ] && action; # action executes if the condition is true
```

```
[ condition ] || action; # action executes if the condition is false
```

`&&` is the logical AND operation and `||` is the logical OR operation. This is a very helpful trick while writing Bash scripts.
Performing mathematical comparisons: usually, conditions are enclosed in square brackets `[]`. Note that there is a space between `[` or `]` and operands. It will show an error if no space is provided.

```
[$var -eq 0 ] or [ $var -eq 0]
```

Perform mathematical tests on variables and values, like this:

```
[ $var -eq 0 ]  # It returns true when $var equal to 0.
[ $var -ne 0 ] # It returns true when $var is not equal to 0
```

Other important operators include the following:

- -gt: Greater than
- -lt: Less than
- -ge: Greater than or equal to
- -le: Less than or equal to

The -a operator is a logical AND and the -o operator is the logical OR. Multiple test conditions can be combined:

```
[ $var1 -ne 0 -a $var2 -gt 2 ]  # using and -a
[ $var1 -ne 0 -o var2 -gt 2 ] # OR -o
```

Filesystem-related tests are as follows:

Test different filesystem-related attributes using different condition flags

- [-f $file_var]: This returns true if the given variable holds a regular file path or filename
- [-x $var]: This returns true if the given variable holds a file path or filename that is executable
- [-d $var]: This returns true if the given variable holds a directory path or directory name
- [-e $var]: This returns true if the given variable holds an existing file
- [-c $var]: This returns true if the given variable holds the path of a character device file
- [-b $var]: This returns true if the given variable holds the path of a block device file
- [-w $var]: This returns true if the given variable holds the path of a file that is writable
- [-r $var]: This returns true if the given variable holds the path of a file that is readable
- [-L $var]: This returns true if the given variable holds the path of a symlink

Consider this example:

```
fpath="/etc/passwd"
if [ -e $fpath ]; then
    echo File exists;
else
    echo Does not exist;
fi
```

String comparisons: When using string comparison, it is best to use double square brackets, since the use of single brackets can sometimes lead to errors

Note that the double square bracket is a Bash extension. If the script will be run using ash or dash (for better performance), you cannot use the double square.

Test if two strings are identical:

- `[[ $str1 = $str2 ]]`: This returns true when `str1` equals `str2`, that is, the text contents of `str1` and `str2` are the same
- `[[ $str1 == $str2 ]]`: It is an alternative method for string equality check

Test if two strings are not identical:

- `[[ $str1 != $str2 ]]`: This returns true when `str1` and `str2` mismatch

Find alphabetically larger string:
Strings are compared alphabetically by comparing the ASCII value of the characters. For example, "A" is 0x41 and "a" is 0x61. Thus "A" is less than "a", and "AAa" is less than "Aaa".

- `[[ $str1 > $str2 ]]`: This returns true when `str1` is alphabetically greater than `str2`
- `[[ $str1 < $str2 ]]`: This returns true when `str1` is alphabetically lesser than `str2`

A space is required after and before =; if it is not provided, it is not a comparison, but it becomes an assignment statement.

Test for an empty string:

- `[[ -z $str1 ]]`: This returns true if `str1` holds an empty string
- `[[ -n $str1 ]]`: This returns true if `str1` holds a nonempty string

It is easier to combine multiple conditions using logical operators such as `&&` and `||`, as in the following code:

```
if [[ -n $str1 ]] && [[ -z $str2 ]] ;
    then
        commands;
    fi
```

Consider this example:

```
str1="Not empty "
str2=""
if [[ -n $str1 ]] && [[ -z $str2 ]];
then
    echo str1 is nonempty and str2 is empty string.
fi
```

This will be the output:

str1 is nonempty and str2 is empty string.

The test command can be used for performing condition checks. This reduces the number of braces used and can make your code more readable. The same test conditions enclosed within `[]` can be used with the test command.

 Note that test is an external program which must be forked, while `[` is an internal function in Bash and thus more efficient. The test program is compatible with Bourne shell, ash, dash, and others.

Consider this example:

```
if  [ $var -eq 0 ]; then echo "True"; fi
can be written as
if  test $var -eq 0 ; then echo "True"; fi
```

Customizing bash with configuration files

Most commands you type on the command line can be placed in a special file, to be evaluated when you log in or start a new bash session. It's common to customize your shell by putting function definitions, aliases, and environment variable settings in one of these files.

Common commands to put into a configuration file include the following:

```
# Define my colors for ls
LS_COLORS='no=00:di=01;46:ln=00;36:pi=40;33:so=00;35:bd=40;33;01'
export LS_COLORS
# My primary prompt
PS1='Hello $USER'; export PS1
# Applications I install outside the normal distro paths
PATH=$PATH:/opt/MySpecialApplication/bin; export PATH
# Shorthand for commands I use frequently
function lc () {/bin/ls -C $* ; }
```

What customization file should I use?

Linux and Unix have several files that might hold customization scripts. These configuration files are divided into three camps—those sourced on login, those evaluated when an interactive shell is invoked, and files evaluated whenever a shell is invoked to process a script file.

How to do it...

These files are evaluated when a user logs into a shell:

```
/etc/profile, $HOME/.profile, $HOME/.bash_login, $HOME/.bash_profile /
```

Note that /etc/profile, $HOME/.profile and $HOME/.bash_profile may not be sourced if you log in via a graphical login manager. That's because the graphical window manager doesn't start a shell. When you open a terminal window, a shell is created, but it's not a login shell.

If a .bash_profile or .bash_login file is present, a .profile file will not be read.

These files will be read by an interactive shell such as a X11 terminal session or using `ssh` to run a single command like: `ssh 192.168.1.1 ls /tmp`.

```
/etc/bash.bashrc $HOME/.bashrc
```

Run a shell script like this:

```
$> cat myscript.sh
#!/bin/bash
echo "Running"
```

None of these files will be sourced unless you have defined the BASH_ENV environment variable:

```
$> export BASH_ENV=~/.bashrc
$> ./myscript.sh
```

Use `ssh` to run a single command, as with the following:

```
ssh 192.168.1.100 ls /tmp
```

This will start a bash shell which will evaluate `/etc/bash.bashrc` and `$HOME/.bashrc`, but not `/etc/profile` or `.profile`.

Invoke a ssh login session, like this:

```
ssh 192.168.1.100
```

This creates a new login bash shell, which will evaluate the following:

```
/etc/profile
/etc/bash.bashrc
$HOME/.profile or .bashrc_profile
```

 DANGER: Other shells, such as the traditional Bourne shell, ash, dash, and ksh, also read this file. Linear arrays (lists) and associative arrays, are not supported in all shells. Avoid using these in `/etc/profile` or `$HOME/.profile`.

Use these files to define non-exported items such as aliases desired by all users. Consider this example:

```
alias l "ls -l"
/etc/bash.bashrc /etc/bashrc
```

Use these files to hold personal settings. They are useful for setting paths that must be inherited by other bash instances. They might include lines like these:

```
CLASSPATH=$CLASSPATH:$HOME/MyJavaProject; export CLASSPATH
$HOME/.bash_login $HOME/.bash_profile $HOME/.profile
```

If .bash_login or .bash_profile are present, .profile will not be read. A .profile file may be read by other shells.

Use these files to hold your personal values that need to be defined whenever a new shell is created. Define aliases and functions here if you want them available in an X11 terminal session:

$HOME/.bashrc, /etc/bash.bashrc

Exported variables and functions are propagated to subordinate shells, but aliases are not. You must define BASH_ENV to be the .bashrc or .profile, where aliases are defined in order to use them in a shell script.

This file is evaluated when a user logs out of a session:

$HOME/.bash_logout

For example, if the user logs in remotely they should clear the screen when they log out.

```
$> cat ~/.bash_logout
# Clear the screen after a remote login/logout.
clear
```

2
Have a Good Command

In this chapter, we will cover the following recipes:

- Concatenating with `cat`
- Recording and playing back terminal sessions
- Finding files and file listing
- Playing with `xargs`
- Translating with `tr`
- Checksum and verification
- Cryptographic tools and hashes
- Sorting unique and duplicate lines
- Temporary file naming and random numbers
- Splitting files and data
- Slicing filenames based on extensions
- Renaming and moving files in bulk
- Spell–checking and dictionary manipulation
- Automating interactive input
- Making commands quicker by running parallel processes
- Examining a directory, files and subdirectories in it

Introduction

Unix-like systems have the best command-line tools. Each command performs a simple function to make our work easier. These simple functions can be combined with other commands to solve complex problems. Combining simple commands is an art; you will get better at it as you practice and gain experience. This chapter introduces some of the most interesting and useful commands, including `grep`, `awk`, `sed`, and `find`.

Concatenating with cat

The `cat` command displays or concatenates the contents of a file, but `cat` is capable of more. For example, `cat` can combine standard input data with data from a file. One way of combining the `stdin` data with file data is to redirect `stdin` to a file and then append two files. The `cat` command can do this in a single invocation. The next recipes show basic and advanced usages of `cat`.

How to do it...

The `cat` command is a simple and frequently used command and it stands for **conCATenate**.

The general syntax of `cat` for reading contents is as follows:

```
$ cat file1 file2 file3 ...
```

This command concatenates data from the files specified as command-line arguments and sends that data to `stdout`.

- To print contents of a single file, execute the following command:

```
$ cat file.txt
This is a line inside file.txt
This is the second line inside file.txt
```

- To print contents of more than one file, execute the following command:

```
$ cat one.txt two.txt
This line is from one.txt
This line is from two.txt
```

The `cat` command not only reads from files and concatenates the data but also reads from the standard input.

The pipe operator redirects data to the cat command's standard input as follows:

```
OUTPUT_FROM_SOME COMMANDS | cat
```

The `cat` command can also concatenate content from files with input from a terminal.

Combine `stdin` and data from another file, like this:

```
$ echo 'Text through stdin' | cat - file.txt
```

In this example, – acts as the filename for the `stdin` text.

There's more...

The `cat` command has many other options for viewing files. You can view the complete list by typing `man cat` in a terminal session.

Getting rid of extra blank lines

Some text files contain two or more blank lines together. If you need to remove the extra blank lines, use the following syntax:

```
$ cat -s file
```

Consider the following example:

```
$ cat multi_blanks.txt
line 1


line 2


line 3
```

```
line 4

$ cat -s multi_blanks.txt # Squeeze adjacent blank lines
line 1
line 2
line 3

line 4
```

We can remove all blank lines with t r, as discussed in the *Translating with tr* recipe in this chapter.

Displaying tabs as ^I

It is hard to distinguish tabs and repeated space characters. Languages such as Python may treat tabs and spaces differently. Mixtures of tabs and spaces may look similar in an editor, but appear as different indentations to the interpreter. It is difficult to identify the difference between tabs and spaces when viewing a file in a text editor. cat can also identify tabs. This helps you to debug indentation errors.

The cat command's -T option displays tab characters as ^I:

```
$ cat file.py
def function():
    var = 5
        next = 6
    third = 7

$ cat -T file.py
def function():
^Ivar = 5
^I^Inext = 6
^Ithird = 7^I
```

Line numbers

The cat command's -n flag prefixes a line number to each line. Consider this example:

```
$ cat lines.txt
line
line
line

$ cat -n lines.txt
     1 line
```

```
2 line
3 line
```

The cat command never changes a file. It sends output to stdout after modifying the input according to the options. Do not attempt to use redirection to overwrite your input file. The shell creates the new output file before it opens the input file. The cat command will not let you use the same file as input and redirected output. Trying to trick cat with a pipe and redirecting the output will empty the input file.

```
$> echo "This will vanish" > myfile
$> cat -n myfile >myfile
cat: myfile: input file is output file
$> cat myfile | cat -n >myfile
$> ls -l myfile
-rw-rw-rw-. 1 user user 0 Aug 24 00:14 myfile   ;# myfile has 0
bytes
```

The -n option generates line numbers for all lines, including blank lines. If you want to skip numbering blank lines, use the -b option.

Recording and playing back terminal sessions

Recording a screen session as a video is useful, but a video is an overkill for debugging terminal sessions or providing a shell tutorial.

The shell provides another option. The script command records your keystrokes and the timing of keystrokes as you type, and saves your input and the resulting output in a pair of files. The scriptreplay command will replay the session.

Getting ready

The `script` and `scriptreplay` commands are available in most GNU/Linux distributions. You can create tutorials of command-line hacks and tricks by recording the terminal sessions. You can also share the recorded files for others to playback and see how to perform a particular task with the command line. You can even invoke other interpreters and record the keystrokes sent to that interpreter. You cannot record vi, emacs, or other applications that map characters to particular locations on the screen.

How to do it...

Start recording the terminal session with the following command:

```
$ script -t 2> timing.log -a output.session
```

A full example looks like this:

```
$ script -t 2> timing.log -a output.session

# This is a demonstration of tclsh
$ tclsh
% puts [expr 2 + 2]
4
% exit
$ exit
```

 Note that this recipe will not work with shells that do not support redirecting only `stderr` to a file, such as the `csh` shell.

The `script` command accepts a filename as an argument. This file will hold the keystrokes and the command results. When you use the `-t` option, the script command sends timing data to `stdout`. The timing data can be redirected to a file (`timing.log`), which records the timing info for each keystroke and output. The previous example used `2>` to redirect `stderr` to `timing.log`.

Using the two files, `timing.log` and `output.session`, we can replay the sequence of command execution as follows:

```
$ scriptreplay timing.log output.session
# Plays the sequence of commands and output
```

How it works...

We often record desktop videos to prepare tutorials. However, videos require a considerable amount of storage, while a terminal script file is just a text file, usually only in the order of kilobytes.

You can share the `timing.log` and `output.session` files to anyone who wants to replay a terminal session in their terminal.

Finding files and file listing

The `find` command is one of the great utilities in the Unix/Linux command-line toolbox. It is useful both at the command line and in shell scripts. Like `cat` and `ls`, `find` has many features, and most people do not use it to its fullest. This recipe deals with some common ways to utilize `find` to locate files.

Getting ready

The `find` command uses the following strategy: `find` descends through a hierarchy of files, matches files that meet the specified criteria, and performs some actions. The default action is to print the names of files and folders, which can be specified with the `-print` option.

How to do it...

To list all the files and folders descending from a given directory, use this syntax:

```
$ find base_path
```

The `base_path` can be any location from which `find` should start descending (for example, `/home/slynux/`).

Here's an example of this command:

```
$ find . -print
.history
Downloads
Downloads/tcl.fossil
Downloads/chapter2.doc
...
```

The . specifies the current directory and .. specifies the parent directory. This convention is followed throughout the Unix filesystem.

The print option separates each file or folder name with a \n (newline). The -print0 option separates each name with a null character '\0'. The main use for -print0 is to pass filenames containing newlines or whitespace characters to the xargs command. The xargs command will be discussed in more detail later:

```
$> echo "test" > "file name"
$> find . -type f -print | xargs ls -l
ls: cannot access ./file: No such file or directory
ls: cannot access name: No such file or directory
$> find . -type f -print0 | xargs -0 ls -l
-rw-rw-rw-. 1 user group 5  Aug 24 15:00 ./file name
```

There's more...

The previous examples demonstrated using find to list all the files and folders in a filesystem hierarchy. The find command can select files based on glob or regular expression rules, depth in the filesystem tree, date, type of file, and more.

Search based on name or regular expression match

The -name argument specifies a selection pattern for the name. The -name argument accepts both glob-style wildcards and regular expressions. In the following example, '*.txt' matches all the file or folder names ending with .txt and prints them.

> Note the single quotes around *.txt. The shell will expand glob wildcards with no quotes or using double-quotes ("). The single quotes prevent the shell from expanding the *.txt and passes that string to the find command.

```
$ find /home/slynux -name '*.txt' -print
```

The `find` command has an option `-iname` (ignore case), which is similar to `-name`, but it matches filenames regardless of case.

Consider the following example:

```
$ ls
example.txt  EXAMPLE.txt  file.txt
$ find . -iname "example*" -print
./example.txt
./EXAMPLE.txt
```

The `find` command supports logical operations with the selection options. The `-a` and `-and` options perform a logical **AND**, while the `-o` and `-or` option perform a logical **OR**.

```
$ ls
new.txt  some.jpg  text.pdf    stuff.png
$ find . \( -name '*.txt' -o -name '*.pdf' \) -print
./text.pdf
./new.txt
```

The previous command will print all the `.txt` and `.pdf` files, since the `find` command matches both `.txt` and `.pdf` files. `\(` and `\)` are used to treat `-name "*.txt" -o -name "*.pdf"` as a single unit.

The following command demonstrates using the `-and` operator to select only the file that starts with an s and has an e in the name somewhere.

```
$ find . \( -name '*e*' -and -name 's*' \)
./some.jpg
```

The `-path` argument restricts the match to files that match a path as well as a name. For example, `$ find /home/users -path '*/slynux/*' -name '*.txt' -print` will find `/home/users/slynux/readme.txt`, but not `/home/users/slynux.txt`.

 The `-regex` argument is similar to `-path`, but `-regex` matches the file paths based on regular expressions.

Regular expressions are more complex than glob wildcards and support more precise pattern matching. A typical example of text matching with regular expressions is to recognize all e-mail addresses. An e-mail address takes the `name@host.root` form. It can be generalized as `[a-z0-9]+@[a-z0-9]+\.[a-z0-9]+`. The characters inside the square brackets represent a set of characters. In this case, `a-z` and `0-9` The + sign signifies that the previous class of characters can occur one or more times. A period is a single character wildcard (like a ? in glob wildcards), so it must be escaped with a backslash to match an actual dot in the e-mail address. So, this regular expression translates to 'a sequence of letters or numbers, followed by an `@`, followed by a sequence of letters or numbers, followed by a period, and ending with a sequence of letters or numbers'. See the *Using regular expressions* recipe in `Chapter 4`, *Texting and Driving* for more details.

This command matches the `.py` or `.sh` files:

```
$ ls
new.PY  next.jpg  test.py script.sh
$ find . -regex '.*\.(py\|sh\)$'
./test.py
script.sh
```

The `-iregex` option ignores the case for regular expression matches.

Consider this example:

```
$ find . -iregex '.*\(\.py\|\.sh\)$'
./test.py
./new.PY
./script.sh
```

Negating arguments

The `find` command can also exclude things that match a pattern using `!`:

```
$ find . ! -name "*.txt" -print
```

This will match all the files whose names do not end in `.txt`. The following example shows the result of the command:

```
$ ls
list.txt  new.PY  new.txt  next.jpg  test.py

$ find . ! -name "*.txt" -print
.
./next.jpg
./test.py
```

```
./new.PY
```

Searching based on the directory depth

The `find` command walks through all the subdirectories until it reaches the bottom of each subdirectory tree. By default, the `find` command will not follow symbolic links. The `-L` option will force it to follow symbolic links. If a link references a link that points to the original, `find` will be stuck in a loop.

The `-maxdepth` and `-mindepth` parameters restrict how far the `find` command will traverse. This will break the `find` command from an otherwise infinite search.

The `/proc` filesystem contains information about your system and running tasks. The folder hierarchy for a task is quite deep and includes symbolic links that loop back on themselves. Each process running your system has an entry in `proc`, named for the process ID. Under each process ID is a folder called `cwd`, which is a link to that task's current working directory.

The following example shows how to list all the tasks that are running in a folder with a file named `bundlemaker.def`:

```
$ find -L /proc -maxdepth 3 -name 'bundlemaker.def' 2>/dev/null
```

- The `-L` option tells the `find` command to follow symbolic links
- The `/proc` is a folder to start searching
- The `-maxdepth 3` option limits the search to only the current folder, not subfolders
- The `-name 'bundlemaker.def'` option is the file to search for
- The `2>/dev/null` redirects error messages about recursive loops to the null device

The `-mindepth` option is similar to `-maxdepth`, but it sets the minimum depth for which `find` will report matches. It can be used to find and print files that are located with a minimum level of depth from the base path. For example, to print all files whose names begin with f and that are at least two subdirectories distant from the current directory, use the following command:

```
$ find . -mindepth 2 -name "f*" -print
./dir1/dir2/file1
./dir3/dir4/f2
```

Files with names starting with f in the current directory or in dir1 and dir3 will not be printed.

 The −maxdepth and −mindepth option should be early in the find command. If they are specified as later arguments, it may affect the efficiency of find as it has to do unnecessary checks. For example, if −maxdepth is specified after a −type argument, the find command will first find the files having the specified −type and then filter out the files that don't match the proper depth. However, if the depth was specified before the −type, find will collect the files having the specified depth and then check for the file type, which is the most efficient way to search.

Searching based on file type

Unix-like operating systems treat every object as a file. There are different kinds of file, such as regular files, directory, character devices, block devices, symlinks, hardlinks, sockets, FIFO, and so on.

The find command filters the file search with the −type option. Using −type, we can tell the find command to match only files of a specified type.

List only directories including descendants:

```
$ find . -type d -print
```

It is hard to list directories and files separately. But find helps to do it. List only regular files as follows:

```
$ find . -type f -print
```

List only symbolic links as follows:

```
$ find . -type l -print
```

The following table shows the types and arguments find recognizes:

File type	Type argument
Regular file	f
Symbolic link	l
Directory	d
Character special device	c

Block device	b
Socket	s
FIFO	p

Searching by file timestamp

Unix/Linux filesystems have three types of timestamp on each file. They are as follows:

- **Access time** (-atime): The timestamp when the file was last accessed
- **Modification time** (-mtime): The timestamp when the file was last modified
- **Change time** (-ctime): The timestamp when the metadata for a file (such as permissions or ownership) was last modified

> Unix does not store file creation time by default; however, some filesystems (ufs2, ext4, zfs, btrfs, jfs) save the creation time. The creation time can be accessed with the stat command.
> Given that some applications modify a file by creating a new file and then deleting the original, the creation date may not be accurate.
> The -atime, -mtime, and -ctime option are the time parameter options available with find. They can be specified with integer values in *number of days*. The number may be prefixed with – or + signs. The – sign implies less than, whereas the + sign implies greater than.

Consider the following example:

- Print files that were accessed within the last seven days:

  ```
  $ find . -type f -atime -7 -print
  ```

- Print files that have an access time exactly seven days old:

  ```
  $ find . -type f -atime 7 -print
  ```

- Print files that have an access time older than seven days:

  ```
  $ find . -type f -atime +7 -print
  ```

The -mtime parameter will search for files based on the modification time; -ctime searches based on the change time.

The `-atime`, `-mtime`, and `-ctime` use time measured in days. The `find` command also supports options that measure in minutes. These are as follows:

- `-amin` (access time)
- `-mmin` (modification time)
- `-cmin` (change time)

To print all the files that have an access time older than seven minutes, use the following command:

```
$ find . -type f -amin +7 -print
```

The `-newer` option specifies a reference file with a modification time that will be used to select files modified more recently than the reference file.

Find all the files that were modified more recently than `file.txt` file:

```
$ find . -type f -newer file.txt -print
```

The `find` command's timestamp flags are useful for writing backup and maintenance scripts.

Searching based on file size

Based on the file sizes of the files, a search can be performed:

```
# Files having size greater than 2 kilobytes
$ find . -type f -size +2k

# Files having size less than 2 kilobytes
$ find . -type f -size -2k

# Files having size 2 kilobytes
$ find . -type f -size 2k
```

Instead of `k`, we can use these different size units:

- `b`: 512 byte blocks
- `c`: Bytes
- `w`: Two-byte words
- `k`: Kilobytes (1,024 bytes)
- `M`: Megabytes (1,024 kilobytes)
- `G`: Gigabytes (1,024 megabytes)

Matching based on file permissions and ownership

It is possible to match files based on the file permissions. We can list out the files with specified file permissions:

```
$ find . -type f -perm 644 -print
# Print files having permission 644
```

The -perm option specifies that find should only match files with their permission set to a particular value. Permissions are explained in more detail in the *Working with file permissions, ownership, and the sticky bit* recipe in Chapter 3, *File In, File Out*.

As an example usage case, we can consider the case of the Apache web server. The PHP files in the web server require proper permissions to execute. We can find PHP files that don't have proper executing permissions:

```
$ find . -type f -name "*.php" ! -perm 644 -print
PHP/custom.php
$ ls -l PHP/custom.php
-rw-rw-rw-.  root    root    513 Mar 13  2016  PHP/custom.php
```

We can also search files based on ownership. The files owned by a specific user can be found with the -user USER option.

The USER argument can be a username or UID.

For example, to print a list of all files owned by the slynux user, you can use the following command:

```
$ find . -type f -user slynux -print
```

Performing actions on files with find

The find command can perform actions on the files it identifies. You can delete files, or execute an arbitrary Linux command on the files.

Deleting based on file matches

The find command's -delete flag removes files that are matched instead of displaying them. Remove the .swp files from the current directory:

```
$ find . -type f -name "*.swp" -delete
```

Executing a command

The `find` command can be coupled with many of the other commands using the `-exec` option.

Consider the previous example. We used `-perm` to find files that do not have proper permissions. Similarly, in the case where we need to change the ownership of all files owned by a certain user (for example, `root`) to another user (for example, `www-data`, the default Apache user in the web server), we can find all the files owned by `root` using the `-user` option and use `-exec` to perform the ownership change operation.

> You must run the `find` command as root if you want to change the ownership of files or directories.

The `find` command uses an open/close curly brace pair `{ }` to represent the filename. In the next example, each time `find` identifies a file it will replace the `{ }` with the filename and change the ownership of the file. For example, if the `find` command finds two files with the `root` owner it will change both so they're owned by `slynux`:

```
# find . -type f -user root -exec chown slynux {} \;
```

> Note that the command is terminated with `\;`. The semicolon must be escaped or it will be grabbed by your command shell as the end of the `find` command instead of the end of the `chown` command.

Invoking a command for each file is a lot of overhead. If the command accepts multiple arguments (as `chown` does) you can terminate the command with a plus (+) instead of a semicolon. The plus causes `find` to make a list of all the files that match the search parameter and execute the application once with all the files on a single command line.

Another usage example is to concatenate all the C program files in a given directory and write them to a single file, say, `all_c_files.txt`. Each of these examples will perform this action:

```
$ find . -type f -name '*.c' -exec cat {} \;>all_c_files.txt
$ find . -type f -name '*.c' -exec cat {} > all_c_files.txt \;
$ fine . -type f -name '*.c' -exec cat {} >all_c_files.txt +
```

To redirect the data from `find` to the `all_c_files.txt` file, we used the > operator instead of >> (append) because the entire output from the `find` command is a single data stream (`stdin`); >> is necessary when multiple data streams are to be appended to a single file.

The following command will copy all the `.txt` files that are older than 10 days to a directory OLD:

```
$ find . -type f -mtime +10 -name "*.txt" -exec cp {} OLD \;
```

The `find` command can be coupled with many other commands.

 We cannot use multiple commands along with the `-exec` parameter. It accepts only a single command, but we can use a trick. Write multiple commands in a shell script (for example, `commands.sh`) and use it with `-exec` as follows:

```
-exec ./commands.sh {} \;
```

The `-exec` parameter can be coupled with `printf` to produce `joutput`. Consider this example:

```
$ find . -type f -name "*.txt" -exec printf "Text file: %s\n" {} \;
Config file: /etc/openvpn/easy-rsa/openssl-1.0.0.cnf
Config file: /etc/my.cnf
```

Skipping specified directories when using the find command

Skipping certain subdirectories may improve performance during the operation of `find`. For example, when searching for files in a development source tree under a version control system such as `Git`, the filesystem contains a directory in each of the subdirectories where version-control-related information is stored. These directories may not contain useful files and should be excluded from the search.

The technique of excluding files and directories is known as **pruning**. The following example shows how to use the `-prune` option to exclude files that match a pattern.

```
$ find devel/source_path  -name '.git' -prune -o -type f -print
```

The `-name ".git" -prune` is the pruning section, which specifies that `.git` directories should be excluded. The `-type f -print` section describes the action to be performed.

Playing with xargs

Unix commands accept data either from the standard input (`stdin`) or as command line arguments. Previous examples have shown how to pass data from one application's standard output to another's standard input with a pipe.

We can invoke applications that accept command-line arguments in other ways. The simplest is to use the back-tic symbol to run a command and use its output as a command line:

```
$ gcc `find '*.c'`
```

This solution works fine in many situations, but if there are a lot of files to be processed, you'll see the dreaded `Argument list too long` error message. The `xargs` program solves this problem.

The `xargs` command reads a list of arguments from `stdin` and executes a command using these arguments in the command line. The `xargs` command can also convert any one-line or multiple-line text inputs into other formats, such as multiple lines (specified number of columns) or a single line, and vice versa.

Getting ready

The `xargs` command should be the first command to appear after a pipe operator. It uses standard input as the primary data source and executes another command using the values it reads from `stdin` as command-line arguments for the new command. This example will search for the main string in a collection of C files:

```
ls *.c | xargs grep main
```

How to do it...

The `xargs` command supplies arguments to a target command by reformatting the data received through `stdin`. By default, `xargs` will execute the `echo` command. In many respects, the `xargs` command is similar to the actions performed by the `find` command's `-exec` option:

- Converting multiple lines of input to a single-line output:

  Xarg's default `echo` command can be used to convert multiple-line input to single-line text, like this:

  ```
  $ cat example.txt # Example file
  1 2 3 4 5 6
  7 8 9 10
  11 12

  $ cat example.txt | xargs
  1 2 3 4 5 6 7 8 9 10 11 12
  ```

- Converting single-line into multiple-line output:

  The `-n` argument to `xargs` limits the number of elements placed on each command line invocation. This recipe splits the input into multiple lines of *N* items each:

  ```
  $ cat example.txt | xargs -n 3
  1 2 3
  4 5 6
  7 8 9
  10 11 12
  ```

How it works...

The `xargs` command works by accepting input from `stdin`, parsing the data into individual elements, and invoking a program with these elements as the final command line arguments. By default, `xargs` will split the input based on whitespace and execute `/bin/echo`.

Splitting the input into elements based on whitespace becomes an issue when file and folder names have spaces (or even newlines) in them. The `My Documents` folder would be parsed into two elements `My` and `Documents`, neither of which exists.

Most problems have solutions and this is no exception.

We can define the delimiter used to separate arguments. To specify a custom delimiter for input, use the -d option:

```
$ echo "split1Xsplit2Xsplit3Xsplit4" | xargs -d X
split1 split2 split3 split4
```

In the preceding code, stdin contains a string consisting of multiple X characters. We define X to be the input delimiter with the -d option.

Using -n along with the previous command, we can split the input into multiple lines of two words each as follows:

```
$ echo "splitXsplitXsplitXsplit" | xargs -d X -n 2
split split
split split
```

The xargs command integrates well with the find command. The output from find can be piped to xargs to perform more complex actions than the -exec option can handle. If the filesystem has files with spaces in the name, the find command's -print0 option will use a 0 (NULL) to delimit the elements, which works with the xargs -0 option to parse these. The following example searches for .docx files on a Samba mounted filesystem, where names with capital letters and spaces are common. It uses grep to report files with images:

```
$ find /smbMount -iname '*.docx' -print0 | xargs -0 grep -L image
```

There's more...

The previous examples showed how to use xargs to organize a set of data. The next examples show how to format sets of data on a command line.

Passing formatted arguments to a command by reading stdin

Here is a small echo script to make it obvious as to how xargs provides command arguments:

```
#!/bin/bash
#Filename: cecho.sh

echo $*'#'
```

When arguments are passed to the `cecho.sh` shell, it will print the arguments terminated by the # character. Consider this example:

```
$ ./cecho.sh arg1 arg2
arg1 arg2 #
```

Here's a common problem:

- I have a list of elements in a file (one per line) to be provided to a command (say, `cecho.sh`). I need to apply the arguments in several styles. In the first method, I need one argument for each invocation, like this:

```
./cecho.sh arg1
./cecho.sh arg2
./cecho.sh arg3
```

- Next, I need to provide one or two arguments each for each execution of the command, like this:

```
./cecho.sh arg1 arg2
./cecho.sh arg3
```

- Finally, I need to provide all arguments at once to the command:

```
./cecho.sh arg1 arg2 arg3
```

Run the `cecho.sh` script and note the output before going through the following section. The `xargs` command can format the arguments for each of these requirements. The list of arguments is in a file called `args.txt`:

```
$ cat args.txt
arg1
arg2
arg3
```

For the first form, we execute the command multiple times with one argument per execution. The `xargs -n` option can limit the number of command line arguments to one:

```
$ cat args.txt | xargs -n 1 ./cecho.sh
arg1 #
arg2 #
arg3 #
```

To limit the number of arguments to two or fewer, execute this:

```
$ cat args.txt | xargs -n 2 ./cecho.sh
arg1 arg2 #
arg3 #
```

Finally, to execute the command at once with all the arguments, do not use any -n argument:

```
$ cat args.txt | xargs ./cecho.sh
arg1 arg2 arg3 #
```

In the preceding examples, the arguments added by xargs were placed at the end of the command. However, we may need to have a constant phrase at the end of the command and want xargs to substitute its argument in the middle, like this:

```
./cecho.sh -p arg1 -l
```

In the preceding command execution, arg1 is the only variable text. All others should remain constant. The arguments from args.txt should be applied like this:

```
./cecho.sh -p arg1 -l
./cecho.sh -p arg2 -l
./cecho.sh -p arg3 -l
```

The xargs-I option specifies a replacement string to be replaced with the arguments xargs parses from the input. When -I is used with xargs, it will execute as one command execution per argument. This example solves the problem:

```
$ cat args.txt | xargs -I {} ./cecho.sh -p {} -l
-p arg1 -l #
-p arg2 -l #
-p arg3 -l #
```

The -I {} specifies the replacement string. For each of the arguments supplied for the command, the {} string will be replaced with arguments read through stdin.

 When used with -I, the command is executed in a loop. When there are three arguments, the command is executed three times along with the {} command. Each time, {} is replaced with arguments one by one.

Using xargs with find

The `xargs` and `find` command can be combined to perform tasks. However, take care to combine them carefully. Consider this example:

```
$ find . -type f -name "*.txt" -print | xargs rm -f
```

This is dangerous. It may cause removal of unexpected files. We cannot predict the delimiting character (whether it is `'\n'` or `' '`) for the output of the `find` command. If any filenames contain a space character (`' '`) `xargs` may misinterpret it as a delimiter. For example, `bashrc text.txt` would be misinterpreted by `xargs` as `bashrc` and `text.txt`. The previous command would not delete `bashrc text.txt`, but would delete `bashrc`.

Use the `-print0` option of `find` to produce an output delimited by the null character (`'\0'`); you use `find` output as `xargs` input.

This command will `find` and remove all `.txt` files and nothing else:

```
$ find . -type f -name "*.txt" -print0 | xargs -0 rm -f
```

Counting the number of lines of C code in a source code directory

At some point, most programmers need to count the **Lines of Code (LOC)** in their C program files The code for this task is as follows:

```
$ find source_code_dir_path -type f -name "*.c" -print0 | xargs -0 wc -l
```

 If you want more statistics about your source code, a utility called `SLOCCount`, is very useful. Modern GNU/Linux distributions usually have packages or you can get it from `http://www.dwheeler.com/sloccount/`.

While and subshell trick with stdin

The `xargs` command places arguments at the end of a command; thus, `xargs` cannot supply arguments to multiple sets of commands. We can create a subshell to handle complex situations. The subshell can use a `while` loop to read arguments and execute commands in a trickier way, like this:

```
$ cat files.txt | ( while read arg; do cat $arg; done )
# Equivalent to cat files.txt | xargs -I {} cat {}
```

Here, by replacing `cat $arg` with any number of commands using a `while` loop, we can perform many command actions with the same arguments. We can pass the output to other commands without using pipes. Subshell `( )` tricks can be used in a variety of problematic environments. When enclosed within subshell operators, it acts as a single unit with multiple commands inside, like so:

```
$ cmd0 | ( cmd1 ; cmd2 ; cmd3) | cmd4
```

If `cmd1` is `cd /` within the subshell, the path of the working directory changes. However, this change resides inside the subshell only. The `cmd4` command will not see the directory change.

The shell accepts a `-c` option to invoke a subshell with a command-line script. This can be combined with `xargs` to solve the problem of needing multiple substitutions. The following example finds all C files and echoes the name of each file, preceded by a newline (the `-e` option enables backslash substitutions). Immediately after the filename is a list of all the times `main` appears in that file:

```
find . -name '*.c' | xargs -I ^ sh -c "echo -ne '\n ^: '; grep main ^"
```

Translating with tr

The `tr` command is a versatile tool in the Unix command–warrior's kit. It is used to craft elegant one-liner commands. It performs substitution of characters, deletes selected characters, and can squeeze repeated characters from the standard input. Tr is short for **translate**, since it translates a set of characters to another set. In this recipe, we will see how to use `tr` to perform basic translation between sets.

Getting ready

The `tr` command accepts input through **stdin (standard input)** and cannot accept input through command-line arguments. It has this invocation format:

```
tr [options] set1 set2
```

Input characters from `stdin` are mapped from the first character in `set1` to the first character in `set2`, and so on and the output is written to `stdout` (standard output). `set1` and `set2` are character classes or a set of characters. If the length of sets is unequal, `set2` is extended to the length of `set1` by repeating the last character; otherwise if the length of `set2` is greater than that of `set1`, all the characters exceeding the length of `set1` are ignored from `set2`.

How to do it...

To perform translation of characters in the input from uppercase to lowercase, use this command:

```
$ echo "HELLO WHO IS THIS" | tr 'A-Z' 'a-z'
hello who is this
```

The `'A-Z'` and `'a-z'` are the sets. We can specify custom sets as needed by appending characters or character classes.

The `'ABD-}'`, `'aA.,'`, `'a-ce-x'`, `'a-c0-9'`, and so on are valid sets. We can define sets easily. Instead of writing continuous character sequences, we can use the `'startchar-endchar'` format. It can also be combined with any other characters or character classes. If `startchar-endchar` is not a valid continuous character sequence, they are then taken as a set of three characters (for example, `startchar`, `-`, and `endchar`). You can also use special characters such as `'\t'`, `'\n'`, or any ASCII characters.

How it works...

Using `tr` with the concept of sets, we can map characters from one set to another set easily. Let's go through an example on using `tr` to encrypt and decrypt numeric characters:

```
$ echo 12345 | tr '0-9' '9876543210'
87654 #Encrypted

$ echo 87654 | tr '9876543210' '0-9'
12345 #Decrypted
```

The `tr` command can be used to encrypt text. **ROT13** is a well-known encryption algorithm. In the ROT13 scheme, characters are shifted by 13 positions, thus the same function can encrypt and decrypt text:

```
$ echo "tr came, tr saw, tr conquered." | tr 'a-zA-Z' 'n-za-mN-ZA-M'
```

The output will be the following:

```
ge pnzr, ge fnj, ge pbadhrerq.
```

By sending the encrypted text again to the same ROT13 function, we get this:

```
$ echo ge pnzr, ge fnj, ge pbadhrerq. | tr 'a-zA-Z' 'n-za-mN-ZA-M'
```

The output will be the following:

```
tr came, tr saw, tr conquered.
```

The `tr` can convert each tab character to a single space, as follows:

```
$ tr '\t' ' ' < file.txt
```

There's more...

We saw some basic translations using the `tr` command. Let's see what else can `tr` help us achieve.

Deleting characters using tr

The `tr` command has an option `-d` to delete a set of characters that appear on `stdin` using the specified set of characters to be deleted, as follows:

```
$ cat file.txt | tr -d  '[set1]'
#Only set1 is used, not set2
```

Consider this example:

```
$ echo "Hello 123 world 456" | tr -d '0-9'
Hello world
# Removes the numbers from stdin and print
```

Complementing character sets

We can use a set to complement `set1` using the `-c` flag. `set2` is optional in the following command:

```
tr -c [set1] [set2]
```

If only `set1` is present, `tr` will delete all characters that are not in `set1`. If `set2` is also present, `tr` will translate characters that aren't in `set1` into values from `set2`. If you use the `-c` option by itself, you must use `set1` and `set2`. If you combine the `-c` and `-d` options, you only use `set1` and all other characters will be deleted.

The following example deletes all the characters from the input text, except the ones specified in the complement set:

```
$ echo hello 1 char 2 next 4 | tr -d -c '0-9 \n'
124
```

This example replaces all characters that aren't in `set1` with spaces:

```
$ echo hello 1 char 2 next 4 | tr -c '0-9' ' '
      1     2     4
```

Squeezing characters with tr

The `tr` command can perform many text-processing tasks. For example, it can remove multiple occurrences of a character in a string. The basic form for this is as follows:

```
tr -s '[set of characters to be squeezed]'
```

If you commonly put two spaces after a period, you'll need to remove extra spaces without removing duplicated letters:

```
$ echo "GNU is        not      UNIX.  Recursive    right ?" | tr -s ' '
GNU is not UNIX. Recursive right ?
```

The `tr` command can also be used to get rid of extra newlines:

```
$ cat multi_blanks.txt | tr -s '\n'
line 1
line 2
line 3
line 4
```

In the preceding usage of `tr`, it removes the extra `'\n'` characters. Let's use `tr` in a tricky way to add a given list of numbers from a file, as follows:

```
$ cat sum.txt
1
2
3
4
5

$ cat sum.txt | echo $[ $(tr '\n' '+' ) 0 ]
15
```

How does this hack work?

Here, the `tr` command replaces `'\n'` with the `'+'` character, hence, we form the string `1+2+3+..5+`, but at the end of the string we have an extra + operator. In order to nullify the effect of the + operator, 0 is appended.

The `$[ operation ]` performs a numeric operation. Hence, it forms this string:

```
echo $[ 1+2+3+4+5+0 ]
```

If we used a loop to perform the addition by reading numbers from a file, it would take a few lines of code. With `tr`, a one–liner does the trick.

Even trickier is when we have a file with letters and numbers and we want to sum the numbers:

```
$ cat test.txt
first 1
second 2
third 3
```

We can use `tr` to strip out the letters with the −d option, then replace the spaces with +:

```
$ cat test.txt | tr -d [a-z] | echo "total: $[$(tr ' ' '+')]"
total: 6
```

Character classes

The `tr` command can use different character classes as sets. Here are the supported character classes:

- `alnum`: Alphanumeric characters

- `alpha`: Alphabetic characters
- `cntrl`: Control (nonprinting) characters
- `digit`: Numeric characters
- `graph`: Graphic characters
- `lower`: Lowercase alphabetic characters
- `print`: Printable characters
- `punct`: Punctuation characters
- `space`: Whitespace characters
- `upper`: Uppercase characters
- `xdigit`: Hexadecimal characters

We can select the required classes, like this:

```
tr [:class:] [:class:]
```

Consider this example:

```
tr '[:lower:]' '[:upper:]'
```

Checksum and verification

Checksum programs are used to generate a relatively small unique key from files. We can recalculate the key to confirm that a file has not changed. Files may be modified deliberately (adding a new user changes the password file), accidentally (a data read error from a CD-ROM drive), or maliciously (a virus is inserted). Checksums let us verify that a file contains the data we expect it to.

Checksums are used by backup applications to check whether a file has been modified and needs to be backed up.

Most software distributions also have a checksum file available. Even robust protocols such as TCP can allow a file to be modified in transit. Hence, we need to know whether the received file is the original one or not by applying some kind of test.

By comparing the checksum of the file we downloaded with the checksum calculated by the distributer, we can verify that the received file is correct. If the checksum calculated from the original file at the source location matches the one calculated at the destination, the file has been received successfully.

Some system validation suites maintain a checksum of the critical files. If malware modifies a file, we can detect this from the changed checksum.

In this recipe, we will see how to compute checksums to verify the integrity of data.

Getting ready

Unix and Linux support several checksum programs, but the most robust and widely used algorithms are **MD5** and **SHA-1**. The **ms5sum** and **sha1sum** programs generate checksum strings by applying the corresponding algorithm to the data. Let's see how to generate a checksum from a file and verify the integrity of that file.

How to do it...

To compute the md5sum, use the following command:

```
$ md5sum filename
68b329da9893e34099c7d8ad5cb9c940 filename
```

The md5sum is a 32-character hexadecimal string as given.

We can redirect the checksum output to a file for later use, as follows:

```
$ md5sum filename > file_sum.md5
```

How it works...

The syntax for the md5sum checksum calculation is as follows:

```
$ md5sum file1 file2 file3 ..
```

When multiple files are used, the output will contain a checksum for each of the files, one checksum report per line:

```
[checksum1]     file1
[checksum1]     file2
[checksum1]     file3
```

The integrity of a file can be verified with the generated file, like this:

```
$ md5sum -c file_sum.md5
# It will output a message whether checksum matches or not
```

If we need to check all the files using all .md5 information available, use this:

```
$ md5sum -c *.md5
```

SHA-1 is another commonly used checksum algorithm. It generates a 40-character hex code from the input. The sha1sum command calculates an SHA-1 checksum. Its usage is similar to md5sum. Simply replace md5sum with sha1sum in all the commands previously mentioned. Instead of file_sum.md5, change the output filename to file_sum.sha1.

Checksums are useful to verify the integrity of files downloaded from the Internet. ISO images are susceptible to erroneous bits. A few wrong bits and the ISO may be unreadable, or, worse, it might install applications that fail in strange ways. Most file repositories include an md5 or sha1 file you can use to verify that files were downloaded correctly.

MD5SUMS	2016-10-13	11:00	256	
MD5SUMS-metalink	2016-10-13	09:53	576	
MD5SUMS-metalink.gpg	2016-10-13	09:53	933	
MD5SUMS.gpg	2016-10-13	11:00	933	
SHA1SUMS	2016-10-13	11:00	288	
SHA1SUMS.gpg	2016-10-13	11:00	933	
SHA256SUMS	2016-10-13	11:00	384	
SHA256SUMS.gpg	2016-10-13	11:00	933	
ubuntu-16.10-desktop-amd64.iso	2016-10-12	21:28	1.5G	Deskto

This is the MD5 sum checksum that is created:

```
3f50877c05121f7fd8544bef2d722824 *ubuntu-16.10-desktop-amd64.iso
e9e9a6c6b3c8c265788f4e726af25994 *ubuntu-16.10-desktop-i386.iso
7d6de832aee348bacc894f0a2ab1170d *ubuntu-16.10-server-amd64.iso
e532cfbc738876b353c7c9943d872606 *ubuntu-16.10-server-i386.iso
```

There's more...

Checksums are also useful when used with a number of files. Let's see how to apply checksums to a collection of files and verify the accuracy.

Checksum for directories

Checksums are calculated for files. Calculating the checksum for a directory requires recursively calculating the checksums for all the files in the directory.

The `md5deep` or `sha1deep` commands traverse a file tree and calculate checksums for all files. These programs may not be installed on your system. Use `apt-get` or `yum` to install the `md5deep` package. An example of this command is as follows:

```
$ md5deep -rl directory_path > directory.md5
```

The `-r` option allows md5deep to recurse into sub-directories. The `-l` option enables displaying the relative path, instead of the default absolute path.

```
# -r to enable recursive traversal
# -l to use relative path. By default it writes absolute file
path in output
```

The `find` and `md5sum` commands can be used to calculate checksums recursively:

```
$ find directory_path -type f -print0 | xargs -0 md5sum >> directory.md5
```

To verify, use this command:

```
$ md5sum -c directory.md5
```

- The **md5** and **SHA-1 checksums** are unidirectional hash algorithms, which cannot be reversed to form the original data. These are also used to generate a unique key from a given data:

  ```
  $ md5sum file
  8503063d5488c3080d4800ff50850dc9  file
  $ sha1sum file
  1ba02b66e2e557fede8f61b7df282cd0a27b816b  file
  ```

  These hashes are commonly used to store passwords. Only the hash for a password is stored. When a user needs to be authenticated, the password is read and converted to the hash and that hash is compared to the stored hash. If they are the same, the password is authenticated and access is provided. Storing plain–text password strings is risky and poses a security risk.

Although commonly used, md5sum and SHA-1 are no longer considered secure. This is because the rise in computing power in recent times that makes it easier to crack them. It is recommended that you use tools such as `bcrypt` or **sha512sum** instead. Read more about this at `http://codahale.com/how-to-safely-store-a-password/`.

- Shadow-like hash (salted hash)

The next recipe shows how to generate a shadow-like salted hash for passwords. The hash for user passwords in Linux is stored in the `/etc/shadow` file. A typical line in `/etc/shadow` will look like this:

```
test:$6$fG4eWdUi$ohTKOlEUzNk77.4S8MrYe07NTRV4M3LrJnZP9p.qc1bR5c.
EcOruzPXfEu1uloBFUa18ENRH7F70zhodas3cR.:14790:0:99999:7:::
```

`$6$fG4eWdUi$ohTKOlEUzNk77.4S8MrYe07NTRV4M3LrJnZP9p.qc1bR5c.EcOr`
`uzPXfEu1uloBFUa18ENRH7F70zhodas3cR` is the hash corresponding to its password.

In some situations, we need to write scripts to edit passwords or add users. In that case, we must generate a shadow password string and write a similar line to the preceding one to the shadow file. We can generate a shadow password using `openssl`.

Shadow passwords are usually salted passwords. SALT is an extra string used to obfuscate and make the encryption stronger. Salt consists of random bits that are used as one of the inputs to a key derivation function that generates the salted hash for the password.

For more details on salt, refer to this Wikipedia page at `http://en.wikipedia.org/wiki/Salt_(cryptography)`.

```
$ opensslpasswd -1 -salt SALT_STRING PASSWORD
$1$SALT_STRING$323VkWkSLHuhbt1zkSsUG.
```

Replace SALT_STRING with a random string and PASSWORD with the password you want to use.

Cryptographic tools and hashes

Encryption techniques are used to protect data from unauthorized access. Unlike the checksum algorithms we just discussed, encryption programs can reconstruct the original data with no loss. There are many algorithms available and we will discuss those most commonly used in the Linux/Unix world.

How to do it...

Let's see how to use tools such as `crypt`, `gpg`, and `base64`:

- The `crypt` command is not commonly installed on Linux systems. It's a simple and relatively insecure cryptographic utility that accepts input from `stdin`, requests a `passphrase`, and sends encrypted output to `stdout`:

  ```
  $ crypt <input_file >output_file
  Enter passphrase:
  ```

  We can provide a passphrase on the command line:

  ```
  $ crypt PASSPHRASE <input_file >encrypted_file
  ```

  In order to decrypt the file, use this:

  ```
  $ crypt PASSPHRASE -d <encrypted_file >output_file
  ```

- gpg (GNU privacy guard) is a widely used tool for protecting files to ensure that data is not read until it reaches its intended destination.

  gpg signatures are also widely used in e-mail communications to "sign" e-mail messages, proving the authenticity of the sender.

  In order to encrypt a file with gpg, use this:

  ```
  $ gpg -c filename
  ```

  This command reads the passphrase interactively and generates `filename.gpg`. In order to decrypt a gpg file, use the following command:

  ```
  $ gpg filename.gpg
  ```

This command reads a passphrase and decrypts the file.

 We are not covering gpg in much detail in this book. For more information, refer to
http://en.wikipedia.org/wiki/GNU_Privacy_Guard.

- **Base64** is a group of similar encoding schemes that represent binary data in an ASCII string format by translating it into a **radix-64** representation. These programs are used to transmit binary data via e-mail. The base64 command encodes and decodes the Base64 string. To encode a binary file into the Base64 format, use this:

  ```
  $ base64 filename > outputfile
  ```

  Alternatively, use this command:

  ```
  $ cat file | base64 > outputfile
  ```

  It can read from stdin.

  Decode Base64 data as follows:

  ```
  $ base64 -d file > outputfile
  ```

  Alternatively, use this:

  ```
  $ cat base64_file | base64 -d > outputfile
  ```

Sorting unique and duplicate lines

Sorting text files is a common task. The sort command sorts text files and stdin. It can be coupled with other commands to produce the required output. uniq is often used with sort to extract unique (or duplicate) lines. The following recipes illustrate some sort and uniq use cases.

Getting ready

The sort and uniq commands accept input as filenames or from stdin (standard input) and output the result by writing to stdout.

How to do it...

1. We can sort a set of files (for example, `file1.txt` and `file2.txt`), like this:

   ```
   $ sort file1.txt file2.txt > sorted.txt
   ```

   Alternatively, use this:

   ```
   $ sort file1.txt file2.txt -o sorted.txt
   ```

2. For a numerical sort, we use this:

   ```
   $ sort -n file.txt
   ```

3. To sort in the reverse order, we use the following command:

   ```
   $ sort -r file.txt
   ```

4. To sort by months (in the order Jan, Feb, March,...), use this:

   ```
   $ sort -M months.txt
   ```

5. To merge two already sorted files, use this command:

   ```
   $ sort -m sorted1 sorted2
   ```

6. To find the unique lines from a sorted file, use this:

   ```
   $ sort file1.txt file2.txt | uniq
   ```

7. To check whether a file has already been sorted, use the following code:

   ```
   #!/bin/bash
   #Desc: Sort
   sort -C filename ;
   if [ $? -eq 0 ]; then
       echo Sorted;
   else
       echo Unsorted;
   fi
   ```

   Replace `filename` with the file you want to check and run the script.

How it works...

As shown in the examples, `sort` accepts numerous parameters to define how the data is to be sorted. The sort command is useful with the `uniq` command, which expects sorted input.

There are numerous scenarios where the `sort` and `uniq` commands can be used. Let's go through the various options and usage techniques.

To check whether a file is already sorted, we exploit the fact that `sort` returns an exit code (`$?`) of 0 if the file is sorted and nonzero otherwise.

```
if sort -c fileToCheck ; then echo sorted ; else echo unsorted ; fi
```

There's more...

These were some basic usages of the `sort` command. Here are sections for using it to accomplish complex tasks:

Sorting according to keys or columns

We can use a column with sort if the input data is formatted like this:

```
$ cat data.txt
1   mac     2000
2   winxp       4000
3   bsd     1000
4   linux       1000
```

We can sort this in many ways; currently it is sorted numerically, by the serial number (the first column). We can also sort by the second or third column.

The `-k` option specifies the characters to sort by. A single digit specifies the column. The `-r` option specifies sorting in reverse order. Consider this example:

```
# Sort reverse by column1
$ sort -nrk 1   data.txt
4   linux       1000
3   bsd     1000
2   winxp       4000
1   mac     2000
# -nr means numeric and reverse

# Sort by column 2
$ sort -k 2   data.txt
```

```
3   bsd     1000
4   linux     1000
1   mac     2000
2   winxp     4000
```

 Always be careful about the -n option for numeric sort. The sort command treats alphabetical sort and numeric sort differently. Hence, in order to specify numeric sort, the −n option should be provided.

When −k is followed by a single integer, it specifies a column in the text file. Columns are separated by space characters. If we need to specify keys as a group of characters (for example, characters 4-5 of column 2), we define the range as two integers separated by a period to define a character position, and join the first and last character positions with a comma:

```
$ cat data.txt


1 alpha 300
2 beta 200
3 gamma 100
$ sort -bk 2.3,2.4 data.txt    ;# Sort m, p, t
3 gamma 100
1 alpha 300
2 beta 200
```

The highlighted characters are to be used as numeric keys. To extract them, use their positions in the lines as the key format (in the previous example, they are 2 and 3).

To use the first character as the key, use this:

```
$ sort -nk 1,1 data.txt
```

To make the sort's output xargs compatible with the \0 terminator, use this command:

```
$ sort -z data.txt | xargs -0
# Use zero terminator to make safe use with xargs
```

Sometimes, the text may contain unnecessary extraneous characters such as spaces. To sort them in dictionary order, ignoring punctuations and folds, use this:

```
$ sort -bd unsorted.txt
```

The −b option is used to ignore leading blank lines from the file and the −d option specifies sorting in dictionary order.

uniq

The `uniq` command finds the unique lines in a given input (`stdin` or a filename command line argument) and either reports or removes the duplicated lines.

This command only works with sorted data. Hence, `uniq` is often used with the `sort` command.

To produce the unique lines (all lines in the input are printed and duplicate lines are printed once), use this:

```
$ cat sorted.txt
bash
foss
hack
hack

$ uniq sorted.txt
bash
foss
hack
```

Alternatively, use this:

```
$ sort unsorted.txt | uniq
```

Display only unique lines (the lines that are not repeated or duplicated in the input file):

```
$ uniq -u sorted.txt
bash
foss
```

Alternatively, use this command:

```
$ sort unsorted.txt | uniq -u
```

To count how many times each of the lines appears in the file, use the following command:

```
$ sort unsorted.txt | uniq -c
   1 bash
   1 foss
   2 hack
```

To find duplicate lines in the file, use this:

```
$ sort unsorted.txt   | uniq -d
hack
```

To specify keys, we can use a combination of the −s and −w arguments:

- −s: This specifies the number for the first *N* characters to be skipped
- −w: This specifies the maximum number of characters to be compared

The following example describes using the comparison key as the index for the uniq operation:

```
$ cat data.txt
u:01:gnu
d:04:linux
u:01:bash
u:01:hack
```

To test only the bold characters (skip the first two characters and use the next two) we use −s 2 to skip the first characters and −w 2 to use the next two:

```
$ sort data.txt | uniq -s 2 -w 2
d:04:linux
u:01:bash
```

When the output from one command is passed as input to the xargs command, it's best to use a zero-byte terminator for each element of data. Passing output from uniq to xargs is no exception to this rule. If a zero-byte terminator is not used, the default space characters are used to split the arguments in the xargs command. For example, a line with the text this is a line from stdin will be taken as four separate arguments by the xargs command instead of a single line. When a zero-byte terminator, \0, is used as the delimiter character, the full line including spaces is interpreted as a single argument.

The −z option generates zero-byte-terminated output:

```
$ uniq -z file.txt
```

This command removes all the files, with filenames read from files.txt:

```
$ uniq -z file.txt | xargs -0 rm
```

If a filename appears multiple time, the uniq command writes the filename only once to stdout, thus avoiding a rm: cannot remove FILENAME: No such file or directory error.

Temporary file naming and random numbers

Shell scripts often need to store temporary data. The most suitable location to do this is /tmp (which will be cleaned out by the system on reboot). There are two methods to generate standard filenames for temporary data.

How to do it...

The mktemp command will create a unique temporary file or folder name:

1. Create a temporary file:

   ```
   $ filename=`mktemp`
   $ echo $filename
   /tmp/tmp.8xvhkjF5fH
   ```

   This creates a temporary file, stores the name in filename, and then displays the name.

2. Create a temporary directory:

   ```
   $ dirname=`mktemp -d`
   $ echo $dirname
   tmp.NI8xzW7VRX
   ```

   This creates a temporary directory, stores the name in filename, and displays the name.

   - To generate a filename without creating a file or directory, use this:

     ```
     $ tmpfile=`mktemp -u`
     $ echo $tmpfile
     /tmp/tmp.RsGmilRpcT
     ```

     Here, the filename is stored in $tmpfile, but the file won't be created.

   - To create the temporary filename based on a template, use this:

     ```
     $mktemp test.XXX
     test.2tc
     ```

How it works...

The `mktemp` command is straightforward. It generates a file with a unique name and returns its filename (or directory name, in the case of directories).

When providing custom templates, X will be replaced by a random alphanumeric character. Also note that there must be at least three X characters in the template for `mktemp` to work.

Splitting files and data

Splitting a large file into smaller pieces is sometimes necessary. Long ago, we had to split files to transport large datasets on floppy disks. Today, we split files for readability, for generating logs, or for working around size-restrictions on e-mail attachments. These recipes will demonstrate ways of splitting files in different chunks.

How to do it...

The split command was created to split files. It accepts a filename as an argument and creates a set of smaller files in which the first part of the original file is in the alphabetically first new file, the next set in the alphabetically next file, and so on.

For example, a 100 KB file can be divided into smaller files of 10k each by specifying the split size. The split command supports M for MB, G for GB, c for byte, and w for word.

```
$ split -b 10k data.file
$ ls
data.file  xaa  xab  xac  xad  xae  xaf  xag  xah  xai  xaj
```

The preceding code will split `data.file` into ten files of `10k` each. The new files are named `xab`, `xac`, `xad`, and so on. By default, split uses alphabetic suffixes. To use numeric suffixes, use the `-d` argument. It is also possible to specify a suffix length using `-a` length:

```
$ split -b 10k data.file -d -a 4

$ ls
data.file x0009  x0019  x0029  x0039  x0049  x0059  x0069  x0079
```

There's more...

The split command has more options. Let's go through them.

Specifying a filename prefix for the split files

All the previous split filenames start with x. If we are splitting more than one file, we'll want to name the pieces, so it's obvious which goes with which. We can use our own filename prefix by providing a prefix as the last argument.

Let's run the previous command with the split_file prefix:

```
$ split -b 10k data.file -d -a 4 split_file
$ ls
data.file          split_file0002   split_file0005   split_file0008
strtok.c
split_file0000   split_file0003   split_file0006   split_file0009
split_file0001   split_file0004   split_file0007
```

To split files based on the number of lines in each split rather than chunk size, use this:

```
-l no_of_lines:
 # Split into files of 10 lines each.
 $ split -l 10 data.file
```

The csplit utility splits files based on context instead of size. It can split based on line count or regular expression pattern. It's particularly useful for splitting log files.

Look at the following example log:

```
$ cat server.log
SERVER-1
[connection] 192.168.0.1 success
[connection] 192.168.0.2 failed
[disconnect] 192.168.0.3 pending
[connection] 192.168.0.4 success
SERVER-2
[connection] 192.168.0.1 failed
[connection] 192.168.0.2 failed
[disconnect] 192.168.0.3 success
[connection] 192.168.0.4 failed
SERVER-3
[connection] 192.168.0.1 pending
[connection] 192.168.0.2 pending
[disconnect] 192.168.0.3 pending
[connection] 192.168.0.4 failed
```

We may need to split the files into `server1.log`, `server2.log`, and `server3.log` from the contents for each `SERVER` in each file. This can be done as follows:

```
$ csplit server.log /SERVER/ -n 2 -s {*}  -f server -b "%02d.log"        $
rm server00.log
$ ls
server01.log   server02.log   server03.log   server.log
```

The details of the command are as follows:

- `/SERVER/`: This is the line used to match a line by which a split is to be carried out.
- `/[REGEX]/`: This is the format. It copies from the current line (first line) up to the matching line that contains `SERVER` excluding the match line.
- `{*}`: This specifies repeating a split based on the match up to the end of the file. We can specify the number of times it is to be continued by placing a number between the curly braces.
- `-s`: This is the flag to make the command silent rather than printing other messages.
- `-n`: This specifies the number of digits to be used as suffix. 01, 02, 03, and so on.
- `-f`: This specifies the filename prefix for split files (`server` is the prefix in the previous example).
- `-b`: This specifies the suffix format. `"%02d.log"` is similar to the `printf` argument format in C, Here, the *filename = prefix + suffix*, that is, `"server"` + `"%02d.log"`.

We remove `server00.log` since the first split file is an empty file (the match word is the first line of the file).

Slicing filenames based on extensions

Many shell scripts perform actions that involve modifying filenames. They may need to rename the files and preserve the extension, or convert files from one format to another and change the extension, while preserving the name, extracting a portion of the filename, and so on.

The shell has built-in features for manipulating filenames.

How to do it...

The % operator will extract the name from name.extension. This example extracts sample from sample.jpg:

```
file_jpg="sample.jpg"
name=${file_jpg%.*}
echo File name is: $name
```

The output is this:

File name is: sample

The # operator will extract the extension:

Extract .jpg from the filename stored in the file_jpg variable:

```
extension=${file_jpg#*.}
echo Extension is: jpg
```

The output is as follows:

Extension is: jpg

How it works...

To extract the name from the filename formatted as name.extension, we use the % operator.

${VAR%.*} is interpreted as follows:

- Remove the string match from $VAR for the wildcard pattern that appears to the right of % (.* in the previous example). Evaluating from right to left finds the wildcard match.
- Store the filename as VAR=sample.jpg. Therefore, the wildcard match for .* from right to left is .jpg. Thus, it is removed from the $VAR string and the output is sample.

% is a nongreedy operation. It finds the minimal match for the wildcard from right to left. The %% operator is similar to %, but it is greedy. This means that it finds the maximal match of the string for the wildcard. Consider this example, where we have this:

VAR=hack.fun.book.txt

Use the % operator for a nongreedy match from right to left and match .txt:

```
$ echo ${VAR%.*}
```

The output will be: hack.fun.book.

Use the %% operator for a greedy match, and match .fun.book.txt:

```
$ echo ${VAR%%.*}
```

The output will be: hack.

The # operator extracts the extension from the filename. It is similar to %, but it evaluates from left to right.

${VAR#*.} is interpreted as follows:

- Remove the string match from $VARIABLE for the wildcard pattern match that appears to the right of # (*. in the previous example). Evaluating from the left to right should make the wildcard match.

Similarly, as in the case of %%, the operator ## is a greedy equivalent to #.

It makes greedy matches by evaluating from left to right and removes the match string from the specified variable. Let's use this example:

```
VAR=hack.fun.book.txt
```

The # operator performs a nongreedy match from left to right and matches hack:

```
$ echo ${VAR#*.}
```

The output will be: fun.book.txt.

The ## operator performs a greedy match from left to right and matches hack.fun.book:

```
$ echo ${VAR##*.}
```

The output will be: txt.

 The ## operator is preferred over the # operator to extract the extension from a filename, since the filename may contain multiple . characters. Since ## makes a greedy match, it always extracts extensions only.

Here is a practical example to extract different portions of a domain name such as URL=`www.google.com`:

```
$ echo ${URL%.*} # Remove rightmost .*
www.google

$ echo ${URL%%.*} # Remove right to leftmost  .* (Greedy operator)
www


$ echo ${URL#*.} # Remove leftmost  part before *.
google.com


$ echo ${URL##*.} # Remove left to rightmost  part before *.
(Greedy operator) com
```

Renaming and moving files in bulk

We frequently need to move and perhaps rename a set of files. System housekeeping often requires moving files with a common prefix or file type to a new folder. Images downloaded from a camera may need to be renamed and sorted. Music, video, and e-mail files all need to be reorganized eventually.

There are custom applications for many of these operations, but we can write our own custom scripts to do it **our** way.

Let's see how to write scripts to perform these kinds of operation.

Getting ready

The `rename` command changes filenames using Perl regular expressions. By combining the `find`, `rename`, and `mv` commands, we can perform a lot of things.

How to do it...

The following script uses find to locate PNG and JPEG files, then uses the ## operator and mv to rename them as image-1.EXT, image-2.EXT, and so on. This changes the file's name, but not its extension:

```bash
#!/bin/bash
#Filename: rename.sh
#Desc: Rename jpg and png files

count=1;
for img in `find . -iname '*.png' -o -iname '*.jpg' -type f -maxdepth 1`
do
  new=image-$count.${img##*.}

  echo "Renaming $img to $new"
  mv "$img" "$new"
  let count++

done
```

The output is as follows:

```
$ ./rename.sh
Renaming hack.jpg to image-1.jpg
Renaming new.jpg to image-2.jpg
Renaming next.png to image-3.png
```

The preceding script renames all the .jpg and .png files in the current directory to new filenames in the format image-1.jpg, image-2.jpg, image-3.png, image-4.png, and so on.

How it works...

The previous script uses a for loop to iterate through the names of all files ending with a .jpg or .png extension. The find command performs this search, using the -o option to specify multiple -iname options for case-insensitive matches. The -maxdepth 1 option restricts the search to the current directory, not any subdirectories.

The count variable is initialized to 1 to track the image number. Then the script renames the file using the mv command. The new name of the file is constructed using ${img##*.}, which parses the extension of the filename currently being processed (refer to the *Slicing filenames based on extensions* recipe in this chapter for an interpretation of ${img##*.}).

`let count++` is used to increment the file number for each execution of the loop.

Here are other ways to perform rename operations:

- Rename `*.JPG` to `*.jpg` like this:

  ```
  $ rename *.JPG *.jpg
  ```

- Use this to replace spaces in the filenames with the "_" character:

  ```
  $ rename 's/ /_/g' *
  ```

  # 's/ /_/g' is the replacement part in the filename and `*` is the wildcard for the target files. It can be `*.txt` or any other wildcard pattern.

- Use these to convert any filenames from uppercase to lowercase and vice versa:

  ```
  $ rename 'y/A-Z/a-z/' *
  $ rename 'y/a-z/A-Z/' *
  ```

- Use this to recursively move all the `.mp3` files to a given directory:

  ```
  $ find path -type f -name "*.mp3" -exec mv {} target_dir \;
  ```

- Use this to recursively rename all the files by replacing spaces with the _ character:

  ```
  $ find path -type f -exec rename 's/ /_/g' {} \;
  ```

Spell–checking and dictionary manipulation

Most Linux distributions include a dictionary file. However, very few people are aware of this, thus spelling errors abound. The `aspell` command-line utility is a spell checker. Let's go through a few scripts that make use of the dictionary file and the spell checker.

How to do it...

The `/usr/share/dict/` directory contains one or perhaps more dictionary files, which are text files with a list of words. We can use this list to check whether a word is a dictionary word or not:

```
$ ls /usr/share/dict/
american-english  british-english
```

To check whether the given word is a dictionary word, use the following script:

```
#!/bin/bash
#Filename: checkword.sh
word=$1
grep "^$1$" /usr/share/dict/british-english -q
if [ $? -eq 0 ]; then
  echo $word is a dictionary word;
else
  echo $word is not a dictionary word;
fi
```

The usage is as follows:

```
$ ./checkword.sh ful
ful is not a dictionary word

$ ./checkword.sh fool
fool is a dictionary word
```

How it works...

In `grep`, `^` is the word-start marker character and the `$` character is the word-end marker. The `-q` option suppresses any output, making the `grep` command quiet.

Alternatively, we can use the spell-check, `aspell`, to check whether a word is in a dictionary or not:

```
#!/bin/bash
#Filename: aspellcheck.sh
word=$1

output=`echo \"$word\" | aspell list`

if [ -z $output ]; then
        echo $word is a dictionary word;
else
```

```
        echo $word is not a dictionary word;
    fi
```

The `aspell list` command returns output text when the given input is not a dictionary word, and does not output anything when the input is a dictionary word. A `-z` command checks whether `$output` is an empty string or not.

The `look` command will display lines that begin with a given string. You might use it to find the lines in a log file that start with a given date, or to find words in the dictionary that start with a given string. By default, `look` searches `/usr/share/dict/words`, or you can provide a file to search.

```
$ look word
```

Alternatively, this can be used:

```
$ grep "^word" filepath
```

Consider this example:

```
$ look android
android
android's
androids
```

Use this to find lines with a given date in `/var/log/syslog`:

```
$look 'Aug 30' /var/log/syslog
```

Automating interactive input

We looked at commands that accept arguments on the command line. Linux also supports many interactive applications ranging from `passwd` to `ssh`.

We can create our own interactive shell scripts. It's easier for casual users to interact with a set of prompts rather than remember command line flags and the proper order. For instance, a script to back up a user's work, but not to back up and lock files, might look like this:

```
$ backupWork.sh
```

- What folder should be backed up? `notes`
- What type of files should be backed up? `.docx`

Automating interactive applications can save you time when you need to rerun the same application and frustration while you're developing one.

Getting ready

The first step to automating a task is to run it and note what you do. The script command discussed earlier may be of use.

How to do it...

Examine the sequence of interactive inputs. From the previous code, we can formulate the steps of the sequence like this:

```
notes[Return]docx[Return]
```

In addition to the preceding steps, type `notes`, press `Return`, type `docx`, and finally press `Return` to convert into a single string like this:

```
"notes\ndocx\n"
```

The \n character is sent when we press Return. By appending the return (\n) characters, we get the string that is passed to `stdin` (standard input).

By sending the equivalent string for the characters typed by the user, we can automate passing input to the interactive processes.

How it works...

Let's write a script that reads input interactively for an automation example:

```
#!/bin/bash
# backup.sh
# Backup files with suffix. Do not backup temp files that start with ~
read -p " What folder should be backed up: " folder
read -p " What type of files should be backed up: " suffix
find $folder -name "*.$suffix" -a ! -name '~*' -exec cp {} \
    $BACKUP/$LOGNAME/$folder
echo "Backed up files from $folder to $BACKUP/$LOGNAME/$folder"
```

Let's automate the sending of input to the command:

```
$ echo -e "notes\ndocx\n" | ./backup.sh
Backed up files from notes to /BackupDrive/MyName/notes
```

This style of automating an interactive script can save you a lot of typing during developing and debugging. It also insures that you perform the same test each time and don't end up chasing a phantom bug because you mis-typed.

We used echo -e to produce the input sequence. The -e option signals to echo to interpret escape sequences. If the input is large we can use an input file and the redirection operator to supply input:

```
$ echo -e "notes\ndocx\n"  > input.data
$ cat input.data
notes
docx
```

You can manually craft the input file without the echo commands by hand–typing. Consider this example:

```
$ ./interactive.sh < input.data
```

This redirects interactive input data from a file.

If you are a reverse engineer, you may have played with buffer overflow exploits. To exploit them we need to redirect a shell code such as \xeb\x1a\x5e\x31\xc0\x88\x46, which is written in hex. These characters cannot be typed directly on the keyboard as keys for these characters are not present. Therefore, we use:

```
echo -e \xeb\x1a\x5e\x31\xc0\x88\x46"
```

This will redirect the byte sequence to a vulnerable executable.

These echo and redirection techniques automate interactive input programs. However, these techniques are fragile, in that there is no validity checking and it's assumed that the target application will always accept data in the same order. If the program asks for input in a changing order, or some inputs are not always required, these methods fail.

The expect program can perform complex interactions and adapt to changes in the target application. This program is in worldwide use to control hardware tests, validate software builds, query router statistics, and much more.

There's more...

The expect application is an interpreter similar to the shell. It's based on the TCL language. We'll discuss the spawn, expect, and send commands for simple automation. With the power of the TCL language behind it, expect can do much more complex tasks. You can learn more about the TCL language at the www.tcl.tk website.

Automating with expect

expect does not come by default on all Linux distributions. You may have to install the expect package with your package manager (apt-get or yum).

Expect has three main commands:

Commands	Description
spawn	Runs the new target application.
expect	Watches for a pattern to be sent by the target application.
send	Sends a string to the target application.

The following example spawns the backup script and then looks for the patterns *folder* and *file* to determine if the backup script is asking for a folder name or a filename. It will then send the appropriate reply. If the backup script is rewritten to request files first and then folders, this automation script still works.

```
#!/usr/bin/expect
#Filename: automate_expect.tcl
spawn ./backup .sh
expect {
  "*folder*" {
      send "notes\n"
      exp_continue
   }
  "*type*" {
      send "docx\n"
      exp_continue
   }
}
```

Run it as:

```
$ ./automate_expect.tcl
```

The `spawn` command's parameters are the target application and arguments to be automated.

The `expect` command accepts a set of patterns to look for and an action to perform when that pattern is matched. The action is enclosed in curly braces.

The `send` command is the message to be sent. This is similar to echo -n -e in that it does not automatically include the newline and does understand backslash symbols.

Making commands quicker by running parallel processes

Computing power constantly increases not only because processors have higher clock cycles but also because they have multiple cores. This means that in a single hardware processor there are multiple logical processors. It's like having several computers, instead of just one.

However, multiple cores are useless unless the software makes use of them. For example, a program that does huge calculations may only run on one core while the others will sit idle. The software has to be aware and take advantage of the multiple cores if we want it to be faster.

In this recipe, we will see how we can make our commands run faster.

How to do it...

Let's take an example of the `md5sum` command we discussed in the previous recipes. This command performs complex computations, making it CPU-intensive. If we have more than one file that we want to generate a checksum for, we can run multiple instances of `md5sum` using a script like this:

```
#/bin/bash
#filename: generate_checksums.sh
PIDARRAY=()
for file in File1.iso File2.iso
do
  md5sum $file &
  PIDARRAY+=("$!")
done
wait ${PIDARRAY[@]}
```

When we run this, we get the following output:

```
$ ./generate_checksums.sh
330dcb53f253acdf76431cecca0fefe7  File1.iso
bd1694a6fe6df12c3b8141dcffaf06e6  File2.iso
```

The output will be the same as running the following command:

```
md5sum File1.iso File2.iso
```

However, if the md5sum commands run simultaneously, you'll get the results quicker if you have a multi-core processor (you can verify this using the time command).

How it works...

We exploit the Bash operand &, which instructs the shell to send the command to the background and continue with the script. However, this means our script will exit as soon as the loop completes, while the md5sum processes are still running in the background. To prevent this, we get the PIDs of the processes using $!, which in Bash holds the PID of the last background process. We append these PIDs to an array and then use the wait command to wait for these processes to finish.

There's more...

The Bash & operand works well for a small number of tasks. If you had a hundred files to checksum, the script would try to start a hundred processes and might force your system into swapping, which would make the tasks run slower.

The GNU parallel command is not part of all installations, but again it can be loaded with your package manager. The parallel command optimizes the use of your resources without overloading any of them.

The parallel command reads a list of files on stdin and uses options similar to the find command's -exec argument to process these files. The {} symbol represents the file to be processed, and the {.} symbol represents the filename without a suffix.

The following command uses **Imagemagick's** convert command to make new, resized images of all the images in a folder:

```
ls *jpg | parallel convert {} -geometry 50x50 {.}Small.jpg
```

Examining a directory, files and subdirectories in it

One of the commonest problems we deal with is finding misplaced files and sorting out mangled file hierarchies. This section will discuss tricks for examining a portion of the filesystem and presenting the contents.

Getting ready

The find command and loops we discussed give us tools to examine and report details in a directory and its contents.

How to do it...

The next recipes show two ways to examine a directory. First we'll display the hierarchy as a tree, then we'll see how to generate a summary of files and folders under a directory.

Generating a tree view of a directory.

Sometimes it's easier to visualize a file system if it's presented graphically.

The next recipe pulls together several of the tools we discussed. It uses the find command to generate a list of all the files and sub-folders under the current folder.

The -exec option creates a subshell which uses echo to send the filenames to the tr command's stdin. There are two tr commands. The first deletes all alphanumeric characters, and any dash (-), underbar (_), or period (.). This passes only the slashes (/) in the path to the second tr command, which translates those slashes to spaces. Finally, the basename command strips the leading path from the filename and displays it.

Use these to view a tree of the folders in /var/log:

```
$ cd /var/log
$ find . -exec sh -c 'echo -n {} | tr -d "[:alnum:]_.\-" | \
    tr "/" " "; basename {}' \;
```

This output is generated:

```
mail
  statistics
gdm
  ::0.log
  ::0.log.1
cups
        error_log
        access_log
... access_l
```

Generating a summary of files and sub-directories

We can generate a list of subdirectories, and the number of files in them, with a combination of the `find` command, `echo`, and `wc` commands, which will be discussed in greater detail in the next chapter.

Use the following to get a summary of files in the current folder:

```
for d in `find . -type d`;
  do
  echo `find $d -type f | wc -l` files in $d;
done
```

If this script is run in `/var/log`, it will generate output like this:

```
103 files in .
17 files in ./cups
0 files in ./hp
0 files in ./hp/tmp
```

3
File In, File Out

In this chapter, we will be covering the following recipes:

- Generating files of any size
- The intersection and set difference (A-B) on text files
- Finding and deleting duplicate files
- Working with file permissions, ownership, and the sticky bit
- Making files immutable
- Generating blank files in bulk
- Finding symbolic links and their targets
- Enumerating file type statistics
- Using loopback files
- Creating ISO files and hybrid ISO
- Finding the difference between files, and patching
- Using head and tail for printing the last or first 10 lines
- Listing only directories - alternative methods
- Fast command-line navigation using `pushd` and `popd`
- Counting the number of lines, words, and characters in a file
- Printing the directory tree
- Manipulating video and image files

Introduction

Unix provides a file-style interface to all devices and system features. The special files provide direct access to devices such as USB sticks and disk drives and provide access to system functions such as memory usage, sensors, and the process stack. For example, the command terminal we use is associated with a device file. We can write to the terminal by writing to the corresponding device file. We can access directories, regular files, block devices, character-special devices, symbolic links, sockets, named pipes, and so on as files. Filename, size, file type, modification time, access time, change time, inode, links associated, and the filesystem the file is on are all attributes and properties files can have. This chapter deals with recipes to handle operations or properties related to files.

Generating files of any size

A file of random data is useful for testing. You can use such files to test application efficiency, to confirm that an application is truly input-neutral, to confirm there's no size limitations in your application, to create loopback filesystems (**loopback files** are files that can contain a filesystem itself and these files can be mounted similarly to a physical device using the `mount` command), and more. Linux provides general utilities to construct such files.

How to do it...

The easiest way to create a large file of a given size is with the `dd` command. The `dd` command clones the given input and writes an exact copy to the output. Input can be `stdin`, a device file, a regular file, and so on. Output can be `stdout`, a device file, a regular file, and so on. An example of the `dd` command is as follows:

```
$ dd if=/dev/zero of=junk.data bs=1M count=1
1+0 records in
1+0 records out
1048576 bytes (1.0 MB) copied, 0.00767266 s, 137 MB/s
```

This command creates a file called `junk.data` containing exactly 1 MB of zeros.

Let's go through the parameters:

- `if` defines the `input` file
- `of` defines the `output` file
- `bs` defines bytes in a block
- `count` defines the number of blocks to be copied

Be careful while using the `dd` command as root, as it operates on a low level with the devices. A mistake could wipe your disk or corrupt the data. Double-check your `dd` command syntax, especially your of = parameter for accuracy.

In the previous example, we created a 1 MB file, by specifying `bs` as 1 MB with a count of 1. If `bs` was set to 2M and `count` to 2, the total file size would be 4 MB.

We can use various units for **blocksize (bs)**. Append any of the following characters to the number to specify the size:

Unit size	Code
Byte (1 B)	C
Word (2 B)	W
Block (512 B)	B
Kilobyte (1024 B)	K
Megabyte (1024 KB)	M
Gigabyte (1024 MB)	G

We can generate a file of any size using **bs**. Instead of MB we can use any other unit notations, such as the ones mentioned in the previous table.

`/dev/zero` is a character special device, which returns the zero byte (\0).

If the input parameter (`if`) is not specified, dd will read input from `stdin`. If the output parameter (`of`) is not specified, `dd` will use `stdout`.

The `dd` command can be used to measure the speed of memory operations by transferring a large quantity of data to `/dev/null` and checking the command output (for example, `1048576 bytes (1.0 MB) copied, 0.00767266 s, 137 MB/s`, as seen in the previous example).

The intersection and set difference (A-B) on text files

Intersection and set difference operations are common in mathematics classes on set theory. Similar operations on strings are useful in some scenarios.

Getting ready

The `comm` command is a utility to perform a comparison between two sorted files. It displays lines that are unique to file 1, file 2, and lines in both files. It has options to suppress one more column, making it easy to perform intersection and difference operations.

- **Intersection**: The intersection operation will print the lines the specified files have in common with one another
- **Difference**: The difference operation will print the lines the specified files contain and that are not the same in all of those files
- **Set difference**: The set difference operation will print the lines in file A that do not match those in all of the set of files specified (B plus C, for example)

How to do it...

Note that `comm` takes two sorted files as input. Here are our sample input files:

```
$ cat A.txt
apple
orange
gold
silver
steel
iron

$ cat B.txt
orange
gold
cookies
carrot

$ sort A.txt -o A.txt ; sort B.txt -o B.txt
```

1. First, execute `comm` without any options:

```
$ comm A.txt B.txt
apple
        carrot
        cookies
                gold
iron
                orange
silver
steel
```

The first column of the output contains lines that are only in `A.txt`. The second column contains lines that are only in `B.txt`. The third column contains the common lines from `A.txt` and `B.txt`. Each of the columns are delimited using the tab (`\t`) character.

2. In order to print the intersection of two files, we need to remove the first and second columns and print the third column. The `-1` option removes the first column, and the `-2` option removes the second column, leaving the third column:

```
$ comm A.txt B.txt -1 -2
gold
orange
```

3. Print only the lines that are uncommon between the two files by removing column 3:

```
$ comm A.txt B.txt   -3
apple
        carrot
        cookies
iron
silver
steel
```

This output uses two columns with blanks to show the unique lines in file1 and file2. We can make this more readable as a list of unique lines by merging the two columns into one, like this:

```
apple
carrot
cookies
iron
silver
steel
```

4. The lines can be merged by removing the tab characters with `tr` (discussed in `Chapter 2`, *Have a Good Command*)

```
$ comm A.txt B.txt  -3 | tr -d '\t'
apple
carrot
cookies
iron
silver
steel
```

5. By removing the unnecessary columns, we can produce the set difference for `A.txt` and `B.txt`, as follows:

- Set difference for `A.txt`:

  ```
  $ comm A.txt B.txt -2 -3
  ```

  `-2 -3` removes the second and third columns

- Set difference for `B.txt`:

  ```
  $ comm A.txt B.txt -1 -3
  ```

  `-2 -3` removes the second and third columns

How it works...

These command-line options reduce the output:

- `-1`: Removes the first column
- `-2`: Removes the second column
- `-3`: Removes the third column

The set difference operation enables you to compare two files and print all the lines that are in the `A.txt` or `B.txt` file excluding the common lines in `A.txt` and `B.txt`. When `A.txt` and `B.txt` are given as arguments to the `comm` command, the output will contain column-1 with the set difference for `A.txt` with regard to `B.txt` and column-2 will contain the set difference for `B.txt` with regard to `A.txt`.

The `comm` command will accept a – character on the command line to read one file from `stdin`. This provides a way to compare more than one file with a given input.

Suppose we have a `C.txt` file, like this:

```
$> cat C.txt
pear
orange
silver
mithral
```

We can compare the `B.txt` and `C.txt` files with `A.txt`, like this:

```
$> sort B.txt C.txt | comm - A.txt
        apple
carrot
cookies
                gold
        iron
mithral
                orange
pear
                silver
        steel
```

Finding and deleting duplicate files

If you need to recover backups or you use your laptop in a disconnected mode or download images from a phone, you'll eventually end up with duplicates: files with the same content. You'll probably want to remove duplicate files and keep a single copy. We can identify duplicate files by examining the content with shell utilities. This recipe describes finding duplicate files and performing operations based on the result.

Getting ready

We identify the duplicate files by comparing file content. Checksums are ideal for this task. Files with the same content will produce the same checksum values.

How to do it...

Follow these steps for finding or deleting duplicate files:

1. Generate some test files:

```
$ echo "hello" > test ; cp test test_copy1 ; cp test test_copy2;
$ echo "next" > other;
# test_copy1 and test_copy2 are copy of test
```

2. The code for the script to remove the duplicate files uses awk, an interpreter that's available on all Linux/Unix systems:

```bash
#!/bin/bash
#Filename: remove_duplicates.sh
#Description: Find and remove duplicate files and
# keep one sample of each file.
ls -lS --time-style=long-iso | awk 'BEGIN {
  getline; getline;
  name1=$8; size=$5
}
{
  name2=$8;
  if (size==$5)
{
  "md5sum "name1 | getline; csum1=$1;
  "md5sum "name2 | getline; csum2=$1;
  if ( csum1==csum2 )
  {
    print name1; print name2
   }
};

size=$5; name1=name2;
}' | sort -u > duplicate_files


  cat duplicate_files | xargs -I {} md5sum {} | \
  sort | uniq -w 32 | awk '{ print $2 }' | \
  sort -u > unique_files

  echo Removing..
  comm duplicate_files unique_files -3 | tee /dev/stderr | \
      xargs rm
  echo Removed duplicates files successfully.
```

3. Run the code as follows:

```
$ ./remove_duplicates.sh
```

How it works...

The preceding code will find the copies of the same file in a directory and remove all except one copy of the file. Let's go through the code and see how it works.

`ls -lS` lists the details of the files in the current folder sorted by file size. The `--time-style=long-iso` option tells `ls` to print dates in the ISO format. `awk` reads the output of `ls -lS` and performs comparisons on columns and rows of the input text to find duplicate files.

The logic behind the code is as follows:

- We list the files sorted by size, so files of the same size will be adjacent. The first step in finding identical files is to find ones with the same size. Next, we calculate the checksum of the files. If the checksums match, the files are duplicates and one set of the duplicates are removed.
- The `BEGIN{}` block of `awk` is executed before the main processing. It reads the "total" lines and initializes the variables. The bulk of the processing takes place in the `{}` block, when `awk` reads and processes the rest of the `ls` output. The `END{}` block statements are executed after all input has been read. The output of `ls -lS` is as follows:

```
total 16
-rw-r--r-- 1 slynux slynux 5 2010-06-29 11:50 other
-rw-r--r-- 1 slynux slynux 6 2010-06-29 11:50 test
-rw-r--r-- 1 slynux slynux 6 2010-06-29 11:50 test_copy1
-rw-r--r-- 1 slynux slynux 6 2010-06-29 11:50 test_copy2
```

- The output of the first line tells us the total number of files, which in this case is not useful. We use `getline` to read the first line and then dump it. We need to compare each of the lines and the following line for size. In the `BEGIN` block, we read the first line and store the name and size (which are the eighth and fifth columns). When `awk` enters the `{}` block, the rest of the lines are read, one by one. This block compares the size obtained from the current line and the previously stored size in the `size` variable. If they are equal, it means that the two files are duplicates by size and must be further checked by `md5sum`.

We have played some tricks on the way to the solution.

The external command output can be read inside `awk` as follows:

```
"cmd"| getline
```

Once the line is read, the entire line is in `$0` and each column is available in `$1`, `$2`, ..., `$n`. Here, we read the md5sum checksum of files into the `csum1` and `csum2` variables. The `name1` and `name2` variables store the consecutive filenames. If the checksums of two files are the same, they are confirmed to be duplicates and are printed.

We need to find a file from each group of duplicates so we can remove all other duplicates. We calculate the `md5sum` value of the duplicates and print one file from each group of duplicates by finding unique lines, comparing `md5sum` from each line using `-w 32` (the first 32 characters in the `md5sum` output; usually, the `md5sum` output consists of a 32-character hash followed by the filename). One sample from each group of duplicates is written to `unique_files`.

Now, we need to remove the files listed in `duplicate_files`, excluding the files listed in `unique_files`. The `comm` command prints files in `duplicate_files` but not in `unique_files`.

For that, we use a set difference operation (refer to the recipes on intersection, difference, and set difference).

`comm` only processes sorted input. Therefore, `sort -u` is used to filter `duplicate_files` and `unique_files`.

The `tee` command is used to pass filenames to the `rm` command as well as `print`. The `tee` command sends its input to both `stdout and a file`. We can also print text to the terminal by redirecting to `stderr`. `/dev/stderr` is the device corresponding to `stderr` (standard error). By redirecting to a `stderr` device file, text sent to `stdin` will be printed in the terminal as standard error.

Working with file permissions, ownership, and the sticky bit

File permissions and ownership are one of the distinguishing features of the Unix/Linux filesystems. These features protect your information in a multi-user environment. Mismatched permissions and ownership can also make it difficult to share files. These recipes explain how to use a file's permission and ownership effectively.

Each file possesses many types of permissions. Three sets of permissions (user, group, and others) are commonly manipulated.

The **user** is the owner of the file, who commonly has all access permitted. The **group** is the collection of users (as defined by the system administrator) that may be permitted some access to the file. **Others** are any users other than the owner or members of the owner's group.

The `ls` command's `-l` option displays many aspects of the file including type, permissions, owner, and group:

```
-rw-r--r-- 1 slynux users  2497  2010-02-28 11:22 bot.py
drwxr-xr-x 2 slynux users  4096  2010-05-27 14:31 a.py
-rw-r--r-- 1 slynux users  539   2010-02-10 09:11 cl.pl
```

The first column of the output defines the file type as follows:

- −: This is used if it is a regular file
- d: This is used if it is a directory
- c: This is used for a character device
- b: This is used for a block device
- l: This is used if it is a symbolic link
- s: This is used for a socket
- p: This is used for a pipe

The next nine characters are divided into three groups of three letters each (--- --- ---). The first three characters correspond to the permissions of the user (owner), the second sets of three characters correspond to the permissions of the group, and the third sets of three characters correspond to the permissions of others. Each character in the nine-character sequence (nine permissions) specifies whether permission is set or unset. If the permission is set, a character appears in the corresponding position, otherwise a − character appears in that position, which means that the corresponding permission is unset (unavailable).

The three common letters in the trio are:

- r Read: When this is set, the file, device, or directory can be read.
- w Write: When this is set, the file, device, or directory can be modified. On folders, this defines whether files can be created or deleted.
- x execute: When this is set, the file, can be executed. On folders, this defines whether the files in the folder can be accessed.

Let's take a look at what each of these three character sets mean for the user, group, and others:

- **User** (permission string: `rwx-----`): These define the options a user has. Usually, the user's permission is `rw-` for a data file and `rwx` for a script or executable. The user has one more special permission called `setuid` (`S`), which appears in the position of execute (`x`). The `setuid` permission enables an executable file to be executed effectively as its owner, even when the executable is run by another user. An example of a file with `setuid` permission set is `-rwS------`.
- **Group** (permission string: `---rwx---`): The second set of three characters specifies the group permissions. Instead of `setuid`, the group has a `setgid` (`S`) bit. This enables the item to run an executable file with an effective group as the owner group. But the group, which initiates the command, may be different. An example of group permission is `----rwS---`.
- **Others** (permission string: `------rwx`): Other permissions appear as the last three characters in the permission string. If these are set, anyone can access this file or folder. As a rule you will want to set these bits to `---`.

Directories have a special permission called a **sticky bit**. When a sticky bit is set for a directory, only the user who created the directory can delete the files in the directory, even if the group and others have write permissions. The sticky bit appears in the position of execute character (`x`) in the others permission set. It is represented as character `t` or `T`. The `t` character appears in the `x` position if the execute permission is unset and the sticky bit is set. If the sticky bit and the execute permission are set, the `T` character appears in the `x` position. Consider this example:

```
------rwt  ,  ------rwT
```

A typical example of a directory with sticky bit turned on is `/tmp`, where anyone can create a file, but only the owner can delete one.

In each of the `ls -l` output lines, the string `slynux users` corresponds to the user and group. Here, `slynux` is the owner who is a member of the group users.

How to do it...

In order to set permissions for files, we use the `chmod` command.

Assume that we need to set the permission, rwx rw- r-.

Set these permissions with chmod:

```
$ chmod u=rwx g=rw o=r filename
```

The options used here are as follows:

- u: This specifies user permissions
- g: This specifies group permissions
- o: This specifies others permissions

Use + to add permission to a user, group, or others, and use – to remove the permissions.

Add the executable permission to a file, which has the permission, rwx rw- r-:

```
$ chmod o+x filename
```

This command adds the x permission for others.

Add the executable permission to all permission categories, that is, for user, group, and others:

```
$ chmod a+x filename
```

Here a means all.

In order to remove a permission, use –. For example, **$ chmod a-x filename**.

Permissions can be denoted with three-digit octal numbers in which each digit corresponds to user, group, and other, in that order.

Read, write, and execute permissions have unique octal numbers, as follows:

- r = 4
- w = 2
- x = 1

We calculate the required combination of permissions by adding the octal values. Consider this example:

- rw- = 4 + 2 = 6
- r-x = 4 + 1 = 5

The permission `rwx rw- r--` in the numeric method is as follows:

- `rwx` = 4 + 2 + 1 = 7
- `rw-` = 4 + 2 = 6
- `r--` = 4

Therefore, `rwx rw- r--` is equal to `764`, and the command to set the permissions using octal values is $ `chmod 764 filename`.

There's more...

Let's examine more tasks we can perform on files and directories.

Changing ownership

The `chown` command will change the ownership of files and folders:

```
$ chown user.group filename
```

Consider this example:

```
$ chown slynux.users test.sh
```

Here, `slynux` is the user, and `users` is the group.

Setting the sticky bit

The sticky bit can be applied to directories. When the sticky bit is set, only the owner can delete files, even though others have write permission for the folder.

The sticky bit is set with the `+t` option to `chmod`:

```
$ chmod a+t directory_name
```

Applying permissions recursively to files

Sometimes, you may need to change the permissions of all the files and directories inside the current directory recursively. The `-R` option to `chmod` supports recursive changes:

```
$ chmod 777 . -R
```

The -R option specifies to change the permissions recursively.

We used . to specify the path as the current working directory. This is equivalent to $ chmod 777 "$(pwd)" -R.

Applying ownership recursively

The chown command also supports the -R flag to recursively change ownership:

```
$ chown user.group . -R
```

Running an executable as a different user (setuid)

Some executables need to be executed as a user other than the current user. For example, the http server may be initiated during the boot sequence by root, but the task should be owned by the httpd user. The setuid permission enables the file to be executed as the file owner when any other user runs the program.

First, change the ownership to the user that needs to execute it and then log in as the user. Then, run the following commands:

```
$ chmod +s executable_file
# chown root.root executable_file
# chmod +s executable_file
$ ./executable_file
```

Now it executes as the root user regardless of who invokes it.

The setuid is only valid for Linux ELF binaries. You cannot set a shell script to run as another user. This is a security feature.

Making files immutable

The Read, Write, Execute, and Setuid fields are common to all Linux file systems. The **Extended File Systems** (ext2, ext3, and ext4) support more attributes.

One of the extended attributes makes files immutable. When a file is made immutable, any user or super user cannot remove the file until the immutable attribute is removed from the file. You can determine the type of filesystem with the df -T command, or by looking at the /etc/mtab file. The first column of the file specifies the partition device path (for example, /dev/sda5) and the third column specifies the filesystem type (for example, ext3).

Making a file immutable is one method for securing files from modification. One example is to make the `/etc/resolv.conf` file immutable. The `resolv.conf` file stores a list of DNS servers, which convert domain names (such as packtpub.com) to IP addresses. The DNS server is usually your ISP's DNS server. However, if you prefer a third-party server, you can modify `/etc/resolv.conf` to point to that DNS. The next time you connect to your ISP, `/etc/resolv.conf` will be overwritten to point to ISP's DNS server. To prevent this, make `/etc/resolv.conf` immutable.

In this recipe, we will see how to make files immutable and make them mutable when required.

Getting ready

The `chattr` command is used to change extended attributes. It can make files immutable, as well as modify attributes to tune filesystem sync or compression.

How to do it...

To make the files immutable, follow these steps:

1. Use `chattr` to make a file immutable:

   ```
   # chattr +i file
   ```

2. The file is now immutable. Try the following command:

   ```
   rm file
   rm: cannot remove `file': Operation not permitted
   ```

3. In order to make it writable, remove the immutable attribute, as follows:

   ```
   chattr -i file
   ```

Generating blank files in bulk

Scripts must be tested before they are used on a live system. We may need to generate thousands of files to confirm that there are no memory leaks or processes left hanging. This recipe shows how to generate blank files.

Getting ready

The `touch` command creates blank files or modifies the timestamp of existing files.

How to do it...

To generate blank files in bulk, follow these steps:

1. Invoking the touch command with a non-existent filename creates an empty file:

   ```
   $ touch filename
   ```

2. Generate bulk files with a different name pattern:

   ```
   for name in {1..100}.txt
   do
       touch $name
   done
   ```

In the preceding code, `{1..100}` will be expanded to a string 1, 2, 3, 4, 5, 6, 7...100. Instead of `{1..100}.txt`, we can use various shorthand patterns such as `test{1..200}.c`, `test{a..z}.txt`, and so on.

If a file already exists, the `touch` command changes all timestamps associated with the file to the current time. These options define a subset of timestamps to be modified:

- `touch -a`: This modifies the access time
- `touch -m`: This modifies the modification time

Instead of the current time, we can specify the time and date:

```
$ touch -d "Fri Jun 25 20:50:14 IST 1999" filename
```

The date string used with `-d` need not be in this exact format. It will accept many simple date formats. We can omit time from the string and provide only dates such as *Jan 20, 2010*.

Finding symbolic links and their targets

Symbolic links are common in Unix-like systems. Reasons for using them range from convenient access, to maintaining multiple versions of the same library or program. This recipe will discuss the basic techniques for handling symbolic links.

Symbolic links are pointers to other files or folders. They are similar in function to aliases in MacOS X or shortcuts in Windows. When symbolic links are removed, it does not affect the original file.

How to do it...

The following steps will help you handle symbolic links:

1. To create a symbolic link run the following command:

   ```
   $ ln -s target symbolic_link_name
   ```

   Consider this example:

   ```
   $ ln -l -s /var/www/ ~/web
   ```

   This creates a symbolic link (called **web**) in the current user's home directory, which points to /var/www/.

2. To verify the link was created, run this command:

   ```
   $ ls -l ~/web
   lrwxrwxrwx 1 slynux slynux 8 2010-06-25 21:34 web -> /var/www
   ```

   web -> /var/www specifies that web points to /var/www.

3. To print symbolic links in the current directory, use this command:

   ```
   $ ls -l | grep "^l"
   ```

4. To print all symbolic links in the current directory and subdirectories, run this command:

   ```
   $ find . -type l -print
   ```

5. To display the target path for a given symbolic link, use the `readlink` command:

```
$ readlink web
/var/www
```

How it works...

When using `ls` and `grep` to display symbolic links in the current folder, the `grep ^l` command filters the `ls -l` output to only display lines starting with l. The ^ specifies the start of the string. The following l specifies that the string must start with l, the identifier for a link.

When using `find`, we use the argument `-typel`, which instructs find to search for symbolic link files. The `-print` option prints the list of symbolic links to the standard output (`stdout`). The initial path is given as the current directory.

Enumerating file type statistics

Linux supports many file types. This recipe describes a script that enumerates through all the files inside a directory and its descendants, and prints a report with details on types of files (files with different file types), and the count of each file type. This recipe is an exercise on writing scripts to enumerate through many files and collect details.

Getting ready

On Unix/Linux systems, file types are not defined by the file extension (as Microsoft Windows does). Unix/Linux systems use the file command, which examines the file's contents to determine a file's type. This recipe collects file type statistics for a number of files. It stores the count of files of the same type in an associative array.

 The associative arrays are supported in bash version 4 and newer.

How to do it...

To enumerate file type statistics, follow these steps:

1. To print the type of a file, use the following command:

   ```
   $ file filename
   ```

   ```
   $ file /etc/passwd
   /etc/passwd: ASCII text
   ```

2. Print the file type without the filename:

   ```
   $ file -b filename
   ASCII text
   ```

3. The script for file statistics is as follows:

   ```bash
   #!/bin/bash
   # Filename: filestat.sh

   if [ $# -ne 1 ];
   then
     echo "Usage is $0 basepath";
     exit
   fi
   path=$1

   declare -A statarray;

   while read line;
   do
     ftype=`file -b "$line" | cut -d, -f1`
     let statarray["$ftype"]++;

   done < (find $path -type f -print)

   echo ============ File types and counts =============
   for ftype in "${!statarray[@]}";
   do
     echo $ftype :  ${statarray["$ftype"]}
   done
   ```

   The usage is as follows:

   ```
   $ ./filestat.sh /home/slynux/temp
   ```

5. A sample output is shown as follows:

```
$ ./filetype.sh /home/slynux/programs
============ File types and counts ============
Vim swap file : 1
ELF 32-bit LSB executable : 6
ASCII text : 2
ASCII C program text : 10
```

How it works...

This script relies on the associative array `statarray`. This array is indexed by the type of file: **PDF**, **ASCII**, and so on. Each index holds the count for that type of file. It is defined by the `declare -A statarray` command.

The script then consists of two loops: a while loop, that processes the output from the find command, and a `for` loop, that iterates through the indices of the `statarray` variable and generates output.

The while loop syntax looks like this:

```
while read line;
do something
done < filename
```

For this script, we use the output of the find command instead of a file as input to `while`.

The `(find $path -type f -print)` command is equivalent to a filename, but it substitutes the filename with a subprocess output.

 Note that the first < is for input redirection and the second < is for converting the subprocess output to a filename. Also, there is a space between these two so the shell won't interpret it as the << operator.

The `find` command uses the `-typef` option to return a list of files under the subdirectory defined in $path. The filenames are read one line at a time by the `read` command. When the read command receives an **EOF (End of File)**, it returns a *fail* and the `while` command exits.

Within the `while` loop, the file command is used to determine a file's type. The `-b` option is used to display the file type without the name.

The file command provides more details than we need, such as image encoding and resolution (in the case of an image file). The details are comma-separated, as in the following example:

```
$ file a.out -b
ELF 32-bit LSB executable, Intel 80386, version 1 (SYSV),
dynamically linked (uses shared libs), for GNU/Linux 2.6.15, not
stripped
```

We need to extract only `ELF 32-bit LSB executable` from the previous details. Hence, we use the `-d`, option to specify , as the delimiter and `-f1` to select the first field.

`<(find $path -type f -print)` is equivalent to a filename, but it substitutes the filename with a subprocess output. Note that the first < is for input redirection and the second < is for converting the subprocess output to a filename. Also, there is a space between these two so that the shell won't interpret it as the << operator.

In Bash 3.x and higher, we have a new operator <<< that lets us use a string output as an input file. Using this operator, we can write the done line of the loop, as follows:

```
done <<< "`find $path -type f -print`"
```

`${!statarray[@]}` returns the list of array indexes.

Using loopback files

Linux filesystems normally exist on devices such as disks or memory sticks. A file can also be mounted as a filesystem. This filesystem-in-a-file can be used for testing, for customized filesystems, or even as an encrypted disk for confidential information.

How to do it...

To create a 1 GB ext4 filesystem in a file, follow these steps:

1. Use `dd` to create a 1 GB file:

```
$ dd if=/dev/zero of=loobackfile.img bs=1G count=1
1024+0 records in
1024+0 records out
1073741824 bytes (1.1 GB) copied, 37.3155 s, 28.8 MB/s
```

The size of the created file exceeds 1 GB because the hard disk is a block device, and hence, storage must be allocated by integral multiples of blocks size.

2. Format the 1 GB file to ext4 using the `mkfs` command:

```
$ mkfs.ext4 loopbackfile.img
```

3. Check the file type with the file command:

```
$ file loobackfile.img
loobackfile.img: Linux rev 1.0 ext4 filesystem data,
UUID=c9d56c42-
f8e6-4cbd-aeab-369d5056660a (extents) (large files) (huge files)
```

4. Create a mount point and mount the loopback file with `mkdir` and mount:

```
# mkdir /mnt/loopback
# mount -o loop loopbackfile.img /mnt/loopback
```

The `-o loop` option is used to mount loopback filesystems.

This is a short method that attaches the loopback filesystem to a device chosen by the operating system named something similar to `/dev/loop1` or `/dev/loop2`.

5. To specify a specific loopback device, run the following command:

```
# losetup /dev/loop1 loopbackfile.img
# mount /dev/loop1 /mnt/loopback
```

6. To umount (`unmount`), use the following syntax:

```
# umount mount_point
```

Consider this example:

```
# umount /mnt/loopback
```

7. We can also use the device file path as an argument to the `umount` command:

```
# umount /dev/loop1
```

Note that the mount and umount commands should be executed as a root user, since it is a privileged command.

How it works...

First we had to create a file to make a loopback filesystem. For this, we used dd, which is a generic command for copying raw data. It copies data from the file specified in the if parameter to the file specified in the of parameter. We instruct dd to copy data in blocks of size 1 GB and copy one such block, creating a 1 GB file. The /dev/zero file is a special file, which will always return 0 when you read from it.

We used the mkfts.ext4 command to create an ext4 filesystem in the file. A filesystem is needed on any device that can be mounted. Common filesystems include ext4, ext3, and vfat.

The mount command attaches the loopback file to a **mountpoint** (/mnt/loopback in this case). A mountpoint makes it possible for users to access the files stored on a filesystem. The mountpoint must be created using the mkdir command before executing the mount command. We pass the -o loop option to mount to tell it that we are mounting a loopback file, not a device.

When mount knows it is operating on a loopback file, it sets up a device in /dev corresponding to the loopback file and then mounts it. If we wish to do it manually, we use the losetup command to create the device and then the mount command to mount it.

There's more...

Let's explore some more possibilities with loopback files and mounting.

Creating partitions inside loopback images

Suppose we want to create a loopback file, partition it, and finally mount a sub-partition. In this case, we cannot use mount -o loop. We must manually set up the device and mount the partitions in it.

To partition a file of zeros:

```
# losetup /dev/loop1 loopback.img
# fdisk /dev/loop1
```

 `fdisk` is a standard partitioning tool on Linux systems. A very concise tutorial on creating partitions using `fdisk` is available at http://www.tldp.org/HOWTO/Partition/fdisk_partitioning.html (make sure to use `/dev/loop1` instead of `/dev/hdb` in this tutorial).

Create partitions in `loopback.img` and mount the first partition:

```
# losetup -o 32256 /dev/loop2 loopback.img
```

Here, `/dev/loop2` represents the first partition,`-o` is the offset flag, and `32256` bytes are for a DOS partition scheme. The first partition starts 32256 bytes from the start of the hard disk.

We can set up the second partition by specifying the required offset. After mounting, we can perform all regular operations as we can on physical devices.

Mounting loopback disk images with partitions more quickly

We can manually pass partition offsets to `losetup` to mount partitions inside a loopback disk image. However, there is a quicker way to mount all the partitions inside such an image using `kpartx`. This utility is usually not installed, so you will have to install it using your package manager:

```
# kpartx -v -a diskimage.img
add map loop0p1 (252:0): 0 114688 linear /dev/loop0 8192
add map loop0p2 (252:1): 0 15628288 linear /dev/loop0 122880
```

This creates mappings from the partitions in the disk image to devices in `/dev/mapper`, which you can then mount. For example, to mount the first partition, use the following command:

```
# mount /dev/mapper/loop0p1 /mnt/disk1
```

When you're done with the devices (and unmounting any mounted partitions using `umount`), remove the mappings by running the following command:

```
# kpartx -d diskimage.img
loop deleted : /dev/loop0
```

Mounting ISO files as loopback

An ISO file is an archive of an optical media. We can mount ISO files in the same way that we mount physical disks using loopback mounting.

We can even use a nonempty directory as the mount path. Then, the mount path will contain data from the devices rather than the original contents, until the device is unmounted. Consider this example:

```
# mkdir /mnt/iso
# mount -o loop linux.iso /mnt/iso
```

Now, perform operations using files from /mnt/iso. ISO is a read-only filesystem.

Flush changing immediately with sync

Changes on a mounted device are not immediately written to the physical device. They are only written when the internal memory buffer is full. We can force writing with the sync command:

```
$ sync
```

Creating ISO files and hybrid ISO

An ISO image is an archive format that stores the exact image of an optical disk such as CD-ROM, DVD-ROM, and so on. ISO files are commonly used to store content to be burned to optical media.

This section will describe how to extract data from an optical disk into an ISO file that can be mounted as a loopback device, and then explain ways to generate your own ISO file systems that can be burned to an optical media.

We need to distinguish between bootable and non-bootable optical disks. Bootable disks are capable of booting from themselves and also running an operating system or another product. Bootable DVDs include installation kits and *Live* systems such as Knoppix and Puppy.

Non-bootable ISOs cannot do that. Upgrade kits, source code DVDs, and so on are non-bootable.

 Note that copying files from a bootable CD-ROM to another CD-ROM is not sufficient to make the new one bootable. To preserve the bootable nature of a CD-ROM, it must be copied as a disk image using an ISO file.

Many people use flash drives as a replacement for optical disks. When we write a bootable ISO to a flash drive, it will not be bootable unless we use a special hybrid ISO image designed specifically for the purpose.

These recipes will give you an insight into ISO images and manipulations.

Getting ready

As mentioned previously, Unix handles everything as files. Every device is a file. Hence, if we want to copy an exact image of a device, we need to read all data from it and write to a file. An optical media reader will be in the /dev folder with a name such as /dev/cdrom, /dev/dvd, or perhaps /dev/sd0. Be careful when accessing an sd*. Multiple disk-type devices are named sd#. Your hard drive may be sd0 and the CD-ROM sd1, for instance.

The cat command will read any data, and redirection will write that data to a file. This works, but we'll also see better ways to do it.

How to do it...

In order to create an ISO image from /dev/cdrom, use the following command:

```
# cat /dev/cdrom > image.iso
```

Though this will work, the preferred way to create an ISO image is with dd:

```
# dd if=/dev/cdrom of=image.iso
```

The mkisofs command creates an ISO image in a file. The output file created by mkisofs can be written to CD-ROM or DVD-ROM with utilities such as cdrecord. The mkisofs command will create an ISO file from a directory containing all the files to be copied to the ISO file:

```
$ mkisofs -V "Label" -o image.iso source_dir/
```

The $-o$ option in the `mkisofs` command specifies the ISO file path. The `source_dir` is the path of the directory to be used as content for the ISO file and the $-V$ option specifies the label to use for the ISO file.

There's more...

Let's learn more commands and techniques related to ISO files.

Hybrid ISO that boots off a flash drive or hard disk

Bootable ISO files cannot usually be transferred to a USB storage device to create a bootable USB stick. However, special types of ISO files called hybrid ISOs can be flashed to create a bootable device.

We can convert standard ISO files into hybrid ISOs with the `isohybrid` command. The `isohybrid` command is a new utility and most Linux distros don't include this by default. You can download the `syslinux package` from http://www.syslinux.org. The command may also be available in your yum or `apt-get` repository as `syslinux-utils`.

This command will make an ISO file bootable:

```
# isohybrid image.iso
```

The ISO file can now be written to USB storage devices.

To write the ISO to a USB storage device, use the following command:

```
# dd if=image.iso of=/dev/sdb1
```

Use the appropriate device instead of /dev/sdb1, or you can use *cat*, as follows:

```
# cat image.iso >> /dev/sdb1
```

Burning an ISO from the command line

The `cdrecord` command burns an ISO file to a CD-ROM or DVD-ROM.

To burn the image to the CD-ROM, run the following command:

```
# cdrecord -v dev=/dev/cdrom image.iso
```

Useful options include the following:

- Specify the burning speed with the -speed option:

    -speed SPEED

    Consider this example:

    # cdrecord -v dev=/dev/cdrom image.iso -speed 8

    Here, 8 is the speed specified as 8x.

- A CD-ROM can be burned in multi-sessions such that we can burn data multiple times on a disk. Multisession burning can be done with the -multi option:

    # cdrecord -v dev=/dev/cdrom image.iso -multi

Playing with the CD-ROM tray

If you are on a desktop computer, try the following commands and have fun:

    $ eject

This command will eject the tray.

    $ eject -t

This command will close the tray.

For extra points, write a loop that opens and closes the tray a number of times. It goes without saying that one would never slip this into a co-workers .bashrc while they are out getting a coffee.

Finding the difference between files, and patching

When multiple versions of a file are available, it is useful to highlight the differences between files rather than comparing them manually. This recipe illustrates how to generate differences between files. When working with multiple developers, changes need to be distributed to the others. Sending the entire source code to other developers is time consuming. Sending a difference file instead is helpful, as it consists of only lines which are changed, added, or removed, and line numbers are attached with it. This difference file is called a **patch file**. We can add the changes specified in the patch file to the original source code with the `patch` command. We can revert the changes by patching again.

How to do it...

The `diff` utility reports the differences between two files.

1. To demonstrate diff behavior, create the following files:

   File 1: `version1.txt`

   ```
   this is the original text
   line2
   line3
   line4
   happy hacking !
   ```

   File 2: `version2.txt`

   ```
   this is the original text
   line2
   line4
   happy hacking !
   GNU is not UNIX
   ```

2. Nonunified `diff` output (without the `-u` flag) is:

   ```
   $ diff version1.txt version2.txt
   3d2
   <line3
   6c5
   > GNU is not UNIX
   ```

3. The unified `diff` output is:

```
$ diff -u version1.txt version2.txt
--- version1.txt    2010-06-27 10:26:54.384884455 +0530
+++ version2.txt    2010-06-27 10:27:28.782140889 +0530
@@ -1,5 +1,5 @@
this is the original text
line2
-line3
line4
happy hacking !
-
+GNU is not UNIX
```

The `-u` option produces a unified output. Unified diff output is more readable and is easier to interpret.

In unified `diff`, the lines starting with + are the added lines and the lines starting with - are the removed lines.

4. A patch file can be generated by redirecting the `diff` output to a file:

```
$ diff -u version1.txt version2.txt > version.patch
```

The `patch` command can apply changes to either of the two files. When applied to `version1.txt`, we get the `version2.txt` file. When applied to `version2.txt`, we generate `version1.txt`.

5. This command applies the patch:

```
$ patch -p1 version1.txt < version.patch
patching file version1.txt
```

We now have `version1.txt` with the same contents as `version2.txt`.

6. To revert the changes, use the following command:

```
$ patch -p1 version1.txt < version.patch
patching file version1.txt
Reversed (or previously applied) patch detected!  Assume -R? [n] y
#Changes are reverted.
```

As shown, patching an already patched file reverts the changes. To avoid prompting the user with y/n, we can use the -R option along with the `patch` command.

There's more...

Let's go through additional features available with `diff`.

Generating difference against directories

The `diff` command can act recursively against directories. It will generate a difference output for all the descendant files in the directories. Use the following command:

```
$ diff -Naur directory1 directory2
```

The interpretation of each of the options in this command is as follows:

- `-N`: This is used for treating missing files as empty
- `-a`: This is used to consider all files as text files
- `-u`: This is used to produce unified output
- `-r`: This is used to recursively traverse through the files in the directories

Using head and tail for printing the last or first 10 lines

When examining a large file, thousands of lines long, the `cat` command, which will display all the line,s is not suitable. Instead, we want to view a subset (for example, the first 10 lines of the file or the last 10 lines of the file). We may need to print the first *n* lines or last *n* lines or print all except the last *n* lines or all except the first *n* lines, or the lines between two locations.

The `head` and `tail` commands can do this.

How to do it...

The `head` command reads the beginning of the input file.

1. Print the first 10 lines:

```
$ head file
```

2. Read the data from `stdin`:

```
$ cat text | head
```

3. Specify the number of first lines to be printed:

```
$ head -n 4 file
```

This command prints the first four lines.

4. Print all lines excluding the last M lines:

```
$ head -n -M file
```

 Note that it is negative M.

For example, to print all the lines except the last five lines, use the following command line:

```
$ seq 11 | head -n -5
1
2
3
4
5
6
```

This command prints lines 1 to 5:

```
$ seq 100 | head -n 5
```

5. Printing everything except the last lines is a common use for `head`. When examining log files we most often want to view the most recent (that is, the last) lines.

6. To print the last 10 lines of a file, use this command:

```
$ tail file
```

7. To read from `stdin`, use the following command:

```
$ cat text | tail
```

8. Print the last five lines:

```
$ tail -n 5 file
```

9. To print all lines excluding the first M lines, use this command:

```
$ tail -n +(M+1)
```

For example, to print all lines except the first five lines, *M + 1 = 6*, the command is as follows:

```
$ seq 100 | tail -n +6
```

This will print from 6 to 100.

One common use for `tail` is to monitor new lines in a growing file, for instance, a system log file. Since new lines are appended to the end of the file, `tail` can be used to display them as they are written. To monitor the growth of the file, `tail` has a special option `-f` or `--follow`, which enables `tail` to follow the appended lines and display them as data is added:

```
$ tail -f growing_file
```

You will probably want to use this on logfiles. The command to monitor the growth of the files would be this:

```
# tail -f /var/log/messages
```

Alternatively, this command can be used:

```
$ dmesg | tail -f
```

The `dmesg` command returns contents of the kernel ring buffer messages. We can use this to debug USB devices, examine disk behavior, or monitor network connectivity. The `-f` tail can add a sleep interval `-s` to set the interval during which the file updates are monitored.

The `tail` command can be instructed to terminate after a given process ID dies.

Suppose a process `Foo` is appending data to a file that we are monitoring. The `-f` tail should be executed until the process `Foo` dies.

```
$ PID=$(pidof Foo)
$ tail -f file --pid $PID
```

When the process `Foo` terminates, `tail` also terminates.

Let's work on an example.

1. Create a new file `file.txt` and open the file in your favorite text editor.
2. Now run the following commands:

```
$ PID=$(pidof gedit)
$ tail -f file.txt --pid $PID
```

3. Add new lines to the file and make frequent file saves.

When you add new lines to the end of the file, the new lines will be written to the terminal by the `tail` command. When you close the edit session, the `tail` command will terminate.

Listing only directories - alternative methods

Listing only directories via scripting is deceptively difficult. This recipe introduces multiple ways of listing only directories.

Getting ready

g ready There are multiple ways of listing directories only. The `dir` command is similar to `ls`, but with fewer options. We can also list directories with `ls` and `find`.

How to do it...

Directories in the current path can be displayed in the following ways:

1. Use `ls` with `-d` to print directories:

```
$ ls -d */
```

2. Use `ls -F` with `grep`:

```
$ ls -F | grep "/$"
```

3. Use `ls -l` with `grep`:

```
$ ls -l | grep "^d"
```

4. Use `find` to print directories:

```
$ find . -type d -maxdepth 1 -print
```

How it works...

When the `-F` parameter is used with `ls`, all entries are appended with some type of file character such as @, *, |, and so on. For directories, entries are appended with the / character. We use `grep` to filter only entries ending with the /$ end-of-line indicator.

The first character of any line in the `ls -l` output is the type of file character. For a directory, the type of file character is d. Hence, we use `grep` to filter lines starting with "d."^ is a start-of-line indicator.

The `find` command can take the parameter type as directory and `maxdepth` is set to 1 since we don't want it to search inside the subdirectories.

Fast command-line navigation using pushd and popd

When navigating around multiple locations in the filesystem, a common practice is to cd to paths you copy and paste. This is not efficient if we are dealing with several locations. When we need to navigate back and forth between locations, it is time consuming to type or paste the path with each `cd` command. Bash and other shells support `pushd` and `popd` to cycle between directories.

Getting ready

`pushd` and `popd` are used to switch between multiple directories without retyping directory paths. `pushd` and `popd` create a stack of paths-a **LastInFirstOut** (**LIFO**) list of the directories we've visited.

How to do it...

The `pushd` and `popd` commands replace cd for changing your working directory.

1. To push and change a directory to a path, use this command:

   ~ $ pushd /var/www

   Now the stack contains `/var/www` ~ and the current directory is changed to `/var/www`.

2. Now, push the next directory path:

   /var/www $ pushd /usr/src

   Now the stack contains `/usr/src/var/www` ~ and the current directory is `/usr/src`.

   You can push as many directory paths as needed.

3. View the stack contents:

   ```
   $ dirs
   /usr/src /var/www ~ /usr/share /etc
   0        1          2 3        4
   ```

4. Now when you want to switch to any path in the list, number each path from 0 to n, then use the path number for which we need to switch. Consider this example:

   $ pushd +3

   Now it will rotate the stack and switch to the `/usr/share` directory.

   `pushd` will always add paths to the stack. To remove paths from the stack, use `popd`.

5. Remove a last pushed path and change to the next directory:

   $ popd

   Suppose the stack is `/usr/src` `/var/www` ~ `/usr/share` `/etc`, and the current directory is `/usr/src`. The `popd` command will change the stack to `/var/www` ~ `/usr/share` `/etc` and change the current directory to `/var/www`.

6. To remove a specific path from the list, use `popd +num`. `num` is counted as 0 to n from left to right.

There's more...

Let's go through the essential directory navigation practices.

pushd and popd are useful when there are more than three directory paths used. However, when you use only two locations, there is an alternative and easier way, that is, cd -.

The current path is `/var/www`.

```
/var/www $  cd /usr/src
/usr/src $ # do something
```

Now, to switch back to `/var/www`, you don't have to type `/var/www`, just execute:

```
/usr/src $ cd -
```

To switch to `/usr/src`:

```
/var/www $ cd -
```

Counting the number of lines, words, and characters in a file

Counting the number of lines, words, and characters in a text file is frequently useful. This book includes some tricky examples in other chapters where the counts are used to produce the required output. **Counting LOC (Lines of Code)** is a common application for developers. We may need to count a subset of files, for example, all source code files, but not object files. A combination of `wc` with other commands can perform that.

The `wc` utility counts lines, words, and characters. It stands for **word count**.

How to do it...

The `wc` command supports options to count the number of lines, words, and characters:

1. Count the number of lines:

   ```
   $ wc -l file
   ```

2. To use `stdin` as input, use this command:

   ```
   $ cat file | wc -l
   ```

3. Count the number of words:

   ```
   $ wc -w file
   $ cat file | wc -w
   ```

4. Count the number of characters:

   ```
   $ wc -c file
   $ cat file | wc -c
   ```

   To count the characters in a text string, use this command:

   ```
   echo -n 1234 | wc -c
   4
   ```

   Here, `-n` deletes the final newline character.

5. To print the number of lines, words, and characters, execute `wc` without any options:

   ```
   $ wc file
   1435    15763   112200
   ```

   Those are the number of lines, words, and characters.

6. Print the length of the longest line in a file with the `-L` option:

   ```
   $ wc file -L
   205
   ```

Printing the directory tree

Graphically representing directories and filesystems as a tree hierarchy makes them easier to visualize. This representation is used by monitoring scripts to present the filesystem in an easy-to-read format.

Getting ready

The tree command prints graphical trees of files and directories. The tree command does not come with preinstalled Linux distributions. You must install it using the package manager.

How to do it...

The following is a sample Unix filesystem tree to show an example:

```
$ tree ~/unixfs
unixfs/
|-- bin
|    |-- cat
|    `-- ls
|-- etc
|    `-- passwd
|-- home
|    |-- pactpub
|    |    |-- automate.sh
|    |    `-- schedule
|    `-- slynux
|-- opt
|-- tmp
`-- usr
8 directories, 5 files
```

The `tree` command supports several options:

- To display only files that match a pattern, use the `-P` option:

```
$ tree path -P PATTERN # Pattern should be wildcard in single
quotes
```

Consider this example:

```
$ tree PATH -P '*.sh' # Replace PATH with a directory path
|-- home
|    |-- packtpub
|    |     `-- automate.sh
```

- To display only files that do not match a pattern, use the `-I` option:

```
$ tree path -I PATTERN
```

- To print the size along with files and directories, use the `-h` option:

```
$ tree -h
```

There's more...

The tree command can generate output in HTML as well as to a terminal.

HTML output for tree

This command creates an HTML file with the tree output:

```
$ tree PATH -H http://localhost -o out.html
```

Replace `http://localhost` with the URL where you are planning to host the file. Replace PATH with a real path for the base directory. For the current directory, use . as PATH.

The web page generated from the directory listing will look as follows:

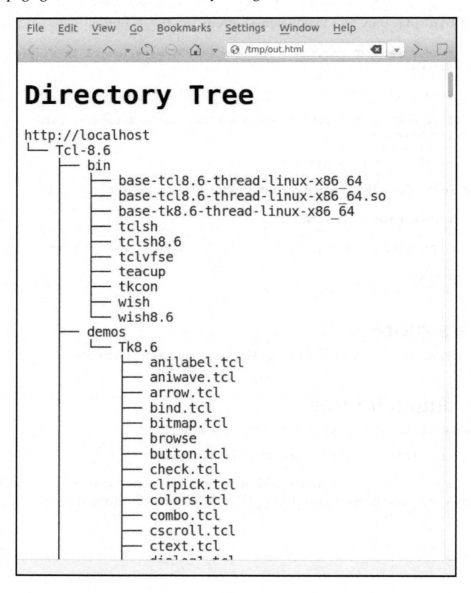

Manipulating video and image files

Linux and Unix support many applications and tools for working with images and video files. Most Linux distributions include the **imageMagick** suite with the **convert** application for manipulating images. The full-function video editing applications such as **kdenlive** and **openshot** are built on top of the **ffmpeg** and **mencoder** command line applications.

The convert application has hundreds of options. We'll just use the one that extracts a portion of an image.

`ffmpeg` and `mencoder` have enough options and features to fill a book all by themselves. We'll just look at a couple simple uses.

This section has some recipes for manipulating still images and videos.

Getting ready

Most Linux distributions include the **ImageMagick** tools. If your system does not include them, or if they are out of date, there are instructions for downloading and installing the latest tools on the ImageMagick website at `www.imagemagick.org`.

Like ImageMagick, many Linux distributions already include the `ffmpeg` and `mencoder` toolsets. The latest releases can be found at the `ffmpeg` and `mencoder` websites at `http://www.ffmpeg.org` and `http://www.mplayerhq.hu`.

Building and installing the video tools will probably require loading codecs and other ancillary files with confusing version dependencies. If you intend to use your Linux system for audio and video editing, it's simplest to use a Linux distribution that's designed for this, such as the Ubuntu Studio distributions.

Here are some recipes for a couple of common audio-video conversions:

Extracting Audio from a movie file (mp4)

Music videos are fun to watch, but the point of music is to listen to it. Extracting the audio portion from a video is simple:

How to do it...

The following command accepts an mp4 video file (FILE.mp4) and extracts the audio portion into a new file (OUTPUTFILE.mp3) as an mp3:

```
ffmpeg -i FILE.mp4 -acodec libmp3lame OUTPUTFILE.mp3
```

Making a video from a set of still images

Many cameras support taking pictures at intervals. You can use this feature to do your own time-lapse photography or create stop-action videos. There are examples of this on www.cwflynt.com. You can convert a set of still images into a video with the OpenShot video editing package or from a command line using the mencoder tool.

How to do it...

This script will accept a list of images and will create an MPEG video file from it:

```
$ cat stills2mpg.sh
echo $* | tr ' ' '\n' >files.txt
mencoder mf://@files.txt -mf fps=24 -ovc lavc \
-lavcopts vcodec=msmpeg4v2 -noskip -o movie.mpg
```

To use this script, copy/paste the commands into a file named stills2mpg.sh, make it executable and invoke it as follows:

```
./stills2mpg.sh file1.jpg file2.jpg file3.jpg ...
```

Alternatively, use this to invoke it:

```
./stills2mpg.sh *.jpg
```

How it works...

The `mencoder` command requires that the input file be formatted as one image file per line. The first line of the script echoes the command line arguments to the tr command to convert the space delimiters to newlines. This transforms the single-line list into a list of files arranged one per line.

You can change the speed of the video by resetting the **FPS (frames-per-second)** parameter. For example, setting the fps value to 1 will make a slide show that changes images every second.

Creating a panned video from a still camera shot

If you decide to create your own video, you'll probably want a panned shot of some landscape at some point. You can record a video image with most cameras, but if you only have a still image you can still make a panned video.

How to do it...

Cameras commonly take a larger image than will fit on a video. You can create a motion-picture pan using the convert application to extract sections of a large image, and stitch them together into a video file with `mencoder`:

```
$> makePan.sh
# Invoke as:
# sh makePan.sh OriginalImage.jpg prefix width height xoffset yoffset
# Clean out any old data
rm -f tmpFiles
# Create 200 still images, stepping through the original xoffset and
yoffset
# pixels at a time
for o in `seq 1 200`
 do
 x=$[ $o+$5 ]
 convert -extract $3x$4+$x+$6 $1 $2_$x.jpg
 echo $2_$x.jpg >> tmpFiles
done
#Stitch together the image files into a mpg video file
mencoder mf://@tmpFiles -mf fps=30 -ovc lavc -lavcopts \
        vcodec=msmpeg4v2 -noskip -o $2.mpg
```

How it works...

This script is more complex than the ones we've looked at so far. It uses seven command-line arguments to define the input image, a prefix to use for the output files, the width and height for the intermediate images, and the starting offset into the original image.

Within the `for` loop, it creates a set of image files and stores the names in a file named `tmpFiles`. Finally, the script uses `mencoder` to merge the extracted image files into an MPEG video that can be imported into a video editor such as kdenlive or OpenShot.

4
Texting and Driving

In this chapter, we will cover the following recipes:

- Using regular expressions
- Searching and mining text inside a file with grep
- Cutting a file column-wise with cut
- Using sed to perform text replacement
- Using awk for advanced text processing
- Finding the frequency of words used in a given file
- Compressing or decompressing JavaScript
- Merging multiple files as columns
- Printing the nth word or column in a file or line
- Printing text between line numbers or patterns
- Printing lines in the reverse order
- Parsing e-mail address and URLs from text
- Removing a sentence in a file containing a word
- Replacing a pattern with text in all the files in a directory
- Text slicing and parameter operations

Introduction

Shell scripting includes many problem-solving tools. There is a rich set of tools for text processing. These tools include utilities, such as sed, awk, grep, and cut, which can be combined to perform text processing needs.

These utilities process files by character, line, word, column, or row to process text files in many ways.

Regular expressions are a basic pattern-matching technique. Most text-processing utilities support regular expressions. With regular expression strings, we can filter, strip, replace, and search within text files.

This chapter includes a collection of recipes to walk you through many solutions to text processing problems.

Using regular expressions

Regular expressions are at the heart of pattern-based text-processing. To use regular expressions effectively, one needs to understand them.

Everyone who uses `ls` is familiar with glob style patterns. Glob rules are useful in many situations, but are too limited for text processing. Regular expressions allow you to describe patterns in finer detail than glob rules.

A typical regular expression to match an e-mail address might look like this:

```
[a-z0-9_]+@[a-z0-9]+\.[a-z]+.
```

If this looks weird, don't worry; it is really simple once you understand the concepts through this recipe.

How to do it...

Regular expressions are composed of text fragments and symbols with special meanings. Using these, we can construct a regular expression to match any text. Regular expressions are the basis for many tools. This section describes regular expressions, but does not introduce the Linux/Unix tools that use them. Later recipes will describe the tools.

Regular expressions consist of one or more elements combined into a string. An element may be a position marker, an identifier, or a count modifier. A position marker anchors the regular expression to the beginning or end of the target string. An identifier defines one or more characters. The count modifier defines how many times an identifier may occur.

Before we look at some sample regular expressions, let's look at the rules.

Position markers

A position marker anchors a regular expression to a position in the string. By default, any set of characters that match a regular expression can be used, regardless of position in the string.

regex	Description	Example
^	This specifies that the text that matches the regular expression must start at the beginning of the string	^tux matches a line that starts with tux
$	This specifies that the text that matches the regular expression must end with the last character in the target string	tux$ matches a line that ends with tux

Identifiers

Identifiers are the basis of regular expressions. These define the characters that must be present (or absent) to match the regular expression.

regex	Description	Example
A character	The regular expression must match this letter.	A will match the letter A
.	This matches any one character.	"Hack." matches Hack1, Hacki, but not Hack12 or Hackil; only one additional character matches
[]	This matches any one of the characters enclosed in the brackets. The enclosed characters may be a set or a range.	coo[kl] matches cook or cool; [0-9] matches any single digit
[^]	This matches any one of the characters except those that are enclosed in square brackets. The enclosed characters may be a set or a range.	9[^01] matches 92 and 93, but not 91 and 90; A[^0-9] matches an A followed by anything except a digit

Count modifiers

An Identifier may occur once, never, or many times. The Count Modifier defines how many times a pattern may appear.

regex	Description	Example
?	This means that the preceding item must match one or zero times	`colou?r` matches `color` or `colour`, but not `colouur`
+	This means that the preceding item must match one or more times	`Rollno-9+` matches `Rollno-99` and `Rollno-9`, but not `Rollno-`
*	This means that the preceding item must match zero or more times	`co*l` matches `cl`, `col`, and `coool`
{n}	This means that the preceding item must match n times	`[0-9]{3}` matches any three-digit number; `[0-9]{3}` can be expanded as `[0-9][0-9][0-9]`
{n, }	This specifies the minimum number of times the preceding item should match	`[0-9]{2,}` matches any number that is two digits or longer
{n, m}	This specifies the minimum and maximum number of times the preceding item should match	`[0-9]{2,5}` matches any number that has two digits to five digits

Other

Here are other characters that fine–tune how a regular expression will be parsed.

()	This treats the terms enclosed as one entity	`ma(tri)?x` matches `max` or `matrix`
|	This specifies alternation-; one of the items on either of side of | should match	`Oct (1st | 2nd)` matches `Oct 1st` or `Oct 2nd`
\	This is the escape character for escaping any of the special characters mentioned previously	`a\.b` matches `a.b`, but not `ajb`; it ignores the special meaning of `.` because of `\`

For more details on the regular expression components available, you can refer to
`http://www.linuxforu.com/2011/04/sed-explained-part-1/`.

There's more...

Let's see a few examples of regular expressions:

This regular expression would match any single word:

```
( +[a-zA-Z]+ +)
```

The initial + characters say we need 1 or more spaces.

The `[a-zA-Z]` set is all upper- and lower-case letters. The following plus sign says we need at least one letter and can have more.

The final + characters say we need to terminate the word with one or more spaces.

 This would not match the last word in a sentence. To match the last word in a sentence or the word before a comma, we write the expression like this:

```
( +[a-zA-Z]+[?,\.]? +)
```

The `[?,\.]?` phrase means we might have a question mark, comma, or a period, but at most one. The period is escaped with a backslash because a bare period is a wildcard that will match anything.

It's easier to match an IP address. We know we'll have four three-digit numbers separated by periods.

The `[0-9]` phrase defines a number. The `{1,3}` phrase defines the count as being at least one digit and no more than three digits:

```
[0-9]{1,3}\.[0-9]{1,3}\.[0-9]{1,3}\.[0-9]{1,3}
```

We can also define an IP address using the `[[:digit:]]` construct to define a number:

```
[[:digit:]]{1,3}\.[[:digit:]]{1,3}\.[[:digit:]]{1,3}\.[[:digit:]]{1,3}
```

We know that an IP address is in the range of four integers (each from 0 to 255), separated by dots (for example, `192.168.0.2`).

This regex will match an IP address in the text being processed. However, it doesn't check for the validity of the address. For example, an IP address of the form `123.300.1.1` will be matched by the regex despite being an invalid IP.

How it works...

Regular expressions are parsed by a complex state machine that tries to find the best match for a regular expression with a string of target text. That text can be the output of a pipe, a file, or even a string you type on the command line. If there are multiple ways to fulfill a regular expression, the engine will usually select the largest set of characters that match.

For example, given the string `this is a test` and a regular expression `s.*s`, the match will be `s is a tes`, not `s is`.

For more details on the regular expression components available, you can refer to `http://www.linuxforu.com/2011/04/sed-explained-part-1/`.

There's more...

The previous tables described the special meanings for characters used in regular expressions.

Treatment of special characters

Regular expressions use some characters, such as $, ^, ., *, +, {, and }, as special characters. But, what if we want to use these characters as normal text characters? Let's see an example of a regex, `a.txt`.

This will match the character a, followed by any character (due to the . character), which is then followed by the `txt` string. However, we want . to match a literal . instead of any character. In order to achieve this, we precede the character with a backward slash \ (doing this is called escaping the character). This indicates that the regex wants to match the literal character rather than its special meaning. Hence, the final regex becomes `a\.txt`.

Visualizing regular expressions

Regular expressions can be tough to understand. Fortunately, there are utilities available to help in visualizing regex. The page at http://www.regexper.com lets you enter a regular expression and creates a graph to help you understand it. Here is a screenshot describing a simple regular expression:

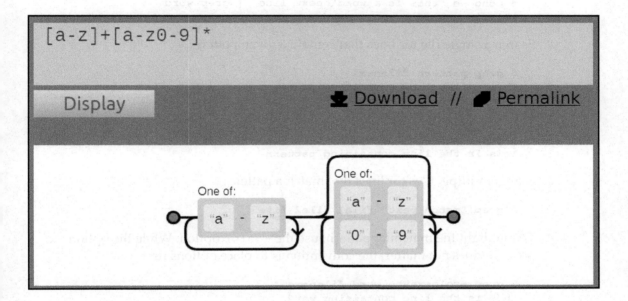

Searching and mining text inside a file with grep

If you forget where you left your keys, you've just got to search for them. If you forget what file has some information, the grep command will find it for you. This recipe will teach you how to locate files that contain patterns.

How to do it...

The `grep` command is the magic Unix utility for searching text. It accepts regular expressions and can produce reports in various formats.

1. Search `stdin` for lines that match a pattern:

```
$ echo -e "this is a word\nnext line" | grep word
this is a word
```

2. Search a single file for lines that contain a given pattern:

```
$ grep pattern filename
this is the line containing pattern
```

Alternatively, this performs the same search:

```
$ grep "pattern" filename
this is the line containing pattern
```

3. Search multiple files for lines that match a pattern:

```
$ grep "match_text" file1 file2 file3 ...
```

4. To highlight the matching pattern, use the `-color` option. While the option position does not matter, the convention is to place options first.

```
$ grep -color=auto word filename
this is the line containing word
```

5. The `grep` command uses basic regular expressions by default. These are a subset of the rules described earlier. The `-E` option will cause `grep` to use the **Extended Regular Expression** syntax. The `egrep` command is a variant of `grep` that uses extended regular expression by default:

```
$ grep -E "[a-z]+" filename
```

Or:

```
$ egrep "[a-z]+" filename
```

6. The `-o` option will report only the matching characters, not the entire line:

```
$ echo this is a line. | egrep -o "[a-z]+\."
line
```

7. The `-v` option will print all lines, except those containing `match_pattern`:

```
$ grep -v match_pattern file
```

The `-v` option added to `grep` inverts the match results.

8. The `-c` option will count the number of lines in which the pattern appears:

```
$ grep -c "text" filename
10
```

It should be noted that `-c` counts the number of matching lines, not the number of times a match is made. Consider this example:

```
$ echo -e "1 2 3 4\nhello\n5 6" | egrep  -c "[0-9]"
2
```

Even though there are six matching items, `grep` reports 2, since there are only two matching lines. Multiple matches in a single line are counted only once.

9. To count the number of matching items in a file, use this trick:

```
$ echo -e "1 2 3 4\nhello\n5 6" | egrep -o "[0-9]" | wc -l
6
```

10. The `-n` option will print the line number of the matching string:

```
$ cat sample1.txt
gnu is not unix
linux is fun
bash is art
$ cat sample2.txt
planetlinux
$ grep linux -n sample1.txt
2:linux is fun
```

Or

```
$ cat sample1.txt | grep linux -n
```

If multiple files are used, the `-c` option will print the filename with the result:

```
$ grep linux -n sample1.txt sample2.txt
sample1.txt:2:linux is fun
sample2.txt:2:planetlinux
```

11. The −b option will print the offset of the line in which a match occurs. Adding the −o option will print the exact character or byte offset where the pattern matches:

```
$ echo gnu is not unix | grep -b -o "not"
7:not
```

Character positions are numbered from 0, not from 1.

12. The −l option lists which files contain the pattern:

```
$ grep -l linux sample1.txt sample2.txt
sample1.txt
sample2.txt
```

The inverse of the −l argument is −L. The −L argument returns a list of nonmatching files.

There's more...

The grep command is one of the most versatile Linux/Unix commands. It also includes options to search through folders, select files to search, and more options for identifying patterns.

Recursively searching many files

To recursively search for a text in files contained in a file hierarchy, use the following command:

```
$ grep "text" . -R -n
```

In this command, . specifies the current directory.

The options −R and −r mean the same thing when used with grep.

Consider this example:

```
$ cd src_dir
$ grep "test_function()" . -R -n
./miscutils/test.c:16:test_function();
```

test_function() exists in line number 16 of miscutils/test.c. The –R option is particularly useful if you are searching for a phrase in a website or source code tree. It is equivalent to this command:

```
$ find . -type f | xargs grep "test_function()"
```

Ignoring case in patterns

The –i argument matches patterns without considering the uppercase or lowercase:

```
$ echo hello world | grep -i "HELLO"
hello
```

grep by matching multiple patterns

The –e argument specifies multiple patterns for matching:

```
$ grep -e "pattern1" -e "pattern2"
```

This will print the lines that contain either of the patterns and output one line for each match. Consider this example:

```
$ echo this is a line of text | grep -o -e "this" -e "line"
this
line
```

Multiple patterns can be defined in a file. The –f option will read the file and use the line-separated patterns:

```
$ grep -f pattern_filesource_filename
```

Consider the following example:

```
$ cat pat_file
hello
cool

$ echo hello this is cool | grep -f pat_file
hello this is cool
```

Including and excluding files in a grep search

grep can include or exclude files in which to search with wild card patterns.

To recursively search only for the .c and .cpp files, use the -include option:

```
$ grep "main()" . -r  --include *.{c,cpp}
```

Note that some{string1,string2,string3} expands as somestring1 somestring2 somestring3.

Use the -exclude flag to exclude all README files from the search:

```
$ grep "main()" . -r --exclude "README"
```

The --exclude-dir option will exclude the named directories from the search:

```
$ grep main . -r -exclude-dir CVS
```

To read a list of files to exclude from a file, use --exclude-from FILE.

Using grep with xargs with the zero-byte suffix

The xargs command provides a list of command-line arguments to another command. When filenames are used as command-line arguments, use a zero-byte terminator for the filenames instead of the default space terminator. Filenames can contain space characters, which will be misinterpreted as name separators, causing a filename to be broken into two filenames (for example, New file.txt might be interpreted as two filenames New and file.txt). Using the zero-byte suffix option solves this problem. We use xargs to accept stdin text from commands such as grep and find. These commands can generate output with a zero-byte suffix. The xargs command will expect 0 byte termination when the -0 flag is used.

Create some test files:

```
$ echo "test" > file1
$ echo "cool" > file2
$ echo "test" > file3
```

The -l option tells `grep` to output only the filenames where a match occurs. The -Z option causes `grep` to use the zero-byte terminator (\0) for these files. These two options are frequently used together. The -0 argument to `xargs` makes it read the input and separate filenames at the zero-byte terminator:

```
$ grep "test" file* -lZ | xargs -0 rm
```

Silent output for grep

Sometimes, instead of examining at the matched strings, we are only interested in whether there was a match or not. The quiet option (-q), causes `grep` to run silently and not generate any output. Instead, it runs the command and returns an exit status based on success or failure. The return status is 0 for success and nonzero for failure.

The `grep` command can be used in quiet mode, for testing whether a match text appears in a file or not:

```
#!/bin/bash
#Filename: silent_grep.sh
#Desc: Testing whether a file contain a text or not

if [ $# -ne 2 ]; then
  echo "Usage: $0 match_text filename"
  exit 1
fi

match_text=$1
filename=$2
grep -q "$match_text" $filename

if [ $? -eq 0 ]; then
  echo "The text exists in the file"
else
  echo "Text does not exist in the file"
fi
```

The `silent_grep.sh` script accepts two command-line arguments, a match word (Student), and a file name (student_data.txt):

```
$ ./silent_grep.sh Student student_data.txt
The text exists in the file
```

Printing lines before and after text matches

Context-based printing is one of the nice features of grep. When grep finds lines that match the pattern, it prints only the matching lines. We may need to see *n* lines before or after the matching line. The -B and -A options display lines before and after the match, respectively.

The -A option prints lines after a match:

```
$ seq 10 | grep 5 -A 3
5
6
7
8
```

The -B option prints lines before the match:

```
$ seq 10 | grep 5 -B 3
2
3
4
5
```

The -A and -B options can be used together, or the -C option can be used to print the same number of lines before and after the match:

```
$ seq 10 | grep 5 -C 3
2
3
4
5
6
7
8
```

If there are multiple matches, then each section is delimited by a -- line:

```
$ echo -e "a\nb\nc\na\nb\nc" | grep a -A 1
a
b
--
a
b
```

Cutting a file column-wise with cut

The cut command splits a file by column instead of lines. This is useful for processing files with fixed-width fields, **Comma Separated Values** (CSV files), or space delimited files such as the standard log files.

How to do it...

The cut command extracts data between character locations or columns. You can specify the delimiter that separates each column. In the cut terminology, each column is known as a **field**.

1. The -f option defines the fields to extract:

   ```
   cut -f FIELD_LIST filename
   ```

   FIELD_LIST is a list of columns that are to be displayed. The list consists of column numbers delimited by commas. Consider this example:

   ```
   $ cut -f 2,3 filename
   ```

   Here, the second and the third columns are displayed.

2. The cut command also reads input from stdin.

   Tab is the default delimiter for fields. Lines without delimiters will be printed. The -s option will disable printing lines without delimiter characters. The following commands demonstrate extracting columns from a tab delimited file:

   ```
   $ cat student_data.txt
   No  Name  Mark  Percent
   1   Sarath  45   90
   2   Alex   49    98
   3   Anu   45    90

   $ cut -f1 student_data.txt
   No
   1
   2
   3
   ```

3. To extract multiple fields provide multiple field numbers separated by commas, using the following options:

```
$ cut -f2,4 student_data.txt
Name      Percent
Sarath    90
Alex      98
Anu       90
```

4. The `--complement` option will display all the fields except those defined by `-f`. This command displays all fields except 3:

```
$ cut -f3 --complement student_data.txt
No   Name    Percent
1    Sarath  90
2    Alex    98
3    Anu     90
```

5. The `-d` option will set the delimiter. The following command shows how to use `cut` with a colon-separated list:

```
$ cat delimited_data.txt
No;Name;Mark;Percent
1;Sarath;45;90
2;Alex;49;98
3;Anu;45;90

$ cut -f2 -d";" delimited_data.txt
Name
Sarath
Alex
Anu
```

There's more

The `cut` command has more options to define the columns displayed.

Specifying the range of characters or bytes as fields

A report with fixed-width columns will have varying numbers of spaces between the columns. You can't extract values based on field position, but you can extract them based on the character location. The `cut` command can select based on bytes or characters as well as fields.

It's unreasonable to enter every character position to extract, so cut accepts these notations as well as the comma-separated list:

N-	From the Nth byte, character, or field, to the end of the line
N-M	From the Nth to M^{th} (included) byte, character, or field
-M	From the first to M^{th} (included) byte, character, or field

We use the preceding notations to specify fields as a range of bytes, characters, or fields with the following options:

- −b for bytes
- −c for characters
- −f for defining fields

Consider this example:

```
$ cat range_fields.txt
abcdefghijklmnopqrstuvwxyz
abcdefghijklmnopqrstuvwxyz
abcdefghijklmnopqrstuvwxyz
abcdefghijklmnopqrstuvwxy
```

Display the second to fifth characters:

```
$ cut -c2-5 range_fields.txt
bcde
bcde
bcde
bcde
```

Display the first two characters:

```
$ cut -c -2  range_fields.txt
ab
ab
ab
ab
```

Replace `-c` with `-b` to count in bytes.

The `-output-delimiter` option specifies the output delimiter. This is particularly useful when displaying multiple sets of data:

```
$ cut range_fields.txt -c1-3,6-9 --output-delimiter ","
abc,fghi
abc,fghi
abc,fghi
abc,fghi
```

Using sed to perform text replacement

`sed` stands for **stream editor**. It's most commonly used for text replacement. This recipe covers many common `sed` techniques.

How to do it...

The `sed` command can replace occurrences of a pattern with another string. The pattern can be a simple string or a regular expression:

```
$ sed 's/pattern/replace_string/' file
```

Alternatively, `sed` can read from `stdin`:

```
$ cat file | sed 's/pattern/replace_string/'
```

If you use the `vi` editor, you will notice that the command to replace the text is very similar to the one discussed here. By default, `sed` only prints the substituted text, allowing it to be used in a pipe.

```
$ cat /etc/passwd | cut -d : -f1,3 | sed 's/:/ - UID: /'
root - UID: 0
bin - UID: 1
...
```

1. The `-I` option will cause `sed` to replace the original file with the modified data:

```
$ sed -i 's/text/replace/' file
```

2. The previous example replaces the first occurrence of the pattern in each line. The
   -g parameter will cause sed to replace every occurrence:

   ```
   $ sed 's/pattern/replace_string/g' file
   ```

The /#g option will replace from the Nth occurrence onwards:

```
$ echo thisthisthisthis | sed 's/this/THIS/2g'
thisTHISTHISTHIS

$ echo thisthisthisthis | sed 's/this/THIS/3g'
thisthisTHISTHIS

$ echo thisthisthisthis | sed 's/this/THIS/4g'
thisthisthisTHIS
```

The sed command treats the character following s as the command delimiter.
This allows us to change strings with a / character in them:

```
sed 's:text:replace:g'
sed 's|text|replace|g'
```

When the delimiter character appears inside the pattern, we have to escape it
using the \ prefix, as follows:

```
sed 's|te\|xt|replace|g'
```

\| is a delimiter appearing in the pattern replaced with escape.

There's more...

The sed command supports regular expressions as the pattern to be replaced and has more
options to control its behavior.

Removing blank lines

Regular expression support makes it easy to remove blank lines. The ^$ regular expression defines a line with nothing between the beginning and end == a blank line. The final /d tells sed to delete the lines, rather than performing a substitution.

```
$ sed '/^$/d' file
```

Performing replacement directly in the file

When a filename is passed to sed, it usually prints to stdout. The -I option will cause sed to modify the contents of the file in place:

```
$ sed 's/PATTERN/replacement/' -i filename
```

For example, replace all three-digit numbers with another specified number in a file, as follows:

```
$ cat sed_data.txt
11 abc 111 this 9 file contains 111 11 88 numbers 0000

$ sed -i 's/\b[0-9]\{3\}\b/NUMBER/g' sed_data.txt
$ cat sed_data.txt
11 abc NUMBER this 9 file contains NUMBER 11 88 numbers 0000
```

The preceding one-liner replaces three-digit numbers only. \b[0-9]\{3\}\b is the regular expression used to match three-digit numbers. [0-9] is the range of digits from 0 to 9. The {3} string defines the count of digits. The backslash is used to give a special meaning for { and } and \b stands for a blank, the word boundary marker.

It's a useful practice to first try the sed command without -i to make sure your regex is correct. After you are satisfied with the result, add the -i option to make changes to the file. Alternatively, you can use the following form of sed:

```
sed -i .bak 's/abc/def/' file
```

In this case, sed will perform the replacement on the file and also create a file called file.bak, which contains the original contents.

Matched string notation (&)

The & symbol is the matched string. This value can be used in the replacement string:

```
$ echo this is an example | sed 's/\w\+/[&]/g'
[this] [is] [an] [example]
```

Here, the `\w\+` regex matches every word. Then, we replace it with `[&]`, which corresponds to the word that is matched.

Substring match notation (\1)

& corresponds to the matched string for the given pattern. Parenthesized portions of a regular expression can be matched with `\#`:

```
$ echo this is digit 7 in a number | sed 's/digit \([0-9]\)/\1/'
this is 7 in a number
```

The preceding command replaces `digit 7` with 7. The substring matched is 7. `\(pattern\)` matches the substring. The pattern is enclosed in () and is escaped with backslashes. For the first substring match, the corresponding notation is `\1`, for the second, it is `\2`, and so on.

```
$ echo seven EIGHT | sed 's/\([a-z]\+\) \([A-Z]\+\)/\2 \1/'
EIGHT seven
```

(`[a-z]\+\`) matches the first word and `\([A-Z]\+\)` matches the second word; `\1` and `\2` are used for referencing them. This type of referencing is called **back referencing**. In the replacement part, their order is changed as `\2 \1`, and hence, it appears in the reverse order.

Combining multiple expressions

Multiple `sed` commands can be combined with pipes, patterns separated by semicolons, or the `-e PATTERN` option:

```
sed 'expression' | sed 'expression'
```

The preceding command is equivalent to the following commands:

```
$ sed 'expression; expression'
```

Or:

```
$ sed -e 'expression' -e expression
```

Consider these examples:

```
$ echo abc | sed 's/a/A/' | sed 's/c/C/'
AbC
$ echo abc | sed 's/a/A/;s/c/C/'
AbC
$ echo abc | sed -e 's/a/A/' -e 's/c/C/'
AbC
```

Quoting

The sed expression is commonly quoted with single quotes. Double quotes can be used. The shell will expand double quotes before invoking sed. Using double quotes is useful when we want to use a variable string in a sed expression.

Consider this example:

```
$ text=hello
$ echo hello world | sed "s/$text/HELLO/"
HELLO world
```

$text is evaluated as hello.

Using awk for advanced text processing

The awk command processes data streams. It supports associative arrays, recursive functions, conditional statements, and more.

Getting ready

The structure of an awk script is:

```
awk ' BEGIN{ print "start" } pattern { commands } END{ print "end"}' file
```

The awk command can also read from stdin.

An awk script includes up to three parts–:BEGIN, END, and a common statement block with the pattern match option. These are optional and any of them can be absent in the script.

Awk will process the file line by line. The commands following BEGIN will be evaluated before <code>awk</code> starts processing the file. Awk will process each line that matches PATTERN with the commands that follow PATTERN. Finally, after processing the entire file, <CODE>awk</CODE> will process the commands that follow END.

How to do it...

Let's write a simple awk script enclosed in single quotes or double quotes:

```
awk 'BEGIN { statements } { statements } END { end statements }'
```

Or:

```
awk "BEGIN { statements } { statements } END { end statements }"
```

This command will report the number of lines in a file:

```
$ awk 'BEGIN { i=0 } { i++ } END{ print i}' filename
```

Or:

```
$ awk "BEGIN { i=0 } { i++ } END{ print i }" filename
```

How it works...

The awk command processes arguments in the following order:

1. First, it executes the commands in the BEGIN { commands } block.
2. Next, awk reads one line from the file or stdin, and executes the commands block if the optional pattern is matched. It repeats this step until the end of file.
3. When the end of the input stream is reached, it executes the END { commands } block.

The BEGIN block is executed before awk starts reading lines from the input stream. It is an optional block. The commands, such as variable initialization and printing the output header for an output table, are common comamnds in the BEGIN block.

The END block is similar to the BEGIN block. It gets executed when awk completes reading all the lines from the input stream. This is commonly printing results after analyzing all the lines.

The most important block holds the common commands with the pattern block. This block is also optional. If it is not provided, { print } gets executed to print each line read. This block gets executed for each line read by awk. It is like a while loop, with statements to execute inside the body of the loop.

When a line is read, awk checks whether the pattern matches the line. The pattern can be a regular expression match, conditions, a range of lines, and so on. If the current line matches the pattern, awk executes the commands enclosed in { }.

The pattern is optional. If it is not used, all lines are matched:

```
$ echo -e "line1\nline2" | awk 'BEGIN{ print "Start" } { print } \
    END{ print "End" } '
Start
line1
line2
End
```

When print is used without an argument, awk prints the current line.

The print command can accept arguments. These arguments are separated by commas, they are printed with a space delimiter. Double quotes are used as the concatenation operator.

Consider this example:

```
$ echo | awk '{ var1="v1"; var2="v2"; var3="v3"; \
    print var1,var2,var3 ; }'
```

The preceding command will display this:

```
v1 v2 v3
```

The echo command writes a single line into the standard output. Hence, the statements in the { } block of awk are executed once. If the input to awk contains multiple lines, the commands in awk will be executed multiple times.

Concatenation is done with quoted strings:

```
$ echo | awk '{ var1="v1"; var2="v2"; var3="v3"; \
    print var1 "-" var2 "-" var3 ; }'
v1-v2-v3
```

{ } is like a block in a loop, iterating through each line of a file.

It's a common practice to place initial variable assignments such as var=0; in the BEGIN block. The END{ } block contains commands to print the results.

There's more...

The awk command differs from commands such as grep, find, and tr, in that it does more than a single function with options to change the behavior. The awk command is a program that interprets and executes programs and includes special variables just like the shell.

Special variables

Some special variables that can be used with awk are as follows:

- NR: This stands for the current record number, which corresponds to the current line number when awk uses lines as records.
- NF: This stands for the number of fields, and corresponds to the number of fields in the current record being processed. The default field delimiter is a space.
- $0: This is a variable that contains the text of the current record.
- $1: This is a variable that holds the text of the first field.
- $2: This is a variable that holds the text of the second field.

Consider this example:

```
$ echo -e "line1 f2 f3\nline2 f4 f5\nline3 f6 f7" | \

awk '{
    print "Line no:"NR",No of fields:"NF, "$0="$0,
    "$1="$1,"$2="$2,"$3="$3
}'
Line no:1,No of fields:3 $0=line1 f2 f3 $1=line1 $2=f2 $3=f3
Line no:2,No of fields:3 $0=line2 f4 f5 $1=line2 $2=f4 $3=f5
Line no:3,No of fields:3 $0=line3 f6 f7 $1=line3 $2=f6 $3=f7
```

We can print the last field of a line as `print $NF`, the next to last as `$(NF-1)`, and so on.

`awk` also supports a `printf()` function with the same syntax as in C.

The following command prints the second and third field of every line:

```
$awk '{ print $3,$2 }' file
```

We can use NR to count the number of lines in a file:

```
$ awk 'END{ print NR }' file
```

Here, we only use the END block. Awk updates NR as each line is read. When `awk` reaches the end of the file, NR will contain the last line number. You can sum up all the numbers from each line of `field 1` as follows:

```
$ seq 5 | awk 'BEGIN{ sum=0; print "Summation:" }
{ print $1"+"; sum+=$1 } END { print "=="; print sum }'
Summation:
1+
2+
3+
4+
5+
==
15
```

Passing an external variable to awk

Using the `-v` argument, we can pass external values other than `stdin` to `awk`, as follows:

```
$ VAR=10000
$ echo | awk -v VARIABLE=$VAR '{ print VARIABLE }'
10000
```

There is a flexible alternate method to pass many variable values from outside `awk`. Consider the following example:

```
$ var1="Variable1" ; var2="Variable2"
$ echo | awk '{ print v1,v2 }' v1=$var1 v2=$var2
Variable1 Variable2
```

When an input is given through a file rather than standard input, use the following command:

```
$ awk '{ print v1,v2 }' v1=$var1 v2=$var2 filename
```

In the preceding method, variables are specified as key-value pairs, separated by a space, and (v1=$var1 v2=$var2) as command arguments to awk soon after the BEGIN, { }, and END blocks.

Reading a line explicitly using getline

The awk program reads an entire file by default. The getline function will read one line. This can be used to read header information from a file in the BEGIN block and then process actual data in the main block.

The syntax is getline var. The var variable will contain the line. If getline is called without an argument, we can access the content of the line with $0, $1, and $2.

Consider this example:

```
$ seq 5 | awk 'BEGIN { getline; print "Read ahead first line", $0 }
{ print $0 }'
Read ahead first line 1
2
3
4
5
```

Filtering lines processed by awk with filter patterns

We can specify conditions for lines to be processed:

```
$ awk 'NR < 5' # first four lines
$ awk 'NR==1,NR==4' #First four lines
$ # Lines containing the pattern linux (we can specify regex)
$ awk '/linux/'
$ # Lines not containing the pattern linux
$ awk '!/linux/'
```

Setting delimiters for fields

By default, the delimiter for fields is a space. The -F option defines a different field delimiter.

```
$ awk -F: '{ print $NF }' /etc/passwd
```

Or:

```
awk 'BEGIN { FS=":" } { print $NF }' /etc/passwd
```

We can set the output field separator by setting `OFS="delimiter"` in the `BEGIN` block.

Reading the command output from awk

Awk can invoke a command and read the output. Place a command string within quotes and use the vertical bar to pipe the output to `getline`:

```
"command" | getline output ;
```

The following code reads a single line from `/etc/passwd` and displays the login name and home folder. It resets the field separator to a `:` in the `BEGIN` block and invokes `grep` in the main block.

```
$ awk 'BEGIN {FS=":"} { "grep root /etc/passwd" | getline; \
    print $1,$6 }'
root /root
```

Associative arrays in Awk

Awk supports variables that contain a number or string and also supports associative arrays. An associative array is an array that's indexed by strings instead of numbers. You can recognize an associative array by the index within square brackets:

```
arrayName[index]
```

An array can be assigned a value with the equal sign, just like simple user-defined variables:

```
myarray[index]=value
```

Using loop inside awk

Awk supports a numeric `for` loop with a syntax similar to `C`:

```
for(i=0;i<10;i++) { print $i ; }
```

Awk also supports a list style for loop that will display the contents of an array:

```
for(i in array) { print array[i]; }
```

The following example shows how to collect data into an array and then display it. This script reads lines from /etc/password, splits them into fields at the : markers, and creates an array of names in which the index is the login ID and the value is the user's name:

```
$ awk 'BEGIN {FS=":"} {nam[$1]=$5} END {for {i in nam} \
    {print i,nam[i]}}' /etc/passwd
root root
ftp FTP User
userj Joe User
```

String manipulation functions in awk

The language of awk includes many built-in string manipulation functions:

- length(string): This returns the string length.
- index(string, search_string): This returns the position at which search_string is found in the string.
- split(string, array, delimiter): This populates an array with the strings created by splitting a string on the delimiter character.
- substr(string, start-position, end-position): This returns the substring of the string between the start and end character offsets.
- sub(regex, replacement_str, string): This replaces the first occurring regular expression match from the string with replacment_str.
- gsub(regex, replacment_str, string): This is like sub(), but it replaces every regular expression match.
- match(regex, string): This returns whether a regular expression (regex) match is found in the string. It returns a non-zero output if a match is found, otherwise it returns zero. Two special variables are associated with match(). They are RSTART and RLENGTH. The RSTART variable contains the position at which the regular expression match starts. The RLENGTH variable contains the length of the string matched by the regular expression.

Finding the frequency of words used in a given file

Computers are good at counting. We frequently need to count items such as the number of sites sending us spam, the number of downloads different web pages get, or how often words are used in a piece of text. This recipes show how to calculate word usage in a piece of text. The techniques are also applicable to log files, database output, and more.

Getting ready

We can use the associative arrays of awk to solve this problem in different ways. **Words** are alphabetic characters, delimited by space or a period. First, we should parse all the words in a given file and then the count of each word needs to be found. Words can be parsed using regex with tools such as sed, awk, or grep.

How to do it...

We just explored the logic and ideas about the solution; now let's create the shell script as follows:

```
#!/bin/bash
#Name: word_freq.sh
#Desc: Find out frequency of words in a file

if [ $# -ne 1 ];
then
  echo "Usage: $0 filename";
  exit -1
fi

filename=$1
egrep -o "\b[[:alpha:]]+\b" $filename | \
  awk '{ count[$0]++ }
    END {printf("%-14s%s\n","Word","Count") ;
      for(ind in count)
        { printf("%-14s%d\n",ind,count[ind]);
        }
      }
```

The script will generate this output:

```
$ ./word_freq.sh words.txt
Word          Count
used            1
this            2
counting        1
```

How it works...

The `egrep` command converts the text file into a stream of words, one word per line. The `\b[[:alpha:]]+\b` pattern matches each word and removes whitespace and punctuation. The `-o` option prints the matching character sequences as one word in each line.

The `awk` command counts each word. It executes the statements in the `{ }` block for each line, so we don't need a specific loop for doing that. The count is incremented by the `count[$0]++` command, in which `$0` is the current line and `count` is an associative array. After all the lines are processed, the `END{ }` block prints the words and their count.

The body of this procedure can be modified using other tools we've looked at. We can merge capitalized and non-capitalized words into a single count with the `tr` command, and sort the output using the sort command, like this:

```
egrep -o "\b[[:alpha:]]+\b" $filename | tr [A=Z] [a-z] | \
  awk '{ count[$0]++ }
    END{ printf("%-14s%s\n","Word","Count") ;
      for(ind in count)
        { printf("%-14s%d\n",ind,count[ind]);
        }
      }' | sort
```

See also

- The *Using awk for advanced text processing* recipe in this chapter explains the `awk` command
- The *Arrays and associative arrays* recipe in `Chapter 1`, *Shell Something Out*, explains arrays in Bash

Compressing or decompressing JavaScript

JavaScript is widely used in websites. While developing the JavaScript code, we use whitespaces, comments, and tabs for readability and maintenance of the code. This increases the file size, which slows page loading. Hence, most professional websites use compressed JavaScript speed page loading. This compression (also known as **minified JS**) is accomplished by removing the whitespace and newline characters. Once JavaScript is compressed, it can be decompressed by replacing enough whitespace and newline characters to make it readable. This recipe produces similar functionality in the shell.

Getting ready

We are going to write a JavaScript compressor tool as well as a decompressing tool. Consider the following JavaScript:

```
$ cat sample.js
function sign_out()
{

    $("#loading").show();
    $.get("log_in",{logout:"True"},

    function(){
      window.location="";
    });
}
```

Our script needs to perform these steps to compress the JavaScript:

1. Remove newline and tab characters.
2. Remove duplicated spaces.
3. Replace comments that look like /* content */.

To decompress or to make the JavaScript more readable, we can use the following tasks:

- Replace ; with ;\n
- Replace { with {\n, and } with \n}

How to do it...

Using these steps, we can use the following command chain:

```
$ cat sample.js |  \
tr -d '\n\t' |  tr -s ' ' \
| sed 's:/\*.*\*/::g' \
| sed 's/ \?\([{}();,:]\) \?/\1/g'
```

The output is as follows:

```
function sign_out(){$("#loading").show();$.get("log_in",
{logout:"True"},function(){window.location="";});}
```

The following decompression script makes the obfuscated code readable:

```
$ cat obfuscated.txt | sed 's/;/;\n/g; s/{/{\n\n/g; s/}/\n\n}/g'
```

Or:

```
$ cat obfuscated.txt | sed 's/;/;\n/g' | sed 's/{/{\n\n/g' | sed
's/}/\n\n}/g'
```

> There is a limitation in the script: that it even gets rid of extra spaces where their presence is intentional. For example, if you have a line like the following: `var a = "hello world"`
> The two spaces will be converted into one space. You can fix problems such as this using the pattern-matching tools we have discussed. Also, when dealing with a mission-critical JavaScript code, it is advised that you use well-established tools to do this.

How it works...

The compression command performs the following tasks:

- Removing the \n and \t characters:

   ```
   tr -d '\n\t'
   ```

- Removing extra spaces:

   ```
   tr -s ' ' or sed 's/[ ]\+/ /g'
   ```

- Removing comments:

```
sed 's:/\*.*\*/::g'
```

: is used as a `sed` delimiter to avoid the need to escape / since we need to use /*
and */.

In sed, * is escaped as *.

.* matches all the text in between /* and */.

- Removing all the spaces preceding and suffixing the {, }, (,), ;, :, and ,
characters:

```
sed 's/ \?\([{}();,:]\) \?/\1/g'
```

The preceding `sed` statement works like this:

- / \?\([{}();,:]\) \?/ in the `sed` code is the match part, and /\1 /g is the
replacement part.
- \([{}();,:]\) is used to match any one character in the [{ } ( ) ; , :]
set (spaces inserted for readability). \(and \) are group operators used to
memorize the match and back reference in the replacement part. (and) are
escaped to give them a special meaning as a group operator. \? precedes and
follows the group operators to match the space character that may precede or
follow any of the characters in the set.
- In the replacement part, the match string (that is, the combination of :, a space
(optional), a character from the set, and again an optional space) is replaced with
the character matched. It uses a back reference to the character matched and
memorized using the group operator (). Back-referenced characters refer to a
group match using the \1 symbol.

The decompression command works as follows:

- s/;/;\n/g replaces ; with ;\n
- s/{/{\n\n/g replaces { with {\n\n
- s/}/\n\n}/g replaces } with \n\n}

See also

- The *Using sed to perform text replacement* recipe in this chapter explains the `sed` command
- The *Translating with tr* recipe in `Chapter 2`, *Have a Good Command*, explains the `tr` command

Merging multiple files as columns

The can command can be used to merge two files by row, one file after the other. Sometimes we need to merge two or more files side by side, joining the lines from file 1 with the lines from file 2.

How to do it...

The `paste` command performs column-wise concatenation:

```
$ paste file1 file2 file3 ...
```

Here is an example:

```
$ cat file1.txt
1
2
3
4
5
$ cat file2.txt
slynux
gnu
bash
hack
$ paste file1.txt file2.txt
1 slynux
2 gnu
3 bash
4 hack
5
```

The default delimiter is tab. We can specify the delimiter with −d:

```
$ paste file1.txt file2.txt -d ","
1,slynux
2,gnu
3,bash
4,hack
5,
```

See also

- The *Cutting a file column-wise with cut* recipe in this chapter explains how to extract data from text files

Printing the nth word or column in a file or line

We often need to extract a few columns of useful data from a file. For example, in a list of students ordered by their scores, we want to get the fourth highest scorer. This recipe shows how to do this.

How to do it...

The awk command is frequently used for this task.

1. To print the fifth column, use the following command:

   ```
   $ awk '{ print $5 }' filename
   ```

2. We can print multiple columns and insert a custom string between the columns.

   The following command will print the permission and filename of each file in the current directory:

   ```
   $ ls -l | awk '{ print $1 " : " $8 }'
   -rw-r--r-- :  delimited_data.txt
   -rw-r--r-- :  obfuscated.txt
   -rw-r--r-- :  paste1.txt
   -rw-r--r-- :  paste2.txt
   ```

See also

- The *Using awk for advanced text processing* recipe in this chapter explains the awk command
- The *Cutting a file column-wise with cut* recipe in this chapter explains how to extract data from text files

Printing text between line numbers or patterns

We may need to print a selected portion of a file, either a range of line numbers or a range matched by a start and end pattern.

Getting ready

Awk, grep, or sed will select lines to print, based on condition. It's simplest to use grep to print lines that include a pattern. Awk is the most versatile tool.

How to do it...

To print the text between line numbers or patterns, follow these steps:

1. Print the lines of a text in a range of line numbers, M to N:

    ```
    $ awk 'NR==M, NR==N' filename
    ```

    Awk can read from stdin:

    ```
    $ cat filename | awk 'NR==M, NR==N'
    ```

2. Replace M and N with numbers:

    ```
    $ seq 100 | awk 'NR==4,NR==6'
    4
    5
    6
    ```

3. Print the lines of text between a `start_pattern` and `end_pattern`:

```
$ awk '/start_pattern/, /end _pattern/' filename
```

Consider this example:

```
$ cat section.txt
line with pattern1
line with pattern2
line with pattern3
line end with pattern4
line with pattern5

$ awk '/pa.*3/, /end/' section.txt
line with pattern3
line end with pattern4
```

The patterns used in `awk` are regular expressions.

See also

- The *Using awk for advanced text processing* recipe in this chapter explains the `awk` command

Printing lines in the reverse order

This recipe may not seem useful, but it can be used to emulate the stack data structure in Bash.

Getting ready

The simplest way to accomplish this is with the `tac` command (the reverse of cat). The task can also be done with `awk`.

How to do it...

We will first see how to do this with `tac`.

1. The syntax of `tac` is as follows:

   ```
   tac file1 file2 ...
   ```

   The `tac` command can also read from `stdin`:

   ```
   $ seq 5 | tac
   5
   4
   3
   2
   1
   ```

   The default line separator for `tac` is \n. The -s option will redefine this:

   ```
   $ echo "1,2" | tac -s ,
   2
   1
   ```

2. This `awk` script will print lines in the reverse order:

   ```
   seq 9 | \
     awk '{ lifo[NR]=$0 } \
       END { for(lno=NR;lno>-1;lno--) { print lifo[lno]; }
             }'
   ```

   \ in the shell script is used to break a single-line command sequence into multiple lines.

How it works...

The `awk` script stores each of the lines into an associative array using the line number as the index (NR returns the line number). After reading all the lines, `awk` executes the END block. The NR variable is maintained by `awk`. It holds the current line number. When `awk` starts the END block, NR is the count of lines. Using lno=NR in the { } block iterates from the last line number to 0, to print the lines in reverse order.

Parsing e-mail address and URLs from text

Parsing elements such as e-mail addresses and URLs is a common task. Regular expressions make finding these patterns easy.

How to do it...

The regular expression pattern to match an e-mail address is as follows:

```
[A-Za-z0-9._]+@[A-Za-z0-9.]+\.[a-zA-Z]{2,4}
```

Consider the following example:

```
$ cat url_email.txt
this is a line of text contains,<email> #slynux@slynux.com.
</email> and email address, blog "http://www.google.com",
test@yahoo.com dfdfdfdddfdf;cool.hacks@gmail.com<br />
<a href="http://code.google.com"><h1>Heading</h1>
```

As we are using extended regular expressions (+, for instance), we should use `egrep`:

```
$ egrep -o '[A-Za-z0-9._]+@[A-Za-z0-9.]+\.[a-zA-Z]{2,4}'
url_email.txt
slynux@slynux.com
test@yahoo.com
cool.hacks@gmail.com
```

The `egrep` regex pattern for an HTTP URL is as follows:

```
http://[a-zA-Z0-9\-\.]+\.[a-zA-Z]{2,4}
```

Consider this example:

```
$ egrep -o "http://[a-zA-Z0-9.]+\.[a-zA-Z]{2,3}" url_email.txt
http://www.google.com
http://code.google.com
```

How it works...

Regular expressions are easy to design part-by-part. In the e-mail regex, we all know that an e-mail address takes the `name@domain.some_2-4_letter_suffix` form. Writing this pattern in the regex language will look like this:

```
[A-Za-z0-9.]+@[A-Za-z0-9.]+\.[a-zA-Z]{2,4}
```

`[A-Za-z0-9.]+` means we need one or more characters in the `[]` block (+ means at least one, maybe more). This string is followed by an `@` character. Next, we will see the domain name, a string of letters or numbers, a period, and then 2-4 more letters. The `[A-Za-z0-9]+` pattern defines an alpha-numeric string. The `\.` pattern means that a literal period must appear. The `[a-zA-Z]{2,4}` pattern defines 2, 3, or 4 letters.

An HTTP URL is similar to an e-mail, but we don't need the `name@` match part of the e-mail regex:

```
http://[a-zA-Z0-9.]+\.[a-zA-Z]{2,3}
```

See also

- The *Using sed to perform text replacement* recipe in this chapter explains the `sed` command
- The *Using regular expressions* recipe in this chapter explains how to use regular expressions

Removing a sentence in a file containing a word

Removing a sentence that contains a specific word is a simple task with regular expressions. This recipe demonstrates techniques for solving similar problems.

Getting ready

`sed` is the best utility for making substitutions. This recipe uses `sed` to replace the matched sentence with a blank.

How to do it...

Let's create a file with some text to carry out the substitutions. Consider this example:

```
$ cat sentence.txt
Linux refers to the family of Unix-like computer operating systems
that use the Linux kernel. Linux can be installed on a wide variety
of computer hardware, ranging from mobile phones, tablet computers
and video game consoles, to mainframes and supercomputers. Linux is
predominantly known for its use in servers.
```

To remove the sentence containing the words `mobile phones`, use the following `sed` expression:

```
$ sed 's/ [^.]*mobile phones[^.]*\.//g' sentence.txt
Linux refers to the family of Unix-like computer operating systems
that use the Linux kernel. Linux is predominantly known for its use
in servers.
```

 This recipe assumes that no sentence spans more than one line, for example, a sentence should always begin and end on the same line in the text.

How it works...

The `sed` regex `'s/ [^.]*mobile phones[^.]*\.//g'` has the `'s/substitution_pattern/replacement_string/g` format. It replaces every occurrence of `substitution_pattern` with the replacement string.

The substitution pattern is the regex for a sentence. Every sentence begins with a space and ends with .. The regular expression must match the text in the format `"space" some text MATCH_STRING some text "dot"`. A sentence may contain any characters except a "dot", which is the delimiter. The `[^.]` pattern matches any character except a period. The `*` pattern defines any number of those characters. The `mobile phones` text match string is placed between the pattern for non-period characters. Every match sentence is replaced by `//` (nothing).

See also

- The *Using sed to perform text replacement* recipe in this chapter explains the sed command
- The *Using regular expressions* recipe in this chapter explains how to use regular expressions

Replacing a pattern with text in all the files in a directory

We often need to replace a particular text with a new text in every file in a directory. An example would be changing a common URI everywhere in a website's source directory.

How to do it...

We can use find to locate the files to have text modified. We can use sed to do the actual replacement.

To replace the Copyright text with the Copyleft word in all .cpp files, use the following command:

```
find . -name *.cpp -print0 | \
    xargs -I{} -0 sed -i 's/Copyright/Copyleft/g' {}
```

How it works...

We use find on the current directory (.) to find the files with a .cpp suffix. The find command uses -print0 to print a null separated list of files (use -print0 when filenames have spaces in them). We pipe the list to xargs, which will pass the filenames to sed, which makes the modifications.

There's more...

If you recall, `find` has an `-exec` option, which can be used to run a command on each of the files that match the search criteria. We can use this option to achieve the same effect or replace the text with a new one:

```
$ find . —name *.cpp —exec sed —i 's/Copyright/Copyleft/g' \{\} \;
```

Or:

```
$ find . —name *.cpp —exec sed —i 's/Copyright/Copyleft/g' \{\} \+
```

These commands perform the same function, but the first form will call `sed` once for every file, while the second form will combine multiple filenames and pass them together to `sed`.

Text slicing and parameter operations

This recipe walks through some simple text-replacement techniques and parameter-expansion shorthands available in Bash. A few simple techniques can help avoid writing multiple lines of code.

How to do it...

Let's get into the tasks.

Replace some text from a variable:

```
$ var="This is a line of text"
$ echo ${var/line/REPLACED}
This is a REPLACED of text"
```

The `line` word is replaced with REPLACED.

We can produce a substring by specifying the start position and string length, using the following syntax:

```
${variable_name:start_position:length}
```

Print from the fifth character onwards:

```
$ string=abcdefghijklmnopqrstuvwxyz
$ echo ${string:4}
efghijklmnopqrstuvwxyz
```

Print eight characters starting from the fifth character:

```
$ echo ${string:4:8}
efghijkl
```

The first character in a string is at position 0. We can count from the last letter as −1. When −1 is inside a parenthesis, (−1) is the index for the last letter:

```
echo ${string:(-1)}
z
$ echo ${string:(-2):2}
yz
```

See also

- The *Using sed to perform text replacement* recipe in this chapter explains other character manipulation tricks

5
Tangled Web? Not At All!

In this chapter, we will cover the following recipes:

- Downloading from a web page
- Downloading a web page as plain text
- A primer on cURL
- Accessing unread Gmail e-mails from the command line
- Parsing data from a website
- Image crawler and downloader
- Web photo album generator
- Twitter command-line client
- Accessing word definitions via a web server
- Finding broken links in a website
- Tracking changes to a website
- Posting to a web page and reading the response
- Downloading a video from the Internet
- Summarizing text with OTS
- Translating text from the command line

Introduction

The Web has become the face of technology and the central access point for data processing. Shell scripts cannot do everything that languages such as PHP can do on the Web, but there are many tasks for which shell scripts are ideally suited. We will explore recipes to download and parse website data, send data to forms, and automate website-usage tasks and similar activities. We can automate many activities that we perform interactively through a browser with a few lines of scripting. The functionality provided by the HTTP protocol and command-line utilities enables us to write scripts to solve many web-automation needs.

Downloading from a web page

Downloading a file or a web page is simple. A few command-line download utilities are available to perform this task.

Getting ready

wget is a flexible file download command-line utility that can be configured with many options.

How to do it...

A web page or a remote file can be downloaded using wget:

```
$ wget URL
```

For example:

```
$ wget knopper.net
--2016-11-02 21:41:23--  http://knopper.net/
Resolving knopper.net... 85.214.68.145
Connecting to knopper.net|85.214.68.145|:80...
connected.
HTTP request sent, awaiting response... 200 OK
Length: 6899 (6.7K) [text/html]
Saving to: "index.html.1"


100% [=============================] 45.5K=0.1s
```

```
2016-11-02 21:41:23 (45.5 KB/s) - "index.html.1" saved
[6899/6899]
```

It is also possible to specify multiple download URLs:

```
$ wget URL1 URL2 URL3 ..
```

How it works...

By default, the downloaded files are named the same as the URL, and the download information and progress is written to stdout.

The -O option specifies the output filename. If a file with that name already exists, it will be replaced by the downloaded file:

```
$ wget http://www.knopper.net -O knopper.html.
```

The -o option specifies a logfile instead of printing logs to stdout:

```
$ wget ftp://ftp.example.com/somefile.img -O dloaded_file.img -o log
```

Using the preceding command will print nothing on the screen. The log or progress will be written to the log and the output file will be dloaded_file.img.

There is a chance that downloads might break due to unstable Internet connections. The -t option specifies how many times the utility will retry before giving up:

```
$ wget -t 5 URL
```

Use a value of 0 to force wget to keep trying infinitely:

```
$ wget -t 0 URL
```

There's more...

The wget utility has options to fine-tune behavior and solve problems.

Restricting the download speed

When there is limited bandwidth with many applications sharing it, a large file can devour all the bandwidth and starve other processes (perhaps interactive users). The `wget` option `–limit-rate` will specify the maximum bandwidth for the download job, allowing all applications fair access to the Internet:

```
$ wget  --limit-rate 20k http://example.com/file.iso
```

In this command, `k` (kilobyte) specifies the speed limit. You can also use `m` for megabyte.

The `–quota` (or `–Q`) option specifies the maximum size of the download. `wget` will stop when the quota is exceeded. This is useful when downloading multiple files to a system with limited space:

```
$ wget -Q 100m http://example.com/file1 http://example.com/file2
```

Resume downloading and continue

If `wget` gets interrupted before the download is complete, it can be resumed where it left off with the `–c` option:

```
$ wget -c URL
```

Copying a complete website (mirroring)

`wget` can download a complete website by recursively collecting the URL links and downloading them like a crawler. To download the pages, use the `--mirror` option:

```
$ wget --mirror --convert-links exampledomain.com
```

Alternatively, use the following command:

```
$ wget -r -N -l -k DEPTH URL
```

The `–l` option specifies the depth of web pages as levels. This means that it will traverse only that number of levels. It is used along with `–r` (recursive). The `–N` argument is used to enable time stamping for the file. URL is the base URL for a website for which the download needs to be initiated. The `–k` or `--convert-links` option instructs `wget` to convert the links to other pages to the local copy.

Exercise discretion when mirroring other websites. Unless you have permission, only perform this for your personal use and don't do it too frequently.

Accessing pages with HTTP or FTP authentication

The `--user` and `--password` arguments provide the username and password to websites that require authentication.

```
$ wget --user username --password pass URL
```

It is also possible to ask for a password without specifying the password inline. For this, use `--ask-password` instead of the `--password` argument.

Downloading a web page as plain text

Web pages are simply text with HTML tags, JavaScript, and CSS. The HTML tags define the content of the web page, which we can parse for specific content. Bash scripts can parse web pages. An HTML file can be viewed in a web browser to see it properly formatted or processed with tools described in the previous chapter.

Parsing a text document is simpler than parsing HTML data because we aren't required to strip off the HTML tags. **Lynx** is a command-line web browser that downloads a web page as plain text.

Getting ready

Lynx is not installed in all distributions, but is available via the package manager.

```
# yum install lynx
```

Alternatively, you can execute the following command:

```
apt-get install lynx
```

How to do it...

The `-dump` option downloads a web page as pure ASCII. The next recipe shows how to send that ASCII version of the page to a file:

```
$ lynx URL -dump > webpage_as_text.txt
```

This command will list all the hyperlinks (`<a href="link">`) separately under a heading `References`, as the footer of the text output. This lets us parse links separately with regular expressions.

Consider this example:

```
$lynx -dump http://google.com > plain_text_page.txt
```

You can see the plain text version of `text` using the `cat` command:

```
$ cat plain_text_page.txt
Search [1]Images [2]Maps [3]Play [4]YouTube [5]News [6]Gmail
[7]Drive
[8]More »
[9]Web History | [10]Settings | [11]Sign in

[12]St. Patrick's Day 2017

   _____

   Google Search  I'm Feeling Lucky    [13]Advanced search
      [14]Language tools

   [15]Advertising Programs    [16]Business Solutions    [17]+Google
      [18]About Google

                 © 2017 - [19]Privacy - [20]Terms

References
 . . .
```

A primer on cURL

cURL transfers data to or from a server using the HTTP, HTTPS, or FTP protocols. It supports `POST`, cookies, authentication, downloading partial files from a specified offset, referer, user agent string, extra headers, limiting speed, maximum file size, progress bar, and more. cURL is useful for maintaining a website, retrieving data, and checking server configurations.

Getting ready

Unlike `wget`, cURL is not included in all Linux distros; you may have to install it with your package manager.

By default, cURL dumps downloaded files to `stdout`, and progress information to `stderr`. To disable displaying progress information, use the `--silent` option.

How to do it...

The `curl` command performs many functions, including downloading, sending different HTTP requests, and specifying HTTP headers.

- To dump the downloaded file to `stdout`, use the following command:

  ```
  $ curl URL
  ```

- The `-O` option specifies sending the downloaded data into a file with the filename parsed from the URL. Note that the URL must be a full page URL, not just a site name.

  ```
  $ curl www.knopper.net/index.htm --silent -O
  ```

- The `-o` option specifies the output file name. With this option you can specify only the site name to retrieve the home page.

  ```
  $curl www.knopper.net -o knoppix_index.html
  % Total % Received % Xferd  Avg  Speed Time   Time    Time
  Current
  Dload Upload Total Spent Left  Speed
  100 6889 100 6889  0 0     10902  0      --:-- --:-- --:-- 26033
  ```

- The `-silent` option prevents the `curl` command from displaying progress information:

  ```
  $ curl URL --silent
  ```

- The `-progress` option displays progress bar while downloading:

  ```
  $ curl http://knopper.net -o index.html --progress
  ################################## 100.0%
  ```

How it works...

cURL downloads web pages or remote files to your local system. You can control the destination filename with the -O and -o options, and verbosity with the -silent and -progress options.

There's more...

In the preceding sections, you learned how to download files. cURL supports more options to fine tune its behavior.

Continuing and resuming downloads

cURL can resume a download from a given offset. This is useful if you have a per-day data limit and a large file to download.

```
$ curl URL/file -C offset
```

offset is an integer value in bytes.

cURL doesn't require us to know the exact byte offset, if we want to resume downloading a file. If you want cURL to figure out the correct resume point, use the -C - option, as follows:

```
$ curl -C - URL
```

cURL will automatically figure out where to restart the download of the specified file.

Setting the referer string with cURL

The **Referer** field in the HTTP header identifies the page that led to the current web page. When a user clicks on a link on web page A to go to web page B, the referer header string for page B will contain the URL of page A.

Some dynamic pages check the referer string before returning the HTML data. For example, a web page may display a Google logo when a user navigates to a website from Google, and display a different page when the user types the URL.

A web developer can write a condition to return a Google page if the referer is www.google.com, or return a different page if not.

You can use `--referer` with the `curl` command to specify the referer string, as follows:

```
$ curl --referer Referer_URL target_URL
```

Consider this example:

```
$ curl --referer http://google.com http://knopper.org
```

Cookies with cURL

`curl` can specify and store the cookies encountered during HTTP operations.

The `-cookieCOOKIE_IDENTIFER` option specifies which cookies to provide. Cookies are defined as `name=value`. Multiple cookies should be delimited with a semicolon (;):

```
$ curl http://example.com --cookie "user=username;pass=hack"
```

The `-cookie-jar` option specifies the file to store cookies in:

```
$ curl URL --cookie-jar cookie_file
```

Setting a user agent string with cURL

Some web pages that check the user agent won't work if there is no user agent specified. For example, some old websites require **Internet Explorer** (**IE**). If a different browser is used, they display a message that the site must be viewed with IE. This is because the website checks for a user agent. You can set the user agent with `curl`.

The `--user-agent` or `-A` option sets the user agent:

```
$ curl URL --user-agent "Mozilla/5.0"
```

Additional headers can be passed with cURL. Use `-H "Header"` to pass additional headers:

```
$ curl -H "Host: www.knopper.net" -H "Accept-language: en" URL
```

 There are many different user agent strings across multiple browsers and crawlers on the Web. You can find a list of some of them at http://www.useragentstring.com/pages/useragentstring.php.

Specifying a bandwidth limit on cURL

When bandwidth is shared among multiple users, we can limit the download rate with the `--limit-rate` option:

```
$ curl URL --limit-rate 20k
```

The rate can be specified with k (kilobyte) or m (megabyte).

Specifying the maximum download size

The `--max-filesize` option specifies the maximum file size:

```
$ curl URL --max-filesize bytes
```

The `curl` command will return a non-zero exit code if the file size exceeds the limit or a zero if the download succeeds.

Authenticating with cURL

The `curl` command's `-u` option performs HTTP or FTP authentication.

The username and password can be specified using `-u username:password`:

```
$ curl -u user:pass http://test_auth.com
```

If you prefer to be prompted for the password, provide only a username:

```
$ curl -u user http://test_auth.com
```

Printing response headers excluding data

Examining headers is sufficient for many checks and statistics. For example, we don't need to download an entire page to confirm it is reachable. Just reading the HTTP response is sufficient.

Another use case for examining the HTTP header is to check the `Content-Length` field to determine the file size or the `Last-Modified` field to see if the file is newer than a current copy before downloading.

The −I or −head option outputs only the HTTP headers, without downloading the remote file:

```
$ curl -I http://knopper.net
HTTP/1.1 200 OK
Date: Tue, 08 Nov 2016 17:15:21 GMT
Server: Apache
Last-Modified: Wed, 26 Oct 2016 23:29:56 GMT
ETag: "1d3c8-1af3-b10500"
Accept-Ranges: bytes
Content-Length: 6899
Content-Type: text/html; charset=ISO-8859-1
```

See also

- The *Posting to a web page and reading the response* recipe in this chapter

Accessing unread Gmail e-mails from the command line

Gmail is a widely-used free e-mail service from Google: http://mail.google.com/. It allows you to read your mail via a browser or an authenticated RSS feeds. We can parse the RSS feeds to report the sender name and subject. This is a quick way to scan unread e-mails without opening the web browser.

How to do it...

Let's go through a shell script to parse the RSS feeds for Gmail to display the unread mails:

```
#!/bin/bash
#Desc: Fetch gmail tool

username='PUT_USERNAME_HERE'
password='PUT_PASSWORD_HERE'

SHOW_COUNT=5 # No of recent unread mails to be shown

echo
curl -u $username:$password --silent \
    "https://mail.google.com/mail/feed/atom" | \
```

```
        tr -d '\n' | sed 's:</entry>:\n:g' |\
        sed -n
's/.*<title>\(.*\)<\/title.*<author><name>\([^<]*\)<\/name><email>
  \([^<]*\).*/From: \2 [\3] \nSubject: \1\n/p' | \
head -n $(( $SHOW_COUNT * 3 ))
```

The output resembles this:

```
$ ./fetch_gmail.sh
From: SLYNUX [ slynux@slynux.com ]
Subject: Book release - 2

From: SLYNUX [ slynux@slynux.com ]
Subject: Book release - 1
.
... 5 entries
```

If you use a Gmail account with two-factor authentication, you will have to generate a new key for this script and use it. Your regular password won't work.

How it works...

The script uses cURL to download the RSS feed. You can view the format of the incoming data by logging in to your Gmail account and viewing https://mail.google.com/mail/feed/atom.

cURL reads the RSS feed with the user authentication provided by the -u user:pass argument. When you use -u user without the password cURL, it will interactively ask for the password.

- tr -d '\n': This removes the newline characters
- sed 's:</entry>:\n:g': This replaces every </entry> element with a newline, so each e-mail entry is delimited by a new line and, hence, mails can be parsed one-by-one.

The next block of script that needs to be executed as one single expression uses sed to extract the relevant fields:

```
sed 's/.*<title>\(.*\)<\/title.*<author><name>\([^<]*\)<\/name><email>
\([^<]*\).*/Author: \2 [\3] \nSubject: \1\n/'
```

This script matches the title with the `<title>\(.*\)<\/title` regular expression, the sender name with the `<author><name>\([^<]*\)<\/name>` regular expression, and e-mail using `<email>\([^<]*\)`. Sed uses back referencing to display the author, title, and subject of the e-mail into an easy to read format:

```
Author: \2 [\3] \nSubject: \1\n
```

`\1` corresponds to the first substring match (title), `\2` for the second substring match (name), and so on.

The `SHOW_COUNT=5` variable is used to take the number of unread mail entries to be printed on the terminal.

`head` is used to display only the `SHOW_COUNT*3` lines from the first line. `SHOW_COUNT` is multiplied by three in order to show three lines of output.

See also

- The *A primer on cURL* recipe in this chapter explains the `curl` command
- The *Using sed to perform text replacement* recipe in `Chapter 4`, *Texting and Driving*, explains the `sed` command

Parsing data from a website

The `lynx`, `sed`, and `awk` commands can be used to mine data from websites. You might have come across a list of actress rankings in a *Searching and mining text inside a file with grep* recipe in `Chapter 4`, *Texting and Driving*; it was generated by parsing the `http://www.johntorres.net/BoxOfficefemaleList.html` web page.

How to do it...

Let's go through the commands used to parse details of actresses from the website:

```
$ lynx -dump -nolist \
    http://www.johntorres.net/BoxOfficefemaleList.html
    grep -o "Rank-.*" | \
    sed -e 's/ *Rank-\([0-9]*\) *\(.*\)/\1\t\2/' | \
    sort -nk 1 > actresslist.txt
```

The output is as follows:

```
# Only 3 entries shown. All others omitted due to space limits
1    Keira Knightley
2    Natalie Portman
3    Monica Bellucci
```

How it works...

Lynx is a command-line web browser; it can dump a text version of a website as we will see in a web browser, instead of returning the raw HTML as wget or cURL does. This saves the step of removing HTML tags. The -nolist option shows the links without numbers. Parsing and formatting the lines that contain Rank is done with sed:

```
sed -e 's/ *Rank-\([0-9]*\) *\(.*\)/\1\t\2/'
```

These lines are then sorted according to the ranks.

See also

- The *Using sed to perform text replacement* recipe in Chapter 4, *Texting and Driving,* explains the sed command
- The *Downloading a web page as plain text* recipe in this chapter explains the lynx command

Image crawler and downloader

Image crawlers download all the images that appear in a web page. Instead of going through the HTML page to pick the images by hand, we can use a script to identify the images and download them automatically.

How to do it...

This Bash script will identify and download the images from a web page:

```
#!/bin/bash
#Desc: Images downloader
#Filename: img_downloader.sh
```

```
if [ $# -ne 3 ];
then
  echo "Usage: $0 URL -d DIRECTORY"
  exit -1
fi
while [ $# -gt 0 ]
do
  case $1 in
  -d) shift; directory=$1; shift ;;
  *) url=$1; shift;;
  esac
done

mkdir -p $directory;
baseurl=$(echo $url | egrep -o "https?://[a-z.\-]+")

echo Downloading $url
curl -s $url | egrep -o "<img[^>]*src=[^>]*>" | \
  sed 's/<img[^>]*src=\"\([^"]*\).*/\1/g' | \
  sed "s,^/,$baseurl/," > /tmp/$$.list

cd $directory;

while read filename;
do
  echo Downloading $filename
  curl -s -O "$filename" --silent
done < /tmp/$$.list
```

An example usage is as follows:

```
$ url=https://commons.wikimedia.org/wiki/Main_Page
$ ./img_downloader.sh $url -d images
```

How it works...

The image downloader script reads an HTML page, strips out all tags except `<img>`, parses `src="URL"` from the `<img>` tag, and downloads them to the specified directory. This script accepts a web page URL and the destination directory as command-line arguments.

The `[ $# -ne 3 ]` statement checks whether the total number of arguments to the script is three, otherwise it exits and returns a usage example. Otherwise, this code parses the URL and destination directory:

```
while [ -n "$1" ]
do
```

```
      case $1 in
      -d) shift; directory=$1; shift ;;
       *) url=${url:-$1}; shift;;
    esac
done
```

The `while` loop runs until all the arguments are processed. The `shift` command shifts arguments to the left so that `$1` will take the next argument's value; that is, `$2`, and so on. Hence, we can evaluate all arguments through `$1` itself.

The `case` statement checks the first argument (`$1`). If that matches `-d`, the next argument must be a directory name, so the arguments are shifted and the directory name is saved. If the argument is any other string it is a URL.

The advantage of parsing arguments in this way is that we can place the -d argument anywhere in the command line:

```
$ ./img_downloader.sh -d DIR URL
```

Or:

```
$ ./img_downloader.sh URL -d DIR
```

`egrep -o "<img src=[^>]*>"` will print only the matching strings, which are the `<img>` tags including their attributes. The `[^>]*` phrase matches all the characters except the closing `>`, that is, `<img src="image.jpg">`.

`sed's/<img src=\"\([^"]*\).*/\1/g'` extracts the `url` from the `src="url"` string.

There are two types of image source paths: relative and absolute. **Absolute paths** contain full URLs that start with `http://` or `https://`. Relative URLs starts with `/` or `image_name` itself. An example of an absolute URL is `http://example.com/image.jpg`. An example of a relative URL is `/image.jpg`.

For relative URLs, the starting `/` should be replaced with the base URL to transform it to `http://example.com/image.jpg`. The script initializes `baseurl` by extracting it from the initial URL with the following command:

```
baseurl=$(echo $url | egrep -o "https?://[a-z.\-]+")
```

The output of the previously described `sed` command is piped into another sed command to replace a leading `/` with `baseurl`, and the results are saved in a file named for the script's PID: (`/tmp/$$.list`).

```
sed "s,^/,$baseurl/," > /tmp/$$.list
```

The final `while` loop iterates through each line of the list and uses curl to download the images. The `--silent` argument is used with `curl` to avoid extra progress messages from being printed on the screen.

See also

- The *A primer on cURL* recipe in this chapter explains the `curl` command
- The *Using sed to perform text replacement* recipe in Chapter 4, *Texting and Driving* explains the `sed` command
- The *Searching and mining text inside a file with grep* recipe in Chapter 4, *Texting and Driving*, explains the `grep` command

Web photo album generator

Web developers frequently create photo albums of full-size and thumbnail images. When a thumbnail is clicked, a large version of the picture is displayed. This requires resizing and placing many images. These actions can be automated with a simple Bash script. The script creates thumbnails, places them in exact directories, and generates the code fragment for `<img>` tags automatically.

Getting ready

This script uses a `for` loop to iterate over every image in the current directory. The usual Bash utilities such as `cat` and `convert` (from the Image Magick package) are used. These will generate an HTML album, using all the images, in `index.html`.

How to do it...

This Bash script will generate an HTML album page:

```
#!/bin/bash
#Filename: generate_album.sh
#Description: Create a photo album using images in current directory

echo "Creating album.."
mkdir -p thumbs
cat <<EOF1 > index.html
```

```
<html>
<head>
<style>

body
{
  width:470px;
  margin:auto;
  border: 1px dashed grey;
  padding:10px;
}

img
{
  margin:5px;
  border: 1px solid black;

}
</style>
</head>
<body>
<center><h1> #Album title </h1></center>
<p>
EOF1

for img in *.jpg;
do
  convert "$img" -resize "100x" "thumbs/$img"
  echo "<a href=\"$img\" >" >>index.html
  echo "<img src=\"thumbs/$img\" title=\"$img\" /></a>" >> index.html
done

cat <<EOF2 >> index.html

</p>
</body>
</html>
EOF2

echo Album generated to index.html
```

Run the script as follows:

```
$ ./generate_album.sh
Creating album..
Album generated to index.html
```

How it works...

The initial part of the script is used to write the header part of the HTML page.

The following script redirects all the contents up to EOF1 to index.html:

```
cat <<EOF1 > index.html
contents...
EOF1
```

The header includes the HTML and CSS styling.

for img in *.jpg *.JPG; iterates over the filenames and evaluates the body of the loop.

convert "$img" -resize "100x" "thumbs/$img" creates images 100px-wide as thumbnails.

The following statement generates the required <img> tag and appends it to index.html:

```
echo "<a href=\"$img\" >"
echo "<img src=\"thumbs/$img\" title=\"$img\" /></a>" >> index.html
```

Finally, the footer HTML tags are appended with cat as in the first part of the script.

See also

- The *Web photo album generator* recipe in this chapter explains EOF and stdin redirection

Twitter command-line client

Twitter is the hottest micro-blogging platform, as well as the latest buzz word for online social media now. We can use Twitter API to read tweets on our timeline from the command line!

Let's see how to do it.

Getting ready

Recently, Twitter stopped allowing people to log in using plain HTTP Authentication, so we must use OAuth to authenticate ourselves. A full explanation of OAuth is out of the scope of this book, so we will use a library which makes it easy to use OAuth from Bash scripts. Perform the following steps:

1. Download the `bash-oauth` library from `https://github.com/livibetter/bash-oauth/archive/master.zip`, and unzip it to any directory.
2. Go to that directory and then inside the subdirectory `bash-oauth-master`, run `make install-all` as root.
3. Go to `https://apps.twitter.com/` and register a new app. This will make it possible to use OAuth.
4. After registering the new app, go to your app's settings and change **Access type** to **Read and Write**.
5. Now, go to the **Details** section of the app and note two things, **Consumer Key** and **Consumer Secret**, so that you can substitute these in the script we are going to write.

Great, now let's write the script that uses this.

How to do it...

This Bash script uses the OAuth library to read tweets or send your own updates:

```
#!/bin/bash
#Filename: twitter.sh
#Description: Basic twitter client

oauth_consumer_key=YOUR_CONSUMER_KEY
oauth_consumer_scret=YOUR_CONSUMER_SECRET

config_file=~/.$oauth_consumer_key-$oauth_consumer_secret-rc

if [[ "$1" != "read" ]] && [[ "$1" != "tweet" ]];
then
  echo -e "Usage: $0 tweet status_message\n    OR\n    $0 read\n"
  exit -1;
fi

#source /usr/local/bin/TwitterOAuth.sh
```

```
source bash-oauth-master/TwitterOAuth.sh
TO_init

if [ ! -e $config_file ]; then
 TO_access_token_helper
 if (( $? == 0 )); then
   echo oauth_token=${TO_ret[0]} > $config_file
   echo oauth_token_secret=${TO_ret[1]} >> $config_file
 fi
fi

source $config_file

if [[ "$1" = "read" ]];
then
TO_statuses_home_timeline '' 'YOUR_TWEET_NAME' '10'
  echo $TO_ret | sed 's/,"/\n/g' | sed 's/":/~/' | \
    awk -F~ '{} \
      {if ($1 == "text") \
        {txt=$2;} \
       else if ($1 == "screen_name") \
        printf("From: %s\n Tweet: %s\n\n", $2, txt);} \
      {}' | tr '"' ' '

elif [[ "$1" = "tweet" ]];
then
  shift
  TO_statuses_update '' "$@"
  echo 'Tweeted :)'
fi
```

Run the script as follows:

```
$./twitter.sh read
Please go to the following link to get the PIN:
https://api.twitter.com/oauth/authorize?
oauth_token=LONG_TOKEN_STRING
PIN: PIN_FROM_WEBSITE
Now you can create, edit and present Slides offline.
- by A Googler
$./twitter.sh tweet "I am reading Packt Shell Scripting Cookbook"
Tweeted :)
$./twitter.sh read | head -2
From: Clif Flynt
Tweet: I am reading Packt Shell Scripting Cookbook
```

How it works...

First of all, we use the source command to include the `TwitterOAuth.sh` library, so we can use its functions to access Twitter. The `TO_init` function initializes the library.

Every app needs to get an OAuth token and token secret the first time it is used. If these are not present, we use the `TO_access_token_helper` library function to acquire them. Once we have the tokens, we save them to a `config` file so we can simply source it the next time the script is run.

The `TO_statuses_home_timeline` library function fetches the tweets from Twitter. This data is retuned as a single long string in JSON format, which starts like this:

```
[{"created_at":"Thu Nov 10 14:45:20 +0000
"016","id":7...9,"id_str":"7...9","text":"Dining...
```

Each tweet starts with the `"created_at"` tag and includes a `text` and a `screen_name` tag. The script will extract the text and screen name data and display only those fields.

The script assigns the long string to the `TO_ret` variable.

The JSON format uses quoted strings for the key and may or may not quote the value. The key/value pairs are separated by commas, and the key and value are separated by a colon (`:`).

The first `sed` replaces each `"` character set with a newline, making each key/value a separate line. These lines are piped to another `sed` command to replace each occurrence of `":` with a tilde (~), which creates a line like this:

```
screen_name~"Clif_Flynt"
```

The final `awk` script reads each line. The `-F~` option splits the line into fields at the tilde, so `$1` is the key and `$2` is the value. The `if` command checks for `text` or `screen_name`. The text is first in the tweet, but it's easier to read if we report the sender first; so the script saves a `text` return until it sees a `screen_name`, then prints the current value of `$2` and the saved value of the text.

The `TO_statuses_update` library function generates a tweet. The empty first parameter defines our message as being in the default format, and the message is a part of the second parameter.

See also

- The *Using sed to perform text replacement* recipe in `Chapter 4`, *Texting and Driving*, explains the `sed` command
- The *Searching and mining text inside a file with grep* recipe in `Chapter 4`, *Texting and Driving*, explains the `grep` command

Accessing word definitions via a web server

Several dictionaries on the Web offer an API to interact with their website via scripts. This recipe demonstrates how to use a popular one.

Getting ready

We are going to use `curl`, `sed`, and `grep` for this define utility. There are a lot of dictionary websites where you can register and use their APIs for personal use for free. In this example, we are using Merriam-Webster's dictionary API. Perform the following steps:

1. Go to `http://www.dictionaryapi.com/register/index.htm`, and register an account for yourself. Select **Collegiate Dictionary** and **Learner's Dictionary**:
2. Log in using the newly created account and go to **My Keys** to access the keys. Note the key for the learner's dictionary.

How to do it...

This script will display a word definition:

```
#!/bin/bash
#Filename: define.sh
#Desc: A script to fetch definitions from dictionaryapi.com

key=YOUR_API_KEY_HERE

if [ $# -ne 2 ];
then
  echo -e "Usage: $0 WORD NUMBER"
  exit -1;
fi
```

```
curl --silent \
http://www.dictionaryapi.com/api/v1/references/learners/xml/$1?key=$key | \
  grep -o \<dt\>.*\</dt\> | \
  sed 's$</*[a-z]*>$$g' | \
  head -n $2 | nl
```

Run the script like this:

```
$ ./define.sh usb 1
1   :a system for connecting a computer to another device (such as
a printer, keyboard, or mouse) by using a special kind of cord a
USB cable/port USB is an abbreviation of "Universal Serial Bus."How
it works...
```

How it works...

We use `curl` to fetch the data from the dictionary API web page by specifying our API `Key` (`$apikey`), and the word we want the definition for (`$1`). The result contains definitions in the `<dt>` tags, selected with `grep`. The `sed` command removes the tags. The script selects the required number of lines from the definitions and uses `nl` to add a line number to each line.

See also

- The *Using sed to perform text replacement* recipe in `Chapter 4` explains the `sed` command
- The *Searching and mining text inside a file with grep* recipe in `Chapter 4`, *Texting and Driving*, explains the `grep` command

Finding broken links in a website

Websites must be tested for broken links. It's not feasible to do this manually for large websites. Luckily, this is an easy task to automate. We can find the broken links with HTTP manipulation tools.

Getting ready

We can use lynx and curl to identify the links and find broken ones. Lynx has the -traversal option, which recursively visits pages on the website and builds a list of all hyperlinks. cURL is used to verify each of the links.

How to do it...

This script uses lynx and curl to find the broken links on a web page:

```bash
#!/bin/bash
#Filename: find_broken.sh
#Desc: Find broken links in a website

if [ $# -ne 1 ];
then
  echo -e "$Usage: $0 URL\n"
  exit 1;
fi

echo Broken links:

mkdir /tmp/$$.lynx
cd /tmp/$$.lynx

lynx -traversal $1 > /dev/null
count=0;

sort -u reject.dat > links.txt

while read link;
do
  output=`curl -I $link -s \
| grep -e "HTTP/.*OK" -e "HTTP/.*200"`
  if [[ -z $output ]];
  then
    output=`curl -I $link -s | grep -e "HTTP/.*301"`
    if [[ -z $output ]];
      then
      echo "BROKEN: $link"
      let count++
    else
      echo "MOVED: $link"
    fi
  fi
done < links.txt
```

```
[ $count -eq 0 ] && echo No broken links found.
```

How it works...

`lynx -traversal URL` will produce a number of files in the working directory. It includes a `reject.dat` file, which will contain all the links in the website. `sort -u` is used to build a list by avoiding duplicates. Then, we iterate through each link and check the header response using `curl -I`. If the first line of the header contains HTTP/ and either `OK` or `200`, it means that the link is valid. If the link is not valid, it is rechecked and tested for a `301`-*link moved*-reply. If that test also fails, the broken link is printed on the screen.

From its name, it might seem like `reject.dat` should contain a list of URLs that were broken or unreachable. However, this is not the case, and lynx just adds all the URLs there.

Also note that `lynx` generates a file called `traverse.errors`, which contains all the URLs that had problems in browsing. However, `lynx` will only add URLs that return `HTTP 404 (not found)`, and so we will lose other errors (for instance, `HTTP 403 Forbidden`). This is why we manually check for statuses.

See also

- The *Downloading a web page as plain text* recipe in this chapter explains the `lynx` command
- The *A primer on cURL* recipe in this chapter explains the `curl` command

Tracking changes to a website

Tracking website changes is useful for both web developers and users. Checking a website manually is impractical, but a change tracking script can be run at regular intervals. When a change occurs, it generates a notification.

Getting ready

Tracking changes in terms of Bash scripting means fetching websites at different times and taking the difference using the `diff` command. We can use `curl` and `diff` to do this.

How to do it...

This Bash script combines different commands, to track changes in a web page:

```bash
#!/bin/bash
#Filename: change_track.sh
#Desc: Script to track changes to webpage

if [ $# -ne 1 ];
then
  echo -e "$Usage: $0 URL\n"
  exit 1;
fi

first_time=0
# Not first time

if [ ! -e "last.html" ];
then
  first_time=1
  # Set it is first time run
fi

curl --silent $1 -o recent.html

if [ $first_time -ne 1 ];
then
  changes=$(diff -u last.html recent.html)
  if [ -n "$changes" ];
  then
    echo -e "Changes:\n"
    echo "$changes"
  else
    echo -e "\nWebsite has no changes"
  fi
else
  echo "[First run] Archiving.."

fi


cp recent.html last.html
```

Let's look at the output of the `track_changes.sh` script on a website you control. First we'll see the output when a web page is unchanged, and then after making changes.

Note that you should change `MyWebSite.org` to your website name.

- First, run the following command:

```
$ ./track_changes.sh http://www.MyWebSite.org
[First run] Archiving..
```

- Second, run the command again:

```
$ ./track_changes.sh http://www.MyWebSite.org
Website has no changes
```

- Third, run the following command after making changes to the web page:

```
$ ./track_changes.sh http://www.MyWebSite.org

Changes:

--- last.html      2010-08-01 07:29:15.000000000 +0200
+++ recent.html    2010-08-01 07:29:43.000000000 +0200
@@ -1,3 +1,4 @@
<html>
  +added line :)
  <p>data</p>
</html>
```

How it works...

The script checks whether the script is running for the first time using `[ ! -e "last.html" ];`. If `last.html` doesn't exist, it means that it is the first time, and the web page must be downloaded and saved as `last.html`.

If it is not the first time, it downloads the new copy (`recent.html`) and checks the difference with the diff utility. Any changes will be displayed as diff output. Finally, `recent.html` is copied to `last.html`.

Note that changing the website you are checking will generate a huge diff file the first time you examine it. If you need to track multiple pages, you can create a folder for each website you intend to watch.

See also

- The *A primer on cURL* recipe in this chapter explains the `curl` command

Posting to a web page and reading the response

POST and GET are two types of request in HTTP to send information to or retrieve information from a website. In a GET request, we send parameters (name-value pairs) through the web page URL itself. The POST command places the key/value pairs in the message body instead of the URL. POST is commonly used when submitting long forms or to conceal information submitted from a casual glance.

Getting ready

For this recipe, we will use the sample `guestbook` website included in the **tclhttpd** package. You can download tclhttpd from `http://sourceforge.net/projects/tclhttpd` and then run it on your local system to create a local web server. The guestbook page requests a name and URL which it adds to a guestbook to show who has visited a site when the user clicks on the **Add me to your guestbook** button.

This process can be automated with a single `curl` (or `wget`) command.

How to do it...

Download the tclhttpd package and `cd` to the `bin` folder. Start the tclhttpd daemon with this command:

```
tclsh httpd.tcl
```

The format to POST and read the HTML response from the generic website resembles this:

```
$ curl URL -d "postvar=postdata2&postvar2=postdata2"
```

Consider the following example:

```
$ curl http://127.0.0.1:8015/guestbook/newguest.html \
-d "name=Clif&url=www.noucorp.com&http=www.noucorp.com"
```

The curl command prints a response page like this:

```
<HTML>
<Head>
<title>Guestbook Registration Confirmed</title>
</Head>
<Body BGCOLOR=white TEXT=black>
<a href="www.noucorp.com">www.noucorp.com</a>

<DL>
<DT>Name
<DD>Clif
<DT>URL
<DD>
</DL>
www.noucorp.com

</Body>
```

-d is the argument used for posting. The string argument for -d is similar to the GET request semantics. var=value pairs are to be delimited by &.

You can post the data using wget using --post-data "string". Consider the following example:

```
$ wget http://127.0.0.1:8015/guestbook/newguest.cgi \
--post-data "name=Clif&url=www.noucorp.com&http=www.noucorp.com" \
-O output.html
```

Use the same format as cURL for name-value pairs. The text in output.html is the same as that returned by the cURL command.

The string to the post arguments (for example, to -d or --post-data) should always be given in quotes. If quotes are not used, & is interpreted by the shell to indicate that this should be a background process.

If you look at the website source (use the **View Source** option from the web browser), you will see an HTML form defined, similar to the following code:

```
<form action="newguest.cgi" " method="post" >
<ul>
<li> Name: <input type="text" name="name" size="40" >
<li> Url: <input type="text" name="url" size="40" >
<input type="submit" >
</ul>
</form>
```

Here, `newguest.cgi` is the target URL. When the user enters the details and clicks on the **Submit** button, the name and URL inputs are sent to `newguest.cgi` as a POST request, and the response page is returned to the browser.

See also

- The *A primer on cURL* recipe in this chapter explains the `curl` command
- The *Downloading from a web page* recipe in this chapter explains the `wget` command

Downloading a video from the Internet

There are many reasons for downloading a video. If you are on a metered service, you might want to download videos during off-hours when the rates are cheaper. You might want to watch videos where the bandwidth doesn't support streaming, or you might just want to make certain that you always have that video of cute cats to show your friends.

Getting ready

One program for downloading videos is `youtube-dl`. This is not included in most distributions and the repositories may not be up-to-date, so it's best to go to the `youtube-dl` main site at `http://yt-dl.org`.

You'll find links and information on that page for downloading and installing `youtube-dl`.

How to do it...

Using `youtube-dl` is easy. Open your browser and find a video you like. Then copy/paste that URL to the `youtube-dl` command line:

```
youtube-dl https://www.youtube.com/watch?v=AJrs13fHQ74
```

While `youtube-dl` is downloading the file it will generate a status line on your terminal.

How it works...

The `youtube-dl` program works by sending a `GET` message to the server, just as a browser would do. It masquerades as a browser so that YouTube or other video providers will download a video as if the device were streaming.

The `-list-formats` (`-F`) option will list the available formats a video is available in, and the `-format` (`-f`) option will specify which format to download. This is useful if you want to download a higher-resolution video than your Internet connection can reliably stream.

Summarizing text with OTS

The **Open Text Summarizer** (**OTS**) is an application that removes the fluff from a piece of text to create a succinct summary.

Getting ready

The `ots` package is not part of most Linux standard distributions, but it can be installed with the following command:

```
apt-get install libots-devel
```

How to do it...

The `OTS` application is easy to use. It reads text from a file or from `stdin` and generates the summary to `stdout`.

```
ots LongFile.txt | less
```

Or

```
cat LongFile.txt | ots | less
```

The `OTS` application can also be used with `curl` to summarize information from websites. For example, you can use `ots` to summarize longwinded blogs:

```
curl http://BlogSite.org | sed -r 's/<[^>]+>//g' | ots | less
```

How it works...

The `curl` command retrieves the page from a blog site and passes the page to `sed`. The `sed` command uses a regular expression to replace all the HTML tags, a string that starts with a less-than symbol and ends with a greater-than symbol, with a blank. The stripped text is passed to `ots`, which generates a summary that's displayed by less.

Translating text from the command line

Google provides an online translation service you can access via your browser. Andrei Neculau created an **awk** script that will access that service and do translations from the command line.

Getting ready

The command line translator is not included on most Linux distributions, but it can be installed directly from Git like this:

```
cd ~/bin
wget git.io/trans
chmod 755 ./trans
```

How to do it...

The `trans` application will translate into the language in your locale environment variable by default.

```
$> trans "J'adore Linux"

J'adore Linux

I love Linux

Translations of J'adore Linux
French -> English

J'adore Linux
I love Linux
```

You can control the language being translated from and to with an option before the text. The format for the option is as follows:

```
from:to
```

To translate from English to French, use the following command:

```
$> trans en:fr "I love Linux"
J'aime Linux
```

How it works...

The `trans` program is about 5,000 lines of awk code that uses `curl` to communicate with the Google, Bing, and Yandex translation services.

6
Repository Management

In this chapter, we will cover the following recipes:

- Creating a new git repository
- Cloning a remote git repository
- Adding and committing changes with git
- Creating and merging branches with git
- Sharing your work
- Pushing a branch to a server
- Retrieving the latest sources for the current branch
- Checking the status of a git repository
- Viewing git history
- Finding bugs
- Committing message ethics
- Using fossil
- Creating a new fossil repository
- Cloning a remote fossil repository
- Opening a fossil project
- Adding and Committing Changes with Fossil
- Using branches and forks with fossil
- Sharing your work with fossil

- Updating your local fossil repository
- Checking the status of a fossil repository
- Viewing fossil history

Introduction

The more time you spend developing applications the more you come to appreciate software that tracks your revision history. A revision control system lets you create a sandbox for new approaches to problems, maintain multiple branches of released code, and provide a development history in the event of intellectual property disputes. Linux and Unix support many source code control systems ranging from the early and primitive SCCS and RCS to concurrent systems such as **CVS** and **SVN** and the modern distributed development systems such as **GIT** and **FOSSIL**.

The big advantage of Git and Fossil over older systems such as CVS and SVN is that a developer can use them without being connected to a network. Older systems such as CVS and RCS worked fine when you were at the office, but you could not check the new code or examine the old code while working remotely.

Git and Fossil are two different revision control systems with some similarities and some differences. Both support the distributed development model of revision control. Git provides source code control and has a number of add-on applications for more information while Fossil is a single executable that provides revision control, trouble tickets, a Wiki, web pages and technical notes.

Git is used for the Linux kernel development and has been adopted by many open source developers. Fossil was designed for the SQLite development team and is also widely used in both the open source and closed source communities.

Git is included with most Linux distributions. If it's not available on your system, you can install it with either yum (Redhat or SuSE) or apt-get (Debian or Ubuntu).

```
$ sudo yum install git-all
$ sudo apt-get install git-all
```

Fossil is available as source or executable from
`http://www.fossil-scm.org`.

Using Git

The git system uses the `git` command with many subcommands to perform individual actions. We'll discuss git clone, git commit, git branch, and others.

To use git you need a code repository. You can either create one yourself (for your projects) or clone a remote repository.

Creating a new git repository

If you are working on your own project, you will want to create your own repository. You can create the repository on your local system, or on a remote site such as GitHub.

Getting ready

All projects in git need a master folder that holds the rest of the project files.

```
$ mkdir MyProject
$ cd MyProject
```

How to do it...

The `git init` command creates the `.git` subfolder within your current working directory and initializes the files that configure `git`.

```
$ git init
```

How it works...

The `git init` command initializes a `git` repository for local use. If you want to allow remote users access this repository, you need to enable that with the `update-server-info` command:

```
$ git update-server-info
```

Cloning a remote git repository

If you intend to access someone else's project, either to contribute new code or just to use the project, you'll need to clone the code to your system.

You need to be online to clone a repository. Once you've copied the files to your system, you can commit new code, backtrack to older revisions, and so on. You can't send any new code changes upstream to the site you cloned from until you are online again.

How to do it...

The `git clone` command copies files from the remote site to your local system. The remote site might be an anonymous repository such as GitHub, or a system where you need to log in with an account name and perhaps password.

Clone from a known remote site such as GitHub:

```
$ git clone http://github.com/ProjectName
```

Clone from a login/password protected site (perhaps your own server):

```
$ git clone clif@172.16.183.130:gitTest
clif@172.16.183.130's password:
```

Adding and committing changes with git

With distributed version control systems such as git, you do most of your work with your local copy of the repository. You can add new code, change code, test, revise, and finally commit the fully tested code. This encourages frequent small commits on your local repository and one large commit when the code is stable.

How to do it...

The `git add` command adds a change in your working code to the staging area. It does not change the repository, it just marks this change as one to be included with the next commit:

```
$ vim SomeFile.sh
$ git add SomeFile.sh
```

Doing a `git add` after every edit session is a good policy if you want to be certain you don't accidently leave out a change when you commit your changes.

You can also add new files to your repository with the git add command:

```
$ echo "my test file" >testfile.txt
$ git add testfile.txt
```

Alternatively, you can add multiple files:

```
$ git add *.c
```

The `git commit` command commits the changes to the repository:

```
$ vim OtherFile.sh
$ git add OtherFile.sh
$ git commit
```

The `git commit` command will open the editor defined in your **EDITOR** shell variable and pre-populate like this:

```
# Please enter the commit message for your changes. Lines starting
# with '#' will be ignored, and an empty message aborts the commit.
#
# Committer: Clif Flynt <clif@cflynt.com>
#
# On branch branch1
# Changes to be committed:
#    (use "git reset HEAD <file>..." to unstage)
#
#       modified:   SomeFile.sh
#       modified:   OtherFile.sh
```

After you enter a comment your changes will be saved in your local copy of the repository.

This does not push your changes to the main repository (perhaps `github`), but other developers can **pull** the new code from your repository if they have an account on your system.

You can shorten the add/commit events with the −a and −m arguments to commit:

- −a: This adds the new code before committing
- −m: This defines a message without going into the editor

```
git commit −am "Add and Commit all modified files."
```

Creating and merging branches with git

If you are maintaining an application you may need to return to an earlier branch to test. For instance, the bug you're fixing may have been around, but unreported, for a long time. You'll want to find when the bug was introduced to track down the code that introduced it. (Refer to `git bisect` in the *Finding bugs* recipe in this chapter.)

When you add new features, you should create a new branch to identify your changes. The project maintainer can then merge the new branch into the master branch after the new code is tested and validated. You can change and create new branches with the git's `checkout` subcommand.

Getting ready...

Use `git init` or `git clone` to create the project on your system.

How to do it...

To change to a previously defined branch:

```
$ git checkout OldBranchName
```

How it works...

The checkout subcommand examines the `.git` folder on your system and restores the snapshot associated with the desired branch.

Note that you cannot change to an existing branch if you have uncommitted changes in your current workspace.

You can create a new branch when you have uncommitted changes in the current workspaces. To create a new branch, use git checkout's −b option:

```
$ git checkout -b MyBranchName
Switched to a new branch 'MyBranchName'
```

This defines your current working branch to be `MyBranchName`. It sets a pointer to match `MyBranchName` to the previous branch. As you add and commit changes, the pointer will diverge further from the initial branch.

When you've tested the code in your new branch, you can merge the changes back into the branch you started from.

There's more...

You can view the branches with the `git branch` command:

```
$ git branch
* MyBranchName
master
```

The current branch is highlighted with an asterisk (*).

Merging branches

After you've edited, added, tested, and committed, you'll want to merge your changes back into the initial branch.

How to do it...

After you've created a new branch and added and committed your changes, change back to the original branch and use the `git merge` command to merge the changes in your new branch:

```
$ git checkout originalBranch
$ git checkout -b modsToOriginalBranch
# Edit, test
$ git commit -a -m "Comment on modifications to originalBranch"
$ git checkout originalBranch
$ git merge modsToOriginalBranch
```

How it works...

The first `git checkout` command retrieves the snapshot for the starting branch. The second `git checkout` command marks your current working code as also being a new branch.

The `git commit` command (or commands) move the snapshot pointer for the new branch further and further away from the original branch. The third `git checkout` command restores your code to the initial state before you made your edits and commits.

The `git merge` command moves the snapshot pointer for the initial branch to the snapshot of the branch you are merging.

There's more...

After you merge a branch, you may not need it any longer. The `-d` option will delete the branch:

```
$ git branch -d MyBranchName
```

Sharing your work

Git lets you work without connecting to the Internet. Eventually, you'll want to share your work.

There are two ways to do this, creating a patch or pushing your new code to the master repository.

Making a patch...

A patch file is a description of the changes that have been committed. Another developer can apply your patch files to their code to use your new code.

The format-patch command will collect your changes and create one or more patch files. The patch files will be named with a number, a description and `.patch`.

How to do it...

The format-patch command requires an identifier to tell Git what the first patch should be. Git will create as many patch files as it needs to change code from what it was then to what it should be.

There are several ways to identify the starting snapshot. One common use for a set of patches is to submit the changes you've made to a given branch to the package maintainer.

For example, suppose you've created a new branch off the master for a new feature. When you've completed your testing, you may send a set of patch files to the project maintainer so they can validate your work and merge the new feature into the project.

The `format-patch` sub-command with the name of a parent branch will generate the patch file to create your current branch:

```
$ git checkout master
$ git checkout -b newFeature
# Edits, adds and commits.
$ git format-patch master
0001-Patch-add-new-feature-to-menu.patch
0002-Patch-support-new-feature-in-library.patch
```

Another common identifier is a git snapshot **SHA1**. Each git snapshot is identified by an SHA1 string.

You can view a log of all the commits in your repository with the `git log` command:

```
$ git log
commit 82567395cb97876e50084fd29c93ccd3dfc9e558
Author: Clif Flynt <clif@example.com>
Date:   Thu Dec 15 13:38:28 2016 -0500

Fixed reported bug #1

commit 721b3fee54e73fd9752e951d7c9163282dcd66b7
Author: Clif Flynt <clif@example.com>
Date:   Thu Dec 15 13:36:12 2016 -0500

Created new feature
```

The `git format-patch` command with an SHA1 identifier looks like this:

```
$ git format-patch SHA1
```

You can use a unique leading segment of the SHA1 identifier or the full, long string:

```
$ git format-patch 721b
$ git format-patch 721b3fee54e73fd9752e951d7c9163282dcd66b7
```

You can also identify a snapshot by its distance from your current location with a -# option.

This command will make a patch file for the most recent change to the master branch:

```
$ git format-patch -1 master
```

This command will make a patch file for the two most recent changes to the `bleedingEdge` branch:

```
$ git format-patch -2 bleedingEdge
```

Applying a patch

The `git apply` command applies a patch to your working code set. You'll have to check out the appropriate snapshot before running this command.

You can test that the patch is valid with the `--check` option.

If your environment is correct for this patch, there will be no return. If you don't have the correct branch checked out, the patch `-check` command will generate an error condition:

```
$ git apply --check 0001-Patch-new-feature.patch
error: patch failed: feature.txt:2
error: feature.txt: patch does not apply
```

When the `--check` option does not generate an error message, use the `git apply` command to apply the patch:

```
$ git apply 0001-Patch-new-feature.patch
```

Pushing a branch to a server

Eventually, you'll want to share your new code with everyone, not just send patches to individuals.

The `git push` command will push a branch to the master.

How to do it...

If you have a unique branch, it can always be pushed to the master repository:

```
$ git push origin MyBranchName
```

If you've modified an existing branch, you may receive an error message as follows:

- `remote: error:` Refusing to update checked out branch: `refs/heads/master`
- `remote: error:` By default, updating the current branch in a non-bare repository

In this case, you need to push your changes to a new branch on the remote site:

```
$ git push origin master:NewBranchName
```

You'll also need to alert the package maintainer to merge this branch into the master:

```
# On remote
$ git merge NewBranchName
```

Retrieving the latest sources for the current branch. If there are multiple developers on a project, you'll need to synchronize with the remote repository occasionally to retrieve data that's been pushed by other developers.

The get fetch and git pull commands will download data from the remote site to your local repository.

 Update your repository without changing the working code.

The git fetch and git pull command will download new code but not modify your working code set.

```
get fetch SITENAME
```

The site you cloned your repository from is named origin:

```
$ get fetch origin
```

To fetch from another developer's repository, use the following command:

```
$ get fetch Username@Address:Project
```

 Update your repository and the working code.

The git pull command performs a fetch and then merges the changes into your current code. This will fail if there are conflicts you need to resolve:

```
$ git pull origin
$ git pull Username@Address:Project
```

Checking the status of a git repository

After a concentrated development and debugging session you are likely to forget all the changes you've made. The `>git status` command will remind you.

How to do it...

The `git status` command reports the current status of your project. It will tell you what branch you are on, whether you have uncommitted changes and whether you are out of sync with the origin repository:

```
$ git status
# On branch master
# Your branch is ahead of 'origin/master' by 1 commit.
#
# Changed but not updated:
#    (use "git add <file>..." to update what will be committed)
#    (use "git checkout -- <file>..." to discard changes in working
 directory)
#
#modified:    newFeature.tcl
```

How it works...

The previous recipe shows `git status` output when a change has been added and committed and one file was modified but not yet committed.

This line indicates that there has been a commit that hasn't been pushed:

```
# Your branch is ahead of 'origin/master' by 1 commit.
```

Lines in this format report on files that have been modified, but not yet committed:

```
#modified:    newFeature.tcl
git config --global user.name "Your Name"
git config --global user.email you@example.com
```

If the identity used for this commit is wrong, you can fix it with the following command:

```
git commit --amend --author='Your Name <you@example.com>'
1 files changed, 1 insertions(+), 0 deletions(-)
create mode 100644 testfile.txt
```

Viewing git history

Before you start working on a project, you should review what's been done. You may need to review what's been done recently to keep up with other developer's work.

The `git log` command generates a report to help you keep up with a project's changes.

How to do it...

The `git log` command generates a report of SHA1 IDs, the author who committed that snapshot, the date it was committed, and the log message:

```
$ git log
commit fa9ef725fe47a34ab8b4488a38db446c6d664f3e
Author: Clif Flynt <clif@noucorp.com>
Date:   Fri Dec 16 20:58:40 2016 -0500
Fixed bug # 1234
```

Finding bugs

Even the best testing groups let bugs slip out into the field. When that happens, it's up to the developers to figure out what the bug is and how to fix it.

Git has tools to help.

Nobody deliberately creates bugs, so the problem is probably caused by fixing an old bug or adding a new feature.

If you can isolate the code that causes the issue, use the `git blame` command to find who committed the code that caused the problem and what the commit SHA code was.

How to do it...

The `git blame` command returns a list of commit hash codes, author, date, and the first line of the commit message:

```
$ git blame testGit.sh
d5f62aa1 (Flynt 2016-12-07 09:41:52 -0500 1) Created testGit.sh
063d573b (Flynt 2016-12-07 09:47:19 -0500 2) Edited on master repo.
2ca12fbf (Flynt 2016-12-07 10:03:47 -0500 3) Edit created remotely
and merged.
```

There's more...

If you have a test that indicates the problem, but don't know the line of code that's at issue, you can use the `git bisect` command to find the commit that introduced the problem.

How to do it...

The `git bisect` command requires two identifiers, one for the last known good code and one for the bad release. The bisect command will identify a revision midway between the good and bad for you to test.

After you test the code, you reset the good or bad pointer. If the test worked, reset the good pointer, if the test failed, reset the bad pointer.

Git will then check out a new snapshot midway between the new good and bad locations:

```
# Pull the current (buggy) code into a git repository
$ git checkout buggyBranch

# Initialize git bisect.
$ git bisect start

# Mark the current commit as bad
$ git bisect bad

# Mark the last known good release tag
# Git pulls a commit at the midpoint for testing.

$ git bisect good v2.5
Bisecting: 3 revisions left to test after this (roughly 2 steps)
[6832085b8d358285d9b033cbc6a521a0ffa12f54] New Feature

# Compile and test
```

```
# Mark as good or bad
# Git pulls next commit to test
$ git bisect good
Bisecting: 1 revision left to test after this (roughly 1 step)
[2ca12fbf1487cbcd0447cf9a924cc5c19f0debf9] Merged. Merge branch
'branch1'
```

How it works...

The git bisect command identifies the version of your code midway between a known good and known bad version. You can now build and test that version. After testing, rerun git bisect to declare that branch as good or bad. After the branch is declared, git bisect will identify a new version, halfway between the new good and bad markers.

Tagging snapshots

Git supports tagging specific snapshots with a mnemonic string and an additional message. You can use the tags to make the development tree clearer with information such as *Merged in new memory management* or to mark specific snapshots along a branch. For example, you can use a tag to mark **release-1.0** and **release-1.1** along the **release-1** branch.

Git supports both lightweight tags (just tagging a snapshot) and tags with associated annotation.

Git tags are local only. git push will not push your tags by default. To send tags to the origin repository, you must include the -tags option:

```
$ git push origin --tags
```

The git tag command has options to add, delete, and list tags.

How to do it...

The git tag command with no argument will list the visible tags:

```
$ git tag
release-1.0
release-1.0beta
release-1.1
```

You can create a tag on your current checkout by adding a tag name:

```
$ git tag ReleaseCandidate-1
```

You can add a tag to a previous commit by appending an SHA-1 identifier to the git tag command:

```
$ git log --pretty=oneline
72f76f89601e25a2bf5bce59551be4475ae78972 Initial checkin
fecef725fe47a34ab8b4488a38db446c6d664f3e Added menu GUI
ad606b8306d22f1175439e08d927419c73f4eaa9 Added menu functions
773fa3a914615556d172163bbda74ef832651ed5 Initial action buttons


$ git tag menuComplete ad606b
```

The -a option will attach annotation to a tag:

```
$ git tag -a tagWithExplanation
# git opens your editor to create the annotation
```

You can define the message on the command line with the -m option:

```
$ git tag -a tagWithShortMessage -m "A short description"
```

The message will be displayed when you use the git show command:

```
$ git show tagWithShortMessage

tag tagWithShortmessage
Tagger: Clif Flynt <clif@cflynt.com>
Date:    Fri Dec 23 09:58:19 2016 -0500

A short description
...
```

The -d option will delete a tag:

```
$ git tag
tag1
tag2
tag3
$ git tag -d tag2
$ git tag
tag2
tag3F
```

Committing message ethics

The commit message is free form text. It can be whatever you think is useful. However, there are comment conventions used in the Git community.

How to do it...

- Use 72 characters or less on each line. Use blank lines to separate paragraphs.
- The first line should be 50 characters or less and summarize why this commit was made. It should be specific enough that someone reading just this line will understand what happened.
- Don't write `Fix bug` or even `Fix bugzilla bug #1234`, write `Remove silly messages that appear each April 1`.

The following paragraphs describe details that will be important to someone following up on your work. Mention any global state variables your code uses, side effects, and so on. If there is a description of the problem you fixed, include the URL for the bug report or feature request.

Using fossil

The fossil application is another distributed version control system. Like Git, it maintains a record of changes regardless of whether the developer has access to the master repository site. Unlike Git, fossil supports an auto-sync mode that will automatically push commits to the remote repository if it's accessible. If the remote site is not available at commit time, fossil saves the changes until the remote site becomes available.

Fossil differs from Git in several respects. The fossil repository is implemented in a single SQLite database instead of a set of folders as Git is implemented. The fossil application includes several other tools such as a web interface, a trouble-ticket system, and a wiki, while Git uses add-on applications to provide these services.

Like Git, the main interface to fossil is the `fossil` command with subcommands to perform specific actions like creating a new repository, cloning an existing repository, adding, committing files, and so on.

Fossil includes a help facility. The fossil help command will generate a list of supported commands, and `fossil help` CMDNAME will display a help page:

```
$ fossil help
Usage: fossil help COMMAND
Common COMMANDs:  (use "fossil help -a|-all" for a complete list)
add         cat         finfo       mv          revert      timeline
...
```

Getting ready

Fossil may not be installed on your system, and is not maintained by all repositories. The definitive site for fossil is `http://www.fossil-scm.org`.

How to do it...

Download a copy of the fossil executable for your platform from `http://www.fossil-scm.org` and move it to your `bin` folder.

Creating a new fossil repository

Fossil is easy to set up and use for your own projects as well as existing projects that you join.

The `fossil new` and `fossil init` commands are identical. You can use either depending on your preference.

How to do it...

The `fossil new` and `fossil init` commands create an empty fossil repository:

```
$ fossil new myProject.fossil
project-id: 855b0e1457da519d811442d81290b93bdc0869e2
server-id:  6b7087bce49d9d906c7572faea47cb2d405d7f72
admin-user: clif (initial password is "f8083e")

$ fossil init myProject.fossil
project-id: 91832f127d77dd523e108a9fb0ada24a5deceedd
server-id:  8c717e7806a08ca2885ca0d62ebebec571fc6d86
admin-user: clif (initial password is "ee884a")
```

How it works...

The `fossil init` and fossil new commands are the same. They create a new empty repository database with the name you request. The `.fossil` suffix is not required, but it's a common convention.

There's more...

Let us look at some more recipes:

Web interface to fossil

The fossil web server provides either local or remote access to many features of the fossil system including configuration, trouble ticket management, a wiki, graphs of the commit history, and more.

The `fossil ui` command starts an http server and attempts to connect your local browser to the fossil server. By default, this interface connects you to the UI and you can perform any required task.

How to do it...

```
$ fossil ui
Listening for HTTP requests on TCP port 8080

#> fossil ui -P 80
Listening for HTTP requests on TCP port 80
```

Making a repository available to remote users

The fossil server command starts a fossil server that allows a remote user to clone your repository. By default, fossil allows anyone to clone a project. Disable the checkin, checkout, clone, and download zip capabilities on the `Admin/Users/Nobody` and `Admin/Users/Anonymous` pages to restrict access to only registered users.

The web interface for configuration is supported when running fossil server, but instead of being the default, you must log in using the credentials provided when you created the repository.

The fossil server can be started with a full path to the repository:

```
$ fossil server /home/projects/projectOne.fossil
```

The fossil server can be started from a folder with the fossil repository without defining the repository:

```
$ cd /home/projects
$ ls
projectOne.fossil
$ fossil server
Listening for HTTP requests on TCP port 8080
```

Cloning a remote fossil repository

Because the fossil repository is contained in a single file, you can clone it simply by copying that file. You can send a fossil repository to another developer as an e-mail attachment, put it on a website, or copy it to a USB memory stick.

The fossil scrub command removes user and password information that the web server may require from the database. This step is recommended before you distribute copies of your repository.

How to do it...

You can clone fossil from a site running fossil in the server mode with the fossil clone command. The fossil clone command distributes the version history, but not the users and password information:

```
$ fossil clone http://RemoteSite:port projectName.fossil
```

How it works...

The fossil clone command copies the repository from the site you've specified to a local file with a name you provide (in the example: projectName.fossil).

Opening a fossil project

The fossil open command extracts the files from a repository. It's usually simplest to create a subfolder under the folder with the fossil repository to hold the project.

How to do it...

Download the fossil repository:

```
$ fossil clone http://example.com/ProjectName project.fossil
```

Make a new folder for your working directory and change to it:

```
$ mkdir newFeature
$ cd newFeature
```

Open the repository in your working folder:

```
$ fossil open ../project.fossil
```

How it works...

The fossil open command extracts all the folders, subfolders, and files that have been checked into the fossil repository.

There's more...

You can use fossil open to extract specific revisions of the code in the repository. This example shows how to check out the 1.0 release to fix an old bug. Make a new folder for your working directory and change it as follows:

```
$ mkdir fix_1.0_Bug
$ cd fix_1.0_Bug
```

Open the repository in your working folder:

```
$ fossil open ../project.fossil release_1.0
```

Adding and committing changes with fossil

Once you've created a repository, you want to add and edit files. The fossil add command adds a new file to a repository and the fossil commit command commits changes to the repository. This is different from Git in which the `add` command marks changes to be added and the commit command actually does the commit.

How to do it...

The next examples show how fossil behaves if you have not defined the EDITOR or VISUAL shell variables. If EDITOR or VISUAL are defined, fossil will use that editor instead of prompting you on the command line:

```
$ echo "example" >example.txt
$ fossil add example.txt
ADDED   example.txt

$ fossil commit
# Enter a commit message for this check-in. Lines beginning with #
are ignored.
#
# user: clif
# tags: trunk
#
# ADDED        example.txt

$ echo "Line 2" >>example.txt
$ fossil commit
# Enter a commit message for this check-in. Lines beginning with #
are ignored.
#
# user: clif
# tags: trunk
#
# EDITED       example.txt
```

There's more...

When you edit a file you only need to commit. By default, the commit will remember all your changes to the local repository. If auto-sync is enabled, the commit will also be pushed to the remote repository:

```
$ vim example.txt
$ vim otherExample.txt
$ fossil commit
# Enter a commit message for this check-in. Lines beginning with #
are ignored.
#
# user: clif
# tags: trunk
#
# EDITED       example.txt, otherExample.txt
```

Using branches and forks with fossil

In an ideal world, a development tree is a straight line with one revision following directly from the previous. In reality, developers frequently work from a stable code base and make changes that are then merged back into the mainline development.

The fossil system distinguishes temporary divergences from the mainline code (for example, a bug fix in your repository) from permanent divergences (like the 1.x release that gets only bug fixes, while new features go into 2.x).

The convention in fossil is to refer to intentional divergences as branches and unintentional divergences as forks. For example, you might create a branch for a new code you are developing, while trying to commit a change to a file after someone else has committed a change to that file would cause a fork unless you first update and resolve collisions.

Branches can be temporary or permanent. A temporary branch might be one you create while developing a new feature. A permanent branch is when you make a release that is intended to diverge from the mainline code.

Both temporary and permanent branches are managed with tags and properties.

When you create a fossil repository with fossil `init` or fossil `new`, it assigns the tag `trunk` to the tree.

The fossil branch command manages branches. There are subcommands to create new branches, list branches, and close branches.

How to do it

1. The first step in working with branches is to create one. The fossil branch new command creates a new branch. It can either create a branch based on your current checkout of the project, or you can create a branch at an earlier state of the project.

2. The fossil branch new command will create a new branch from a given checkin:

```
$ fossil branch new NewBranchName Basis-Id
New branch: 9ae25e77317e509e420a51ffbc43c2b1ae4034da
```

3. The `Basis-Id` is an identifier to tell fossil what code snapshot to branch from. There are several ways to define the `Basis-Id`. The most common of these are discussed in the next section.

4. Note that you need to perform a checkout to update your working folder to the new branch:

```
$ fossil checkout NewBranchName
```

How it works...

`NewBranchName` is the name for your new branch. A convention is to name branches in a way that describes the modification being made. Branch names such as `localtime_fixes` or `bug_1234_fix` are common.

The `Basis-Id` is a string that identifies the node where the branch diverges. This can be the name of a branch if you are diverging from the head of a given branch.

The following commands show how to create a branch from the tip of a trunk:

```
$ fossil branch new test_rework_parse_logic trunk
New branch: 9ae25e77317e509e420a51ffbc43c2b1ae4034da

$ fossil checkout test_rework_parse_logic
```

The fossil commit command allows you to specify a new branch name at commit time with the `--branch` option:

```
$ fossil checkout trunk

# Make Changes

$ fossil commit --branch test_rework_parse_logic
```

There's more...

Merging forks and branches

Branches and forks can both be merged back into their parent branch. The forks are considered temporary and should be merged as soon as the modifications are approved. Branches are considered permanent, but even these may be merged back into the mainline code.

The fossil merge command will merge a temporary fork into another branch.

How to do it...

1. To create a temporary fork and merge it back into an existing branch, you must first check out the branch you intend to work on:

   ```
   $ fossil checkout trunk
   ```

2. Now you can edit and test. When you're satisfied with the new code, commit the new code onto a new branch. The --branch option creates a new branch if necessary and sets your current branch to the new branch:

   ```
   $ fossil commit --branch new_logic
   ```

3. After the code has been tested and verified, you can merge it back into the appropriate branch by performing a checkout of the branch you want to merge into, then invoke the fossil merge command to schedule the merge, and finally commit the merge:

   ```
   $ fossil checkout trunk
   $ fossil merge new_logic
   $ fossil commit
   ```

4. Fossil and Git behave slightly differently in this respect. The git merge command updates the repository, while the fossil merge command doesn't modify the repository until the merge is committed.

Sharing your work with fossil

If you use multiple platforms for development, or if you work on someone else's project, you need to synchronize your local repository with the remote, master repository. Fossil has several ways to handle this.

How to do it...

By default fossil runs in the `autosync` mode. In this mode, your commits are immediately propagated to the remote repository.

The `autosync` setting can be enabled and disabled with the fossil setting command:

```
$ fossil setting autosync off
$ fossil setting autosync on
```

When `autosync` is disabled (fossil is running in manual merge mode), you must use the fossil push command to send changes in your local repository to the remote:

```
$ fossil push
```

How it works...

The `push` command pushes all changes in your local repository to the remote repository. It does not modify any checked out code.

Updating your local fossil repository

The flip side of pushing your work to the remote repository is updating your local repository. You'll need to do this if you do some development on your laptop while the main repository is on your companies server, or if you are working on a project with multiple people and you need to keep up to date on their new features.

How to do it...

The fossil server does not push updates to remote repositories automatically. The `fossil pull` command will pull updates to your repository. It updates the repository, but does not change your working code:

```
$ fossil pull
```

The `fossil checkout` command will update your working code if there were changes in the repository:

```
$ fossil checkout
```

You can combine the pull and checkout subcommands with the `fossil update` command:

```
$ fossil update
UPDATE main.tcl
-------------------------------------------------------------------
------------
updated-to:     47c85d29075b25aa0d61f39d56f61f72ac2aae67 2016-12-20
17:35:49 UTC
tags:           trunk
comment:        Ticket 1234abc workaround (user: clif)
changes:        1 file modified.
"fossil undo" is available to undo changes to the working checkout.
```

Checking the status of a fossil repository

Before you start any new development, you should compare the state of your local repository to the master repository. You don't want to waste time writing code that conflicts with code that's been accepted.

How to do it...

The `fossil status` command will report the current status of your project, whether you have uncommitted edits and whether your working code is at the tip:

```
$ fossil status
repository:     /home/clif/myProject/../myProject.fossil
local-root:     /home/clif/myProject/
config-db:      /home/clif/.fossil
checkout:       47c85d29075b25aa0d61f39d56f61f72ac2aae67 2016-12-20
17:35:49 UTC
parent:         f3c579cd47d383980770341e9c079a87d92b17db 2016-12-20
17:33:38 UTC
tags:           trunk
comment:        Ticket 1234abc workaround (user: clif)
EDITED        main.tcl
```

If there has been a commit made to the branch you're working on since your last checkout, the status will include a line resembling the following:

```
child:          abcdef123456789...   YYYY-MM-DD HH:MM::SS UTC
```

This indicates that there is a commit after your code. You will have to do a `fossil update` to bring your working copy of the code into sync before you can commit to the head of the branch. This may require you to fix conflicts by hand.

Note that fossil can only report the data in your local repository. If commits have been made but not pushed to the server and pulled into your local repository, they won't be displayed. You should invoke `fossil sync` before `fossil status` to confirm that your repository has all the latest information.

Viewing fossil history

The `fossil server` and `fossil ui` commands start fossil's web server and let you view the history of check-ins and navigate through code via your favorite browser.

The timeline tab provides a tree-structured view of the branches, commits, and merges. The web interface supports viewing the source code associated with the commits and performing diffs between different versions.

How to do it...

Start fossil in the UI mode. It will try to find your browser and open the main page. If that
fails, you can point your browser to fossil:

```
$ fossil ui
Listening for HTTP requests on TCP port 8080

$ konqueror 127.0.0.1:8080
```

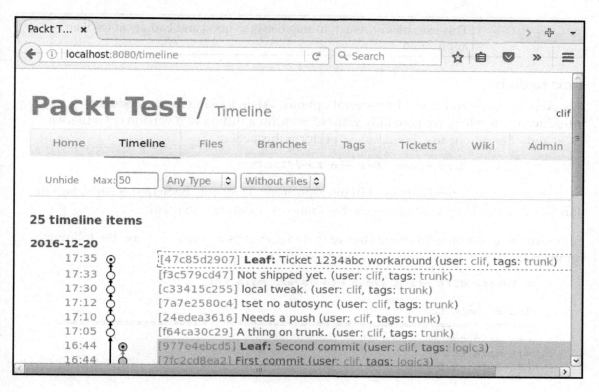

Finding bugs

Fossil provides tools to help locate the commit where a bug was introduced:

Tools	Description
`fossil diff`	This displays the difference between two revisions of a file
`fossil blame`	This generates a report showing the commit information for each line in a file
`fossil bisect`	This uses binary search to step between good and bad versions of an application

How to do it...

The `fossil diff` command has several options. When looking for the code that introduced a problem, we generally want to perform a diff on two versions of a file. The `-from` and `-to` options to `fossil diff` perform this action:

```
$ fossil diff -from ID-1 -to ID-2FILENAME
```

`ID-1` and `ID-2` are identifiers used in the repository. They may be SHA-1 hashes, tags or dates, and so on. The `FILENAME` is the file that was committed to fossil.

For example, to find the difference between two revisions of `main.tcl` use the following command:

```
$ fossil diff -from 47c85 -to 7a7e25 main.tcl

Index: main.tcl
==================================================================
--- main.tcl
+++ main.tcl
@@ -9,10 +9,5 @@

set max 10
set min 1
+ while {$x < $max} {
- for {set x $min} {$x < $max} {incr x} {
-    process $x
- }
-
```

There's more...

The differences between two revisions are useful, but it's more useful to see the entire file annotated to show when lines were added.

The `fossil blame` command generates an annotated listing of a file showing when lines were added:

```
$ fossil blame main.tcl
7806f43641 2016-12-18    clif: # main.tcl
06e155a6c2 2016-12-19    clif: # Clif Flynt
b2420ef6be 2016-12-19    clif: # Packt fossil Test Script
a387090833 2016-12-19    clif:
76074da03c 2016-12-20    clif: for {set i 0} {$i < 10} {incr
i} {
76074da03c 2016-12-20    clif: puts "Buy my book"
2204206a18 2016-12-20    clif: }
7a7e2580c4 2016-12-20    clif:
```

When you know that there's a problem in one version but not in another, you need to center in on the version where the problem was introduced.

The `fossil bisect` command provides support for this. It lets you define a good and bad version of the code and automatically checks out the version between those to be tested. You can then mark this version as good or bad and fossil will repeat the process. Fossil bisect also generates reports showing how many versions have been tested and how many need to be tested.

How to do it...

The `fossil bisect reset` command initializes the good and bad pointers. The `fossil bisect good` and `fossil bisect bad` commands mark versions as good or bad and check out the version of the code that's midway between the good and bad version:

```
$ fossil bisect reset
$ fossil bisect good 63e1e1
$ fossil bisect bad 47c85d
UPDATE main.tcl
--------------------------------------------------------------------
updated-to:   f64ca30c29df0f985105409700992d54e 2016-12-20 17:05:44 UTC
tags:         trunk
comment:      Reworked flaky test. (user: clif)
changes:      1 file modified.
  "fossil undo" is available to undo changes to the working checkout.
    2 BAD      2016-12-20 17:35:49 47c85d29075b25aa
    3 CURRENT  2016-12-20 17:05:44 f64ca30c29df0f98
    1 GOOD     2016-12-19 23:03:22 63e1e1290f853d76
```

After testing the `f64ca` version of the code, you can mark it good or bad and `fossil bisect` will check out the next version for testing.

There's more...

The `fossil bisect status` command generates a report of the available versions and marks the tested versions:

```
$ fossil bisect status
2016-12-20 17:35:49 47c85d2907 BAD
2016-12-20 17:33:38 f3c579cd47
2016-12-20 17:30:03 c33415c255 CURRENT NEXT
2016-12-20 17:12:04 7a7e2580c4
2016-12-20 17:10:35 24edea3616
2016-12-20 17:05:44 f64ca30c29 GOOD
```

Tagging snapshots

Every node in the fossil graph can have one or more tags attached to it. Tags can identify releases, branches, or just particular milestones that you may want to refer to. For example, you may want a release-1 branch with tags for release-1.0, release-1.1, and so on. A tag can be used with checkout or merge instead of using the SHA1 identifier.

Tags are implemented with the fossil tag command. Fossil supports several subcommands to add, cancel, find, and list tags.

The `fossil tag add` command creates a new tag:

```
$ fossil tag add TagName Identifier
```

How to do it...

The `TagName` is whatever you want to call the branch.

Identifier is an identifier for the node to be tagged. The identifier can be one of the following:

1. **A branch name**: Tag the most recent commit on this branch
2. **An SHA1 identifier**: Tag the commit with this SHA1 identifier
3. **A datestamp (YYYY-MM-DD)**: Tag the commit just previous to this datestamp
4. **A timestamp (YYYY-MM-DD HH:MM:SS)**: Tag the commit just previous to this timestamp

```
# Tag the current tip of the trunk as release_1.0
$ fossil add tag release_1.0 trunk

# Tag the last commit on December 15 as beta_release_1
$ fossil add tag beta_release_1 2016-12-16
```

There's more...

A tag can be used as an identifier to create a fork or branch:

```
$ fossil add tag newTag trunk
$ fossil branch new newTagBranch newTag
$ fossil checkout newTagBranch
```

A tag can create a branch with a commit and the `-branch` option:

```
$ fossil add tag myNewTag 2016-12-21
$ fossil checkout myNewTag
# edit and change
$ fossil commit -branch myNewTag
```

7
The Backup Plan

In this chapter, we will cover the following recipes:

- Archiving with `tar`
- Archiving with `cpio`
- Compressing data with `gzip`
- Archiving and compressing with `zip`
- Faster archiving with `pbzip2`
- Creating filesystems with compression
- Backing up snapshots with `rsync`
- Differential archives
- Creating entire disk images using `fsarchiver`

Introduction

Nobody cares about backups until they need them, and nobody makes backups unless forced. Therefore, making backups needs to be automated. With advances in disk drive technology, it's simplest to add a new drive or use the cloud for backups, rather than backing up to a tape drive. Even with cheap drives or cloud storage, backup data should be compressed to reduce storage needs and transfer time. Data should be encrypted before it's stored on the cloud. Data is usually archived and compressed before encrypting. Many standard encryption programs can be automated with shell scripts. This chapter's recipes describe creating and maintaining files or folder archives, compression formats, and encrypting techniques.

Archiving with tar

The `tar` command was written to archive files. It was originally designed to store data on tape, thus the name, **Tape ARchive**. Tar allows you to combine multiple files and directories into a single file while retaining the file attributes, such as owner and permissions. The file created by the `tar` command is often referred to as a **tarball**. These recipes describe creating archives with `tar`.

Getting ready

The `tar` command comes by default with all Unix-like operating systems. It has a simple syntax and creates archives in a portable file format. It supports many arguments to fine-tune its behavior.

How to do it...

The `tar` command creates, updates, examines, and unpacks archives.

1. To create an archive file with tar:

   ```
   $ tar -cf output.tar [SOURCES]
   ```

   The `c` option creates a new archive and the `f` option tells tar the name of a file to use for the archive. The f option must be followed by a filename:

   ```
   $ tar -cf archive.tar file1 file2 file3 folder1 ..
   ```

2. The `-t` option lists the contents of an archive:

   ```
   $ tar -tf archive.tar
   file1
   file2
   ```

3. The `-v` or `-vv` flag includes more information in the output. These features are called verbose (v) and very-verbose (vv). The `-v` convention is common for commands that generate reports by printing to the terminal. The `-v` option displays more details, such as file permissions, owner group, and modification date:

   ```
   $ tar -tvf archive.tar
   -rw-rw-r-- shaan/shaan          0 2013-04-08 21:34 file1
   ```

```
-rw-rw-r-- shaan/shaan          0 2013-04-08 21:34 file2
```

 The filename must appear immediately after the −f and it should be the last option in the argument group. For example, if you want verbose output, you should use the options like this:

```
$ tar -cvf output.tar file1 file2 file3 folder1 ..
```

How it works...

The tar command accepts a list of filenames or wildcards such as *.txt to specify the sources. When finished, tar will archive the source files into the named file.

We cannot pass hundreds of files or folders as command-line arguments. So, it is safer to use the append option (explained later) if many files are to be archived.

There's more...

Let's go through additional features supported by the tar command.

Appending files to an archive

The −r option will append new files to the end of an existing archive:

```
$ tar -rvf original.tar new_file
```

The next example creates an archive with one text file in it:

```
$ echo hello >hello.txt
$ tar -cf archive.tar hello.txt
```

The −t option displays the files in an archive. The −f option defines the archive name:

```
$ tar -tf archive.tar
hello.txt
```

The −r option appends a file:

```
$ tar -rf archive.tar world.txt
$ tar -tf archive.tar
hello.txt
world.txt
```

The archive now contains both the files.

Extracting files and folders from an archive

The -x option extracts the contents of the archive to the current directory:

```
$ tar -xf archive.tar
```

When -x is used, the tar command extracts the contents of the archive to the current directory. The -C option specifies a different directory to receive the extracted files:

```
$ tar -xf archive.tar -C /path/to/extraction_directory
```

The command extracts the contents of an archive to a specified directory. It extracts the entire contents of the archive. We can extract just a few files by specifying them as command arguments:

```
$ tar -xvf file.tar file1 file4
```

The preceding command extracts only file1 and file4, and it ignores other files in the archive.

stdin and stdout with tar

While archiving, we can specify stdout as the output file so another command in a pipe can read it as stdin and process the archive.

This technique will transfer data through a **Secure Shell (SSH)** connection, for example:

```
$ tar cvf - files/ | ssh user@example.com "tar xv -C Documents/"
```

In the preceding example, the files/directory is added to a tar archive which is output to stdout (denoted by -) and extracted to the Documents folder on the remote system.

Concatenating two archives

The -A option will merge multiple tar archives.

Given two tarballs, file1.tar and file2.tar, the following command will merge the contents of file2.tar into file1.tar:

```
$ tar -Af file1.tar file2.tar
```

Verify it by listing the contents:

```
$ tar -tvf file1.tar
```

Updating files in an archive with a timestamp check

The append option appends any given file to the archive. If a file already exists inside the archive, tar will append the file, and the archive will contain duplicates. The update option -u specifies only appending files that are newer than existing files inside the archive.

```
$ tar -tf archive.tar
filea
fileb
filec
```

To append `filea` only if `filea` has been modified since the last time it was added to `archive.tar`, use the following command:

```
$ tar -uf archive.tar filea
```

Nothing happens if the version of `filea` outside the archive and the `filea` inside `archive.tar` have the same timestamp.

Use the `touch` command to modify the file timestamp and then try the `tar` command again:

```
$ tar -uvvf archive.tar filea
-rw-r--r-- slynux/slynux      0 2010-08-14 17:53 filea
```

The file is appended since its timestamp is newer than the one inside the archive, as shown with the -t option:

```
$ tar -tf archive.tar
-rw-r--r-- slynux/slynux      0 2010-08-14 17:52 filea
-rw-r--r-- slynux/slynux      0 2010-08-14 17:52 fileb
-rw-r--r-- slynux/slynux      0 2010-08-14 17:52 filec
-rw-r--r-- slynux/slynux      0 2010-08-14 17:53 filea
```

Note that the new `filea` has been appended to the `tar` archive. When extracting this archive, tar will select the latest version of `filea`.

Comparing files in the archive and filesystem

The -d flag compares files inside an archive with those on the filesystem. This feature can be used to determine whether or not a new archive needs to be created.

```
$ tar -df archive.tar
afile: Mod time differs
afile: Size differs
```

Deleting files from the archive

The -delete option removes files from an archive:

```
$ tar -f archive.tar --delete file1 file2 ..
```

Alternatively,

```
$ tar --delete --file archive.tar [FILE LIST]
```

The next example demonstrates deleting a file:

```
$ tar -tf archive.tar
filea
fileb
filec
$ tar --delete --file archive.tar filea
$ tar -tf archive.tar
fileb
filec
```

Compression with the tar archive

By default, the tar command archives files, it does not compress them. Tar supports options to compress the resulting archive. Compression can significantly decrease the size of the files. Tarballs are often compressed into one of the following formats:

- **gzip format**: file.tar.gz or file.tgz
- **bzip2 format**: file.tar.bz2
- **Lempel-Ziv-Markov format**: file.tar.lzma

Different `tar` flags are used to specify different compression formats:

- `-j` for **bunzip2**
- `-z` for **gzip**
- `--lzma` for **lzma**

It is possible to use compression formats without explicitly specifying special options as earlier. `tar` can compress based on the extension of the output or decompress based on an input file's extension. The `-a` or - **auto-compress** option causes tar to select a compression algorithm automatically based on file extension:

```
$ tar acvf archive.tar.gz filea fileb filec
filea
fileb
filec
$ tar tf archive.tar.gz
filea
fileb
filec
```

Excluding a set of files from archiving

The `-exclude [PATTEN]` option will exclude files matched by wildcard patterns from being archived.

For example, to exclude all `.txt` files from archiving use the following command:

```
$ tar -cf arch.tar * --exclude "*.txt"
```

Note that the pattern should be enclosed within quotes to prevent the shell from expanding it.

It is also possible to exclude a list of files provided in a list file with the `-x` flag as follows:

```
$ cat list
filea
fileb

$ tar -cf arch.tar * -X list
```

Now it excludes `filea` and `fileb` from archiving.

Excluding version control directories

One use for tarballs is distributing source code. Much source code is maintained using version control systems such as subversion, Git, mercurial, and CVS, (refer to the previous chapter). Code directories under version control often contain special directories such as .svn or .git. These are managed by the version control application and are not useful to anyone except a developer. Thus, they should be eliminated from the tarball of the source code being distributed to users.

In order to exclude version control related files and directories while archiving use the --exclude-vcs option along with tar. Consider this example:

```
$ tar --exclude-vcs -czvvf source_code.tar.gz eye_of_gnome_svn
```

Printing the total bytes

The -totals option will print the total bytes copied to the archive. Note that this is the number of bytes of actual data. If you include a compression option, the file size will be less than the number of bytes archived.

```
$ tar -cf arc.tar * --exclude "*.txt" --totals
Total bytes written: 20480 (20KiB, 12MiB/s)
```

See also

- The *Compressing data with gzip* recipe in this chapter explains the gzip command

Archiving with cpio

The cpio application is another archiving format similar to tar. It is used to store files and directories in an archive with attributes such as permissions and ownership. The cpio format is used in RPM package archives (which are used in distros such as Fedora), initramfs files for the Linux kernel that contain the kernel image, and so on. This recipe will give simple examples of cpio.

How to do it...

The `cpio` application accepts input filenames via `stdin` and it writes the archive to `stdout`. We have to redirect `stdout` to a file to save the `cpio` output:

1. Create test files:

   ```
   $ touch file1 file2 file3
   ```

2. Archive the test files:

   ```
   $ ls file* | cpio -ov > archive.cpio
   ```

3. List files in a `cpio` archive:

   ```
   $ cpio -it < archive.cpio
   ```

4. Extract files from the `cpio` archive:

   ```
   $ cpio -id < archive.cpio
   ```

How it works...

For the archiving command, the options are as follows:

- -o: This specifies the output
- -v: This is used for printing a list of files archived

Using `cpio`, we can also archive using files as absolute paths. `/usr/somedir` is an absolute path as it contains the full path starting from root (/).

A relative path will not start with / but it starts the path from the current directory. For example, `test/file` means that there is a directory named `test` and `file` is inside the `test` directory.

While extracting, `cpio` extracts to the absolute path itself. However, in the case of `tar`, it removes the / in the absolute path and converts it to a relative path.

The options in the command for listing all the files in the given `cpio` archive are as follows:

- `-i` is for specifying the input
- `-t` is for listing

In the command for extraction, `-o` stands for extracting and `cpio` overwrites files without prompting. The `-d` option tells `cpio` to create new directories as needed.

Compressing data with gzip

The **gzip** application is a common compression format in the GNU/Linux platform. The `gzip`, `gunzip`, and `zcat` programs all handle `gzip` compression. These utilities only compress/decompress a single file or data stream. They cannot archive directories and multiple files directly. Fortunately, `gzip` can be used with both tar and `cpio`.

How to do it...

`gzip` will compress a file and `gunzip` will decompress it back to the original:

1. Compress a file with `gzip`:

   ```
   $ gzip filename
   $ ls
   filename.gz
   ```

2. Extract a `gzip` compressed file:

   ```
   $ gunzip filename.gz
   $ ls
   filename
   ```

3. In order to list the properties of a compressed file, use the following command:

   ```
   $ gzip -l test.txt.gz
   compressed          uncompressed  ratio uncompressed_name
   35                  6 -33.3% test.txt
   ```

4. The `gzip` command can read a file from `stdin` and write a compressed file to `stdout`.

   Read data from `stdin` and output the compressed data to `stdout`:

   ```
   $ cat file | gzip -c > file.gz
   ```

   The `-c` option is used to specify output to `stdout`.

   The gzip `-c` option works well with `cpio`:

   ```
   $ ls * | cpio -o | gzip -c > cpiooutput.gz
   $ zcat cpiooutput.gz | cpio -it
   ```

5. We can specify the compression level for `gzip` using `--fast` or the `--best` option to provide low and high compression ratios, respectively.

There's more...

The `gzip` command is often used with other commands and has advanced options to specify the compression ratio.

Gzip with tarball

A gzipped tarball is a tar archive compressed using gzip. We can use two methods to create such tarballs:

- The first method is as follows:

  ```
  $ tar -czvvf archive.tar.gz [FILES]
  ```

  Alternatively, this command can be used:

  ```
  $ tar -cavvf archive.tar.gz [FILES]
  ```

The `-z` option specifies `gzip` compression and the `-a` option specifies that the compression format should be determined from the extension.

- The second method is as follows:

  First, create a tarball:

  ```
  $ tar -cvvf archive.tar [FILES]
  ```

  Then, compress the tarball:

  ```
  $ gzip archive.tar
  ```

If many files (a few hundred) are to be archived in a tarball and need to be compressed, we use the second method with a few changes. The problem with defining many files on the command line is that it can accept only a limited number of files as arguments. To solve this problem, we create a `tar` file by adding files one by one in a loop with the append option (-r), as follows:

```
FILE_LIST="file1  file2 file3  file4  file5"
for f in $FILE_LIST;
  do
  tar -rvf archive.tar $f
done
gzip archive.tar
```

The following command will extract a gzipped tarball:

```
$ tar -xavvf archive.tar.gz -C extract_directory
```

In the preceding command, the -a option is used to detect the compression format.

zcat - reading gzipped files without extracting

The `zcat` command dumps uncompressed data from a `.gz` file to `stdout` without recreating the original file. The `.gz` file remains intact.

```
$ ls
test.gz

$ zcat test.gz
A test file
# file test contains a line "A test file"

$ ls
test.gz
```

Compression ratio

We can specify the compression ratio, which is available in the range 1 to 9, where:

- 1 is the lowest, but fastest
- 9 is the best, but slowest

You can specify any ratio in that range as follows:

```
$ gzip -5 test.img
```

By default, gzip uses a value of -6, favoring a better compression at the cost of some speed.

Using bzip2

bzip2 is similar to gzip in function and syntax. The difference is that bzip2 offers better compression and runs more slowly than gzip.

To compress a file using bzip2 use the command as follows:

```
$ bzip2 filename
```

Extract a bzipped file as follows:

```
$ bunzip2 filename.bz2
```

The way to compress to and extract from tar.bz2 files is similar to tar.gz, discussed earlier:

```
$ tar -xjvf archive.tar.bz2
```

Here -j specifies compressing the archive in the bzip2 format.

Using lzma

The lzma compression delivers better compression ratios than gzip and bzip2.

To compress a file using lzma use the command as follows:

```
$ lzma filename
```

To extract a lzma file, use the following command:

```
$ unlzma filename.lzma
```

A tarball can be compressed with the `-lzma` option:

```
$ tar -cvvf --lzma archive.tar.lzma [FILES]
```

Alternatively, this can be used:

```
$ tar -cavvf archive.tar.lzma [FILES]
```

To extract a tarball created with `lzma` compression to a specified directory, use this command:

```
$ tar -xvvf --lzma archive.tar.lzma -C extract_directory
```

In the preceding command, `-x` is used for extraction. `--lzma` specifies the use of `lzma` to decompress the resulting file.

Alternatively, use this:

```
$ tar -xavvf archive.tar.lzma -C extract_directory
```

See also

- The *Archiving with tar* recipe in this chapter explains the `tar` command

Archiving and compressing with zip

ZIP is a popular compressed archive format available on Linux, Mac, and Windows. It isn't as commonly used as `gzip` or `bzip2` on Linux but is useful when distributing data to other platforms.

How to do it...

1. The following syntax creates a zip archive:

   ```
   $ zip archive_name.zip file1 file2 file3...
   ```

   Consider this example:

   ```
   $ zip file.zip file
   ```

   Here, the `file.zip` file will be produced.

2. The -r flag will archive folders recursively:

   ```
   $ zip -r archive.zip folder1 folder2
   ```

3. The unzip command will extract files and folders from a ZIP file:

   ```
   $ unzip file.zip
   ```

   The unzip command extracts the contents without removing the archive (unlike unlzma or gunzip).

4. The -u flag updates files in the archive with newer files:

   ```
   $ zip file.zip -u newfile
   ```

5. The -d flag deletes one or more files from a zipped archive:

   ```
   $ zip -d arc.zip file.txt
   ```

6. The -l flag to unzip lists the files in an archive:

   ```
   $ unzip -l archive.zip
   ```

How it works...

While being similar to most of the archiving and compression tools we have already discussed, zip, unlike lzma, gzip, or bzip2, won't remove the source file after archiving. While zip is similar to tar, it performs both archiving and compression, while tar by itself does not perform compression.

Faster archiving with pbzip2

Most modern computers have at least two CPU cores. This is almost the same as two real CPUs doing your work. However, just having a multicore CPU doesn't mean a program will run faster; it is important that the program is designed to take advantage of the multiple cores.

The compression commands covered so far use only one CPU. The pbzip2, plzip, pigz, and lrzip commands are multithreaded and can use multiple cores, hence, decreasing the overall time taken to compress your files.

None of these are installed with most distros, but can be added to your system with apt-get or yum.

Getting ready

pbzip2 usually doesn't come preinstalled with most distros, you will have to use your package manager to install it:

```
sudo apt-get install pbzip2
```

How to do it...

1. The pbzip2 command will compress a single file:

   ```
   pbzip2 myfile.tar
   ```

   pbzip2 detects the number of cores on your system and compresses myfile.tar, to myfile.tar.bz2.

2. To compress and archive multiple files or directories, we use pbzip2 in combination with tar, as follows:

   ```
   tar cf sav.tar.bz2 --use-compress-prog=pbzip2 dir
   ```

   Alternatively, this can be used:

   ```
   tar -c directory_to_compress/ | pbzip2 -c > myfile.tar.bz2
   ```

3. Extracting a pbzip2 compressed file is as follows:

   The -d flag will decompress a file:

   ```
   pbzip2 -d myfile.tar.bz2
   ```

   A tar archive can be decompressed and extracted using a pipe:

   ```
   pbzip2 -dc myfile.tar.bz2 | tar x
   ```

How it works...

The `pbzip2` application uses the same compression algorithms as `bzip2`, but it compresses separate chunks of data simultaneously using `pthreads`, a threading library. The threading is transparent to the user, but provides much faster compression.

Like `gzip` or `bzip2`, `pbzip2` does not create archives. It only works on a single file. To compress multiple files and directories, we use it in conjunction with `tar` or `cpio`.

There's more...

There are other useful options we can use with `pbzip2`:

Manually specifying the number of CPUs

The `-p` option specifies the number of CPU cores to use. This is useful if automatic detection fails or you need cores free for other jobs:

```
pbzip2 -p4 myfile.tar
```

This will tell `pbzip2` to use 4 CPUs.

Specifying the compression ratio

The options from `-1` to `-9` specify the fastest and best compression ratios with **1** being the fastest and **9** being the best compression

Creating filesystems with compression

The `squashfs` program creates a read-only, heavily compressed filesystem. The `squashfs` program can compress 2 to 3 GB of data into a 700 MB file. The Linux LiveCD (or LiveUSB) distributions are built using `squashfs`. These CDs make use of a read-only compressed filesystem, which keeps the root filesystem on a compressed file. The compressed file can be loopback-mounted to load a complete Linux environment. When files are required, they are decompressed and loaded into the RAM, run, and the RAM is freed.

The `squashfs` program is useful when you need a compressed archive and random access to the files. Completely decompressing a large compressed archive takes a long time. A loopback-mounted archive provides fast file access since only the requested portion of the archive is decompressed.

Getting ready

Mounting a `squashfs` filesystem is supported by all modern Linux distributions. However, creating `squashfs` files requires `squashfs-tools`, which can be installed using the package manager:

```
$ sudo apt-get install squashfs-tools
```

Alternatively, this can be used:

```
$ yum install squashfs-tools
```

How to do it...

1. Create a `squashfs` file by adding source directories and files with the `mksquashfs` command:

   ```
   $ mksquashfs SOURCES compressedfs.squashfs
   ```

   Sources can be wildcards, files, or folder paths.

   Consider this example:

   ```
   $ sudo mksquashfs /etc test.squashfs
   Parallel mksquashfs: Using 2 processors
   Creating 4.0 filesystem on test.squashfs, block size 131072.
   [=======================================] 1867/1867 100%
   ```

More details will be printed on the terminal. The output is stripped to save space.

2. To mount the `squashfs` file to a mount point, use loopback mounting, as follows:

```
# mkdir /mnt/squash
# mount -o loop compressedfs.squashfs /mnt/squash
```

You can access the contents at `/mnt/squashfs`.

There's more...

The `squashfs` filesystem can be customized by specifying additional parameters.

Excluding files while creating a squashfs file

The `-e` flag will exclude files and folders:

```
$ sudo mksquashfs /etc test.squashfs -e /etc/passwd /etc/shadow
```

The `-e` option excludes `/etc/passwd and /etc/shadow` files from the `squashfs` filesystem.

The `-ef` option reads a file with a list of files to exclude:

```
$ cat excludelist
/etc/passwd
/etc/shadow

$ sudo mksquashfs /etc test.squashfs -ef excludelist
```

If we want to support wildcards in excludes lists, use `-wildcard` as an argument.

Backing up snapshots with rsync

Backing up data is something that needs to be done regularly. In addition to local backups, we may need to back up data to or from remote locations. The `rsync` command synchronizes files and directories from one location to another while minimizing transfer time. The advantages of `rsync` over the `cp` command are that `rsync` compares modification dates and will only copy the files that are newer, `rsync` supports data transfer across remote machines, and `rsync` supports compression and encryption.

How to do it...

1. To copy a source directory to a destination, use the following command:

   ```
   $ rsync -av source_path destination_path
   ```

   Consider this example:

   ```
   $ rsync -av /home/slynux/data
   slynux@192.168.0.6:/home/backups/data
   ```

   In the preceding command:

   - `-a` stands for archiving
   - `-v` (verbose) prints the details or progress on stdout

   The preceding command will recursively copy all the files from the source path to the destination path. The source and destination paths can be either remote or local.

2. To backup data to a remote server or host, use the following command:

   ```
   $ rsync -av source_dir username@host:PATH
   ```

   To keep a mirror at the destination, run the same `rsync` command at regular intervals. It will copy only changed files to the destination.

3. To restore the data from the remote host to `localhost`, use the following command:

   ```
   $ rsync -av username@host:PATH destination
   ```

The `rsync` command uses SSH to connect to the remote machine hence, you should provide the remote machine's address in the `user@host` format, where user is the username and host is the IP address or host name attached to the remote machine. `PATH` is the path on the remote machine from where the data needs to be copied.

Make sure that the OpenSSH server is installed and running on the remote machine. Additionally, to avoid being prompted for a password for the remote machine, refer to the *Password-less auto-login with SSH* recipe in `Chapter 8`, *The Old-Boy Network*.

4. Compressing data during transfer can significantly optimize the speed of the transfer. The `rsync-z` option `specifies` compressing data during transfer:

```
$ rsync -avz source destination
```

5. To synchronize one directory to another directory, use the following command:

```
$ rsync -av /home/test/ /home/backups
```

The preceding command copies the source (`/home/test`) to an existing folder called backups.

6. To copy a full directory inside another directory, use the following command:

```
$ rsync -av /home/test /home/backups
```

This command copies the source (`/home/test`) to a directory named backups by creating that directory.

For the PATH format, if we use / at the end of the source, `rsync` will copy the contents of the end directory specified in the `source_path` to the destination.

If / is not present at the end of the source, `rsync` will copy the end directory itself to the destination.

Adding the `-r` option will force `rsync` to copy all the contents of a directory, recursively.

How it works...

The `rsync` command works with the source and destination paths, which can be either local or remote. Both paths can be remote paths. Usually, remote connections are made using SSH to provide secure, two-way communication. Local and remote paths look like this:

- `/home/user/data` (local path)
- `user@192.168.0.6:/home/backups/data` (remote path)

`/home/user/data` specifies the absolute path in the machine in which the `rsync` command is executed. `user@192.168.0.6:/home/backups/data` specifies that the path is `/home/backups/data` in the machine whose IP address is `192.168.0.6` and is logged in as the `user` user.

There's more...

The `rsync` command supports several command-line options to fine-tune its behavior.

Excluding files while archiving with rsync

The `-exclude` and -exclude-from options specify files that should not be transferred:

```
--exclude PATTERN
```

We can specify a wildcard pattern of files to be excluded. Consider the following example:

```
$ rsync -avz /home/code/app /mnt/disk/backup/code --exclude "*.o"
```

This command excludes the `.o` files from backing up.

Alternatively, we can specify a list of files to be excluded by providing a list file.

Use `--exclude-from FILEPATH`.

Deleting non-existent files while updating rsync backup

By default, `rsync` does not remove files from the destination if they no longer exist at the source. The `–delete` option removes those files from the destination that do not exist at the source:

```
$ rsync -avz SOURCE DESTINATION --delete
```

Scheduling backups at intervals

You can create a `cron` job to schedule backups at regular intervals.

A sample is as follows:

```
$ crontab -ev
```

Add the following line:

```
0 */10 * * * rsync -avz /home/code user@IP_ADDRESS:/home/backups
```

The preceding `crontab` entry schedules `rsync` to be executed every 10 hours.

`*/10` is the hour position of the `crontab` syntax. `/10` specifies executing the backup every 10 hours. If `*/10` is written in the minutes position, it will execute every 10 minutes.

Have a look at the *Scheduling with a cron* recipe in `Chapter 10`, *Administration Calls*, to understand how to configure `crontab`.

Differential archives

The backup solutions described so far are full copies of a filesystem as it exists at that time. This snapshot is useful when you recognize a problem immediately and need the most recent snapshot to recover. It fails if you don't realize the problem until a new snapshot is made and the previous good data has been overwritten by current bad data.

An archive of a filesystem provides a history of file changes. This is useful when you need to return to an older version of a damaged file.

rsync, tar, and cpio can be used to make daily snapshots of a filesystem. However, backing up a full filesystem every day is expensive. Creating a separate snapshot for each day of the week will require seven times as much space as the original filesystem.

Differential backups only save the data that's changed since the last full backup. The dump/restore utilities from Unix support this style of archived backups. Unfortunately, these utilities were designed around tape drives and are not simple to use.

The find utility can be used with tar or cpio to duplicate this type of functionality.

How to do it...

Create an initial full backup with tar:

```
tar -cvz /backup/full.tgz /home/user
```

Use find's -newer flag to determine what files have changed since the full backup was created, and create a new archive:

```
tar -czf day-`date +%j`.tgz `find /home/user -newer
/backup/full.tgz`
```

How it works...

The find command generates a list of all files that have been modified since the creation of the full backup (/backup/full.tgz).

The date command generates a filename based on the Julian date. Thus, the first differential backup of the year will be day-1.tgz, the backup for January 2 will be day-2.tgz, and so on.

The differential archive will be larger each day as more and more files are changed from the initial full backup. When the differential archives grow too large, make a new full backup.

Creating entire disk images using fsarchiver

The `fsarchiver` application can save the contents of a disk partition to a compressed archive file. Unlike `tar` or `cpio`, `fsarchiver` retains extended file attributes and can be restored to a disk with no current filesystem. The `fsarchiver` application recognizes and retains Windows file attributes as well as Linux attributes, making it suitable for migrating Samba-mounted partitions.

Getting ready

The `fsarchiver` application is not installed in most distros by default. You will have to install it using your package manager. For more information, go to `http://www.fsarchiver.org/Installation`.

How to do it...

1. Create a backup of a `filesystem/partition`.

    Use the `savefs` option of `fsarchiver` like this:

    ```
    fsarchiver savefs backup.fsa /dev/sda1
    ```

    Here `backup.fsa` is the final backup file and `/dev/sda1` is the partition to backup

2. Back-up more than one partition at the same time.

    Use the `savefs` option as earlier and pass the partitions as the last parameters to `fsarchiver`:

    ```
    fsarchiver savefs backup.fsa /dev/sda1 /dev/sda2
    ```

3. Restore a partition from a backup archive.

    Use the `restfs` option of `fsarchiver` like this:

    ```
    fsarchiver restfs backup.fsa id=0,dest=/dev/sda1
    ```

id=0 denotes that we want to pick the first partition from the archive to the partition specified as dest=/dev/sda1.

Restore multiple partitions from a backup archive.

As earlier, use the restfs option as follows:

```
fsarchiver restfs backup.fsa id=0,dest=/dev/sda1
id=1,dest=/dev/sdb1
```

Here, we use two sets of the id,dest parameter to tell fsarchiver to restore the first two partitions from the backup to two physical partitions.

How it works...

Like tar, fsarchiver examines the filesystem to create a list of files and then saves those files in a compressed archive file. Unlike tar which only saves information about the files, fsarchiver performs a backup of the filesystem as well. This makes it easier to restore the backup on a fresh partition as it is not necessary to recreate the filesystem.

If you are seeing the /dev/sda1 notation for partitions for the first time, this requires an explanation. /dev in Linux holds special files called device files, which refer to a physical device. The sd in sda1 refers to **SATA** disk, the next letter can be a, b, c, and so on, followed by the partition number.

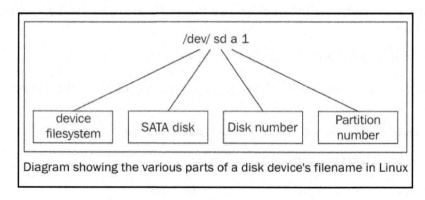

Diagram showing the various parts of a disk device's filename in Linux

8
The Old-Boy Network

In this chapter, we will cover the following recipes:

- Setting up the network
- Let us ping!
- Tracing IP routes
- Listing all available machines on a network
- Running commands on a remote host with SSH
- Running graphical commands on a remote machine
- Transferring files through the network
- Connecting to a wireless network
- Password-less auto-login with SSH
- Port forwarding using SSH
- Mounting a remote drive at a local mount point
- Network traffic and port analysis
- Measuring network bandwidth
- Creating arbitrary sockets
- Building a bridge
- Sharing an Internet connection
- Basic firewall using `iptables`
- Creating a Virtual Private Network

Introduction

Networking is the act of connecting computers to allow them to exchange information. The most widely used networking stack is TCP/IP, where each node is assigned a unique IP address for identification. If you are already familiar with networking, you can skip this introduction.

TCP/IP networks work by passing data packets from node to node. Each data packet contains the IP address of its destination and the port number of the application that can process this data.

When a node receives a packet, it checks to see if it is this packet's destination. If so, the node checks the port number and invokes the appropriate application to process the data. If this node is not the destination, it evaluates what it knows about the network and passes the packet to a node that is closer to the final destination.

Shell scripts can be used to configure the nodes in a network, test the availability of machines, automate execution of commands at remote hosts, and more. This chapter provides recipes that introduce tools and commands related to networking, and shows how to use them effectively.

Setting up the network

Before digging through recipes based on networking, it is essential to have a basic understanding of setting up a network, terminologies, and commands for assigning IP address, adding routes, and so on. This recipe provides an overview of commands used in GNU/Linux networks.

Getting ready

A network interface physically connects a machine to a network, either with a wire or a Wi-Fi link. Linux denotes network interfaces using names such as eth0, eth1, or enp0s25 (referring to Ethernet interfaces). Other interfaces, namely usb0, wlan0, and tun0, are available for USB network interfaces, wireless LAN, and tunnels, respectively.

In this recipe, we will use these commands: ifconfig, route, nslookup, and host.

The `ifconfig` command is used to configure and display details about network interfaces, subnet mask, and so on. It should be available at `/sbin/ifconfig`.

How to do it...

1. List the current network interface configuration:

```
$ ifconfig
lo         Link encap:Local Loopback
inet addr:127.0.0.1  Mask:255.0.0.0
inet6addr: ::1/128 Scope:Host
    UP LOOPBACK RUNNING  MTU:16436  Metric:1
    RX packets:6078 errors:0 dropped:0 overruns:0 frame:0
    TX packets:6078 errors:0 dropped:0 overruns:0 carrier:0
collisions:0 txqueuelen:0
    RX bytes:634520 (634.5 KB)  TX bytes:634520 (634.5 KB)
wlan0      Link encap:EthernetHWaddr 00:1c:bf:87:25:d2
inet addr:192.168.0.82  Bcast:192.168.3.255  Mask:255.255.252.0
inet6addr: fe80::21c:bfff:fe87:25d2/64 Scope:Link
    UP BROADCAST RUNNING MULTICAST  MTU:1500  Metric:1
    RX packets:420917 errors:0 dropped:0 overruns:0 frame:0
    TX packets:86820 errors:0 dropped:0 overruns:0 carrier:0
collisions:0 txqueuelen:1000
    RX bytes:98027420 (98.0 MB)  TX bytes:22602672 (22.6 MB)
```

The leftmost column in the ifconfig output lists the names of network interfaces, and the right-hand columns show the details related to the corresponding network interface.

2. To set the IP address for a network interface, use the following command:

```
# ifconfig wlan0 192.168.0.80
```

You will need to run the preceding command as root

`192.168.0.80` is defined as the address for the wireless device, wlan0

To set the subnet mask along with the IP address, use the following command:

```
# ifconfig wlan0 192.168.0.80  netmask 255.255.252.0
```

3. Many networks use **Dynamic Host Configuration Protocol** (DHCP) to assign IP addresses automatically when a computer connects to the network. The dhclient command assigns the IP address when your machine is connected to a network that assigns IP addresses automatically. If addresses are assigned via DHCP, use dhclient instead of manually choosing an address that might conflict with another machine on the network. Many Linux distributions invoke dhclient automatically when they sense a network cable connection

```
# dhclient eth0
```

There's more...

The ifconfig command can be combined with other shell tools to produce specific reports.

Printing the list of network interfaces

This one-line command sequence displays network interfaces available on a system:

```
$ ifconfig | cut -c-10 | tr -d ' ' | tr -s 'n'
lo
wlan0
```

The first ten characters of each line in ifconfig output is reserved for writing names of network interfaces. Hence, we use cut to extract the first ten characters of each line. tr -d ' ' deletes every space character in each line. Now, the n newline character is squeezed using tr -s 'n' to produce a list of interface names.

Displaying IP addresses

The ifconfig command displays details of every active network interface available on the system. However, we can restrict it to a specific interface using the following command:

```
$ ifconfig iface_name
```

Consider this example:

```
$ ifconfig wlan0
wlan0     Link encap:EthernetHWaddr 00:1c:bf:87:25:d2
inet addr:192.168.0.82 Bcast:192.168.3.255 Mask:255.255.252.0
inet6 addr: fe80::3a2c:4aff:6e6e:17a9/64 Scope:Link
UP BROADCAST RUNNINT MULTICAST  MTU:1500 Metric:1
RX Packets...
```

To control a device, we need the IP address, broadcast address, hardware address, and subnet mask:

- `HWaddr 00:1c:bf:87:25:d2`: This is the hardware address (MAC address)
- `inet addr:192.168.0.82`: This is the IP address
- `Bcast:192.168.3.255`: This is the broadcast address
- `Mask:255.255.252.0`: This is the subnet mask

To extract the IP address from the `ifconfig` output, use this command:

```
$ ifconfig wlan0 | egrep -o "inetaddr:[^ ]*" | grep -o "[0-9.]*"
192.168.0.82
```

The `egrep -o "inetaddr:[^ ]*"` command returns `inet addr:192.168.0.82`. The pattern starts with `inetaddr:` and ends with any non-space character sequence (specified by `[^ ]*`). The next command, `grep -o "[0-9.]*"` reduces its input to only numbers and periods, and prints out an IP4 address.

Spoofing the hardware address (MAC address)

When authentication or filtering is based on the hardware address, we can use hardware address spoofing. The hardware address appears in the `ifconfig` output as `HWaddr 00:1c:bf:87:25:d2`.

The `hw` subcommand of `ifconfig` will define a devices class and the MAC address:

```
# ifconfig eth0 hw ether 00:1c:bf:87:25:d5
```

In the preceding command, `00:1c:bf:87:25:d5` is the new MAC address to be assigned. This is useful when we need to access the Internet through MAC-authenticated service providers that provide access to the Internet for a single machine.

 Note: this definition only lasts until a machine restarts.

Name server and DNS (Domain Name Service)

The underlying addressing scheme for the Internet is the dotted decimal form (like `83.166.169.231`). Humans prefer to use words instead of numbers, so resources on the Internet are identified with strings of words called **URLs** or **domain names**. For example, `www.packtpub.com` is a domain name and it corresponds to an IP address. The site can be identified by the numeric or the string name.

This technique of mapping IP addresses to symbolic names is called **Domain Name Service** (**DNS**). When we enter `www.google.com`, our computer uses the DNS servers to resolve the domain name into the corresponding IP address. While on a local network, we set up the local DNS to name local machines with symbolic names.

Name servers are defined in `/etc/resolv.conf`:

```
$ cat /etc/resolv.conf
# Local nameserver
nameserver 192.168.1.1
# External nameserver
nameserver 8.8.8.8
```

We can add name servers manually by editing that file or with a one-liner:

```
# sudo echo nameserver IP_ADDRESS >> /etc/resolv.conf
```

The easiest method to obtain an IP address is to use the `ping` command to access the domain name. The reply includes the IP address:

```
$ ping google.com
PING google.com (64.233.181.106) 56(84) bytes of data.
```

The number `64.233.181.106` is the IP address of a google.com server.

A domain name may map to multiple IP addresses. In that case, `ping` shows one address from the list of IP addresses. To obtain all the addresses assigned to the domain name, we should use a DNS lookup utility.

DNS lookup

Several DNS lookup utilities provide name and IP address resolution from the command line. The `host` and `nslookup` commands are two commonly installed utilities.

The `host` command lists all of the IP addresses attached to a domain name:

```
$ host google.com
google.com has address 64.233.181.105
google.com has address 64.233.181.99
google.com has address 64.233.181.147
google.com has address 64.233.181.106
google.com has address 64.233.181.103
google.com has address 64.233.181.104
```

The `nslookup` command maps names to IP addresses and will also map IP addresses to names:

```
$ nslookup google.com
Server:      8.8.8.8
Address:     8.8.8.8#53

Non-authoritative answer:
Name:   google.com
Address: 64.233.181.105
Name:   google.com
Address: 64.233.181.99
Name:   google.com
Address: 64.233.181.147
Name:   google.com
Address: 64.233.181.106
Name:   google.com
Address: 64.233.181.103
Name:   google.com
Address: 64.233.181.104

Server:      8.8.8.8
```

The last line in the preceding command-line snippet corresponds to the default name server used for resolution.

It is possible to add a symbolic name to the IP address resolution by adding entries into the `/etc/hosts` file.

Entries in `/etc/hosts` follow this format:

```
IP_ADDRESS name1 name2 ...
```

You can update /etc/hosts like this:

```
# echo IP_ADDRESS symbolic_name>> /etc/hosts
```

Consider this example:

```
# echo 192.168.0.9 backupserver>> /etc/hosts
```

After adding this entry, whenever resolution to backupserver occurs, it will resolve to 192.168.0.9.

If backupserver has multiple names, you can include them on the same line:

```
# echo 192.168.0.9 backupserver backupserver.example.com >> /etc/hosts
```

Showing routing table information

It is common to have interconnected networks. For example, different departments at work or school may be on separate networks. When a device on one network wants to communicate with a device on the other network, it needs to send packets through a device which is common to both networks. This device is called a gateway and its function is to route packets to and from different networks.

The operating system maintains a table called the routing table, which contains the information on how packets are to be forwarded through machines on the network. The route command displays the routing table:

```
$ route
Kernel IP routing table
Destination       Gateway       GenmaskFlags   Metric   Ref   UseIface
192.168.0.0       *             255.255.252.0  U        2     0     0wlan0
link-local        *             255.255.0.0    U        1000  0     0wlan0
default           p4.local      0.0.0.0        UG       0     0     0wlan0
```

Alternatively, you can also use this:

```
$ route -n
Kernel IP routing table
Destination    Gateway       Genmask        Flags Metric Ref   UseIface
192.168.0.0    0.0.0.0       255.255.252.0  U     2      0     0   wlan0
169.254.0.0    0.0.0.0       255.255.0.0    U     1000   0     0   wlan0
0.0.0.0        192.168.0.4   0.0.0.0        UG    0      0     0   wlan0
```

Using −n specifies to display the numeric addresses. By default, route will map the numeric address to a name.

When your system does not know the route to a destination, it sends the packet to a default gateway. The default gateway may be the link to the Internet or an inter-departmental router.

The `route add` command can add a default gateway:

```
# route add default gw IP_ADDRESS INTERFACE_NAME
```

Consider this example:

```
# route add default gw 192.168.0.1 wlan0
```

See also

- The *Using variables and environment variables* recipe of `Chapter 1`, *Shell Something Out*, explains the `PATH` variable
- The *Searching and mining text inside a file with grep* recipe of `Chapter 4`, *Texting and Driving*, explains the `grep` command

Let us ping!

The `ping` command is a basic network command, supported on all major operating systems. Ping is used to verify connectivity between hosts on a network and identify accessible machines.

How to do it...

The ping command uses **Internet Control Message Protocol (ICMP)** packets to check the connectivity of two hosts on a network. When these echo packets are sent to a target, the target responds with a reply if the connection is complete. A ping request can fail if there is no route to the target or if there is no known route from the target back to the requester.

Pinging an address will check whether a host is reachable:

```
$ ping ADDRESS
```

The `ADDRESS` can be a hostname, domain name, or an IP address itself.

By default, `ping` will continuously send packets and the reply information is printed on the terminal. Stop the pinging process by pressing *Ctrl + C*.

Consider the following example:

- When a host is reachable, the output will be similar to the following:

```
$ ping 192.168.0.1
PING 192.168.0.1 (192.168.0.1) 56(84) bytes of data.
64 bytes from 192.168.0.1: icmp_seq=1 ttl=64 time=1.44 ms
^C
--- 192.168.0.1 ping statistics ---
1 packets transmitted, 1 received, 0% packet loss, time 0ms
rtt min/avg/max/mdev = 1.440/1.440/1.440/0.000 ms

$ ping google.com
PING google.com (209.85.153.104) 56(84) bytes of data.
64 bytes from bom01s01-in-f104.1e100.net (209.85.153.104):
icmp_seq=1 ttl=53 time=123 ms
^C
--- google.com ping statistics ---
1 packets transmitted, 1 received, 0% packet loss, time 0ms
rtt min/avg/max/mdev = 123.388/123.388/123.388/0.000 ms
```

- When a host is unreachable, the output will resemble this:

```
$ ping 192.168.0.99
PING 192.168.0.99 (192.168.0.99) 56(84) bytes of data.
From 192.168.0.82 icmp_seq=1 Destination Host Unreachable
From 192.168.0.82 icmp_seq=2 Destination Host Unreachable
```

If the target is not reachable, the ping returns with the `Destination Host Unreachable` error message.

Network administrators generally configure devices such as routers not to respond to `ping`. This is done to lower security risks, as `ping` can be used by attackers (using brute-force) to find out IP addresses of machines.

There's more...

In addition to checking the connectivity between two points in a network, the `ping` command returns other information. The round trip time and lost packet reports can be used to determine whether a network is working properly.

Round Trip Time

The `ping` command displays **Round Trip Time** (**RTT**) for each packet sent and returned. RTT is reported in milliseconds. On an internal network, a RTT of under 1ms is common. When pinging a site on the Internet, RTT are commonly 10-400 ms, and may exceed 1000 ms:

```
--- google.com ping statistics ---
5 packets transmitted, 5 received, 0% packet loss, time 4000ms
rtt min/avg/max/mdev = 118.012/206.630/347.186/77.713 ms
```

Here, the minimum RTT is `118.012` ms, the average RTT is `206.630` ms, and the maximum RTT is `347.186`ms. The `mdev` (`77.713`ms) parameter in the ping output stands for mean deviation.

Sequence number

Each packet that ping sends is assigned a number, sequentially from 1 until ping stops. If a network is near saturation, packets may be returned out of order because of collisions and retries, or may be completely dropped:

```
$> ping example.com
64 bytes from example.com (1.2.3.4): icmp_seq=1 ttl=37 time=127.2 ms
64 bytes from example.com (1.2.3.4): icmp_seq=3 ttl=37 time=150.2 ms
64 bytes from example.com (1.2.3.4): icmp_seq=2 ttl=30 time=1500.3 ms
```

In this example, the second packet was dropped and then retried after a timeout, causing it to be returned out of order and with a longer Round Trip Time.

Time to live

Each ping packet has a predefined number of hops it can take before it is dropped. Each router decrements that value by one. This value shows how many routers are between your system and the site you are pinging. The initial **Time To Live** (**TTL**) value can vary depending on your platform or ping revision. You can determine the initial value by pinging the loopback connection:

```
$> ping 127.0.0.1
64 bytes from 127.0.0.1: icmp_seq=1 ttl=64 time=0.049 ms
$> ping www.google.com
64 bytes from 173.194.68.99: icmp_seq=1 ttl=45 time=49.4 ms
```

In this example, we ping the loopback address to determine what the TTL is with no hops (in this case, 64). Then we ping a remote site and subtract that TTL value from our No-Hop value to determine how many hops are between the two sites. In this case, 64-45 is 19 hops.

The TTL value is usually constant between two sites, but can change when conditions require alternative paths.

Limiting the number of packets to be sent

The `ping` command sends echo packets and waits for the reply of echo indefinitely until it is stopped by pressing *Ctrl* + *C*. The `-c` flag will limit the count of echo packets to be sent:

```
-c COUNT
```

Consider this example:

```
$ ping 192.168.0.1 -c 2
PING 192.168.0.1 (192.168.0.1) 56(84) bytes of data.
64 bytes from 192.168.0.1: icmp_seq=1 ttl=64 time=4.02 ms
64 bytes from 192.168.0.1: icmp_seq=2 ttl=64 time=1.03 ms

--- 192.168.0.1 ping statistics ---
2 packets transmitted, 2 received, 0% packet loss, time 1001ms
rtt min/avg/max/mdev = 1.039/2.533/4.028/1.495 ms
```

In the previous example, the `ping` command sends two echo packets and stops. This is useful when we need to ping multiple machines from a list of IP addresses through a script and check their statuses.

Return status of the ping command

The `ping` command returns the exit status 0 when it succeeds and returns non-zero when it fails. `Successful` means the destination host is reachable, whereas `Failure` is when the destination host is unreachable.

The return status can be obtained as follows:

```
$ ping domain -c2
if [ $? -eq0 ];
then
  echo Successful ;
else
  echo Failure
fi
```

Tracing IP routes

When an application requests a service through the Internet, the server may be at a distant location and connected via many of gateways or routers. The `traceroute` command displays the address of all intermediate gateways a packet visits before reaching its destination. `traceroute` information helps us to understand how many hops each packet takes to reach a destination. The number of intermediate gateways represents the effective distance between two nodes in a network, which may not be related to the physical distance. Travel time increases with each hop. It takes time for a router to receive, decipher, and transmit a packet.

How to do it...

The format for the `traceroute` command is as follows:

```
traceroute destinationIP
```

`destinationIP` may be numeric or a string:

```
$ traceroute google.com
traceroute to google.com (74.125.77.104), 30 hops max, 60 byte packets
 1  gw-c6509.lxb.as5577.net (195.26.4.1)  0.313 ms  0.371 ms  0.457 ms
 2  40g.lxb-fra.as5577.net (83.243.12.2)  4.684 ms  4.754 ms  4.823 ms
 3  de-cix10.net.google.com (80.81.192.108)  5.312 ms  5.348 ms  5.327 ms
 4  209.85.255.170 (209.85.255.170)  5.816 ms  5.791 ms 209.85.255.172
(209.85.255.172)  5.678 ms
 5  209.85.250.140 (209.85.250.140)  10.126 ms  9.867 ms  10.754 ms
 6  64.233.175.246 (64.233.175.246)  12.940 ms 72.14.233.114 (72.14.233.114)
13.736 ms  13.803 ms
 7  72.14.239.199 (72.14.239.199)  14.618 ms 209.85.255.166 (209.85.255.166)
12.755 ms 209.85.255.143 (209.85.255.143)  13.803 ms
 8  209.85.255.98 (209.85.255.98)  22.625 ms 209.85.255.110 (209.85.255.110)
14.122 ms
*
 9  ew-in-f104.1e100.net (74.125.77.104)  13.061 ms  13.256 ms  13.484 ms
```

 Modern Linux distributions also ship with an `mtr` command, which is similar to traceroute but shows real-time data that keeps refreshing. It is useful for checking your network carrier quality.

Listing all available machines on a network

When we monitor a large network, we need to check the availability of all machines. A machine may not be available for two reasons: it is not powered on, or because of a problem in the network. We can write a shell script to determine and report which machines are available on the network.

Getting ready

In this recipe, we demonstrate two methods. The first method uses ping and the second method uses `fping`. The `fping` command is easier for scripts and has more features than the ping command. It may not be part of your Linux distribution, but can be installed with your package manager.

How to do it...

The next example script will find the visible machines on the network using the ping command:

```bash
#!/bin/bash
#Filename: ping.sh
# Change base address 192.168.0 according to your network.

for ip in 192.168.0.{1..255} ;
do
  ping $ip -c 2 &> /dev/null ;

  if [ $? -eq 0 ];
  then
    echo $ip is alive
  fi
done
```

The output resembles this:

```
$ ./ping.sh
192.168.0.1 is alive
192.168.0.90 is alive
```

How it works...

This script uses the `ping` command to find out the available machines on the network. It uses a `for` loop to iterate through a list of IP addresses generated by the expression `192.168.0.{1..255}`. The `{start..end}` notation generates values between start and end. In this case, it creates IP addresses from `192.168.0.1` to `192.168.0.255`.

`ping $ip -c 2 &> /dev/null` runs a `ping` command to the corresponding IP address. The `-c` option causes ping to send only two packets. The `&> /dev/null` redirects both `stderr` and `stdout to /dev/null`, so nothing is printed on the terminal. The script uses `$?` to evaluate the exit status. If it is successful, the exit status is `0`, and the IP address which replied to our ping is printed.

In this script, a separate `ping` command is executed for each address, one after the other. This causes the script to run slowly when an IP address does not reply, since each ping must wait to time out before the next ping begins.

There's more...

The next recipes show enhancements to the ping script and how to use `fping`.

Parallel pings

The previous script tests each address sequentially. The delay for each test is accumulated and becomes large. Running the ping commands in parallel will make this faster. Enclosing the body of the loop in `{ }&` will make the `ping` commands run in parallel. `( )` encloses a block of commands to run as a subshell, and `&` sends it to the background:

```
#!/bin/bash
#Filename: fast_ping.sh
# Change base address 192.168.0 according to your network.

for ip in 192.168.0.{1..255} ;
do
    (
```

```
        ping $ip -c2 &> /dev/null ;

        if [ $? -eq0 ];
        then
         echo $ip is alive
        fi
    ) &
  done
wait
```

In the `for` loop, we execute many background processes and come out of the loop, terminating the script. The `wait` command prevents the script from terminating until all its child processes have exited.

 The output will be in the order that pings reply. This will not be the numeric order in which they were sent if some machines or network segments are slower than others.

Using fping

The second method uses a different command called `fping`. The `fping` command generates ICMP messages to multiple IP addresses and then waits to see which reply. It runs much faster than the first script.

The options available with `fping` include the following:

- The `-a` option with `fping` specifies to display the IP addresses for available machines
- The `-u` option with `fping` specifies to display unreachable machines
- The `-g` option specifies generating a range of IP addresses from the slash-subnet mask notation specified as IP/mask or start and end IP addresses:

    ```
    $ fping -a 192.160.1/24 -g
    ```

Alternatively, this can be used:

    ```
    $ fping -a 192.160.1 192.168.0.255 -g
    ```

- `2>/dev/null` is used to dump error messages printed due to an unreachable host to a null device

It is also possible to manually specify a list of IP addresses as command-line arguments or as a list through `stdin`. Consider the following example:

```
$ fping -a 192.168.0.1 192.168.0.5 192.168.0.6
# Passes IP address as arguments
$ fping -a <ip.list
# Passes a list of IP addresses from a file
```

See also

- The *Playing with file descriptors and redirection* recipe in `Chapter 1`, *Shell Something Out*, explains the data redirection
- The *Comparisons and tests* recipe in `Chapter 1`, *Shell Something Out*, explains numeric comparisons

Running commands on a remote host with SSH

SSH stands for **Secure Shell**. It connects two computers across an encrypted tunnel. SSH gives you access to a shell on a remote computer where you can interactively run a single command and receive the results or start an interactive session.

Getting ready

SSH doesn't come preinstalled with all GNU/Linux distributions. You may have to install the `openssh-server` and `openssh-client` packages using a package manager. By default, SSH runs on port number 22.

How to do it...

1. To connect to a remote host with the SSH server running, use the following command:

   ```
   $ ssh username@remote_host
   ```

The options in this command are as follows:

- `username` is the user that exists at the remote host
- `remote_host` can be the domain name or IP address

Consider this example:

```
$ ssh mec@192.168.0.1
The authenticity of host '192.168.0.1 (192.168.0.1)' can't be
established.
RSA key fingerprint is
2b:b4:90:79:49:0a:f1:b3:8a:db:9f:73:2d:75:d6:f9.
Are you sure you want to continue connecting (yes/no)? yes
Warning: Permanently added '192.168.0.1' (RSA) to the list of
known hosts.
Password:

Last login: Fri Sep  3 05:15:21 2010 from 192.168.0.82
mec@proxy-1:~$
```

SSH will ask for a password, and upon successful authentication it will connect to the login shell on the remote machine.

SSH performs a fingerprint verification to make sure we are actually connecting to the remote computer we want. This is to avoid what is called a **man-in-the-middle attack**, where an attacker tries to impersonate another computer. SSH will, by default, store the fingerprint the first time we connect to a server and verify that it does not change for future connections.

By default, the SSH server runs at port 22. However, certain servers run SSH service at different ports. In that case, use `-p port_num` with the `ssh` command to specify the port.

2. Connect to an SSH server running at port 422:

```
$ ssh user@locahost -p 422
```

When using `ssh` in shell scripts, we do not want an interactive shell, we simply want to execute commands on the remote system and process the command's output.

Issuing a password every time is not practical for an automated script, so password-less login using SSH keys should be configured. The *Password-less auto-login with SSH* recipe in this chapter explains the SSH commands to set this up.

3. To run a command at the remote host and display its output on the local shell, use the following syntax:

```
$ sshuser@host 'COMMANDS'
```

Consider this example:

```
$ ssh mec@192.168.0.1 'whoami'
mec
```

You can submit multiple commands by separating the commands with a semicolon:

```
$ ssh user@host "command1 ; command2 ; command3"
```

Consider the following example:

```
$ ssh mec@192.168.0.1  "echo user: $(whoami);echo OS: $(uname)"
Password:
user: mec
OS: Linux
```

In this example, the commands executed at the remote host are as follows:

```
echo user: $(whoami);
echo OS: $(uname)
```

We can pass a more complex subshell in the command sequence using the ( ) subshell operator.

3. The next example is an SSH-based shell script to collect the uptime of a list of remote hosts. Uptime is the length of time since the last power-on. It's returned by the uptime command.

It is assumed that all systems in IP_LIST have a common user test.

```
#!/bin/bash
#Filename: uptime.sh
#Description: Uptime monitor

IP_LIST="192.168.0.1 192.168.0.5 192.168.0.9"
```

```
USER="test"

for IP in $IP_LIST;
do
utime=$(ssh ${USER}@${IP} uptime  |awk '{ print $3 }' )
  echo $IP uptime:  $utime
done
```

Expected output:

```
$ ./uptime.sh
192.168.0.1 uptime: 1:50,
192.168.0.5 uptime: 2:15,
192.168.0.9 uptime: 10:15,
```

There's more...

The ssh command can be executed with several additional options.

SSH with compression

The SSH protocol supports compressing the data transfer. This feature comes in handy when bandwidth is an issue. Use the -C option with the ssh command to enable compression:

```
$ ssh -C user@hostname COMMANDS
```

Redirecting data into stdin of remote host shell commands

SSH allows you to use output from a task on your local system as input on the remote system:

```
$ echo 'text' | ssh user@remote_host 'echo'
text
```

Alternatively, this can be used:

```
# Redirect data from file as:
$ ssh user@remote_host 'echo'  < file
```

echo on the remote host prints the data received through `stdin`, which in turn is passed to `stdin` from localhost.

This facility can be used to transfer tar archives from a local host to the remote host. This is described in detail in `Chapter 7`, *The Backup plan*:

```
$> tar -czf - LOCALFOLDER | ssh 'tar -xzvf-'
```

Running graphical commands on a remote machine

If you attempt to run a command on a remote machine that uses a graphical window, you will see an error similar to `cannot open display`. This is because the `ssh` shell is attempting (and failing) to connect to the X server on the remote machine.

How to do it...

To run an graphical application on a remote server, you need to set the `$DISPLAY` variable to force the application to connect to the X server on your local machine:

```
ssh user@host "export DISPLAY=:0 ; command1; command2"""
```

This will launch the graphical output on the remote machine.

If you want to show the graphical output on your local machine, use SSH's X11 forwarding option:

```
ssh -X user@host "command1; command2"
```

This will run the commands on the remote machine, but it will display graphics on your machine.

See also

- The *Password-less auto-login with SSH* recipe in this chapter explains how to configure auto-login to execute commands without prompting for a password

Transferring files through the network

A major use for networking computers is resource sharing. Files are a common shared resource. There are different methods for transferring files between systems, ranging from a USB stick and `sneakernet` to network links such as NFS and Samba. These recipes describe how to transfer files using the common protocols FTP, SFTP, RSYNC, and SCP.

Getting ready

The commands for performing file transfer over the network are mostly available by default with Linux installation. Files can be transferred via FTP using the traditional `ftp` command or the newer `lftp`, or via an SSH connection using `scp` or `sftp`. Files can be synchronized across systems with the `rsync` command.

How to do it...

File Transfer Protocol (FTP) is old and is used in many public websites to share files. The service usually runs on port `21`. FTP requires that an FTP server be installed and running on the remote machine. We can use the traditional `ftp` command or the newer `lftp` command to access an FTP-enabled server. The following commands are supported by both `ftp` and `lftp`. FTP is used in many public websites to share files.

To connect to an FTP server and transfer files to and from it, use the following command:

```
$ lftpusername@ftphost
```

It will prompt for a password and then display a logged in prompt:

```
lftp username@ftphost:~>
```

You can type commands in this prompt, as shown here:

- `cd directory`: This will change directory on the remote system
- `lcd`: This will change the directory on the local machine
- `mkdir`: This will create a directory on the remote machine
- `ls`: This will list files in the current directory on the remote machine

- `get FILENAME`: This will download a file to the current directory on the local machine:

      lftp username@ftphost:~> get filename

- `put filename`: This will upload a file from the current directory on the remote machine:

      lftp username@ftphost:~> put filename

- The `quit` command will terminate an `lftp` session

Autocompletion is supported in the `lftp` prompt

There's more...

Let's go through additional techniques and commands used for file transfer through a network.

Automated FTP transfer

The `lftp` and the `ftp` commands open an interactive session with the user. We can automate FTP file transfers with a shell script:

```
#!/bin/bash

#Automated FTP transfer
HOST=example.com'
USER='foo'
PASSWD='password'
lftp  -u ${USER}:${PASSWD} $HOST <<EOF

binary
cd /home/foo
put testfile.jpg

quit
EOF
```

The preceding script has the following structure:

```
<<EOF
DATA
EOF
```

This is used to send data through `stdin` to the `lftp` command. The *Playing with file descriptors and redirection* recipe of `Chapter 1`, *Shell Something Out*, explains various methods for redirection to *stdin*.

The `-u` option logs in to the remote site with our defined `USER` and `PASSWD`. The `binary` command sets the file mode to binary.

SFTP (Secure FTP)

SFTP is a file transfer system that runs on the top of an SSH connection and emulates an FTP interface. It requires an SSH server on the remote system instead of an FTP server. It provides an interactive session with an `sftp` prompt.

Sftp supports the same commands as `ftp` and `lftp`.

To start an `sftp` session, use the following command:

```
$ sftp user@domainname
```

Similar to `lftp`, an `sftp` session can be terminated by typing the `quit` command.

Sometimes, the SSH server will not be running at the default port 22. If it is running at a different port, we can specify the port along with `sftp` as `-oPort=PORTNO`. Consider this example:

```
$ sftp -oPort=422 user@slynux.org
```

`-oPort` should be the first argument of the `sftp` command.

The rsync command

The `rsync` command is widely used for copying files over networks and for taking backup snapshots. This is described in detail in the *Backing up snapshots with rsync*

 recipe of `Chapter 7`, *The Backup Plan*.

SCP (secure copy program)

SCP is a secure file copy command similar to the older, insecure remote copy tool called `rcp`. The files are transferred through an encrypted channel using SSH:

```
$ scp filename user@remotehost:/home/path
```

This will prompt for a password. Like `ssh`, the transfer can be made password-less with the auto-login SSH technique. The *Password-less auto-login with SSH* recipe in this chapter explains SSH auto-login. Once SSH login is automated, the scp command can be executed without an interactive password prompt.

The `remotehost` can be an IP address or domain name. The format of the `scp` command is as follows:

```
$ scp SOURCE DESTINATION
```

SOURCE or DESTINATION can be in the format `username@host:/path`:

```
$ scp user@remotehost:/home/path/filename filename
```

The preceding command copies a file from the remote host to the current directory with the given filename.

If SSH is running at a different port than `22`, use `-oPort` with the same syntax, `sftp`.

Recursive copying with scp

The `-r` parameter tells `scp` to recursively copy a directory between two machines:

```
$ scp -r /home/usernameuser@remotehost:/home/backups
# Copies the directory /home/usernameto the remote backup
```

The `-p` parameter will cause `scp` to retain permissions and modes when copying files.

See also

- The *Playing with file descriptors and redirection* recipe in Chapter 1, *Shell Something Out*, explains the standard input using EOF

Connecting to a wireless network

An Ethernet connection is simple to configure, since it is connected through wired cables with no special requirements like authentication. However, wireless LAN requires an **Extended Service Set IDentification** network identifier (**ESSID**) and may also require a pass-phrase.

Getting ready

To connect to a wired network, we simply assign an IP address and subnet mask with the ifconfig utility. A wireless network connection requires the iwconfig and iwlist utilities.

How to do it...

This script will connect to a wireless LAN with **WEP (Wired Equivalent Privacy)**:

```bash
#!/bin/bash
#Filename: wlan_connect.sh
#Description: Connect to Wireless LAN

#Modify the parameters below according to your settings
######### PARAMETERS ###########
IFACE=wlan0
IP_ADDR=192.168.1.5
SUBNET_MASK=255.255.255.0
GW=192.168.1.1
HW_ADDR='00:1c:bf:87:25:d2'
#Comment above line if you don't want to spoof mac address

ESSID="homenet"
WEP_KEY=8b140b20e7
FREQ=2.462G
################################

KEY_PART=""

if [[ -n $WEP_KEY ]];
then
  KEY_PART="key $WEP_KEY"
fi

if [ $UID -ne 0 ];
then
  echo "Run as root"
  exit 1;
fi

# Shut down the interface before setting new config
/sbin/ifconfig $IFACE down


if [[ -n $HW_ADDR  ]];
```

```
then
   /sbin/ifconfig $IFACE hw ether $HW_ADDR
   echo Spoofed MAC ADDRESS to $HW_ADDR
fi

/sbin/iwconfig $IFACE essid $ESSID $KEY_PART freq $FREQ

/sbin/ifconfig $IFACE $IP_ADDR netmask $SUBNET_MASK

route add default gw $GW $IFACE

echo Successfully configured $IFACE
```

How it works...

The `ifconfig`, `iwconfig`, and `route` commands must be run as root. Hence, a check for the root user is performed before performing any actions in the scripts.

Wireless LAN requires parameters such as `essid`, `key`, and `frequency` to connect to the network. `essid` is the name of the wireless network to connect to. Some networks use a WEP key for authentication, which is usually a five- or ten-letter hex passphrase. The frequency assigned to the network is required by the `iwconfig` command to attach the wireless card with the proper wireless network.

The `iwlist` utility will scan and list the available wireless networks:

```
# iwlist scan
wlan0     Scan completed :
          Cell 01 - Address: 00:12:17:7B:1C:65
                    Channel:11
                    Frequency:2.462 GHz (Channel 11)
                    Quality=33/70  Signal level=-77 dBm
                    Encryption key:on
                    ESSID:"model-2"
```

The `Frequency` parameter can be extracted from the scan result, from the `Frequency:2.462 GHz (Channel 11)` line.

> WEP is used in this example for simplicity. Note that WEP is insecure. If you are administering the wireless network, use a variant of **Wi-Fi Protected Access2 (WPA2)**.

See also

- The *Comparisons and tests* recipe of `Chapter 1`, *Shell Something Out*, explains string comparisons

Password-less auto-login with SSH

SSH is widely used with automation scripting, as it makes it possible to remotely execute commands at remote hosts and read their outputs. Usually, SSH is authenticated with username and password, which are prompted during the execution of SSH commands. Providing passwords in automated scripts is impractical, so we need to automate logins. SSH has a feature which SSH allows a session to auto-login. This recipe describes how to create SSH keys for auto-login.

Getting ready

SSH uses an encryption technique called asymmetric keys consisting of two keys–a public key and a private key for automatic authentication. The `ssh-keygen` application creates an authentication key pair. To automate the authentication, the public key must be placed on the server (by appending the public key to the `~/.ssh/authorized_keys` file) and the private key file of the pair should be present at the `~/.ssh` directory of the user at the client machine. SSH configuration options (for example, path and name of the `authorized_keys` file) can be modified by altering the `/etc/ssh/sshd_config` configuration file.

How to do it...

There are two steps to implement automatic authentication with SSH. They are as follows:

- Creating the SSH key on the local machine
- Transferring the public key to the remote host and appending it to `~/.ssh/authorized_keys` (which requires access to the remote machine)

To create an SSH key, run the `ssh-keygen` command with the encryption algorithm type specified as RSA:

```
$ ssh-keygen -t rsa
Generating public/private rsa key pair.
Enter file in which to save the key (/home/username/.ssh/id_rsa):
```

```
Created directory '/home/username/.ssh'.
Enter passphrase (empty for no passphrase):
Enter same passphrase again:
Your identification has been saved in /home/username/.ssh/id_rsa.
Your public key has been saved in /home/username/.ssh/id_rsa.pub.
The key fingerprint is:
f7:17:c6:4d:c9:ee:17:00:af:0f:b3:27:a6:9c:0a:05 username@slynux-laptop
The key'srandomart image is:
+--[ RSA 2048]----+
|          .      |
|         o . .|
|     E     o o.|
|      ...oo  |
|      .S .+  +o.|
|      .  . .=....|
|      .+.o...|
|       . . + o.  .|
|          ..+     |
+-----------------+
```

You need to enter a passphrase to generate the public-private key pair. It is possible to generate the key pair without entering a passphrase, but it is insecure.

If you intend to write scripts that use automated login to several machines, you should leave the passphrase empty to prevent the script from asking for a passphrase while running.

The `ssh-keygen` program creates two files. `~/.ssh/id_rsa.pub` and `~/.ssh/id_rsa`: `id_rsa.pub` is the generated public key and `id_rsa` is the private key. The public key has to be appended to the `~/.ssh/authorized_keys` file on remote servers where we need to auto-login from the current host.

This command will append a key file:

```
$ ssh USER@REMOTE_HOST \
    "cat >> ~/.ssh/authorized_keys" < ~/.ssh/id_rsa.pub
Password:
```

Provide the login password in the previous command.

The auto-login has been set up from now onwards, so SSH will not prompt for passwords during execution. Test this with the following command:

```
$ ssh USER@REMOTE_HOST uname
Linux
```

You will not be prompted for a password. Most Linux distros include `ssh-copy-id`, which will append your private key to the appropriate `authorized_keys` file on the remote server. This is shorter than the `ssh` technique described earlier:

```
ssh-copy-id USER@REMOTE_HOST
```

Port forwarding using SSH

Port forwarding is a technique which redirects an IP connection from one host to another. For example, if you are using a Linux/Unix system as a firewall you can redirect connections to port `1234` to an internal address such as `192.168.1.10:22` to provide an `ssh` tunnel from the outside world to an internal machine.

How to do it...

You can forward a port on your local machine to another machine and it's also possible to forward a port on a remote machine to another machine. In the following examples, you will get a shell prompt once the forwarding is complete. Keep this shell open to use the port forward and exit it whenever you want to stop the port forward.

1. This command will forward port `8000` on your local machine to port `80` on `www.kernel.org`:

   ```
   ssh -L 8000:www.kernel.org:80user@localhost
   ```

   Replace user with the username on your local machine.

2. This command will forward port 8000 on a remote machine to port `80` of `www.kernel.org`:

   ```
   ssh -L 8000:www.kernel.org:80user@REMOTE_MACHINE
   ```

   Here, replace REMOTE_MACHINE with the hostname or IP address of the remote machine and `user` with the username you have SSH access to.

There's more...

Port forwarding is more useful when using non-interactive mode or reverse port forwarding.

Non-interactive port forward

If you want to just set port forwarding instead of having a shell kept open while port forwarding is effective, use the following form of `ssh`:

```
ssh -fL8000:www.kernel.org:80user@localhost -N
```

The `-f` option instructs `ssh` to fork to background before executing the command. `-N` tells `ssh` that there is no command to run; we only want to forward ports.

Reverse port forwarding

Reverse port forwarding is one of the most powerful features of SSH. This is most useful in situations where you have a machine which isn't publicly accessible from the Internet, but you want others to be able to access a service on this machine. In this case, if you have SSH access to a remote machine which is publicly accessible on the Internet, you can set up a reverse port forward on that remote machine to the local machine which is running the service.

```
ssh -R 8000:localhost:80 user@REMOTE_MACHINE
```

This command will forward port `8000` on the remote machine to port `80` on the local machine. Don't forget to replace `REMOTE_MACHINE` with the hostname of the IP address of the remote machine.

Using this method, if you browse to `http://localhost:8000` on the remote machine, you will connect to a web server running on port `80` of the local machine.

Mounting a remote drive at a local mount point

Having a local mount point to access the remote host filesystem facilitates read and write data transfer operations. SSH is the common transfer protocol. The `sshfs` application uses SSH to enable you to mount a remote filesystem on a local mount point.

Getting ready

`sshfs` doesn't come by default with GNU/Linux distributions. Install `sshfs` with a package manager. `sshfs` is an extension to the FUSE filesystem package that allows users to mount a wide variety of data as if it were a local filesystem. Variants of FUSE are supported on Linux, Unix, Mac OS/X, Windows, and more.

 For more information on FUSE, visit its website at `http://fuse.sourceforge.net/`.

How to do it...

To mount a filesystem location at a remote host to a local mount point:

```
# sshfs -o allow_otheruser@remotehost:/home/path /mnt/mountpoint
Password:
```

Issue the password when prompted. After the password is accepted, the data at `/home/path` on the remote host can be accessed via a local mount point, `/mnt/mountpoint`.

To unmount, use the following command:

```
# umount /mnt/mountpoint
```

See also

- The *Running commands on a remote host with SSH* recipe in this chapter explains the `ssh` command

Network traffic and port analysis

Every application that accesses the network does it via a port. Listing the open ports, the application using a port and the user running the application is a way to track the expected and unexpected uses of your system. This information can be used to allocate resources as well as checking for rootkits or other malware.

Getting ready

Various commands are available for listing ports and services running on a network node. The `lsof` and `netstat` commands are available on most GNU/Linux distributions.

How to do it...

The `lsof` (list open files) command will list open files. The `-i` option limits it to open network connections:

```
$ lsof -i
COMMAND     PID    USER    FD    TYPE DEVICE SIZE/OFF NODE
    NAME

firefox-b 2261 slynux     78u  IPv4  63729       0t0  TCP
    localhost:47797->localhost:42486 (ESTABLISHED)

firefox-b 2261 slynux     80u  IPv4  68270       0t0  TCP
    slynux-laptop.local:41204->192.168.0.2:3128 (CLOSE_WAIT)

firefox-b 2261 slynux     82u  IPv4  68195       0t0  TCP
    slynux-laptop.local:41197->192.168.0.2:3128 (ESTABLISHED)

ssh        3570 slynux     3u  IPv6  30025       0t0  TCP
    localhost:39263->localhost:ssh (ESTABLISHED)

ssh        3836 slynux     3u  IPv4  43431       0t0  TCP
    slynux-laptop.local:40414->boney.mt.org:422 (ESTABLISHED)

GoogleTal 4022 slynux     12u  IPv4  55370       0t0  TCP
    localhost:42486 (LISTEN)

GoogleTal 4022 slynux     13u  IPv4  55379       0t0  TCP
    localhost:42486->localhost:32955 (ESTABLISHED)
```

Each entry in the output of `lsof` corresponds to a service with an active network port. The last column of output consists of lines similar to this:

```
laptop.local:41197->192.168.0.2:3128
```

In this output, `laptop.local:41197` corresponds to the `localhost` and `192.168.0.2:3128` corresponds to the remote host. `41197` is the port used on the current machine, and `3128` is the port to which the service connects at the remote host.

To list the opened ports from the current machine, use the following command:

```
$ lsof -i | grep ":[0-9a-z]+->" -o | grep "[0-9a-z]+" -o  | sort | uniq
```

How it works...

The `:[0-9a-z]+->` regex for grep extracts the host port portion (`:34395->` or `:ssh->`) from the `lsof` output. The next `grep` removes the leading colon and trailing arrow leaving the port number (which is alphanumeric). Multiple connections may occur through the same port and hence, multiple entries of the same port may occur. The output is sorted and passed through `uniq` to display each port only once.

There's more...

There are more utilities that report open port and network traffic related information.

Opened port and services using netstat

`netstat` also returns network service statistics. It has many features beyond what is covered in this recipe.

Use `netstat -tnp` to list opened port and services:

```
$ netstat -tnp
Proto Recv-Q Send-Q Local Address          Foreign Address
      State        PID/Program name

tcp        0      0 192.168.0.82:38163     192.168.0.2:3128
      ESTABLISHED 2261/firefox-bin

tcp        0      0 192.168.0.82:38164     192.168.0.2:3128
      TIME_WAIT    -

tcp        0      0 192.168.0.82:40414     193.107.206.24:422
      ESTABLISHED 3836/ssh

tcp        0      0 127.0.0.1:42486        127.0.0.1:32955
      ESTABLISHED 4022/GoogleTalkPlug

tcp        0      0 192.168.0.82:38152     192.168.0.2:3128
      ESTABLISHED 2261/firefox-bin
```

```
tcp6        0        0 ::1:22                           ::1:39263
    ESTABLISHED -

tcp6        0        0 ::1:39263                        ::1:22
    ESTABLISHED 3570/ssh
```

Measuring network bandwidth

The previous discussion of `ping` and `traceroute` was on measuring the latency of a network and the number of hops between nodes.

The `iperf` application provides more metrics for a networks' performance. The `iperf` application is not installed by default, but it is provided by most distributions' package manager.

How to do it...

The `iperf` application must be installed on both ends of a link (a host and a client). Once `iperf` is installed, start the server end:

```
$ iperf -s
```

Then run the client side to generate throughput statistics:

```
$ iperf -c 192.168.1.36
------------------------------------------------------------
Client connecting to 192.168.1.36, TCP port 5001
TCP window size: 19.3 KByte (default)
------------------------------------------------------------
[  3] local 192.168.1.44 port 46526 connected with 192.168.1.36 port 5001
[ ID] Interval       Transfer     Bandwidth
[  3]  0.0-10.0 sec   113 MBytes  94.7 Mbits/sec
```

The `-m` option instructs `iperf` to also find the **Maximum Transfer Size (MTU)**:

```
$ iperf -mc 192.168.1.36
------------------------------------------------------------
Client connecting to 192.168.1.36, TCP port 5001
TCP window size: 19.3 KByte (default)
------------------------------------------------------------
[  3] local 192.168.1.44 port 46558 connected with 192.168.1.36 port 5001
[ ID] Interval       Transfer     Bandwidth
[  3]  0.0-10.0 sec   113 MBytes  94.7 Mbits/sec
[  3] MSS size 1448 bytes (MTU 1500 bytes, ethernet)
```

Creating arbitrary sockets

For operations such as file transfer and secure shell, there are prebuilt tools such as ftp and ssh. We can also write custom scripts as network services. The next recipe demonstrates how to create simple network sockets and use them for communication.

Getting ready

The netcat or nc command will create network sockets to transfer data over a TCP/IP network. We need two sockets: one listens for connections and the other connects to the listener.

How to do it...

1. Set up the listening socket using the following command:

   ```
   nc -l 1234
   ```

   This will create a listening socket on port 1234 on the local machine.

2. Connect to the socket using the following command:

   ```
   nc HOST 1234
   ```

   If you are running this on the same machine as the listening socket, replace HOST with localhost, otherwise replace it with the IP address or hostname of the machine.

3. Type something and press *Enter* on the terminal where you performed step 2. The message will appear on the terminal where you performed step 1.

There's more...

Network sockets can be used for more than just text communication, as shown in the following sections.

Quickly copying files over the network

We can exploit `netcat` and shell redirection to copy files over the network. This command will send a file to the listening machine:

1. On the listening machine, run the following command:

```
nc -l 1234 >destination_filename
```

2. On the sender machine, run the following command:

```
nc HOST 1234 <source_filename
```

Creating a broadcasting server

You can use `netcan` to create a custom server. The next recipe demonstrates a server that will send the time every 10 seconds. The time can be received by connecting to the port with a client `nc` session of telnet:

```
# A script to echo the date out a port
while [ 1 ]
do
  sleep 10
  date
done | nc -l 12345
echo exited
```

How it works...

Copying files with `nc` works because ns echoes the input from the input of one socket to the output at the other.

The broadcasting server is a bit more complicated. The `while [ 1 ]` loop will run forever. Within the loop, the script sleeps for 10 seconds, then invokes the date command and pipes the output to the `nc` command.

You can use `nc` to create a client, as follows:

```
$ nc 127.0.0.1 12345
```

Building a bridge

If you have two separate networks, you may need a way to pass data from one network to the other. This is commonly done by connecting the two subnets with a router, hub, or switch.

A Linux system can be used for a network bridge.

A bridge is a low-level connection that passes packets based on their MAC address instead of being identified by the IP address. As such it requires fewer machine resources and is more efficient.

You can use a bridge to link virtual machines on private, non-routed networks, or to link separate subnets in a company, for instance, to link a manufacturing subnet to the shipping sub-net so production information can be shared.

Getting ready

The Linux kernel has supported network bridges since the 2.2 kernel. The current tool to define a bridge, is the iproute2 (`ip`) command. This is standard in most distributions.

How to do it...

The ip command performs several actions using the command/subcommand model. To create a bridge, we use the `ip link` commands.

 The Ethernet adapter being attached to the bridge should not be configured with an IP address when it is added to the bridge. The bridge is configured with an address, not the NIC.

In this example, there are two NIC cards: `eth0` is configured and connected to the `192.168.1.0` subnet, while eth1 is not configured but will be connected to the `10.0.0.0` subnet via the bridge:

```
# Create a new bridge named br0
ip link add br0 type bridge

# Add an Ethernet adapter to the bridge
ip link set dev eth1 master br0

# Configure the bridge's IP address
```

```
ifconfig br0 10.0.0.2

# Enable packet forwarding
echo 1 >/proc/sys/net/ipv4/ip_forward
```

This creates the bridge allowing packets to be sent from eth0 to eth1 and back. Before the bridge can be useful, we need to add this bridge to the routing tables.

On machines in the 10.0.0.0/24 network, we add a route to the 192.168.1.0/16 network:

```
route add -net 192.168.1.0/16 gw 10.0.0.2
```

Machines on the 192.168.1.0/16 subnet need to know how to find the 10.0.0.0/24 subnet. If the eth0 card is configured for IP address 192.168.1.2, the route command is as follows:

```
route add -net 10.0.0.0/24 gw 192.168.1.2
```

Sharing an Internet connection

Most firewall/routers have the ability to share an Internet connection with the devices in your home or office. This is called **Network Address Translation (NAT)**. A Linux computer with two **Network Interface Cards (NIC)** can act as a router, providing firewall protection and connection sharing.

Firewalling and NAT support are provided by the support for iptables built into the kernel. This recipe introduces iptables with a recipe that shares a computer's Ethernet link to the Internet through the wireless interface to give other wireless devices access to the Internet via the host's Ethernet NIC.

Getting ready

This recipe uses iptables to define a **Network Address Translation (NAT)**, which lets a networking device share a connection with other devices. You will need the name of your wireless interface, which is reported by the iwconfig command.

How to do it...

1. Connect to the Internet. In this recipe, we are assuming that the primary wired network connection, eth0, is connected to the Internet. Change it according to your setup.

2. Using your distro's network management tool, create a new ad hoc wireless connection with the following settings:
    *   IP address: 10.99.66.55

    *   Subnet mask: 255.255.0.0 (16)

3. Use the following shell script to share the Internet connection:

```bash
#!/bin/bash
#filename: netsharing.sh

echo 1 > /proc/sys/net/ipv4/ip_forward

iptables -A FORWARD -i $1 -o $2 \
    -s 10.99.0.0/16 -m conntrack --ctstate NEW -j ACCEPT

iptables -A FORWARD -m conntrack --ctstate \
    ESTABLISHED,RELATED -j ACCEPT

iptables -A POSTROUTING -t nat -j MASQUERADE
```

4. Run the script:

```
./netsharing.sh eth0 wlan0
```

Here eth0 is the interface that is connected to the Internet and wlan0 is the wireless interface that is supposed to share the Internet with other devices.

5. Connect your devices to the wireless network you just created with the following settings:
    *   IP address: 10.99.66.56 (and so on)
    *   Subnet mask: 255.255.0.0

 To make this more convenient, you might want to install a DHCP and DNS server on your machine, so it's not necessary to configure IPs on devices manually. A handy tool for this is dnsmasq, which performs both DHCP and DNS operations.

How it works

There are three sets of IP addresses set aside for non-routing use. That means that no network interface visible to the Internet can use them. They are only used by machines on a local, internal network. The addresses are `10.x.x.x`, `192.168.x.x`, and `172.16.x.x->172.32.x.x`. In this recipe, we use a portion of the `10.x.x.x` address space for our internal network.

By default, Linux systems will accept or generate packets, but will not echo them. This is controlled by the value `in/proc/sys/net/ipv4/ip_forward`.

Echoing a `1` to that location tells the Linux kernel to forward any packet it doesn't recognize. This allows the wireless devices on the `10.99.66.x` subnet to use `10.99.66.55` as their gateway. They will send a packet destined for an Internet site to `10.99.66.55`, which will then forward it out its gateway on `eth0` to the Internet to be routed to the destination.

The `iptables` command is how we interact with the Linux kernel's iptables subsystem. These commands add rules to forward all packets from the internal network to the outside world and to forward expected packets from the outside world to our internal network.

The next recipe will discuss more ways to use iptables.

Basic firewall using iptables

A firewall is a network service that is used to filter network traffic for unwanted traffic, block it, and allow the desired traffic to pass. The standard firewall tool for Linux is `iptables`, which is integrated into the kernel in recent versions.

How to do it...

`iptables` is present by default on all modern Linux distributions. It's easy to configure for common scenarios:

1. If don't want to contact a given site (for example, a known malware site), you can block traffic to that IP address:

   ```
   #iptables -A OUTPUT -d 8.8.8.8 -j DROP
   ```

If you use `PING 8.8.8.8` in another terminal, then by running the `iptables` command, you will see this:

```
PING 8.8.8.8 (8.8.8.8) 56(84) bytes of data.
64 bytes from 8.8.8.8: icmp_req=1 ttl=56 time=221 ms
64 bytes from 8.8.8.8: icmp_req=2 ttl=56 time=221 ms
ping: sendmsg: Operation not permitted
ping: sendmsg: Operation not permitted
```

Here, the ping fails the third time because we used the `iptables` command to drop all traffic to `8.8.8.8`.

2. You can also block traffic to a specific port:

```
#iptables -A OUTPUT -p tcp -dport 21 -j DROP
$ ftp ftp.kde.org
ftp: connect: Connection timed out
```

If you find messages like this in your `/var/log/secure` or `var/log/messages` file, you have a small problem:

```
Failed password for abel from 1.2.3.4 port 12345 ssh2
Failed password for baker from 1.2.3.4 port 12345 ssh2
```

These messages mean a robot is probing your system for weak passwords. You can prevent the robot from accessing your site with an INPUT rule that will drop all traffic from that site.

```
#iptables -I INPUT -s 1.2.3.4 -j DROP
```

How it works...

`iptables` is the command used to configure the firewall on Linux. The first argument in `iptables` is -A, which instructs `iptables` to append a new rule to the chain, or -I, which places the new rule at the start of the ruleset. The next parameter defines the chain. A chain is a collection of rules, and in earlier recipes we used the OUTPUT chain, which is evaluated for outgoing traffic, whereas the last recipes used the INPUT chain, which is evaluated for incoming traffic.

The -d parameter specifies the destination to match with the packet being sent, and -s specifies the source of a packet. Finally, the -j parameter instructs iptables to jump to a particular action. In these examples, we used the DROP action to drop the packet. Other actions include ACCEPT and REJECT.

In the second example, we use the -p parameter to specify that this rule matches only TCP on the port specified with -dport. This blocks only the outbound FTP traffic.

There's more...

You can clear the changes made to the iptables chains with the -flush parameter:

```
#iptables -flush
```

Creating a Virtual Private Network

A **Virtual Private Network (VPN)** is an encrypted channel that operates across public networks. The encryption keeps your information private. VPNs are used to connect remote offices, distributed manufacturing sites, and remote workers.

We've discussed copying files with nc, or scp, or ssh. With a VPN network, you can mount remote drives via NFS and access resources on the remote network as if they were local.

Linux has clients for several VPN systems, as well as client and server support for OpenVPN.

This section's recipes will describe setting up an OpenVPN server and client. This recipe is to configure a single server to service multiple clients in a hub and spoke model. OpenVPN supports more topologies that are beyond the scope of this chapter.

Getting ready

OpenVPN is not part of most Linux distributions. You can install it using your package manager:

```
apt-get install openvpn
```

Alternatively, this command can also be used:

```
yum install openvpn
```

Note that you'll need to do this on the server and each client.

Confirm that the tunnel device (`/dev/net/tun`) exists. Test this on server and client systems. On modern Linux systems, the tunnel should already exist:

```
ls /dev/net/tun
```

How to do it...

The first step in setting up an OpenVPN network is to create the certificates for the server and at least one client. The simplest way to handle this is to make self-signed certificates with the `easy-rsa` package included with pre-version 2.3 releases of OpenVPN. If you have a later version of OpenVPN, `easy-rsa` should be available via the package manager.

This package is probably installed in `/usr/share/easy-rsa`.

Creating certificates

First, make sure you've got a clean slate with nothing left over from previous installations:

```
# cd /usr/share/easy-rsa
# . ./vars
# ./clean-all
```

NOTE: If you run `./clean-all`, I will be doing a `rm -rf` on `/usr/share/easy-rsa/keys`.

Next, create the **Certificate Authority** key with the `build-ca` command. This command will prompt you for information about your site. You'll have to enter this information several times. Substitute your name, e-mail, site name, and so on for the values in this recipe. The required information varies slightly between commands. Only the unique sections will be repeated in these recipes:

```
# ./build-ca
Generating a 2048 bit RSA private key
......+++
..................................................+++
writing new private key to 'ca.key'
-----
You are about to be asked to enter information that will be incorporated
into your certificate request.
```

```
What you are about to enter is what is called a Distinguished Name or a DN.
There are quite a few fields but you can leave some blank
For somefieldsthere will be a default value,
If you enter '.', the field will be left blank.
-----
Country Name (2 letter code) [US]:
State or Province Name (full name) [CA]:MI
Locality Name (eg, city) [SanFrancisco]:WhitmoreLake
Organization Name (eg, company) [Fort-Funston]:Example
Organizational Unit Name (eg, section) [MyOrganizationalUnit]:Packt
Common Name (eg, your name or your server's hostname) [Fort-Funston
CA]:vpnserver
Name [EasyRSA]:
Email Address [me@myhost.mydomain]:admin@example.com

Next, build the server certificate with the build-key command:
# ./build-key server
Generating a 2048 bit RSA private key
..................................+++
....................+++
writing new private key to 'server.key'
-----
You are about to be asked to enter information that will be incorporated
into your certificate request....
```

```
Please enter the following 'extra' attributes
to be sent with your certificate request
A challenge password []:
```

Create a certificate for at least one client. You'll need a separate client certificate for each machine that you wish to connect to this OpenVPN server:

```
# ./build-key client1
Generating a 2048 bit RSA private key
......................+++
.................................................+++
writing new private key to 'client1.key'
-----
You are about to be asked to enter information that will be incorporated
into your certificate request.
...
```

```
Please enter the following 'extra' attributes
to be sent with your certificate request
A challenge password []:
An optional company name []:
Using configuration from /usr/share/easy-rsa/openssl-1.0.0.cnf
Check that the request matches the signature
Signature ok
The Subject's Distinguished Name is as follows
countryName    :PRINTABLE:'US'
stateOrProvinceName  :PRINTABLE:'MI'
localityName   :PRINTABLE:'WhitmoreLake'
organizationName   :PRINTABLE:'Example'
organizationalUnitName:PRINTABLE:'Packt'
commonName     :PRINTABLE:'client1'
name                 :PRINTABLE:'EasyRSA'
emailAddress:IA5STRING:'admin@example.com'
Certificate is to be certified until Jan  8 15:24:13 2027 GMT (3650 days)
Sign the certificate? [y/n]:y


1 out of 1 certificate requests certified, commit? [y/n]y
Write out database with 1 new entries
Data Base Updated
```

Finally, generate the **Diffie-Hellman** with the `build-dh` command. This will take several seconds and will generate a few screens filled with dots and plusses:

```
# ./build-dh
Generating DH parameters, 2048 bit long safe prime, generator 2
This is going to take a long time
.....................+............+........
```

These steps will create several files in the keys folder. The next step is to copy them to the folders where they'll be used.

Copy server keys to /etc/openvpn:

```
# cp keys/server* /etc/openvpn
# cp keys/ca.crt /etc/openvpn
# cp keys/dh2048.pem /etc/openvpn
```

Copy the client keys to the client system:

```
# scp keys/client1* client.example.com:/etc/openvpn
# scp keys/ca.crt client.example.com:/etc/openvpn
```

Configuring OpenVPN on the server

OpenVPN includes sample configuration files that are almost ready to use. You only need to customize a few lines for your environment. The files are commonly found in `/usr/share/doc/openvpn/examples/sample-config-files`:

```
# cd /usr/share/doc/openvpn/examples/sample-config-files
# cp server.conf.gz /etc/openvpn
# cd /etc/openvpn
# gunzip server.conf.gz
# vim server.conf
```

Set the local IP address to listen on. This is the IP address of the NIC attached to the network you intend to allow VPN connections through:

```
local 192.168.1.125
Modify the paths to the certificates:

ca /etc/openvpn/ca.crt
cert /etc/openvpn/server.crt
key /etc/openvpn/server.key  # This file should be kept secret
```

Finally, check that the `diffie-hellman` parameter file is correct. The OpenVPN sample `config` file may specify a 1024-bit length key, while the `easy-rsa` creates a 2048-bit (more secure) key.

```
#dh dh1024.pem
dh dh2048.pem
```

Configuring OpenVPN on the client

There is a similar set of configurations to do on each client.

Copy the client configuration file to `/etc/openvpn`:

```
# cd /usr/share/doc/openvpn/examples/sample-config-files
# cpclient.conf /etc/openvpn
```

Edit the `client.conf` file:

```
# cd /etc/openvpn
# vim client.conf
```

Change the paths for the certificates to the point to correct folders:

```
ca /etc/openvpn/ca.crt
cert /etc/openvpn/server.crt
key /etc/openvpn/server.key  # This file should be kept secret
```

Set the remote site for your server:

```
#remote my-server-1 1194
remote server.example.com 1194
```

Starting the server

The server can be started now. If everything is configured correctly, you'll see it output several lines of output. The important line to look for is the `Initialization Sequence Completed` line. If that is missing, look for an error message earlier in the output:

```
# openvpnserver.conf
Wed Jan 11 12:31:08 2017 OpenVPN 2.3.4 x86_64-pc-linux-gnu [SSL (OpenSSL)]
[LZO] [EPOLL] [PKCS11] [MH] [IPv6] built on Nov 12 2015
Wed Jan 11 12:31:08 2017 library versions: OpenSSL 1.0.1t  3 May 2016, LZO
2.08...


Wed Jan 11 12:31:08 2017 client1,10.8.0.4
Wed Jan 11 12:31:08 2017 Initialization Sequence Completed
```

Using `ifconfig`, you can confirm that the server is running. You should see the tunnel device (tun) listed:

```
$ ifconfig
tun0      Link encap:UNSPECHWaddr
00-00-00-00-00-00-00-00-00-00-00-00-00-00-00-00
inet addr:10.8.0.1  P-t-P:10.8.0.2  Mask:255.255.255.255
          UP POINTOPOINT RUNNING NOARP MULTICAST  MTU:1500  Metric:1
          RX packets:0 errors:0 dropped:0 overruns:0 frame:0
          TX packets:0 errors:0 dropped:0 overruns:0 carrier:0
          collisions:0 txqueuelen:100
          RX bytes:0 (0.0 B)  TX bytes:0 (0.0 B)
```

Starting and testing a client

Once the server is running, you can start a client. Like the server, the client side of OpenVPN is created with the openvpn command. Again, the important part of this output is the Initialization Sequence Completed line:

```
# openvpn client.conf
Wed Jan 11 12:34:14 2017 OpenVPN 2.3.4 i586-pc-linux-gnu [SSL (OpenSSL)]
[LZO] [EPOLL] [PKCS11] [MH] [IPv6] built on Nov 19 2015
Wed Jan 11 12:34:14 2017 library versions: OpenSSL 1.0.1t  3 May 2016, LZO
2.08...



Wed Jan 11 12:34:17 2017 /sbin/ipaddr add dev tun0 local 10.8.0.6 peer
10.8.0.5
Wed Jan 11 12:34:17 2017 /sbin/ip route add 10.8.0.1/32 via 10.8.0.5
Wed Jan 11 12:34:17 2017 Initialization Sequence Completed
```

Using the ifconfig command, you can confirm that the tunnel has been initialized:

```
$ /sbin/ifconfig

tun0      Link encap:UNSPECHWaddr 00-00-00-00-00-00-00-00...00-00-00-00
inet addr:10.8.0.6  P-t-P:10.8.0.5  Mask:255.255.255.255
          UP POINTOPOINT RUNNING NOARP MULTICAST  MTU:1500  Metric:1
          RX packets:2 errors:0 dropped:0 overruns:0 frame:0
          TX packets:4 errors:0 dropped:0 overruns:0 carrier:0
          collisions:0 txqueuelen:100
          RX bytes:168 (168.0 B)   TX bytes:336 (336.0 B)
```

Use the netstat command to confirm that the new network is routed correctly:

```
$ netstat -rn
Kernel IP routing table
Destination     Gateway         Genmask         Flags  MSS Window  irttIface
0.0.0.0         192.168.1.7     0.0.0.0         UG       0 0        0 eth0
10.8.0.1        10.8.0.5        255.255.255.255 UGH      0 0        0 tun0
10.8.0.5        0.0.0.0         255.255.255.255 UH       0 0        0 tun0
192.168.1.0     0.0.0.0         255.255.255.0   U        0 0        0 eth0
```

This output shows the tunnel device connected to the `10.8.0.x` network, and the gateway is `10.8.0.1`.

Finally, you can test connectivity with the `ping` command:

```
$ ping 10.8.0.1
PING 10.8.0.1 (10.8.0.1) 56(84) bytes of data.
64 bytes from 10.8.0.1: icmp_seq=1 ttl=64 time=1.44 ms
```

9
Put On the Monitor's Cap

In this chapter, we will cover the following recipes:

- Monitoring disk usage
- Calculating the execution time for a command
- Collecting information about logged in users, boot logs, and boot failures
- Listing the top ten CPU– consuming processes in an hour
- Monitoring command outputs with watch
- Logging access to files and directories
- Logging with syslog
- Managing log files with `logrotate`
- Monitoring user logins to find intruders
- Monitoring remote disk usage health
- Determining active user hours on a system
- Measuring and optimizing power usage
- Monitoring disk activity
- Checking disks and filesystems for errors
- Examining disk health
- Getting disk statistics

Introduction

A computing system is a set of hardware and the software components that control it. The software includes the operating system kernel which allocates resources and many modules that perform individual tasks, ranging from reading disk data to serving web pages.

An administrator needs to monitor these modules and applications to confirm that they are working correctly and to understand whether resources need to be reallocated (moving a user partition to a larger disk, providing a faster network, and so on).

Linux provides both interactive programs for examining the system's current performance and modules for logging performance over time.

This chapter describes the commands that monitor system activity and discusses logging techniques.

Monitoring disk usage

Disk space is always a limited resource. We monitor disk usage to know when it's running low, then search for large files or folders to delete, move, or compress. This recipe illustrates disk monitoring commands.

Getting ready

The du (disk usage) and df (disk free) commands report disk usage. These tools report what files and folders are consuming disk space and how much space is available.

How to do it...

To find the disk space used by a file (or files), use the following command:

```
$ du  FILENAME1 FILENAME2 ..
```

Consider this example:

```
$ du file.txt
```

To obtain the disk usage for all files inside a directory, along with the individual disk usage for each file shown in each line, use this command:

```
$ du -a DIRECTORY
```

The -a option outputs results for all files in the specified directory or directories recursively.

> Running du DIRECTORY will output a similar result, but it will show only the size consumed by subdirectories. However, this does not show the disk usage for each of the files. For printing the disk usage by files, -a is mandatory.

Consider this example:

```
$  du -a test
4  test/output.txt
4  test/process_log.sh
4  test/pcpu.sh
16  test
```

The du command can be used on a directory:

```
$ du test
16  test
```

There's more...

The du command includes options to define how the data is reported.

Displaying disk usage in KB, MB, or blocks

By default, the disk usage command displays the total bytes used by a file. A more human-readable format is expressed in units such as KB, MB, or GB. The -h option displays the results in a human-readable format:

```
du -h FILENAME
```

Consider this example:

```
$ du -h test/pcpu.sh
4.0K  test/pcpu.sh
# Multiple file arguments are accepted
```

Alternatively, use it like this:

```
# du -h DIRECTORY
$ du -h hack/
16K  hack/
```

Displaying the grand total sum of disk usage

The −c option will calculate the total size used by files or directories, as well as display individual file sizes:

```
$ du -c FILENAME1 FILENAME2..
du -c process_log.sh pcpu.sh
4   process_log.sh
4   pcpu.sh
8   total
```

Alternatively, use it like one of these:

```
$ du   -c DIRECTORY
$ du -c test/
16   test/
16   total
```

Or:

```
$ du -c *.txt
# Wildcards
```

The −c option can be used with options such as −a and −h to produce the usual output, with an extra line containing the total size.

The −s option (summarize), will print the grand total as the output. The −h flag can be used with it to print in a human-readable format:

```
$ du -sh /usr/bin
256M   /usr/bin
```

Printing sizes in specified units

The −b, −k, and −m options will force du to print the disk usage in specified units. Note that these cannot be used with the −h option:

- Print the size in bytes (by default):

```
$ du -b FILE(s)
```

- Print the size in kilobytes:

```
$ du -k FILE(s)
```

- Print the size in megabytes:

    ```
    $ du -m FILE(s)
    ```

- Print the size in the given BLOCK size specified:

    ```
    $ du -B BLOCK_SIZE FILE(s)
    ```

Here, BLOCK_SIZE is specified in bytes.

Note that the file size returned is not intuitively obvious. With the -b option, du reports the exact number of bytes in the file. With other options, du reports the amount of disk space used by the file. Since disk space is allocated in fixed-size chunks (commonly 4 K), the space used by a 400-byte file will be a single block (4 K):

```
$ du pcpu.sh
4   pcpu.sh
$ du -b pcpu.sh
439 pcpu.sh
$ du -k pcpu.sh
4   pcpu.sh
$ du -m pcpu.sh
1   pcpu.sh
$ du -B 4 pcpu.sh
1024   pcpu.sh
```

Excluding files from the disk usage calculation

The --exclude and -exclude-from options cause du to exclude files from the disk usage calculation.

- The -exclude option can be used with wildcards or a single filename:

    ```
    $ du --exclude "WILDCARD" DIRECTORY
    ```

Consider this example:

```
# Excludes all .txt files from calculation
$ du --exclude "*.txt" *
# Exclude temp.txt from calculation
$ du --exclude "temp.txt" *
```

- The `--exclude` option will exclude one file or files that match a pattern. The `--exclude-from` option allows more files or patterns to be excluded. Each filename or pattern must be on a single line.

```
$ ls *.txt >EXCLUDE.txt
$ ls *.odt >>EXCLUDE.txt
# EXCLUDE.txt contains a list of all .txt and .odt files.
$ du --exclude-from EXCLUDE.txt DIRECTORY
```

The `-max-depth` option restricts how many subdirectories du will examine. A depth of 1 calculates disk usage in the current directory. A depth of 2 calculates usage in the current directory and the next subdirectory:

```
$ du --max-depth 2 DIRECTORY
```

The `-x` option limits du to a single filesystem. The default behavior for du is to follow links and mount points.

The du command requires read permission for all files, and read and execute for all directories. The du command will throw an error if the user running it does not have proper permissions.

Finding the ten largest size files from a given directory

Combine the du and sort commands to find large files that should be deleted or moved:

```
$ du -ak SOURCE_DIR | sort -nrk 1 | head
```

The `-a` option makes du display the size of all the files and directories in the SOURCE_DIR. The first column of the output is the size. The `-k` option causes it to be displayed in kilobytes. The second column contains the file or folder name.

The `-n` option to sort performs a numerical sort. The `-1` option specifies column 1 and the `-r` option reverses the sort order. The head command extracts the first ten lines from the output:

```
$ du -ak /home/slynux | sort -nrk 1 | head -n 4
50220 /home/slynux
43296 /home/slynux/.mozilla
43284 /home/slynux/.mozilla/firefox
43276 /home/slynux/.mozilla/firefox/8c22khxc.default
```

One of the drawbacks of this one-liner is that it includes directories in the result. We can improve the one-liner to output only the large files with the `find` command:

```
$ find . -type f -exec du -k {} \; | sort -nrk 1 | head
```

The find command selects only filenames for du to process, rather than having du traverse the filesystem to select items to report.

Note that the du command reports the number of bytes that a file requires. This is not necessarily the same as the amount of disk space the file is consuming. Space on the disk is allocated in blocks, so a 1-byte file will consume one disk block, usually between 512 and 4096 bytes.

The next section describes using the `df` command to determine how much space is actually available.

Disk free information

The `du` command provides information about the usage, while `df` provides information about free disk space. Use `-h` with `df` to print the disk space in a human-readable format. Consider this example:

```
$ df -h
Filesystem             Size  Used Avail Use% Mounted on
/dev/sda1              9.2G  2.2G  6.6G  25% /
none                  497M  240K  497M   1% /dev
none                  502M  168K  501M   1% /dev/shm
none                  502M   88K  501M   1% /var/run
none                  502M     0  502M   0% /var/lock
none                  502M     0  502M   0% /lib/init/rw
none                  9.2G  2.2G  6.6G  25%
/var/lib/ureadahead/debugfs
```

The `df` command can be invoked with a folder name. In that case, it will report free space for the disk partition that contains that directory. This is useful if you don't know which partition contains a directory:

```
$ df -h /home/user
Filesystem             Size  Used Avail Use% Mounted on
/dev/md1              917G  739G  133G  85% /raid1
```

Calculating the execution time for a command

Execution time is the criteria for analyzing an application's efficiency or comparing algorithms.

How to do it...

1. The `time` command measures an application's execution time.

    Consider the following example:

    ```
    $ time APPLICATION
    ```

    The `time` command executes `APPLICATION`. When `APPLICATION` is complete, the `time` command reports the real, system, and user time statistics to `stderr` and sends the APPLICATION's normal output to `stdout`.

    ```
    $ time ls
    test.txt
    next.txt
    real    0m0.008s
    user    0m0.001s
    sys     0m0.003s
    ```

     An executable binary of the `time` command is found in `/usr/bin/time`. If you are running bash, you'll get the shell built-in `time` by default. The shell built-in `time` has limited options. Use an absolute path (`/usr/bin/time`) to access the extended functionality.

2. The `-o` option will write the time statistics to a file:

    ```
    $ /usr/bin/time -o output.txt COMMAND
    ```

    The filename must appear immediately after the `-o` flag.

    The `-a` flag can be used with `-o` to append the time statistics to a file:

    ```
    $ /usr/bin/time -a -o output.txt COMMAND
    ```

3. The `-f` option specifies the statistics to report and the format for the output. A format string includes one or more parameters prefixed with a `%`. Format parameters include the following:

- Real time: `%e`
- User time: `%U`
- System time: `%S`
- System Page size: `%Z`

We can create a formatted output by combining these parameters with extra text:

```
$ /usr/bin/time -f "FORMAT STRING" COMMAND
```

Consider this example:

```
$ /usr/bin/time -f "Time: %U" -a -o timing.log uname
Linux
```

The `%U` parameter specifies user time.

The **time** command sends the target application's output to `stdout` and the time command output to `stderr`. We can redirect the output with a redirection operator (`>`) and redirect the time information output with the (`2>`) error redirection operator.

Consider the following example:

```
$ /usr/bin/time -f "Time: %U" uname> command_output.txt
2>time.log
$ cat time.log
Time: 0.00
$ cat command_output.txt
Linux
```

4. The format command can report memory usage as well as timing information. The `%M` flag shows the maximum memory used in KB and `%Z` parameter causes the time command to report the system page size:

```
$ /usr/bin/time -f "Max: %M K\nPage size: %Z bytes" \
  ls>
/dev/null
Max: 996 K
Page size: 4096 bytes
```

In this example, the output of the target application is unimportant, so the standard output is directed to `/dev/null` rather than being displayed.

How it works...

The time command reports these times by default:

- **Real**: This is the wall clock time-the time from start to finish of the command. This is the elapsed time including time slices used by other processes and the time the process spends when blocked (for example, time spent waiting for I/O to complete).
- **User**: This is the amount of CPU time spent in user-mode code (outside the kernel) within the process. This is the CPU time used to execute the process. Other processes, and the time these processes spend when blocked do not count toward this figure.
- **Sys**: This is the amount of CPU time spent in the kernel within the process; the CPU time spent in system calls within the kernel, as opposed to the library code, which runs in the user space. Like user time, this is only the CPU time used by the process. Refer to the following table for a brief description of the kernel mode (also known as supervisor mode) and the system call mechanism.

Many details regarding a process can be reported by the `time` command. These include exit status, number of signals received, and number of context switches made. Each parameter can be displayed when a suitable format string is supplied to the `-f` option.

The following table shows some of the interesting parameters:

Parameter	Description
%C	This shows the name and command-line arguments of the command being timed.
%D	This shows the average size of the process's unshared data area, in kilobytes.
%E	This shows the elapsed real (wall clock) time used by the process in [hours:] minutes:seconds.
%x	This shows the exit status of the command.
%k	This shows the number of signals delivered to the process.
%W	This shows the number of times the process was swapped out of the main memory.

Parameter	Description
%Z	This shows the system's page size in bytes. This is a per-system constant, but varies between systems.
%P	This shows the percentage of the CPU that this job got. This is just user + system times divided by the total running time. It also prints a percentage sign.
%K	This shows the average total (data + stack + text) memory usage of the process, in Kilobytes.
%W	This shows the number of times that the program was context-switched voluntarily, for instance, while waiting for an I/O operation to complete.
%c	This shows the number of times the process was context-switched involuntarily (because the time slice expired).

Collecting information about logged in users, boot logs, and boot failures

Linux supports commands to report aspects of the runtime system including logged in users, how long the computer has been powered on, and boot failures. This data is used to allocate resources and diagnose problems.

Getting ready

This recipe introduces the who, w, users, uptime, last, and lastb commands.

How to do it...

1. The who command reports information about the current users:

```
$ who
slynux    pts/0    2010-09-29 05:24 (slynuxs-macbook-pro.local)
slynux    tty7     2010-09-29 07:08 (:0)
```

This output lists the login name, the TTY used by the users, login time, and remote hostname (or X display information) about logged in users.

TTY (the term comes from **TeleTYpewriter**) is the device file associated with a text terminal that is created in /dev when a terminal is newly spawned by the user (for example, /dev/pts/3). The device path for the current terminal can be found out by executing the tty command.

2. The w command provides more detailed information:

```
$ w
07:09:05 up  1:45,  2 users,  load average: 0.12, 0.06, 0.02
USER     TTY     FROM    LOGIN@   IDLE  JCPU PCPU WHAT
slynux   pts/0   slynuxs 05:24   0.00s  0.65s 0.11s sshd: slynux
slynux   tty7    :0      07:08   1:45m  3.28s 0.26s bash
```

This first line lists the current time, system uptime, number of users currently logged on, and the system load averages for the past 1, 5, and 15 minutes. Following this, the details about each login session are displayed with each line containing the login name, the TTY name, the remote host, login time, idle time, total CPU time used by the user since login, CPU time of the currently running process, and the command line of their current process.

Load average in the uptime command's output indicates system load. This is explained in more detail in Chapter 10, *Administration Calls*.

3. The users command lists only the name of logged-in users:

```
$ users
slynux slynux slynux hacker
```

If a user has multiple sessions open, either by logging in remotely several times or opening several terminal windows, there will be an entry for each session. In the preceding output, the slynux user has opened three terminals sessions. The easiest way to print unique users is to filter the output through sort and uniq:

```
$ users | tr ' ' '\n' | sort | uniq
slynux
hacker
```

The tr command replaces each ' ' character with '\n'. Then a combination of sort and uniq reduces the list to a unique entry for each user.

4. The `uptime` command reports how long the system has been powered on:

```
$ uptime
21:44:33 up 6 days, 11:53, 8 users, load average: 0.09, 0.14,
0.09
```

The time that follows the `up` word is how long the system has been powered on. We can write a one-liner to extract the uptime only:

```
$ uptime | sed 's/.*up \(.*\),.*users.*/\1/'
```

This uses `sed` to replace the line of output with only the string between the word up and the comma before users.

5. The `last` command provides a list of users who have logged onto the system since the `/var/log/wtmp` file was created. This may go back a year or more:

```
$ last
aku1   pts/3    10.2.1.3      Tue May 16 08:23 - 16:14   (07:51)
cfly   pts/0    cflynt.com   Tue May 16 07:49    still logged in
dgpx   pts/0    10.0.0.5      Tue May 16 06:19 - 06:27   (00:07)
stvl   pts/0    10.2.1.4      Mon May 15 18:38 - 19:07   (00:29)
```

The `last` command reports who logged in, what `tty` they were assigned, where they logged in from (IP address or local terminal), the login, logout, and session time. Reboots are marked as a login by a pseudo-user named `reboot`.

6. The `last` command allows you to define a user to get only information about that user:

```
$ last USER
```

7. USER can be a real user or the pseudo-user `reboot`:

```
$ last reboot
reboot    system boot   2.6.32-21-generi Tue Sep 28 18:10 - 21:48
(03:37)
reboot    system boot   2.6.32-21-generi Tue Sep 28 05:14 - 21:48
(16:33)
```

8. The `lastb` command will give you a list of the failed login attempts:

```
# lastb
test      tty8          :0              Wed Dec 15 03:56 - 03:56
(00:00)
slynux    tty8          :0              Wed Dec 15 03:55 - 03:55
(00:00)
```

The `lastb` command must be run as the root user.

Both `last` and `lastb` report the contents of `/var/log/wtmp`. The default is to report month, day, and time of the event. However, there may be multiple years of data in that file, and the month/day can be confusing.

The `-F` flag will report the full date:

```
# lastb -F
hacker    tty0          1.2.3.4         Sat Jan 7 11:50:53 2017 -
Sat Jan 7 11:50:53 2017 (00:00)
```

Listing the top ten CPU– consuming processes in an hour

The CPU is another resource that can be exhausted by a misbehaving process. Linux supports commands to identify and control the processes hogging the CPU.

Getting ready

The `ps` command displays details about the processes running on the system. It reports details such as CPU usage, running commands, memory usage, and process status. The `ps` command can be used in a script to identify who consumed the most CPU resource over an hour. For more details on the `ps` command, refer to `Chapter 10`, *Administration Calls*.

How to do it...

This shell script monitors and calculates CPU usages for one hour:

```
#!/bin/bash
#Name: pcpu_usage.sh
#Description: Script to calculate cpu usage by processes for 1 hour

#Change the SECS to total seconds to monitor CPU usage.
#UNIT_TIME is the interval in seconds between each sampling

SECS=3600
UNIT_TIME=60

STEPS=$(( $SECS / $UNIT_TIME ))

echo Watching CPU usage... ;

# Collect data in temp file

for((i=0;i<STEPS;i++))
do
  ps -eocomm,pcpu | egrep -v '(0.0)|(%CPU)' >> /tmp/cpu_usage.$$
  sleep $UNIT_TIME
done

# Process collected data
echo
echo CPU eaters :

cat /tmp/cpu_usage.$$ | \
awk '
{ process[$1]+=$2; }
END{
  for(i in process)
  {
    printf("%-20s %s\n",i, process[i]) ;
  }
}' | sort -nrk 2 | head

#Remove the temporary log file
rm /tmp/cpu_usage.$$
```

The output resembles the following:

```
$ ./pcpu_usage.sh
Watching CPU usage...
CPU eaters :
Xorg            20
firefox-bin     15
bash            3
evince          2
pulseaudio      1.0
pcpu.sh             0.3
wpa_supplicant  0
wnck-applet     0
watchdog/0      0
usb-storage     0
```

How it works...

The CPU usage data is generated by the first loop that runs for one hour (3600 seconds). Once each minute, the `ps -eocomm,pcpu` command generates a report on the system activity at that time. The `-e` option specifies to collect data on all processes, not just this session's tasks. The `-o` option specifies an output format. The `comm` and `pcpu` words specify reporting the command name and percentage of CPU, respectively. This `ps` command generates a line with the command name and current percentage of CPU usage for each running process. These lines are filtered with `grep` to remove lines where there was no CPU usage (%CPU is 0.0) and the COMMAND %CPU header. The interesting lines are appended to a temporary file.

The temporary file is named `/tmp/cpu_usage.$$`. Here, `$$` is a script variable that holds the process ID (PID) of the current script. For example, if the script's PID is `1345`, the temporary file will be named `/tmp/cpu_usage.1345`.

The statistics file will be ready after one hour and will contain 60 sets of entries, corresponding to the system status at each minute. The `awk` script sums the total CPU usage for each process into an associative array named process. This array uses the process name as array index. Finally, `awk` sorts the result with a numeric reverse sort according to the total CPU usage and uses head to limit the report to the top 10 usage entries.

See also

- The *Using awk for advanced text processing* recipe of `Chapter 4`, *Texting and Driving*, explains the `awk` command
- The *Using head and tail for printing the last or first 10 lines* recipe of `Chapter 3`, *File In, File Out*, explains the `tail` command

Monitoring command outputs with watch

The watch command will execute a command at intervals and display that command's output. You can use a terminal session and the screen command described in `chapter 10`, *Administration Calls* to create a customized dashboard to monitor your systems with watch.

How to do it...

The `watch` command monitors the output of a command on the terminal at regular intervals. The syntax of the `watch` command is as follows:

```
$ watch COMMAND
```

Consider this example:

```
$ watch ls
```

Alternatively, it can be used like this:

```
$ watch 'df /home'
```

Consider the following example:

```
# list only directories
$ watch 'ls -l | grep "^d"'
```

This command will update the output at a default interval of two seconds.

The `-n SECONDS` option defines the time interval for updating the output:

```
# Monitor the output of ls -l every of 5 seconds
$ watch -n 5 'ls -l'
```

There's more

The `watch` command can be used with any command that generates output. Some commands change their output frequently, and the changes are more important than the entire output. The watch command will highlight the difference between consecutive runs. Note that this highlight only lasts until the next update.

Highlighting the differences in the watch output

The `-d` option highlights differences between successive runs of the command being watched:

```
$ watch -d 'COMMANDS'

# Highlight new network connections for 30 seconds
$ watch -n 30 -d 'ss | grep ESTAB'
```

Logging access to files and directories

There are many reasons you may need to be notified when a file is accessed. You might want to know when a file is modified so it can be backed up, or you might want to know when files in `/bin` are modified by a hacker.

Getting ready

The `inotifywait` command watches a file or directory and reports when an event occurs. It doesn't come by default with every Linux distribution. You have to install the `inotify-tools` package. It requires the `inotify` support in the Linux kernel. Most new GNU/Linux distributions compile the `inotify` support into the kernel.

How to do it...

The `inotify` command can monitor a directory:

```
#/bin/bash
#Filename: watchdir.sh
#Description: Watch directory access
path=$1
#Provide path of directory or file as argument to script
```

```
$ inotifywait -m -r -e create,move,delete $path  -q
```

A sample output resembles the following:

```
$ ./watchdir.sh .
./ CREATE new
./ MOVED_FROM new
./ MOVED_TO news
./ DELETE news
```

How it works...

The previous script will log create, move, and delete events in the given path. The -m option causes watch to stay active and monitor changes continuously, rather than exiting after an event happens. The -r option enables a recursive watch of the directories (symbolic links are ignored). The -e option specifies the list of events to be watched and -q reduces the verbose messages and prints only the required ones. This output can be redirected to a log file.

The events that `inotifywait` can check include the following:

Event	Description
access	When a read happens to a file
modify	When file contents are modified
attrib	When metadata is changed
move	When a file undergoes a move operation
create	When a new file is created
open	When a file undergoes an open operation
close	When a file undergoes a close operation
delete	When a file is removed

Logging with syslog

Log files related to daemons and system processes are located in the `/var/log` directory. These log files use a standard protocol called **syslog**, handled by the `syslogd` daemon. Every standard application makes use of `syslogd` to log information. This recipe describes how to use `syslogd` to log information from a shell script.

Getting ready

Log files help you deduce what is going wrong with a system. It is a good practice to log progress and actions with log file messages. The logger command will place data into log files with `syslogd`.

These are some of the standard Linux log files. Some distributions use different names for these files:

Log file	Description
`/var/log/boot.log`	Boot log information
`/var/log/httpd`	Apache web server log
`/var/log/messages`	Post boot kernel information
`/var/log/auth.log` `/var/log/secure`	User authentication log
`/var/log/dmesg`	System boot up messages
`/var/log/mail.log` `/var/log/maillog`	Mail server log
`/var/log/Xorg.0.log`	X server log

How to do it...

The `logger` command allows scripts to create and manage log messages:

1. Place a message in the syslog file `/var/log/messages`:

    ```
    $ logger LOG_MESSAGE
    ```

Consider this example:

```
$ logger This is a test log line
```

```
$ tail -n 1 /var/log/messages
Sep 29 07:47:44 slynux-laptop slynux: This is a test log line
```

The `/var/log/messages` log file is a general purpose log file. When the `logger` command is used, it logs to `/var/log/messages` by default.

2. The `-t` flag defines a tag for the message:

    ```
    $ logger -t TAG This is a message
    ```

    ```
    $ tail -n 1 /var/log/messages
    Sep 29 07:48:42 slynux-laptop TAG: This is a message
    ```

The `-p` option to logger and configuration files in `/etc/rsyslog.d` control where log messages are saved.

To save to a custom file, follow these steps:

*   Create a new configuration file in `/etc/rsyslog.d`

*   Add a pattern for a priority and the log file

*   Restart the log daemon

Consider the following example:

```
# cat /etc/rsyslog.d/myConfig
local7.* /var/log/local7
# cd /etc/init.d
# ./syslogd restart
# logger -p local7.info A line to be placed in /var/log/local7
```

3. The -f option will log the lines from another file:

```
$ logger -f /var/log/source.log
```

See also

- The *Using head and tail for printing the last or first 10 lines* recipe of Chapter 3, *File In, File Out*, explains the head and tail commands

Managing log files with logrotate

Log files keep track of events on the system. They are essential for debugging problems and monitoring live machines. Log files grow as time passes and more events are recorded. Since the older data is less useful than the current data, log files are renamed when they reach a size limit and the oldest files are deleted.

Getting ready

The logrotate command can restrict the size of the log file. The system logger facility appends information to the end of a log file without deleting earlier data. Thus a log file will grow larger over time. The logrotate command scans log files defined in the configuration file. It will keep the last 100 kilobytes (for example, specified *SIZE = 100 k*) from the log file and move the rest of the data (older log data) to a new file logfile_name.1. When the old-data file (logfile_name.1) exceeds SIZE, logrotate renames that file to logfile_name.2 and starts a new logfile_name.1. The logrotate command can compress the older logs as logfile_name.1.gz, logfile_name.2.gz, and so on.

How to do it...

The system's `logrotate` configuration files are held in `/etc/logrotate.d`. Most Linux distributions have many files in this folder.

We can create a custom configuration for a log file (say `/var/log/program.log`):

```
$ cat /etc/logrotate.d/program
/var/log/program.log {
missingok
notifempty
size 30k
  compress
weekly
  rotate 5
create 0600 root root
}
```

This is a complete configuration. The `/var/log/program.log` string specifies the log file path. Logrotate will archive old logs in the same directory.

How it works...

The `logrotate` command supports these options in the configuration file:

Parameter	Description
`missingok`	This ignores if the log file is missing and return without rotating the log.
`notifempty`	This only rotates the log if the source log file is not empty.
`size 30k`	This limits the size of the log file for which the rotation is to be made. It can be 1 M for 1 MB.
`compress`	This enables compression with gzip for older logs.
`weekly`	This specifies the interval at which the rotation is to be performed. It can be weekly, yearly, or daily.
`rotate 5`	This is the number of older copies of log file archives to be kept. Since 5 is specified, there will be `program.log.1.gz`, `program.log.2.gz`, and so on up to `program.log.5.gz`.

`create 0600 root root`	This specifies the mode, user, and the group of the log file archive to be created.

The options in the table are examples of what can be specified. More options can be defined in the `logrotate` configuration file. Refer to the man page at `http://linux.die.net/man/8/logrotate`, for more information.

Monitoring user logins to find intruders

Log files can be used to gather details about the state of the system and attacks on the system.

Suppose we have a system connected to the Internet with SSH enabled. Many attackers are trying to log in to the system. We need to design an intrusion detection system to identify users who fail their login attempts. Such attempts may be of a hacker using a dictionary attack. The script should generate a report with the following details:

- User that failed to log in
- Number of attempts
- IP address of the attacker
- Host mapping for the IP address
- Time when login attempts occurred

Getting ready

A shell script can scan the log files and gather the required information. Login details are recorded in `/var/log/auth.log` or `/var/log/secure`. The script scans the log file for failed login attempts and analyzes the data. It uses the `host` command to map the host from the IP address.

How to do it...

The intrusion detection script resembles this:

```
#!/bin/bash
#Filename: intruder_detect.sh
#Description: Intruder reporting tool with auth.log input
AUTHLOG=/var/log/auth.log

if [[ -n $1 ]];
then
  AUTHLOG=$1
  echo Using Log file : $AUTHLOG
fi

# Collect the failed login attempts
LOG=/tmp/failed.$$.log
grep "Failed pass" $AUTHLOG > $LOG

# extract the users who failed
users=$(cat $LOG | awk '{ print $(NF-5) }' | sort | uniq)

# extract the IP Addresses of failed attempts
ip_list="$(egrep -o "[0-9]+\.[0-9]+\.[0-9]+\.[0-9]+" $LOG | sort | uniq)"


printf "%-10s|%-3s|%-16s|%-33s|%s\n" "User" "Attempts" "IP address" \
    "Host" "Time range"

# Loop through IPs and Users who failed.

for ip in $ip_list;
do
  for user in $users;
    do
    # Count attempts by this user from this IP

    attempts=`grep $ip $LOG | grep " $user " | wc -l`

    if [ $attempts -ne 0 ]
    then
      first_time=`grep $ip $LOG | grep " $user " | head -1 | cut -c-16`
      time="$first_time"
      if [ $attempts -gt 1 ]
      then
        last_time=`grep $ip $LOG | grep " $user " | tail -1 | cut -c-16`
        time="$first_time -> $last_time"
      fi
```

```
        HOST=$(host $ip 8.8.8.8 | tail -1 | awk '{ print $NF }' )
        printf "%-10s|%-3s|%-16s|%-33s|%-s\n" "$user" "$attempts" "$ip"\
            "$HOST" "$time";
    fi
  done
done

rm $LOG
```

The output resembles the following:

```
Using Log file : secure
User |Attempts|IP address|Host          |Time range
pi   |1       |10.251.90.93  |3(NXDOMAIN) |Jan  2 03:50:24
root |1       |10.56.180.82  |2(SERVFAIL) |Dec 26 04:31:29
root |6       |10.80.142.25  |example.com |Dec 19 07:46:49  -> Dec 19 07:47:38
```

How it works...

The `intruder_detect.sh` script defaults to using `/var/log/auth.log` as input. Alternatively, we can provide a log file with a command-line argument. The failed logins are collected in a temporary file to reduce processing.

When a login attempt fails, SSH logs lines are similar to this:

```
sshd[21197]: Failed password for bob1 from 10.83.248.32 port 50035
```

The script `greps` for the `Failed passw` string and puts those lines in `/tmp/failed.$$.log`.

The next step is to extract the users who failed to login. The `awk` command extracts the fifth field from the end (the user name) and pipes that to sort and `uniq` to create a list of the users.

Next, the unique IP addresses are extracted with a regular expression and the `egrep` command.

Nested for loops iterate through the IP address and users extracting the lines with each IP address and user combination. If the number of attempts for this IP/User combination is > 0, the time of the first occurrence is extracted with `grep`, head, and cut. If the number of attempts is > 1, then the last time is extracted using tail instead of head.

This login attempt is then reported with the formatted `printf` command.

Finally, the temporary file is removed.

Monitoring remote disk usage health

Disks fill up and sometimes wear out. Even RAIDed storage systems can fail if you don't replace a faulty drive before the others fail. Monitoring the health of the storage systems is part of an administrator's job.

The job gets easier when an automated script checks the devices on the network and generates a one-line report, the date, IP address of the machine, device, capacity of device, used space, free space, percentage usage, and alert status. If the disk usage is under 80 percent, the drive status is reported as SAFE. If the drive is getting full and needs attention, the status is reported as ALERT.

Getting ready

The script uses SSH to log in to remote systems, collect disk usage statistics, and write them to a log file in the central machine. This script can be scheduled to run at a particular time.

The script requires a common user account on the remote machines so the `disklog` script can log in to collect data. We should configure auto-login with SSH for the common user (the *Password-less auto-login with SSH* recipe of `Chapter 8`, *The Old-Boy Network*, explains auto-login).

How to do it...

Here's the code:

```
#!/bin/bash
#Filename: disklog.sh
#Description: Monitor disk usage health for remote systems
```

```
logfile="diskusage.log"

if [[ -n $1 ]]
then
  logfile=$1
fi

    # Use the environment variable or modify this to a hardcoded value
user=$USER

#provide the list of remote machine IP addresses
IP_LIST="127.0.0.1 0.0.0.0"
# Or collect them at runtime with nmap
# IP_LIST=`nmap -sn 192.168.1.2-255 | grep scan | grep cut -c22-`

if [ ! -e $logfile ]
then
  printf "%-8s %-14s %-9s %-8s %-6s %-6s %-6s %s\n" \
    "Date" "IP address" "Device" "Capacity" "Used" "Free" \
    "Percent" "Status" > $logfile
fi
 (
for ip in $IP_LIST;
do
 ssh $user@$ip 'df -H' | grep ^/dev/ > /tmp/$$.df

 while read line;
 do
 cur_date=$(date +%D)
 printf "%-8s %-14s " $cur_date $ip
 echo $line | \
     awk '{ printf("%-9s %-8s %-6s %-6s %-8s",$1,$2,$3,$4,$5); }'

 pusg=$(echo $line | egrep -o "[0-9]+%")
 pusg=${pusg/\%/};
 if [ $pusg -lt 80 ];
 then
 echo SAFE
 else
 echo ALERT
 fi

 done< /tmp/$$.df
done

) >> $logfile
```

The `cron` utility will schedule the script to run at regular intervals. For example, to run the script every day at 10 a.m., write the following entry in `crontab`:

```
00 10 * * * /home/path/disklog.sh /home/user/diskusg.log
```

Run the `crontab -e` command and add the preceding line.

You can run the script manually as follows:

```
$ ./disklog.sh
```

The output for the previous script resembles this:

```
01/18/17 192.168.1.6    /dev/sda1    106G    53G    49G    52%    SAFE
01/18/17 192.168.1.6    /dev/md1     958G   776G   159G    84%    ALERT
```

How it works...

The `disklog.sh` script accepts the log file path as a command-line argument or uses the default log file. The `-e $logfile` checks whether the file exists or not. If the log file does not exist, it is initialized with a column header. The list of remote machine IP addresses can be hardcoded in `IP_LIST`, delimited with spaces, or the `nmap` command can be used to scan the network for available nodes. If you use the `nmap` call, adjust the IP address range for your network.

A for loop iterates through each of the IP addresses. The `ssh` application sends the `df -H` command to each node to retrieve the disk usage information. The `df` output is stored in a temporary file. A `while` loop reads that file line by line and invokes `awk` to extract the relevant data and output it. An `egrep` command extracts the percent full value and strips `%`. If this value is less than 80, the line is marked `SAFE`, else it's marked `ALERT`. The entire output string must be redirected to the `log` file. Hence, the `for` loop is enclosed in a subshell `()` and the standard output is redirected to the log file.

See also

- The *Scheduling with a cron* recipe in `Chapter 10`, *Administration Calls*, explains the `crontab` command

Determining active user hours on a system

This recipe makes use of the system logs to find out how many hours each user has spent on the server and ranks them according to the total usage hours. A report is generated with the details, including rank, user, first logged in date, last logged in date, number of times logged in, and total usage hours.

Getting ready

The raw data about user sessions is stored in a binary format in the /var/log/wtmp file. The last command returns details about login sessions. The sum of the session hours for each user is that user's total usage hours.

How to do it...

This script will determine the active users and generate the report:

```bash
#!/bin/bash
#Filename: active_users.sh
#Description: Reporting tool to find out active users

log=/var/log/wtmp

if [[ -n $1 ]];
then
  log=$1
fi

printf "%-4s %-10s %-10s %-6s %-8s\n" "Rank" "User" "Start" \
  "Logins" "Usage hours"

last -f $log | head -n -2   > /tmp/ulog.$$

cat /tmp/ulog.$$ |   cut -d' ' -f1 | sort | uniq> /tmp/users.$$

(
while read user;
do
  grep ^$user /tmp/ulog.$$ > /tmp/user.$$
  minutes=0

  while read t
  do
```

```
    s=$(echo $t | awk -F: '{ print ($1 * 60) + $2 }')
    let minutes=minutes+s
done< <(cat /tmp/user.$$ | awk '{ print $NF }' | tr -d ')('))

firstlog=$(tail -n 1 /tmp/user.$$ | awk '{ print $5,$6 }')
nlogins=$(cat /tmp/user.$$ | wc -l)
hours=$(echo "$minutes / 60.0" | bc)

printf "%-10s %-10s %-6s %-8s\n"  $user "$firstlog" $nlogins $hours
done< /tmp/users.$$

) | sort -nrk 4 | awk '{ printf("%-4s %s\n", NR, $0) }'
rm /tmp/users.$$ /tmp/user.$$ /tmp/ulog.$$
```

The output resembles the following:

```
$ ./active_users.sh
Rank User        Start      Logins Usage hours
1    easyibaa    Dec 11     531    349
2    demoproj    Dec 10     350    230
3    kjayaram    Dec 9      213    55
4    cinenews    Dec 11     85     139
5    thebenga    Dec 10     54     35
6    gateway2    Dec 11     52     34
7    soft132     Dec 12     49     25
8    sarathla    Nov 1      45     29
9    gtsminis    Dec 11     41     26
10   agentcde    Dec 13     39     32
```

How it works...

The `active_users.sh` script reads from `/var/log/wtmp` or a `wtmp` log file defined on the command line. The `last -f` command extracts the log file contents. The first column in the log file is the username. The `cut` command extracts the first column from the log file. The `sort` and `uniq` commands reduce this to a list of unique users.

The script's outer loop iterates through the users. For each user, `grep` is used to extract the log lines corresponding to a particular user.

The last column of each line is the duration of this login session. These values are summed in the inner `while read t` loop.

The session duration is formatted as (HOUR:SEC). This value is extracted with awk to report the last field and then piped to tr -d to remove the parentheses. A second awk command converts the *HH::MM* string to minutes and the minutes are totaled. When the loop is complete, the total minutes are converted to hours by dividing $minutes with 60.

The first login time for a user is the last line in the temporary file of user data. This is extracted with tail and awk. The number of login sessions is the number of lines in this file, calculated with wc.

The users are sorted by the total usage hours with sort's -nr option for the numeric and descending order and -k4 to specify the sort column (usage hour). Finally, the output of the sort is passed to awk, which prefixes each line with a line number representing the rank of each user.

Measuring and optimizing power usage

Battery capacity is a critical resource on mobile devices, such as notebook computers and tablets. Linux provides tools that measure power consumption, one such command is powertop.

Getting ready

The powertop application doesn't come preinstalled with many Linux distributions, you will have to install it using your package manager.

How to do it...

The powertop application measures per-module power consumption and supports interactively optimizing power consumption:

With no options, powertop presents a display on the terminal:

```
# powertop
```

The `powertop` command takes measurements and displays detailed information about power usage, the processes using the most power, and so on:

```
PowerTOP 2.3   Overview  Idle stats  Frequency stats  Device stats  Tunable

Summary: 1146.1 wakeups/sec,   0.0 GPU ops/secs, 0.0 VFS ops/sec and 73.0% C

Usage Events/s Category Description
407.4 ms/s 258.7 Process /usr/lib/vmware/bin/vmware
64.8 ms/s 313.8 Process /usr/lib64/firefox/firefox
```

The `-html` tag will cause `powertop` to take measurements over a period of time and generate an HTML report with the default filename `PowerTOP.html`, which you can open using any web browser:

```
# powertop --html
```

In the interactive mode, you can optimize power usage. When `powertop` is running, use the arrow or tab keys to switch to the **Tunables** tab; this shows a list of attributes `powertop` can tune to for consuming less power. Choose the ones you want, press Enter to toggle from **Bad** to **Good**.

> If you want to monitor the power consumption from a portable device's battery, it is required to remove the charger and use the battery for `powertop` to make measurements.

Monitoring disk activity

A popular naming convention for monitoring tools is to end the name with the `'top'` word (the command used to monitor processes). The tool to monitor disk I/O is called `iotop`.

Getting ready

The **iotop** application doesn't come preinstalled with most Linux distributions, you will have to install it using your package manager. The iotop application requires root privileges, so you'll need to run it as `sudo` or root user.

How to do it...

The `iotop` application can either perform continuous monitoring or generate reports for a fixed period:

1. For continuous monitoring, use the command as follows:

    ```
    # iotop -o
    ```

    The `-o` option tells `iotop` to show only those processes that are doing active I/O while it is running, which reduces the noise in the output.

2. The `-n` option tells iotop to run for *N* times and exit:

    ```
    # iotop -b -n 2
    ```

3. The `-p` option monitors a specific process:

    ```
    # iotop -p PID
    ```

    `PID` is the process you wish to monitor.

In most modern distributions, instead of finding the PID and supplying it to `iotop`, you can use the `pidof` command and write the preceding command as follows: # iotop -p `pidof cp`

Checking disks and filesystems for errors

Linux filesystems are incredibly robust. Despite that, a filesystem can become corrupted and data can be lost. The sooner you find a problem, the less data loss and corruption you need to worry about.

Getting ready

The standard tool for checking filesystems is `fsck`. This command is installed on all modern distributions. Note that you'll need to run `fsck` as root or via a `sudo`.

How to do it...

Linux will run `fsck` automatically at boot time if the filesystem has been unchecked for a long time or there is a reason (unsafe reboot after a power glitch) to suspect it's been corrupted. You can run `fsck` manually.

1. To check for errors on a partition or filesystem, pass the path to `fsck`:

   ```
   # fsck /dev/sdb3
   fsck from util-linux 2.20.1
   e2fsck 1.42.5 (29-Jul-2012)
   HDD2 has been mounted 26 times without being checked, check forced.
   Pass 1: Checking inodes, blocks, and sizes
   Pass 2: Checking directory structure
   Pass 3: Checking directory connectivity
   Pass 4: Checking reference counts
   Pass 5: Checking group summary information
   HDD2: 75540/16138240 files (0.7% non-contiguous),
   48756390/64529088 blocks
   ```

2. The −A flag checks all the filesystems configured in `/etc/fstab`:

   ```
   # fsck -A
   ```

   This will go through the `/etc/fstab` file, checking each filesystem. The `fstab` file defines the mapping between physical disk partitions and mount points. It's used to mount filesystems during boot.

3. The −a option instructs `fsck` to automatically attempt to fix errors, instead of interactively asking us whether or not to repair them. Use this option with caution:

   ```
   # fsck -a /dev/sda2
   ```

4. The −N option simulates the actions `fsck` will perform:

   ```
   # fsck -AN
   fsck from util-linux 2.20.1
   [/sbin/fsck.ext4 (1) -- /] fsck.ext4 /dev/sda8
   [/sbin/fsck.ext4 (1) -- /home] fsck.ext4 /dev/sda7
   [/sbin/fsck.ext3 (1) -- /media/Data] fsck.ext3 /dev/sda6
   ```

How it works...

The `fsck` application is a frontend for filesystem specific `fsck` applications. When we run `fsck`, it detects the type of the filesystem and runs the appropriate `fsck.fstype` command, where `fstype` is the type of the filesystem. For example, if we run `fsck` on an `ext4` filesystem, it will end up calling the `fsck.ext4` command.

Because of this, `fsck` supports only the common options across all filesystem-specific tools. To find more detailed options, read the application specific man pages such as `fsck.ext4`.

It's very rare, but possible, for `fsck` to lose data or make a badly damaged filesystem worse. If you suspect severe corruption of a filesystem, you should use the `-N` option to list the actions that `fsck` will perform without actually performing them. If `fsck` reports more than a dozen problems it can fix or if these include damaged directory structures, you may want to mount the drive in the read-only mode and try to extract critical data before running `fsck`.

Examining disk health

Modern disk drives run for years with no problems, but when a disk fails, it's a major disaster. Modern disk drives include a **Self-Monitoring, Analysis, and Reporting Technology (SMART)** facility to monitor the disk's health so you can replace an ailing drive before a major failure occurs.

Getting ready

Linux supports interacting with the drives SMART utilities via the `smartmontools` package. This is installed by default on most distributions. If it's not present, you can install it with your package manager:

```
apt-get install smartmontools
```

Alternatively, this command can be used:

```
yum install smartmontools
```

How to do it...

The user interface to `smartmontools` is the `smartctl` application. This application initiates tests on the disk drive and reports the status of the SMART device.

Since the `smartctl` application accesses the raw disk device, you must have root access to run it.

The `-a` option reports the full status of a device:

```
$ smartctl -a /dev/sda
```

The output will be a header of basic information, a set of raw data values and the test results. The header includes details about the drive being tested and a datestamp for this report:

```
smartctl 5.43 2012-06-30 r3573 [x86_64-linux-2.6.32-
642.11.1.el6.x86_64] (local build)
Copyright (C) 2002-12 by Bruce Allen,
http://smartmontools.sourceforge.net

=== START OF INFORMATION SECTION ===
Device Model:     WDC WD10EZEX-00BN5A0
Serial Number:    WD-WCC3F1HHJ4T8
LU WWN Device Id: 5 0014ee 20c75fb3b
Firmware Version: 01.01A01
User Capacity:    1,000,204,886,016 bytes [1.00 TB]
Sector Sizes:     512 bytes logical, 4096 bytes physical
Device is:        Not in smartctl database [for details use: -P
showall]
ATA Version is:   8
ATA Standard is:  ACS-2 (unknown minor revision code: 0x001f)
Local Time is:    Mon Jan 23 11:26:57 2017 EST
SMART support is: Available - device has SMART capability.
SMART support is: Enabled
...
```

The raw data values include error counts, spin-up time, power-on hours, and more. The last two columns (WHEN_FAILED and RAW_VALUE) are of particular interest. In the following sample, the device has been powered on 9823 hours. It was powered on and off 11 times (servers don't get power-cycled a lot) and the current temperature is 30° C. When the value for power on gets close to the manufacturer's **Mean Time Between Failures** (**MTBF**), it's time to start considering replacing the drive or moving it to a less critical system. If the Power Cycle count increases between reboots, it could indicate a failing power supply or faulty cables. If the temperature gets high, you should consider checking the drive's enclosure. A fan may have failed or a filter might be clogged:

```
ID# ATTRIBUTE_NAME           FLAG      VALUE WORST THRESH TYPE      UPDATED
    WHEN_FAILED RAW_VALUE

  9 Power_On_Hours           0x0032    087   087   000    Old_age   Always
        -         9823

 12 Power_Cycle_Count        0x0032    100   100   000    Old_age   Always
        -         11

194 Temperature_Celsius      0x0022    113   109   000    Old_age   Always
        -         30
```

The last section of the output will be the results of the tests:

```
SMART Error Log Version: 1
No Errors Logged

SMART Self-test log structure revision number 1

Num  Test_Description    Status                    Remaining   LifeTime(hours)
        LBA_of_first_error
# 1  Extended offline    Completed without error      00%          9825
        -
```

The -t flag forces the SMART device to run the self-tests. These are non-destructive and can be run on a drive while it is in service. SMART devices can run a long or short test. A short test will take a few minutes, while the long test will take an hour or more on a large device:

```
$ smartctl -t [long][short] DEVICE

$ smartctl -t long /dev/sda

smartctl 5.43 2012-06-30 r3573 [x86_64-linux-2.6.32-642.11.1.el6.x86_64]
(local build)
Copyright (C) 2002-12 by Bruce Allen, http://smartmontools.sourceforge.net

=== START OF OFFLINE IMMEDIATE AND SELF-TEST SECTION ===
Sending command: "Execute SMART Extended self-test routine immediately in
off-line mode".
Drive command "Execute SMART Extended self-test routine immediately in off-
line mode" successful.
Testing has begun.
Please wait 124 minutes for test to complete.
Test will complete after Mon Jan 23 13:31:23 2017

Use smartctl -X to abort test.
```

In a bit over two hours, this test will be completed and the results will be viewable with the smartctl -a command.

How it works

Modern disk drives are much more than a spinning metal disk. They include a CPU, ROM, memory, and custom signal processing chips. The smartctl command interacts with the small operating system running on the disk's CPU to requests tests and reports.

Getting disk statistics

The smartctl command provides many disk statistics and tests the drives. The hdparm command provides more statistics and examines how the disk performs in your system, which may be influenced by controller chips, cables, and so on.

Getting ready

The `hdparm` command is standard on most Linux distributions. You must have root access to use it.

How to do it...

The `-I` option will provide basic information about your device:

```
$ hdparm -I DEVICE
$ hdparm -I /dev/sda
```

The following sample output shows some of the data reported. The model number and firmware are the same as reported by `smartctl`. The configuration includes parameters that can be tuned before a drive is partitioned and a filesystem is created:

```
/dev/sda:

ATA device, with non-removable media
 Model Number:       WDC WD10EZEX-00BN5A0
 Serial Number:      WD-WCC3F1HHJ4T8
 Firmware Revision:  01.01A01
 Transport:          Serial, SATA 1.0a, SATA II Extensions, SATA Rev 2.5,
SATA Rev 2.6, SATA Rev 3.0
Standards:
 Used: unknown (minor revision code 0x001f)
 Supported: 9 8 7 6 5
 Likely used: 9
Configuration:
 Logical  max current
 cylinders 16383 16383
 heads   16 16
 sectors/track 63 63
 --
 CHS current addressable sectors:   16514064
 LBA     user addressable sectors:  268435455
 LBA48   user addressable sectors: 1953525168
 Logical  Sector size:                 512 bytes
 Physical Sector size:               4096 bytes
 device size with M = 1024*1024:    953869 MBytes
 device size with M = 1000*1000:   1000204 MBytes (1000 GB)
 cache/buffer size  = unknown
 Nominal Media Rotation Rate: 7200

 ...
 Security:
```

```
Master password revision code = 65534
  supported
not enabled
not locked
not frozen
not expired: security count
  supported: enhanced erase
128min for SECURITY ERASE UNIT. 128min for ENHANCED SECURITY ERASE UNIT.
Logical Unit WWN Device Identifier: 50014ee20c75fb3b
  NAA  : 5
  IEEE OUI : 0014ee
  Unique ID : 20c75fb3b
Checksum: correct
```

How it works

The `hdparm` command is a user interface into the kernel libraries and modules. It includes support for modifying parameters as well as reporting them. Use extreme caution when changing these parameters!

There's more

The `hdparm` command can test a disk's performance. The `-t` and `-T` options performs timing tests on buffered and cached reads, respectively:

```
# hdparm -t /dev/sda
Timing buffered disk reads: 486 MB in  3.00 seconds = 161.86 MB/sec

# hdparm -T /dev/sda
Timing cached reads:   26492 MB in  1.99 seconds = 13309.38 MB/sec
```

10
Administration Calls

In this chapter, we will cover the following topics:

- Gathering information about processes
- What's what – which, whereis, whatis, and file
- Killing processes, and sending and responding to signals
- Sending messages to user terminals
- The /proc filesystem
- Gathering system information
- Scheduling with a cron
- Database styles and uses
- Writing and reading SQLite databases
- Writing and reading a MySQL database from Bash
- User administration scripts
- Bulk image resizing and format conversion
- Taking screenshots from the terminal
- Managing multiple terminals from one

Introduction

Managing multiple terminals from one GNU/Linux ecosystem consists of the network, each set of hardware, the OS Kernel that allocates resources, interface modules, system utilities, and user programs. An administrator needs to monitor the entire system to keep everything running smoothly. Linux administration tools range from all-in-one GUI applications to command-line tools designed for scripting.

Gathering information about processes

The term **process** in this case means the running instance of a program. Many processes run simultaneously on a computer. Each process is assigned a unique identification number, called a **process ID (PID)**. Multiple instances of the same program with the same name can run at the same time, but they will each have different PIDs and attributes. Process attributes include the user who owns the process, the amount of memory used by the program, the CPU time used by the program, and so on. This recipe shows how to gather information about processes.

Getting ready

Important commands related to process management are `top`, `ps`, and `pgrep`. These tools are available in all Linux distributions.

How to do it...

`ps` reports information about active processes. It provides information about which user owns the process, when the process started, the command path used to execute the process, the PID, the terminal it is attached to (**TTY**, for **TeleTYpe**), the memory used by the process, the CPU time used by the process, and so on. Consider the following example:

```
$ ps
PID TTY          TIME CMD
1220 pts/0    00:00:00 bash
1242 pts/0    00:00:00 ps
```

Be default, `ps` will display the processes initiated from the current terminal (TTY). The first column shows the PID, the second column refers to the terminal (TTY), the third column indicates how much time has elapsed since the process started, and finally we have CMD (the command).

The `ps` command report can be modified with command-line parameters.

The `-f` (`full`) option displays more columns of information:

```
$ ps -f
UID        PID  PPID  C STIME TTY          TIME CMD
slynux    1220  1219  0 18:18 pts/0    00:00:00 -bash
slynux    1587  1220  0 18:59 pts/0    00:00:00 ps -f
```

The -e (every) and -ax (all) options provide a report on every process that is running on the system.

> The -x argument (along with -a) specifies the removal of the default TTY restriction imparted by ps. Usually, if you use ps without arguments, it'll only print processes attached to the current terminal.

The commands ps -e, ps -ef, ps -ax, and ps -axf generate reports on all processes and provide more information than ps:

```
$ ps -e | head -5
PID TTY     TIME CMD
1 ?        00:00:00 init
2 ?        00:00:00 kthreadd
3 ?        00:00:00 migration/0
4 ?        00:00:00 ksoftirqd/0
```

The -e option generates a long report. This example filters the output with head to display the first five entries.

The -o PARAMETER1, PARAMETER2 option specifies the data to be displayed.

> Parameters for -o are delimited with a comma (,). There is no space between the comma operator and the next parameter.
> The -o option can be combined with the -e (every) option (-eo) to list every process running in the system. However, when you use filters similar to the ones that restrict ps to the specified users along with -o, -e is not used. The -e option overrules the filter and displays all the processes.

In this example, comm stands for COMMAND and pcpu represents the percentage of CPU usage:

```
$ ps -eo comm,pcpu | head -5
COMMAND         %CPU
init            0.0
kthreadd        0.0
migration/0     0.0
ksoftirqd/0     0.0
```

How it works...

The following parameters for the −o option are supported:

Parameter	Description
pcpu	Percentage of CPU
pid	Process ID
ppid	Parent process ID
pmem	Percentage of memory
comm	Executable filename
cmd	A simple command
user	The user who started the process
nice	The priority (niceness)
time	Cumulative CPU time
etime	Elapsed time since the process started
tty	The associated TTY device
euid	The effective user
stat	Process state

There's more...

The ps command, grep, and other tools can be combined to produce custom reports.

Showing environment variables for a process

Some processes are dependent on their environment variable definitions. Knowing the environment variables and values can help you debug or customize a process.

The `ps` command does not normally show the environment information of a command. The `e` output modifier at the end of the command adds this information to the output:

```
$ ps e
```

Here's an example of environment information:

```
$ ps -eo pid,cmd  e | tail -n 1
1238 -bash USER=slynux LOGNAME=slynux HOME=/home/slynux
PATH=/usr/local/sbin:/usr/local/bin:/usr/sbin:/usr/bin:/sbin:/bin
MAIL=/var/mail/slynux SHELL=/bin/bash SSH_CLIENT=10.211.55.2 49277 22
SSH_CONNECTION=10.211.55.2 49277 10.211.55.4 22 SSH_TTY=/dev/pts/0
```

Environment information helps trace problems using the `apt-get` package manager. If you use an HTTP proxy to connect to the Internet, you may need to set environment variables using `http_proxy=host:port`. If this is not set, the `apt-get` command will not select the proxy and hence returns an error. Knowing that `http_proxy` is not set makes the problem obvious.

When a scheduling tool, such as `cron` (discussed later in this chapter), is used to run an application, the expected environment variables may not be set. This `crontab` entry will not open a GUI-windowed application:

```
00 10 * * * /usr/bin/windowapp
```

It fails because GUI applications require the `DISPLAY` environment variable. To determine the required environment variables, run `windowapp` manually and then `ps -C windowapp -eo cmd e`.

After you've identified the required environment variables, define them before the command name in `crontab`:

```
00 10 * * * DISPLAY=:0 /usr/bin/windowapp
```

OR

```
DISPLAY=0
00 10 * * * /usr/bin/windowapp
```

The definition `DISPLAY=:0` was obtained from the `ps` output.

Creating a tree view of processes

The ps command can report a process PID, but tracking from a child to the ultimate parent is tedious. Adding f to the end of the ps command creates a tree view of the processes, showing the parent-child relationship between tasks. The next example shows an ssh session invoked from a bash shell running inside xterm:

```
$ ps -u clif f | grep -A2 xterm | head -3
15281  ?        S      0:00 xterm
15284 pts/20   Ss+    0:00 \_ bash
15286 pts/20   S+     0:18 \_ ssh 192.168.1.2
```

Sorting ps output

By default, the ps command output is unsorted. The -sort parameter forces ps to sort the output. The ascending or descending order can be specified by adding the + (ascending) or − (descending) prefix to the parameter:

```
$ ps [OPTIONS] --sort -paramter1,+parameter2,parameter3..
```

For example, to list the top five CPU-consuming processes, use the following:

```
$ ps -eo comm,pcpu --sort -pcpu | head -5
COMMAND          %CPU
Xorg              0.1
hald-addon-stor  0.0
ata/0             0.0
scsi_eh_0         0.0
```

This displays the top five processes, sorted in descending order by percentage of CPU usage.

The grep command can filter the ps output. To report only those Bash processes that are currently running, use the following:

```
$ ps -eo comm,pid,pcpu,pmem | grep bash
bash           1255  0.0  0.3
bash           1680  5.5  0.3
```

Filters with ps for real user or ID, effective user or ID

The ps command can group processes based on the real and effective usernames or IDs specified. The ps command filters the output by checking whether each entry belongs to a specific effective user or a real user from the list of arguments.

- Specify an effective user's list with −u EUSER1, EUSER2, and so on
- Specify a real user's list with −U RUSER1, RUSER2, and so on

Here's an example of this:

```
# display user and percent cpu usage for processes with real user
# and effective user of root
$ ps -u root -U root -o user,pcpu
```

The −o may be used with −e as −eo but when filters are applied, −e should not be used. It overrides the filter options.

TTY filter for ps

The ps output can be selected by specifying the TTY to which the process is attached. Use the -t option to specify the TTY list:

```
$ ps -t TTY1, TTY2 ..
```

Here's an example of this:

```
$ ps -t pts/0,pts/1
   PID TTY          TIME CMD
  1238 pts/0    00:00:00 bash
  1835 pts/1    00:00:00 bash
  1864 pts/0    00:00:00 ps
```

Information about process threads

The −L option to ps will display information about process threads. This option adds an LWP column to the thread ID. Adding the −f option to −L (−Lf) adds two columns: NLWP, the thread count, and LWP, the thread ID:

```
$ ps -Lf
UID  PID  PPID  LWP  C  NLWP  STIME  TTY  TIME
     CMD
user 1611 1     1612 0  2     Jan16  ?    00:00:00
     /usr/lib/gvfs/gvfsd
```

This command lists five processes with a maximum number of threads:

```
$ ps -eLf --sort -nlwp | head -5
UID        PID  PPID   LWP  C NLWP STIME TTY   TIME
    CMD
root        647    1   647  0   64 14:39 ?    00:00:00
    /usr/sbin/console-kit-daemon --no-daemon
root        647    1   654  0   64 14:39 ?    00:00:00
    /usr/sbin/console-kit-daemon --no-daemon
root        647    1   656  0   64 14:39 ?    00:00:00
    /usr/sbin/console-kit-daemon --no-daemon
root        647    1   657  0   64 14:39 ?    00:00:00
    /usr/sbin/console-kit-daemon --no-daemon
```

Specifying the output width and columns to be displayed

The `ps` command supports many options to select fields in order to display and control how they are displayed. Here are some of the more common options:

`-f`	This specifies a full format. It includes the starting time of the parent PID user ID.
`-u userList`	This selects processes owned by the users in the list. By default, it selects the current user.
`-l`	Long listing. It displays the user ID, parent PID, size, and more.

What's what – which, whereis, whatis, and file

There may be several files with the same name. Knowing which executable is being invoked and whether a file is compiled code or a script is useful information.

How to do it...

The `which`, `whereis`, `file`, and `whatis` commands report information about files and directories.

- `which`: The which command reports the location of a command:

```
$ which ls
/bin/ls
```

- We often use commands without knowing the directory where the executable file is stored. Depending on how your PATH variable is defined, you may use a command from /bin, /usr/local/bin, or /opt/PACKAGENAME/bin.

- When we type a command, the terminal looks for the command in a set of directories and executes the first executable file it finds. The directories to search are specified in the PATH environment variable:

```
$ echo $PATH
/usr/local/bin:/usr/bin:/bin:/usr/sbin:/sbin
```

- We can add directories to be searched and export the new PATH. To add /opt/bin to PATH, use the following command:

```
$ export PATH=$PATH:/opt/bin
# /opt/bin is added to PATH
```

- **whereis**: whereis is similar to the which command. It not only returns the path of the command, but also prints the location of the man page (if available) and the path for the source code of the command (if available):

```
$ whereis ls
ls: /bin/ls /usr/share/man/man1/ls.1.gz
```

- **whatis**: The whatis command outputs a one-line description of the command given as the argument. It parses information from the man page:

```
$ whatis ls
ls (1)      - list directory contents
```

The file command reports a file type. Its syntax is as follows:

```
$ file FILENAME
```

- The reported file type may comprise a few words or a long description:

```
$file /etc/passwd
/etc/passwd: ASCII text
$ file /bin/ls
/bin/ls: ELF 32-bit LSB executable, Intel 80386, version 1
(SYSV), dynamically linked (uses shared libs), for GNU/Linux
2.6.15, stripped
```

apropos
Sometimes we need to search for a command that is related to the topic. The `apropos` command will search the man pages for a keyword. Here's the code to do this: **Apropos topic**

Finding the process ID from the given command names

Suppose several instances of a command are being executed. In such a scenario, we need the PID of each process. Both the `ps` and `pgrep` command return this information:

```
$ ps -C COMMAND_NAME
```

Alternatively, the following is returned:

```
$ ps -C COMMAND_NAME -o pid=
```

When = is appended to `pid`, it removes the header PID from the output of `ps`. To remove headers from a column, append = to the parameter.

This command lists the process IDs of Bash processes:

```
$ ps -C bash -o pid=
 1255
 1680
```

The `pgrep` command also returns a list of process IDs for a command:

```
$ pgrep bash
1255
1680
```

`pgrep` requires only a portion of the command name as its input argument to extract a Bash command; `pgrep ash` or `pgrep bas` will also work, for example. But `ps` requires you to type the exact command. `pgrep` supports these output-filtering options.

The `-d` option specifies an output delimiter other than the default new line:

```
$ pgrep COMMAND -d DELIMITER_STRING
$ pgrep bash -d ":"
1255:1680
```

The −u option filters for a list of users:

```
$ pgrep −u root,slynux COMMAND
```

In this command, `root` and `slynux` are users.

The −c option returns the count of matching processes:

```
$ pgrep −c COMMAND
```

Determining how busy a system is

Systems are either unused or overloaded. The `load average` value describes the total load on the running system. It describes the average number of runnable processes, processes with all resources except CPU time slices, on the system.

Load average is reported by the uptime and top commands. It is reported with three values. The first value indicates the average in 1 minute, the second indicates the average in 5 minutes, and the third indicates the average in 15 minutes.

It is reported by uptime:

```
$ uptime
12:40:53 up  6:16,  2 users,  load average: 0.00, 0.00, 0.00
```

The top command

By default, the `top` command displays a list of the top CPU-consuming processes as well as basic system statistics, including the number of tasks in the process list, CPU cores, and memory usage. The output is updated every few seconds.

This command displays several parameters along with the top CPU-consuming processes:

```
$ top
top − 18:37:50 up 16 days, 4:41,7 users,load average 0.08 0.05 .11
Tasks: 395 total,  2 running, 393 sleeping, 0 stopped 0 zombie
```

See also...

- The *Scheduling with a cron* recipe in this chapter explains how to schedule tasks

Killing processes, and sending and responding to signals

You may need to kill processes (if they go rogue and start consuming too many resources) if you need to reduce system load, or before rebooting. Signals are an inter-process communication mechanism that interrupts a running process and forces it to perform some action. These actions include forcing a process to terminate in either a controlled or immediate manner.

Getting ready

Signals send an interrupt to a running program. When a process receives a signal, it responds by executing a signal handler. Compiled applications generate signals with the kill system call. A signal can be generated from the command line (or shell script) with the kill command. The trap command can be used in a script to handle received signals.

Each signal is identified by a name and an integer value. The SIGKILL (9) signal terminates a process immediately. The keystroke events *Ctrl + C* and *Ctrl + Z* send signals to abort or put the task in the background.

How to do it...

1. The kill -1 command will list the available signals:

   ```
   $ kill -1
   SIGHUP 2) SIGINT 3) SIGQUIT 4) SIGILL 5) SIGTRAP
   . . .
   ```

2. Terminate the process:

   ```
   $ kill PROCESS_ID_LIST
   ```

   The kill command issues a SIGTERM signal by default. The process ID list is specified with spaces for delimiters.

3. The -s option specifies the signal to be sent to the process:

   ```
   $ kill -s SIGNAL PID
   ```

The SIGNAL argument is either a signal name or a signal number. There are many signals available for different purposes. The most common ones are as follows:

- SIGHUP 1: Hangup detection on the death of the controlling process or terminal

- SIGINT 2: This is the signal emitted when *Ctrl + C* is pressed

- SIGKILL 9: This is the signal used to forcibly kill the process

- SIGTERM 15: This is the signal used to terminate a process by default

- SIGTSTP 20: This is the signal emitted when *Ctrl + Z* is pressed

4. We frequently use force kill for processes. Use this with caution. This is an immediate action, and it will not save data or perform a normal cleanup operation. The SIGTERM signal should be tried first; SIGKILL should be saved for extreme measures:

```
$ kill -s SIGKILL PROCESS_ID
```

Alternatively, use this to perform the cleanup operation:

```
$ kill -9 PROCESS_ID
```

There's more...

Linux supports other commands to signal or terminate processes.

The kill family of commands

The kill command takes the process ID as the argument. The killall command terminates the process by name:

```
$ killall process_name
```

The -s option specifies the signal to send. By default, killall sends a SIGTERM signal:

```
$ killall -s SIGNAL process_name
```

The -9 option forcibly kills a process by name:

```
$ killall -9 process_name
```

Here's an example of the preceding:

```
$ killall -9 gedit
```

The `-u` owner specifies the process's user:

```
$ killall -u USERNAME process_name
```

The `-I` option makes `killall` run in interactive mode:

The `pkill` command is similar to the `kill` command, but by default it accepts a process name instead of a process ID:

```
$ pkill process_name
$ pkill -s SIGNAL process_name
```

`SIGNAL` is the signal number. The `SIGNAL` name is not supported with `pkill`. The `pkill` command provides many of the same options as the `kill` command. Check the `pkill` man pages for more details.

Capturing and responding to signals

Well-behaved programs save data and shut down cleanly when they receive a `SIGTERM` signal. The `trap` command assigns a signal handler to signals in a script. Once a function is assigned to a signal using the `trap` command, when a script receives a signal, this function is executed.

The syntax is as follows:

```
trap 'signal_handler_function_name' SIGNAL LIST
```

`SIGNAL LIST` is space-delimited. It can include both signal numbers and signal names.

This shell script responds to the `SIGINT` signal:

```
#/bin/bash
#Filename: sighandle.sh
#Description: Signal handler

function handler()
{
  echo Hey, received signal : SIGINT
}

# $$ is a special variable that returns process ID of current
# process/script
```

```
echo My process ID is $$

#handler is the name of the signal handler function for SIGINT signal
trap 'handler' SIGINT

while true;
do
   sleep 1
done
```

Run this script in a terminal. When the script is running, pressing *Ctrl + C* it will show the message by executing the signal handler associated with it. *Ctrl + C* corresponds to a SIGINT signal.

The while loop is used to keep the process running forever without being terminated. This is done so the script can respond to signals. The loop to keep a process alive infinitely is often called the **event loop**.

If the process ID of the script is given, the kill command can send a signal to it:

$ kill -s SIGINT PROCESS_ID

The process ID of the preceding script will be printed when it is executed; alternatively, you can find it with the ps command.

If no signal handlers are specified for signals, a script will call the default signal handlers assigned by the operating system. Generally, pressing *Ctrl + C* will terminate a program, as the default handler provided by the operating system will terminate the process. The custom handler defined here overrides the default handler.

We can define signal handlers for any signals available (kill -l) with the trap command. A single signal handler can process multiple signals.

Sending messages to user terminals

Linux supports three applications to display messages on another user's screen. The write command sends a message to a user, the talk command lets two users have a conversation, and the wall command sends a message to all users.

Before doing something potentially disruptive (say, rebooting the server), the system administrator should send a message to the terminal of every user on the system or network.

Getting ready

The `write` and `wall` commands are part of most Linux distributions. If a user is logged in multiple times, you may need to specify the terminal you wish to send a message to.

You can determine a user's terminals with the `who` command:

```
$> who
user1     pts/0     2017-01-16 13:56 (:0.0)
user1     pts/1     2017-01-17 08:35 (:0.0)
```

The second column (`pts/#`) is the user's terminal identifier.

The `write` and `wall` programs work on a single system. The `talk` program can connect users across a network.

The talk program is not commonly installed. Both the talk program and talk server must be installed and running on any machine where talk is used. Install the talk application as `talk` and `talkd` on Debian-based systems or as `talk` and `talk-server` on Red Hat-based systems. You will probably need to edit `/etc/xinet.d/talk` and `/etc/xinet.d/ntalk` to set the `disable` field to `no`. Once you do this, restart `xinet`:

```
# cd /etc/xinet.d
# vi ntalk
# cd /etc/init.d
#./xinetd restart
```

How to do it...

Sending one message to one user

The write command will send a message to a single user:

```
$ write USERNAME [device]
```

You can redirect a message from a file or an echo or write interactively. An interactive write is terminated with Ctrl-D.

The message can be directed to a specific session by appending the pseudo terminal identifier to the command:

```
$ echo "Log off now. I'm rebooting the system" | write user1 pts/3
```

Holding a conversation with another user

The talk command opens an interactive conversation between two users. The syntax for this is `$ talk user@host`.

The next command initiates a conversation with user2 on their workstation:

```
$ talk user2@workstation2.example.com
```

After typing the talk command, your terminal session is cleared and split into two windows. In one of the windows, you'll see text like this:

```
[Waiting for your party to respond]
```

The person you're trying to talk to will see a message like this:

```
Message from Talk_Daemon@workstation1.example.com
talk: connection requested by user1@workstation.example.com
talk: respond with talk user1@workstation1.example.com
```

When they invoke talk, their terminal session will also be cleared and split. What you type will appear in one window on their screen and what they type will appear on yours:

```
I need to reboot the database server.
How much longer will your processing take?
------------------------------------------------
90% complete. Should be just a couple more minutes.
```

Sending a message to all users

The **wall** (WriteALL) command broadcasts a message to all the users and terminal sessions:

```
$ cat message | wall
```

Or:

```
$ wall < message
Broadcast Message from slynux@slynux-laptop
        (/dev/pts/1) at 12:54 ...

This is a message
```

The message header shows who sent the message: which user and which host.

The write, talk, and wall commands only deliver messages between users when the **write message** option is enabled. Messages from the root are displayed regardless of the **write message** option.

The message option is usually enabled. The mesg command will enable or disable the receiving of messages:

```
# enable receiving messages
$ mesg y
# disable receiving messages
$ mesg n
```

The /proc filesystem

/proc is an in-memory pseudo filesystem that provides user-space access to many of the Linux kernel's internal data structures. Most pseudo files are read-only, but some, such as /proc/sys/net/ipv4/forward (described in Chapter 8, *The Old-Boy Network*), can be used to fine-tune your system's behavior.

How to do it...

The /proc directory contains several files and directories. You can view most files in /proc and their subdirectories with cat, less, or more. They are displayed as plain text.

Every process running on a system has a directory in /proc, named according to the process's PID.

Suppose Bash is running with PID 4295 (pgrep bash); in this case, /proc/4295 will exist. This folder will contain information about the process. The files under /proc/PID include:

- environ: This contains the environment variables associated with the process. cat /proc/4295/environ will display the environment variables passed to the process 4295.
- cwd: This is a symlink to the process's working directory.
- exe: This is a symlink to the process's executable:

```
$ readlink /proc/4295/exe
/bin/bash
```

- `fd`: This is the directory consisting of entries on file descriptors used by the process. The values 0, 1, and 2 are stdin, stdout, and stderr, respectively.
- `io`: This file displays the number of characters read or written by the process.

Gathering system information

Describing a computer system requires many sets of data. This data includes network information, the hostname, kernel version, Linux distribution name, CPU description, memory allocation, disk partitions, and more. This information can be retrieved from the command line.

How to do it...

1. The `hostname` and `uname` commands print the hostname of the current system:

   ```
   $ hostname
   ```

   Alternatively, they print the following:

   ```
   $ uname -n
   server.example.com
   ```

2. The `-a` option to `uname` prints details about the Linux kernel version, hardware architecture, and more:

   ```
   $ uname -a
   server.example.com 2.6.32-642.11.1.e16.x86_64 #1 SMP Fri Nov 18
   19:25:05 UTC 2016 x86_64 x86_64 GNU/Linux
   ```

3. The `-r` option limits the report to the kernel release:

   ```
   $ uname -r
   2.6.32-642.11.1.e16.x86_64
   ```

4. The `-m` option prints the machine type:

   ```
   $ uname -m
   x86_64
   ```

5. The `/proc/` directory holds information about the system, modules, and running processes. `/proc/cpuinfo` contains CPU details:

```
$ cat /proc/cpuinfo
processor     : 0
vendor_id     : GenuineIntel
cpu family    : 6
model         : 63
model name    : Intel(R)Core(TM)i7-5820K CPU @ 3.30GHz
...
```

If the processor has multiple cores, these lines will be repeated n times. To extract only one item of information, use `sed`. The fifth line contains the processor name:

```
$ cat /proc/cpuinfo | sed -n 5p
Intel(R)CORE(TM)i7-5820K CPU @ 3.3 GHz
```

6. `/proc/meminfo` contains information about the memory and current RAM usage:

```
$ cat /proc/meminfo
MemTotal:      32777552 kB
MemFree:       11895296 kB
Buffers:         634628 kB
...
```

The first line of `meminfo` shows the system's total RAM:

```
$ cat /proc/meminfo  | head -1
MemTotal:       1026096 kB
```

7. `/proc/partitions` describes the disk partitions:

```
$ cat /proc/partitions
major minor  #blocks   name
    8         0 976762584 sda
    8         1    512000 sda1
    8         2 976248832 sda2
...
```

The `fdisk` program edits a disk's partition table and also reports the current partition table. Run this command as `root`:

```
$ sudo fdisk -l
```

8. The `lshw` and `dmidecode` applications generate long and complete reports about your system. The report includes information about the motherboard, BIOS, CPU, memory slots, interface slots, disks, and more. These must be run as root. `dmidecode` is commonly available, but you may need to install `lshw`:

```
$ sudo lshw
description: Computer
product: 440BX
vendor: Intel
...

$ sudo dmidecode
SMBIOS 2.8 present
115 structures occupying 4160 bytes.
Table at 0xDCEE1000.

BIOS Information
    Vendor: American Megatrends Inc
...
```

Scheduling with a cron

The GNU/Linux system supports several utilities for scheduling tasks. The `cron` utility is the most widely supported. It allows you to schedule tasks to be run in the background at regular intervals. The `cron` utility uses a table (crontab) with a list of scripts or commands to be executed and the time when they are to be executed.

Cron is used to schedule system housekeeping tasks, such as performing backups, synchronizing the system clocking with `ntpdate`, and removing temporary files.

A regular user might use `cron` to schedule Internet downloads to happen late at night when their ISP allows drop caps and the available bandwidth is higher.

Getting ready

The `cron` scheduling utility comes with all GNU/Linux distributions. It scans the `cron` tables to determine whether a command is due to be run. Each user has their own `cron` table, which is a plain text file. The `crontab` command manipulates the `cron` table.

How to do it...

A `crontab` entry specifies the time to execute a command and the command to be executed. Each line in the `cron` table defines a single command. The command can either be a script or a binary application. When `cron` runs a task, it runs as the user who created the entry, but it does not source the user's `.bashrc`. If the task requires environment variables, they must be defined in the `crontab`.

Each cron table line consists of six space-delimited fields in the following order:

- `Minute` (0 - 59)
- `Hour` (0 - 23)
- `Day` (1 - 31)
- `Month` (1 - 12)
- `Weekday` (0 - 6)
- `COMMAND` (the script or command to be executed at the specified time)

The first five fields specify the time when an instance of the command is to be executed. Multiple values are delimited by commas (no spaces). A star signifies that any time or any day will match. A division sign schedules the event to trigger every /Y interval (*/5 in minutes means every five minutes).

1. Execute the `test.sh` script at the 2nd minute of all hours on all days:

   ```
   02 * * * * /home/slynux/test.sh
   ```

2. Execute **test.sh** on the 5th, 6th, and 7th hours on all days:

   ```
   00 5,6,7 * * * /home/slynux/test.sh
   ```

3. Execute `script.sh` every other hour on Sundays:

   ```
   00 */2 * * 0 /home/slynux/script.sh
   ```

4. Shut down the computer at 2 a.m. every day:

   ```
   00 02 * * * /sbin/shutdown -h
   ```

5. The `crontab` command can be used interactively or with prewritten files.

   Use the `-e` option with `crontab` to edit the `cron` table:

   ```
   $ crontab -e
   02 02 * * * /home/slynux/script.sh
   ```

   When `crontab -e` is entered, the default text editor (usually `vi`) is opened and the user can type the `cron` jobs and save them. The `cron` jobs will be scheduled and executed at specified time intervals.

6. The `crontab` command can be invoked from a script to replace the current crontab with a new one. Here's how you do this:

   - Create a text file (for example, `task.cron`) with the `cron` job in it and then run `crontab` with this filename as the command argument:

     ```
     $ crontab task.cron
     ```

   - Alternatively, specify the `cron` job as an inline function without creating a separate file. For example, refer to the following:

     ```
     $ crontab<<EOF
     02 * * * * /home/slynux/script.sh
     EOF
     ```

   The `cron` job needs to be written between `crontab<<EOF` and `EOF`.

How it works...

An asterisk (*) specifies that the command should be executed at every instance during the given time period. A `*` in the `Hour` field in the `cron` job will cause the command to be executed every hour. To execute the command at multiple instances of a time period, specify the time intervals separated by a comma in this time field. For example, to run the command at the 5th and 10th minute, enter `5,10` in the `Minute` field. A slash (divide by) symbol will cause the command to run as per a division of the time. For example `0-30/6` in the Minutes field will run a command every 5 minutes during the first half of each hour. The string `*/12` in the Hours field will run a command every other hour.

Cron jobs are executed as the user who created `crontab`. If you need to execute commands that require higher privileges, such as shutting down the computer, run the `crontab` command as root.

The commands specified in a cron job are written with the full path to the command. This is because cron does not source your .bashrc, so the environment in which a cron job is executed is different from the bash shell we execute on a terminal. Hence, the PATH environment variable may not be set. If your command requires certain environment variables, you must explicitly set them.

There's more...

The crontab command has more options.

Specifying environment variables

Many commands require environment variables to be set properly for execution. The cron command sets the SHELL variable to "/bin/sh" and also sets LOGNAME and HOME from the values in /etc/passwd. If other variables are required, they can be defined in the crontab. These can be defined for all tasks or individually for a single task.

If the MAILTO environment variable is defined, cron will send the output of the command to that user via an e-mail.

The crontab defines environment variables by inserting a line with a variable assignment statement in the user's cron table.

The following crontab defines an http_proxy environment variable to use a proxy server for Internet interactions:

```
http_proxy=http://192.168.0.3:3128
MAILTO=user@example.com
00 * * * * /home/slynux/download.sh
```

This format is supported by vixie-cron, used in Debian, Ubunto, and CentOS distributions. For other distributions, environment variables can be defined on a per-command basis:

```
00 * * * * http_proxy=http:192.168.0.2:3128;
/home/sylinux/download.sh
```

Running commands at system start-up/boot

Running specific commands when the system starts (or boots) is a common requirement. Some `cron` implementations support a `@reboot` time field to run a job during the reboot process. Note that this feature is not supported by all `cron` implementations and only root is allowed to use this feature on some systems. Now check out the following code:

```
@reboot command
```

This will run the command as your user at runtime.

Viewing the cron table

The `-l` option to crontab will list the current user's crontab:

```
$ crontab -l
02 05 * * * /home/user/disklog.sh
```

Adding the `-u` option will specify a user's crontab to view. You must be logged in as root to use the `-u` option:

```
# crontab -l -u slynux
09 10 * * * /home/slynux/test.sh
```

Removing the cron table

The `-r` option will remove the current user's cron table:

```
$ crontab -r
```

The `-u` option specifies the crontab to remove. You must be a root user to remove another user's crontab:

```
# crontab -u slynux -r
```

Database styles and uses

Linux supports many styles of databases, ranging from simple text files (`/etc/passwd`) to low level B-Tree databases (Berkely DB and bdb), lightweight SQL (sqlite), and fully featured relational database servers, such as Postgres, Oracle, and MySQL.

One rule of thumb for selecting a database style is to use the least complex system that works for your application. A text file and `grep` is sufficient for a small database when the fields are known and fixed.

Some applications require references. For example, a database of books and authors should be created with two tables, one for books and one for the authors, to avoid duplicating the author information for each book.

If the table is read more often than it's modified, then SQLite is a good choice. This database engine does not require a server, which makes it portable and easy to embed in another application (as Firefox does).

If the database is modified frequently by multiple tasks (for example, a webstore's inventory system), then one of the RDBMS systems, such as Postgres, Oracle, or MySQL, is appropriate.

Getting ready

You can create a text-based database with standard shell tools. SqlLite is commonly installed by default; the executable is `sqlite3`. You'll need to install MySQL, Oracle, and Postgres. The next section will explain how to install MySQL. You can download Oracle from www.oracle.com. Postgres is usually available with your package manager.

How to do it...

A text file database can be built with common shell tools.

To create an address list, create a file with one line per address and fields separated by a known character. In this case, the character is a tilde (~):

```
first last~Street~City, State~Country~Phone~
```

For instance:

```
Joe User~123 Example Street~AnyTown, District~1-123-123-1234~
```

Then add a function to find lines that match a pattern and translate each line into a human-friendly format:

```
function  addr {
    grep $1 $HOME/etc/addr.txt | sed 's/~/\n/g'
}
```

When in use, this would resemble the following:

```
$ addr Joe
Joe User
123 Example Street
AnyTown District
1-123-123-1234
```

There's more...

The SQLite, Postgres, Oracle, and MySQL database applications provide a more powerful database paradigm known as relational databases. A relational database stores relations between tables, for example, the relation between a book and its author.

A common way to interact with a relational database is using SQL. This language is supported by SQLite, Postgres, Oracle, MySQL, and other database engines.

SQL is a rich language. You can read books devoted to it. Luckily, you just need a few commands to use SQL effectively.

Creating a table

Tables are defined with the CREATE TABLE command:

```
CREATE TABLE tablename (field1 type1, field2 type2,...);
```

The next line creates a table of books and authors:

```
CREATE TABLE book (title STRING, author STRING);
```

Inserting a row into an SQL database

The insert command will insert a row of data into the database.

```
INSERT INTO table (columns) VALUES (val1, val2,...);
```

The following command inserts the book you're currently reading:

```
INSERT INTO book (title, author) VALUES ('Linux Shell Scripting
Cookbook', 'Clif Flynt');
```

Selecting rows from a SQL database

The select command will select all the rows that match a test:

```
SELECT fields FROM table WHERE test;
```

This command will select book titles that include the word Shell from the book table:

```
SELECT title FROM book WHERE title like '%Shell%';
```

Writing and reading SQLite databases

SQLite is a lightweight database engine that is used in applications ranging from Android apps and Firefox to US Navy inventory systems. Because of the range of use, there are more applications running SQLite than any other database.

A SQLite database is a single file that is accessed by one or more database engines. The database engine is a C library that can be linked to an application; it is loaded as a library to a scripting language, such as TCL, Python, or Perl, or run as a standalone program.

The standalone application sqlite3 is the easiest to use within a shell script.

Getting ready

The sqlite3 executable may not be installed in your installation. If it is not, it can be installed by loading the sqlite3 package with your package manager.

For Debian and Ubuntu, use the following:

```
apt-get install sqlite3 libsqlite3-dev
```

For Red Hat, SuSE, Fedora, and Centos, use the following:

```
yum install sqlite sqlite-devel
```

How to do it...

The sqlite3 command is an interactive database engine that connects to a SQLite database and supports the process of creating tables, inserting data, querying tables, and so on.

The syntax of the `sqlite3` command is this:

```
sqlite3 databaseName
```

If the `databaseName` file exists, `sqlite3` will open it. If the file does not exist, `sqlite3` will create an empty database. In this recipe, we will create a table, insert one row, and retrieve that entry:

```
# Create a books database
$ sqlite3 books.db
sqlite> CREATE TABLE books (title string, author string);
sqlite> INSERT INTO books (title, author) VALUES ('Linux Shell
Scripting Cookbook', 'Clif Flynt');
sqlite> SELECT * FROM books WHERE author LIKE '%Flynt%';
Linux Shell Scripting Cookbook|Clif Flynt
```

How it works...

The `sqlite3` application creates an empty database named `books.db` and displays the `sqlite>` prompt to accept SQL commands.

The `CREATE TABLE` command creates a table with two fields: title and author.

The `INSERT` command inserts one book into the database. Strings in SQL are delimited with single quotes.

The `SELECT` command retrieves the rows that match the test. The percentage symbol (`%`) is the SQL wildcard, similar to a star (`*`) in the shell.

There's more...

A shell script can use `sqlite3` to access a database and provide a simple user interface. The next script implements the previous address database with `sqlite` instead of a flat text file. It provides three commands:

- `init`: This is to create the database
- `insert`: This is to add a new row
- `query`: This is to select rows that match a query

In use, it would look like this:

```
$> dbaddr.sh init
$> dbaddr.sh insert 'Joe User' '123-1234' 'user@example.com'
$> dbaddr.sh query name Joe
Joe User
123-1234
user@example.com
```

The following script implements this database application:

```bash
#!/bin/bash
# Create a command based on the first argument

case $1 in
  init )
    cmd="CREATE TABLE address \
      (name string, phone string, email string);" ;;
  query )
    cmd="SELECT name, phone, email FROM address \
      WHERE $2 LIKE '$3';";;
  insert )
    cmd="INSERT INTO address (name, phone, email) \
      VALUES ( '$2', '$3', '$4' );";;
esac

# Send the command to sqlite3 and reformat the output

echo $cmd | sqlite3 $HOME/addr.db | sed 's/|/\n/g'
```

This script uses the case statement to select the SQL command string. The other command-line arguments are replaced with this string and the string is sent to `sqlite3` to be evaluated. The `$1`, `$2`, `$3`, and `$4` are the first, second, third, and fourth arguments, respectively, to the script.

Writing and reading a MySQL database from Bash

MySQL is a widely used database management system. In 2009, Oracle acquired SUN and with that the MySQL database. The MariaDB package is a fork of the MySQL package that is independent of Oracle. MariaDB can access MySQL databases, but MySQL engines cannot always access MariaDB databases.

Both MySQL and MariaDB have interfaces for many languages, including PHP, Python, C++, Tcl, and more. All of them use the `mysql` command to provide an interactive session in order to access a database. This is the easiest way for a shell script to interact with a MySQL database. These examples should work with either MySQL or MariaDB.

A bash script can convert a text or **Comma-Separated Values (CSV)** file into MySQL tables and rows. For example, we can read all the e-mail addresses stored in a guestbook program's database by running a query from the shell script.

The next set of scripts demonstrates how to insert the contents of the file into a database table of students and generate a report while ranking each student within the department.

Getting ready

MySQL and MariaDB are not always present in the base Linux distribution. They can be installed as either `mysql-server` and `mysql-client` or the `mariadb-server` package. The MariaDB distribution uses MySQL as a command and is sometimes installed when the MySQL package is requested.

MySQL supports a username and password for authentication. You will be prompted for a password during the installation.

Use the `mysql` command to create a new database on a fresh installation. After you create the database with the `CREATE DATABASE` command, you can select it for use with the use command. Once a database is selected, standard SQL commands can be used to create tables and insert data:

```
$> mysql -user=root -password=PASSWORD

Welcome to the MariaDB monitor.  Commands end with ; or \g.
Your MariaDB connection id is 44
Server version: 10.0.29-MariaDB-0+deb8u1 (Debian)

Copyright (c) 2000, 2016, Oracle, MariaDB Corporation Ab and others.

Type 'help;' or '\h' for help. Type '\c' to clear the current input
statement.

MariaDB [(none)]> CREATE DATABASE test1;
Query OK, 1 row affected (0.00 sec)
MariaDB [(none)]> use test1;
```

The `quit` command or Ctrl-D will terminate a `mysql` interactive session.

How to do it...

This recipe consists of three scripts: one to create a database and table, one to insert student data, and one to read and display data from the table.

Create the database and table script:

```bash
#!/bin/bash
#Filename: create_db.sh
#Description: Create MySQL database and table

USER="user"
PASS="user"

mysql -u $USER -p$PASS <<EOF 2> /dev/null
CREATE DATABASE students;
EOF

[ $? -eq 0 ] && echo Created DB || echo DB already exist
mysql -u $USER -p$PASS students <<EOF 2> /dev/null
CREATE TABLE students(
id int,
name varchar(100),
mark int,
dept varchar(4)
);
EOF

[ $? -eq 0 ] && echo Created table students || \
    echo Table students already exist

mysql -u $USER -p$PASS students <<EOF
DELETE FROM students;
EOF
```

This script inserts data in the table:

```bash
#!/bin/bash
#Filename: write_to_db.sh
#Description: Read from CSV and write to MySQLdb

USER="user"
PASS="user"

if [ $# -ne 1 ];
then
  echo $0 DATAFILE
  echo
```

```
    exit 2
fi

data=$1

while read line;
do

  oldIFS=$IFS
  IFS=,
  values=($line)
  values[1]="\"`echo ${values[1]} | tr ' ' '#'`\""
  values[3]="\"`echo ${values[3]}`\""


  query=`echo ${values[@]} | tr ' #' ', '`
  IFS=$oldIFS

  mysql -u $USER -p$PASS students <<EOF
INSERT INTO students VALUES($query);
EOF

done< $data
echo Wrote data into DB
```

The last script queries the database and generates a report:

```
#!/bin/bash
#Filename: read_db.sh
#Description: Read from the database

USER="user"
PASS="user"

depts=`mysql -u $USER -p$PASS students <<EOF | tail -n +2
SELECT DISTINCT dept FROM students;
EOF`

for d in $depts;
do

echo Department : $d

result="`mysql -u $USER -p$PASS students <<EOF
SET @i:=0;
SELECT @i:=@i+1 as rank,name,mark FROM students WHERE dept="$d" ORDER BY
mark DESC;
EOF`"
```

```
echo "$result"
echo

done
```

The data for the input CSV file (`studentdata.csv`) will resemble this:

```
1,Navin M,98,CS
2,Kavya N,70,CS
3,Nawaz O,80,CS
4,Hari S,80,EC
5,Alex M,50,EC
6,Neenu J,70,EC
7,Bob A,30,EC
8,Anu M,90,AE
9,Sruthi,89,AE
10,Andrew,89,AE
```

Execute the scripts in the following sequence:

```
$ ./create_db.sh
Created DB
Created table students

$ ./write_to_db.sh studentdat.csv
Wrote data into DB

$ ./read_db.sh
Department : CS
rank   name   mark
1    Navin M  98
2    Nawaz O  80
3    Kavya N  70

Department : EC
rank   name   mark
1    Hari S  80
2    Neenu J 70
3    Alex M  50
4    Bob A   30

Department : AE
rank   name   mark
1    Anu M    90
2    Sruthi   89
3    Andrew   89
```

How it works...

The first script, `create_db.sh`, creates a database called `students` and a table named `students` inside it. The `mysql` command is used for MySQL manipulations. The `mysql` command specifies the username with `-u` and the password with `-pPASSWORD`. The variables `USER` and `PASS` are used to store the username and password.

The other command argument for the `mysql` command is the database name. If a database name is specified as an argument to the `mysql` command, it will use that database; otherwise, we have to explicitly define the database to be used with the **use** `database_name` command.

The `mysql` command accepts the queries to be executed through standard input (`stdin`). A convenient way of supplying multiple lines through `stdin` is using the `<<EOF` method. The text that appears between `<<EOF` and `EOF` is passed to `mysql` as standard input.

The `CREATE DATABASE` and `CREATE TABLE` commands redirect `stderr` to `/dev/null` to prevent the display of error messages. The script checks the exit status for the `mysql` command stored in `$?` to determine whether a failure has occurred; it assumes that a failure occurs because a table or database already exists. If the database or table already exists, a message is displayed to notify the user; otherwise, the database and table are created.

The `write_to_db.sh` script accepts the filename of the student data CSV file. It reads each line of the CSV file in the `while` loop. On each iteration, a line from the CSV file is read and reformatted into a SQL command. The script stores the data from the comma-separated line in an array. Array assignment is done in this form: `array=(val1 val2 val3)`. Here, the space character is the **InternalFieldSeparator (IFS)**. This data has comma-separated values. By changing the IFS to a comma, we can easily assign values to the array (`IFS=,`).

The data elements in the comma-separated line are `id`, `name`, `mark`, and `department`. The `id` and `mark` values are integers, while `name` and `dept` are strings that must be quoted.

The name could contain space characters that would conflict with the IFS. The script replaces the space in the name with a character (#) and restores it after formulating the query.

To quote the strings, the values in the array are reassigned with a prefix and suffixed with `\"`. The `tr` command substitutes each space in the name with #.

Finally, the query is formed by replacing the space character with a comma and replacing #
with a space. Then, SQL's INSERT command is executed.

The third script, read_db.sh, generates a list of students for each department ordered by
rank. The first query finds distinct names of departments. We use a while loop to iterate
through each department and run the query to display student details in the order of
highest marks obtained. SET @i=0 is an SQL construct to set this: i=0. On each row, it is
incremented and displayed as the rank of the student.

User administration scripts

GNU/Linux is a multiuser operating system that allows many users to log in and perform
activities at the same time. Administration tasks involving user management include setting
the default shell for the user, adding a user to a group, disabling a shell account, adding
new users, removing users, setting a password, setting an expiry date for a user account,
and so on. This recipe demonstrates a user management tool to handle these tasks.

How to do it...

This script performs common user management tasks:

```bash
#!/bin/bash
#Filename: user_adm.sh
#Description: A user administration tool

function usage()
{
  echo Usage:
  echo Add a new user
  echo $0 -adduser username password
  echo
  echo Remove an existing user
  echo $0 -deluser username
  echo
  echo Set the default shell for the user
  echo $0 -shell username SHELL_PATH
  echo
  echo Suspend a user account
  echo $0 -disable username
  echo
  echo Enable a suspended user account
  echo $0 -enable username
```

```
   echo
   echo Set expiry date for user account
   echo $0 -expiry DATE
   echo
   echo Change password for user account
   echo $0 -passwd username
   echo
   echo Create a new user group
   echo $0 -newgroup groupname
   echo
   echo Remove an existing user group
   echo $0 -delgroup groupname
   echo
   echo Add a user to a group
   echo $0 -addgroup username groupname
   echo
   echo Show details about a user
   echo $0 -details username
   echo
   echo Show usage
   echo $0 -usage
   echo

   exit
}

if [ $UID -ne 0 ];
then
   echo Run $0 as root.
   exit 2
fi

case $1 in

   -adduser)  [ $# -ne 3 ] && usage ; useradd $2 -p $3 -m ;;
   -deluser)  [ $# -ne 2 ] && usage ; deluser $2 --remove-all-files;;
   -shell)    [ $# -ne 3 ] && usage ; chsh $2 -s $3 ;;
   -disable)  [ $# -ne 2 ] && usage ; usermod -L $2 ;;
   -enable)   [ $# -ne 2 ] && usage ; usermod -U $2  ;;
   -expiry)   [ $# -ne 3 ] && usage ; chage $2 -E $3 ;;
   -passwd)   [ $# -ne 2 ] && usage ; passwd $2 ;;
   -newgroup) [ $# -ne 2 ] && usage ; addgroup $2 ;;
   -delgroup) [ $# -ne 2 ] && usage ; delgroup $2 ;;
   -addgroup) [ $# -ne 3 ] && usage ; addgroup $2 $3 ;;
   -details)  [ $# -ne 2 ] && usage ; finger $2 ; chage -l $2 ;;
   -usage) usage ;;
   *) usage ;;
esac
```

A sample output resembles the following:

```
# ./user_adm.sh -details test
Login: test                     Name:
Directory: /home/test                     Shell: /bin/sh
Last login Tue Dec 21 00:07 (IST) on pts/1 from localhost
No mail.
No Plan.
Last password change            : Dec 20, 2010
Password expires      : never
Password inactive     : never
Account expires             : Oct 10, 2010
Minimum number of days between password change    : 0
Maximum number of days between password change    : 99999
Number of days of warning before password expires  : 7
```

How it works...

The `user_adm.sh` script performs several common user management tasks. The `usage()` text explains how to use the script when the user provides incorrect parameters or includes the `-usage` parameter. A case statement parses command arguments and executes the appropriate commands.

The valid command options for the `user_adm.sh` script are: `-adduser`, `-deluser`, `-shell`, `-disable`, `-enable`, `-expiry`, `-passwd`, `-newgroup`, `-delgroup`, `-addgroup`, `-details`, and `-usage`. When the `*)` case is matched, it means no option was recognized; hence, `usage()` is invoked.

Run this script as the root. It confirms the user ID (the root's user ID is 0) before the arguments are examined.

When an argument is matched, the `[ $# -ne 3 ] &&` test usage checks the number of arguments. If the number of command arguments does not match the required number, the `usage()` function is invoked and the script exits.

These options are supported by the following scripts:

- `-useradd`: The `useradd` command creates a new user:

    useradd USER -p PASSWORD -m

- The `-m` option creates the home directory.

- `-deluser`: The `deluser` command removes the user:

    deluser USER --remove-all-files

- The `--remove-all-files` option removes all the files associated with the user, including the `home` directory.
- `-shell`: The `chsh` command changes the default shell of the user:

    chsh USER -s SHELL

- `-disable` and `-enable`: The `usermod` command manipulates several attributes related to user accounts. `usermod -L USER` locks the user account and `usermod -U USER` unlocks the user account.
- `-expiry`: The `change` command manipulates user account expiry information:

    chage -E DATE

These options are supported:

- `-m MIN_DAYS`: This sets the minimum number of days between password changes to `MIN_DAYS`

- `-M MAX_DAYS`: This sets the maximum number of days during which a password is valid
- `-W WARN_DAYS`: This sets the number of days to provide a warning before a password change is required
- `-passwd`: The `passwd` command changes a user's password:

    passwd USER

The command will prompt to enter a new password:

- `-newgroup` and `-addgroup`: The `addgroup` command adds a new user group to the system:

    addgroup GROUP

If you include a username, it will add this user to a group:

```
addgroup USER GROUP
-delgroup
```

The delgroup command removes a user group:

```
delgroup GROUP
```

- -details: The finger USER command displays user information, including the home directory, last login time, default shell, and so on. The chage -1 command displays the user account expiry information.

Bulk image resizing and format conversion

All of us download photos from our phones and cameras. Before we e-mail an image or post it to the Web, we may need to resize it or perhaps change the format. We can use scripts to modify these image files in bulk. This recipe describes recipes for image management.

Getting ready

The convert command from the **ImageMagick** suite contains tools for manipulating images. It supports many image formats and conversion options. Most GNU/Linux distributions don't include ImageMagick by default. You need to manually install the package. For more information, point your web browser at www.imagemagick.org.

How to do it...

The convert program will convert a file from one image format to another:

```
$ convert INPUT_FILE OUTPUT_FILE
```

Here's an example of this:

```
$ convert file1.jpg file1.png
```

We can resize an image by specifying the scale percentage or the width and height of the output image. To resize an image by specifying WIDTH or HEIGHT, use this:

```
$ convert imageOrig.png -resize WIDTHxHEIGHT imageResized.png
```

Here's an example of this:

```
$ convert photo.png -resize 1024x768 wallpaper.png
```

If either WIDTH or HEIGHT is missing, then whatever is missing will be automatically calculated to preserve the image aspect ratio:

```
$ convert image.png -resize WIDTHx image.png
```

Here's an example of this:

```
$ convert image.png -resize 1024x image.png
```

To resize the image by specifying the percentage scale factor, use this:

```
$ convert image.png -resize "50%" image.png
```

This script will perform a set of operations on all the images in a directory:

```
#!/bin/bash
#Filename: image_help.sh
#Description: A script for image management

if [ $# -ne 4 -a $# -ne 6 -a $# -ne 8 ];
then
  echo Incorrect number of arguments
  exit 2
fi

while [ $# -ne 0 ];
do

  case $1 in
  -source) shift; source_dir=$1 ; shift ;;
  -scale) shift; scale=$1 ; shift ;;
  -percent) shift; percent=$1 ; shift ;;
  -dest) shift ; dest_dir=$1 ; shift ;;
  -ext) shift ; ext=$1 ; shift ;;
  *) echo Wrong parameters; exit 2 ;;
  esac;

done
```

```
for img in `echo $source_dir/*` ;
do
  source_file=$img
  if [[ -n $ext ]];
  then
    dest_file=${img%.*}.$ext
  else
    dest_file=$img
  fi

  if [[ -n $dest_dir ]];
  then
    dest_file=${dest_file##*/}
    dest_file="$dest_dir/$dest_file"
  fi

  if [[ -n $scale ]];
  then
    PARAM="-resize $scale"
  elif [[ -n $percent ]];    then
    PARAM="-resize $percent%"
  fi

  echo Processing file : $source_file
  convert $source_file $PARAM $dest_file

done
```

The following example scales the images in the `sample_dir` directory to `20%`:

```
$ ./image_help.sh -source sample_dir -percent 20%
Processing file :sample/IMG_4455.JPG
Processing file :sample/IMG_4456.JPG
Processing file :sample/IMG_4457.JPG
Processing file :sample/IMG_4458.JPG
```

To scale images to a width of `1024`, use this:

```
$ ./image_help.sh -source sample_dir -scale 1024x
```

To scale and convert files into a specified destination directory, use this:

```
# newdir is the new destination directory
$ ./image_help.sh -source sample -scale 50% -ext png -dest newdir
```

How it works...

The preceding `image_help.sh` script accepts these arguments:

- `-source`: This specifies the source directory of the images.
- `-dest`: This specifies the destination directory of the converted image files. If `-dest` is not specified, the destination directory will be the same as the source directory.
- `-ext`: This specifies the target file format for conversions.
- `-percent`: This specifies the percentage of scaling.
- `-scale`: This specifies the scaled width and height.
- Both the `-percent` and `-scale` parameters may not appear.
- The script starts by checking the number of command arguments. Either four, six, or eight parameters are valid.

The command line is parsed with a `while` loop and the case statement and values are assigned to appropriate variables. `$#` is a special variable that contains the number of arguments. The `shift` command shifts the command arguments one position to the left. With this, every time the shifting happens, we can access the next command argument as `$1` rather than using `$1`, `$2`, `$3`, and so on.

The case statement is like a switch statement in the C programming language. When a case is matched, the corresponding statements are executed. Each match statement is terminated with `;;`. Once all the parameters are parsed into the variables `percent`, `scale`, `source_dir`, `ext`, and `dest_dir`, a `for` loop iterates through each file in the source directory and the file is converted.

Several tests are done within the `for` loop to fine-tune the conversion.

If the variable `ext` is defined (if `-ext` is given in the command argument), the extension of the destination file is changed from `source_file.extension` to `source_file.$ext`.

If the `-dest` parameter is provided, the destination file path is modified by replacing the directory in the source path with the destination directory.

If -scale or -percent are specified, the resize parameter (`-resize widthx` or `-resize perc%`) is added to the command.

After the parameters are evaluated, the `convert` command is executed with proper arguments.

See also

- The *Slicing filenames based on extensions* recipe in `Chapter 2`, *Have a Good Command*, explains how to extract a portion of the filename

Taking screenshots from the terminal

As GUI applications proliferate, it becomes important to take screenshots, both to document your actions and to report unexpected results. Linux supports several tools for grabbing screenshots.

Getting ready

This section will describe the **xwd** application and a tool from ImageMagick, which was used in the previous recipe. The xwd application is usually installed with the base GUI. You can install ImageMagick using your package manager.

How to do it...

The xwd program extracts visual information from a window, converts it into X Window Dump format, and prints the data to `stdout`. This output can be redirected to a file, and the file can be converted into GIF, PNG, or JPEG format, as shown in the previous recipe.

When xwd is invoked, it changes your cursor to a crosshair. When you move this crosshair to an X Window and click on it, the window is grabbed:

```
$ xwd >step1.xwd
```

ImageMagick's `import` command supports more options for taking screenshots:

To take a screenshot of the whole screen, use this:

```
$ import -window root screenshot.png
```

You can manually select a region and take a screenshot of it using this:

```
$ import screenshot.png
```

To take a screenshot of a specific window, use this:

```
$ import -window window_id screenshot.png
```

The `xwininfo` command will return a window ID. Run the command and click on the window you want. Then, pass this `window_id` value to the `-window` option of `import`.

Managing multiple terminals from one

SSH sessions, Konsoles, and xterms are heavyweight solutions for applications you want to run for a long time, but they perform a check infrequently (such as monitoring log files or disk usage).

The GNU screen utility creates multiple virtual screens in a terminal session. The tasks you start in a virtual screen continue to run when the screen is hidden.

Getting ready

To achieve this, we will use a utility called **GNU screen**. If the screen is not installed on your distribution by default, install it using the package manager:

```
apt-get install screen
```

How to do it...

1. Once the screen utility has created a new window, all the keystrokes go to the task running in that window, except Control-A (*Ctrl-A*), which marks the start of a screen command.
2. **Creating screen windows**: To create a new screen, run the command screen from your shell. You will see a welcome message with information about the screen. Press Space or Return to return to the shell prompt. To create a new virtual terminal, press *Ctrl + A* and then *C* (these are case-sensitive) or type screen again.
3. **Viewing a list of open windows**: While running the screen, pressing *Ctrl+A* followed by a quote (") will list your terminal sessions.

4. **Switching between windows**: The keystrokes *Ctrl* + *A* and *Ctrl* + *N* display the next window and *Ctrl* + *A* and *Ctrl* + *P* the previous window.

5. **Attaching to and detaching screens**: The screen command supports saving and loading screen sessions, called detaching and attaching in screen terminology. To detach from the current screen session, press *Ctrl* + *A* and *Ctrl* + *D*. To attach to an existing screen when starting the screen, use:

```
screen -r -d
```

6. This tells the screen to attach the last screen session. If you have more than one detached session, the screen will output a list; then use:

```
screen -r -d PID
```

Here, `PID` is the PID of the screen session you want to attach.

11
Tracing the Clues

In this chapter, we will cover the following topics:

- Tracing packets with `tcpdump`
- Finding packets with `ngrep`
- Tracing network routes with `ip`
- Tracing system calls with `strace`
- Tracing dynamic library functions with `ltrace`

Introduction

Nothing happens without a trace. On a Linux system, we can trace events via the log files discussed in `Chapter 9`, *Put On The Monitor's Cap*. The `top` command shows which programs use the most CPU time, and `watch`, `df`, and `du` let us monitor disk usage.

This chapter will describe ways to get more information about network packets, CPU usage, disk usage, and dynamic library calls.

Tracing packets with tcpdump

Just knowing which applications are using a given port may not be sufficient information to trace down a problem. Sometimes you need to check the data that is being transferred as well.

Getting ready

You need to be a root user to run `tcpdump`. The `tcpdump` application may not be installed in your system by default. So install it with your package manager:

```
$ sudo apt-get install tcpdump
$ sudo yum install libpcap tcpdump
```

How to do it...

The `tcpdump` application is the frontend to Wireshark and other network sniffer programs. The GUI interface supports many of the options we'll describe shortly.

This application's default behavior is to display every packet seen on the primary Ethernet link. The format of a packet report is as follows:

```
TIMESTAMP SRC_IP:PORT > DEST_IP:PORT: NAME1 VALUE1, NAME2 VALUE2,...
```

The name-value pairs include:

- `Flags`: The flags associated with this packet are as follows:
    - The term `S` stands for **SYN** (**Start Connection**)
    - The term `F` stands for **FIN** (**Finish Connection**)
    - The term `P` stands for **PUSH** (**Push data**)
    - The term `R` stands for **RST** (**Reset Connection**)
    - The period `.` means there are no flags
- `seq`: This refers to the sequence number of the packet. It will be echoed in an ACK to identify the packet being acknowledged.
- `ack`: This refers to the acknowledgement that indicates a packet is received. The value is the sequence number from a previous packet.
- `win`: This indicates the size of the buffer at the destination.
- `options`: This refers to the TCP options defined for this packet. It is reported as a comma-separated set of key-value pairs.

The following output shows requests from a Windows computer to the SAMBA server intermingled with a DNS request. The intermingling of different packets from different sources and applications makes it difficult to track a specific application or traffic on a given host. However, the `tcpdump` command has flags that make our life easier:

```
$ tcpdump
22:00:25.269277 IP 192.168.1.40.49182 > 192.168.1.2.microsoft-ds: Flags
[P.], seq 3265172834:3265172954, ack 850195805, win 257, length 120SMB
PACKET: SMBtrans2 (REQUEST)

22:00:25.269417 IP 192.168.1.44.33150 > 192.168.1.7.domain: 13394+ PTR?
2.1.168.192.in-addr.arpa. (42)

22:00:25.269917 IP 192.168.1.2.microsoft-ds > 192.168.1.40.49182: Flags
[.], ack 120, win 1298, length 0

22:00:25.269927 IP 192.168.1.2.microsoft-ds > 192.168.1.40.49182: Flags
[P.], seq 1:105, ack 120, win 1298, length 104SMB PACKET: SMBtrans2 (REPLY)
```

The `-w` flag sends the `tcpdump` output to a file instead of the terminal. The output format is in binary form, which can be read with the `-r` flag. Sniffing packets must be done with root privileges, but displaying the results from a previously saved file can be done as a normal user.

By default, `tcpdump` runs and collects data until it is killed using Ctrl-C or **SIGTERM**. The `-c` flag limits the number of packets:

```
# tcpdump -w /tmp/tcpdump.raw -c 50
tcpdump: listening on eth0, link-type EN10MB (Ethernet), capture size 65535
bytes
50 packets captured
50 packets received by filter
0 packets dropped by kernel
```

As a rule, we want to examine the activity on a single host, perhaps a single application.

The last values of the `tcpdump` command line form an expression that helps us filter packets. The expression is a set of key-value pairs with modifiers and Boolean operators. The next recipes demonstrate using filters.

Displaying only HTTP packets

The `port` key displays only the packets sent to or from a given port:

```
$ tcpdump -r /tmp/tcpdump.raw port http
```

```
reading from file /tmp/tcpdump.raw, link-type EN10MB (Ethernet)
10:36:50.586005 IP 192.168.1.44.59154 > ord38s04-in-f3.1e100.net.http:
Flags [.], ack 3779320903, win 431, options [nop,nop,TS val 2061350532 ecr
3014589802], length 0

10:36:50.586007 IP ord38s04-in-f3.1e100.net.http > 192.168.1.44.59152:
Flags [.], ack 1, win 350, options [nop,nop,TS val 3010640112 ecr
2061270277], length 0
```

Displaying only HTTP packets generated by this host

If you are trying to track web usage on your network, you may only need to see the packets generated on your site. The `src` modifier specifies only these packets, with given values, in the source file. The `dst` modifier specifies only the destination:

```
$ tcpdump -r /tmp/tcpdump.raw src port http
reading from file /tmp/tcpdump.raw, link-type EN10MB (Ethernet)

10:36:50.586007 IP ord38s04-in-f3.1e100.net.http > 192.168.1.44.59152:
Flags [.], ack 1, win 350, options [nop,nop,TS val 3010640112 ecr
2061270277], length 0
10:36:50.586035 IP ord38s04-in-f3.1e100.net.http > 192.168.1.44.59150:
Flags [.], ack 1, win 350, options [nop,nop,TS val 3010385005 ecr
2061270277], length 0
```

Viewing the packet payload as well as headers

If you need to track down the host that's swamping the network, all you need is headers. If you are trying to debug a web or database application, you probably need to see the contents of the packets as well as the headers.

The `-X` flag will include the packet data in the output.

The host keyword can be combined with port information to limit the report to data to and from a given host.

The two tests are connected with **and** to perform the Boolean **and** operation, and they report only those packets that are to or from noucorp.com and/or the HTTP server. The sample output shows the start of a GET request and the server's reply:

```
$ tcpdump -X -r /tmp/tcpdump.raw host noucorp.com and port http
reading from file /tmp/tcpdump.raw, link-type EN10MB (Ethernet)
11:12:04.708905 IP 192.168.1.44.35652 > noucorp.com.http: Flags [P.], seq
2939551893:2939552200, ack 1031497919, win 501, options [nop,nop,TS val
```

```
2063464654 ecr 28236429], length 307
   0x0000:  4500 0167 1e54 4000 4006 70a5 c0a8 012c   E..g.T@.@.p....,
   0x0010:  98a0 5023 8b44 0050 af36 0095 3d7b 68bf   ..P#.D.P.6..={h.
   0x0020:  8018 01f5 abf1 0000 0101 080a 7afd f8ce   ............z...
   0x0030:  01ae da8d 4745 5420 2f20 4854 5450 2f31   ....GET./.HTTP/1
   0x0040:  2e31 0d0a 486f 7374 3a20 6e6f 7563 6f72   .1..Host:.noucor
   0x0050:  702e 636f 6d0d 0a55 7365 722d 4167 656e   p.com..User-Agen
   0x0060:  743a 204d 6f7a 696c 6c61 2f35 2e30 2028   t:.Mozilla/5.0.(
   0x0070:  5831 313b 204c 696e 7578 2078 3836 5f36   X11;.Linux.x86_6
   0x0080:  343b 2072 763a 3435 2e30 2920 4765 636b   4;.rv:45.0).Geck
   0x0090:  6f2f 3230 3130 3031 3031 2046 6972 6566   o/20100101.Firef
   0x00a0:  6f78 2f34 352e 300d 0a41 6363 6570 743a   ox/45.0..Accept:
...
11:12:04.731343 IP noucorp.com.http > 192.168.1.44.35652: Flags [.], seq
1:1449, ack 307, win 79, options [nop,nop,TS val 28241838 ecr 2063464654],
length 1448
   0x0000:  4500 05dc 0491 4000 4006 85f3 98a0 5023   E.....@.@.....P#
   0x0010:  c0a8 012c 0050 8b44 3d7b 68bf af36 01c8   ...,.P.D={h..6..
   0x0020:  8010 004f a7b4 0000 0101 080a 01ae efae   ...O............
   0x0030:  7afd f8ce 4854 5450 2f31 2e31 2032 3030   z...HTTP/1.1.200
   0x0040:  2044 6174 6120 666f 6c6c 6f77 730d 0a44   .Data.follows..D
   0x0050:  6174 653a 2054 6875 2c20 3039 2046 6562   ate:.Thu,.09.Feb
   0x0060:  2032 3031 3720 3136 3a31 323a 3034 2047   .2017.16:12:04.G
   0x0070:  4d54 0d0a 5365 7276 6572 3a20 5463 6c2d   MT..Server:.Tcl-
   0x0080:  5765 6273 6572 7665 722f 332e 352e 3220   Webserver/3.5.2.
```

How it works...

The `tcpdump` application sets a promiscuous flag that causes the NIC to pass all the packets to the processor. It does this instead of filtering only the ones that pertain to this host. This flag allows the recording of any packet on the physical network that the host is connected to, not just the packets intended for this host.

This application is used to trace issues with overloaded network segments, hosts that generate unexpected traffic, network looping, faulty NICs, malformed packets, and more.

With the `-w` and `-r` option, `tcpdump` saves data in raw format, allowing you to examine it later as a regular user. For example, if there are excessive network packet collisions at 3:00 A.M., you can set up a `cron` job to run `tcpdump` at 3:00 A.M. and then examine the data during normal working hours.

Finding packets with ngrep

The `ngrep` application is a cross between `grep` and `tcpdump`. It watches network ports and displays packets that match a pattern. You must have root privileges to run `ngrep`.

Getting ready

You may not have the `ngrep` package installed. However, it can be installed with most package managers:

```
# apt-get install ngrep
# yum install ngrep
```

How to do it...

The `ngrep` application accepts a pattern to watch for (such as `grep`), a filter string (such as `tcpdump`), and many command-line flags to fine-tune its behavior.

The following example watches the traffic on port 80 and reports any packets with the string `Linux` in them:

```
$> ngrep -q -c 64 Linux port 80
interface: eth0 (192.168.1.0/255.255.255.0)
filter: ( port 80 ) and (ip or ip6)
match: Linux

T 192.168.1.44:36602 -> 152.160.80.35:80 [AP]
  GET /Training/linux_detail/ HTTP/1.1..Host: noucorp.com..Us
  er-Agent: Mozilla/5.0 (X11; Linux x86_64; rv:45.0) Gecko/20
  100101 Firefox/45.0..Accept: text/html,application/xhtml+xm
  l,application/xml;q=0.9,*/*;q=0.8..Accept-Language: en-US,e
  n;q=0.5..Accept-Encoding: gzip, deflate..Referer: http://no
  ucorp.com/Training/..Connection: keep-alive..Cache-Control:
   max-age=0....
```

The `-q` flag directs `ngrep` to only print the headers and payloads.

The `-c` flag defines the number of columns to use for payload data. By default, the number is four, which is not useful for text-based packets.

After the flags is the match string (Linux), followed by a filter expression using the same filter language as `tcpdump`.

How it works...

The ngrep application also sets the promiscuous flag, allowing it to sniff all the visible packets, whether they relate to the host or not.

The previous example displayed all of the HTTP traffic. If the host system is on a wireless network or wired via a hub (instead of a switch), it will display all of the web traffic caused by all the active users.

There's more...

The -x option in ngrep displays a hex dump as well as a printable form. Combining this with -X allows you to search for a binary string (perhaps a virus signature or some known pattern).

This example watches for a binary stream from an HTTPS connection:

```
# ngrep -xX '1703030034' port 443
interface: eth0 (192.168.1.0/255.255.255.0)
filter: ( port 443 ) and (ip or ip6)
match: 0x1703030034
#########################################
T 172.217.6.1:443 -> 192.168.1.44:40698 [AP]
  17 03 03 00 34 00 00 00    00 00 00 00 07 dd b0 02    ....4...........
  f5 38 07 e8 24 08 eb 92    3c c6 66 2f 07 94 8b 25    .8..$...<.f/...%
  37 b3 1c 8d f4 f0 64 c3    99 9e b3 45 44 14 64 23    7.....d....ED.d#
  80 85 1b a1 81 a3 d2 7a    cd                         .......z.
```

The hash marks indicate the packets that were scanned; they do not include the target pattern. There are many more options to ngrep; read the man page for the complete list.

Tracing network routes with ip

The ip utility reports information about the state of your network. It can tell you how many packets are being sent and received, what types of packets are being sent, how the packets are being routed, and more.

Getting ready

The `netstat` utility described in Chapter 8, *The Old-Boy Network* is standard in all Linux distributions; however, it is now being replaced by more efficient utilities, such as `ip`. These new utilities are included in the `iproute2` package, which is already installed on most modern distributions.

How to do it...

The `ip` utility has many features. This recipe will discuss a few that are useful for tracing network behavior.

Reporting routes with ip route

When packets don't reach their destination (`ping` or `traceroute` fail), the first thing an experienced user checks is the cables. The next thing to check is the routing tables. If a system lacks a default gateway (`0.0.0.0`), it will only find machines on its physical network. If you have multiple networks running on the same wires, you'll need to add routes to allow machines attached to one network to send packets to another.

The `ip route` command reports known routes:

```
$ ip route
10.8.0.2 dev tun0  proto kernel  scope link  src 10.8.0.1
192.168.87.0/24 dev vmnet1  proto kernel  scope link  src 192.168.87.1
192.168.1.0/24 dev eth0  proto kernel  scope link  src 192.168.1.44
default via 192.168.1.1 dev eth0  proto static
```

The `ip route` report is space-delimited. After the first element, it consists of a set of keys and values.

The first line in the preceding code describes the `10.8.0.2` address as a tunnel device that uses a kernel protocol, and this address is only valid on this tunnel device. The second line describes the `192.168.87.x` network used to communicate with virtual machines. The third line is the primary network of this system, which is connected to `/dev/eth0`. The last line defines the default route, which routes to `192.168.1.1` through `eth0`.

The keys reported by `ip route` include the following:

- `via`: This refers to the address of the next hop.
- `proto`: This is the protocol identifier of the route. The kernel protocol is a route installed by the kernel, while static routes are defined by an administrator.
- `scope`: This refers to the scope where the address is valid. A link scope is only valid on this device.
- `dev`: This is the device associated with the address.

Tracing recent IP connections and the ARP table

The `ip neighbor` command reports known relationships between the IP address, device, and hardware MAC address. It reports whether the relationship was reestablished recently or has gone stale:

```
$> ip neighbor
192.168.1.1 dev eth0 lladdr 2c:30:33:c9:af:3e STALE
192.168.1.4 dev eth0 lladdr 00:0a:e6:11:c7:dd STALE
172.16.183.138 dev vmnet8 lladdr 00:50:56:20:3d:6c STALE

192.168.1.2 dev eth0 lladdr 6c:f0:49:cd:45:ff REACHABLE
```

The output of the `ip neighbor` command shows that there has been no recent activity between either this system and the default gateway, or this system and the host at `192.168.1.4`. It also shows that there has been no recent activity in the virtual machines and the host at `192.168.1.2` is connected recently.

The current status of `REACHABLE` in the preceding output means that the `arp` table is up to date and the host thinks it knows the MAC address of the remote system. The value of `STALE` here does not indicate that the system is unreachable; it merely means the values in the `arp` table have expired. When your system tries to use one of these routes, it sends an ARP request first to verify the MAC address associated with the IP address.

The relationship between the MAC address and the IP address should only change when the hardware is changed or devices are reassigned.

If devices on a network show intermittent connectivity, it may mean that two devices have been assigned the same IP address. It could also be possible that two DHCP servers are running or someone has manually assigned an address that's already in use.

In the case of two devices with the same IP address, the reported MAC address for a given IP address will change in intervals, and the `ip neighbor` command will help track down the misconfigured device.

Tracing a route

The `traceroute` command discussed in Chapter 8, *The Old-Boy Network* traces a packet's entire path from the current host to its destination. The `route get` command reports the next hop from the current machine:

```
$ ip route get 172.16.183.138
172.16.183.138 dev vmnet8 src 172.16.183.1
cache mtu 1500 hoplimit 64
```

The preceding return shows that the route to the virtual machine is through the vmnet8 interface located at `172.16.183.1`. The packets sent to this site will be split if they are larger than 1,500 bytes and discarded after 64 hops:

```
$ in route get 148.59.87.90
148.59.87.90 via 192.168.1.1 dev eth0 src 192.168.1.3
cache mtu 1500 hoplimit 64
```

To reach an address on the Internet, a packet needs to leave the local network via the default gateway, and the link to this gateway is the host's eth0 device at `192.168.1.3`.

How it works...

The `ip` command runs in the user space and interfaces in the kernel tables. Using this command, a normal user can examine the network configuration whereas a superuser can configure the network.

Tracing system calls with strace

A GNU/Linux computer may have hundreds of tasks running at a time, but it will possess only one Network Interface, one disk drive, one keyboard, and so on. The Linux kernel allocates these limited resources and controls how tasks access them. This prevents two tasks from accidently intermingling data in a disk file, for example.

When you run an application, it uses a combination of **User-Space libraries** (functions such as `printf` and `fopen`) and System-Space Libraries (functions such as `write` and `open`). When your program calls `printf` (or a script invokes the `echo` command), it invokes a user-space library call to `printf` to format the output string; this is followed by a system-space call to the `write` function. The system call makes sure only one task can access a resource at a time.

In a perfect world, all computer programs would run with no problems. In an almost perfect world, you'd have the source code, the program would be compiled with debugging support, and it would fail consistently.

In the real world, you sometimes have to cope with programs where you don't have the source, and it fails intermittently. Developers can't help you unless you give them some data to work with.

The Linux `strace` command reports the system calls that an application makes; this can help us understand what it's doing even if we don't have the source code.

Getting ready

The `strace` command is installed as part of the Developer package; it can be installed separately as well:

```
$ sudo apt-get install strace
$ sudo yum install strace
```

How to do it...

One way to understand `strace` is to write a short C program and use `strace` to see what system calls it makes.

This test program allocates memory, uses the memory, prints a short message, frees the memory, and exits.

The `strace` output shows the system functions this program calls:

```
$ cat test.c
#include <stdio.h>
#include <stdlib.h>
#include <string.h>
```

```
main () {
  char *tmp;
  tmp=malloc(100);
  strcat(tmp, "testing");
  printf("TMP: %s\n", tmp);
  free(tmp);
  exit(0);
}
$ gcc test.c
$ strace ./a.out
execve("./a.out", ["./a.out"], [/* 51 vars */]) = 0
brk(0)                                    = 0x9fc000
mmap(NULL, 4096, PROT_READ|PROT_WRITE, MAP_PRIVATE|MAP_ANONYMOUS, -1, 0) =
0x7fc85c7f5000
access("/etc/ld.so.preload", R_OK)        = -1 ENOENT (No such file or
directory)
open("/etc/ld.so.cache", O_RDONLY)        = 3
fstat(3, {st_mode=S_IFREG|0644, st_size=95195, ...}) = 0
mmap(NULL, 95195, PROT_READ, MAP_PRIVATE, 3, 0) = 0x7fc85c7dd000
close(3)                                  = 0
open("/lib64/libc.so.6", O_RDONLY)        = 3
read(3,
"\177ELF\2\1\1\3\0\0\0\0\0\0\0\0\0\3\0>\0\1\0\0\0000\356\1\16;\0\0\0"...,
832) = 832
fstat(3, {st_mode=S_IFREG|0755, st_size=1928936, ...}) = 0
mmap(0x3b0e000000, 3750184, PROT_READ|PROT_EXEC, MAP_PRIVATE|MAP_DENYWRITE,
3, 0) = 0x3b0e000000
mprotect(0x3b0e18a000, 2097152, PROT_NONE) = 0
mmap(0x3b0e38a000, 24576, PROT_READ|PROT_WRITE,
MAP_PRIVATE|MAP_FIXED|MAP_DENYWRITE, 3, 0x18a000) = 0x3b0e38a000
mmap(0x3b0e390000, 14632, PROT_READ|PROT_WRITE,
MAP_PRIVATE|MAP_FIXED|MAP_ANONYMOUS, -1, 0) = 0x3b0e390000
close(3)                                  = 0
mmap(NULL, 4096, PROT_READ|PROT_WRITE, MAP_PRIVATE|MAP_ANONYMOUS, -1, 0) =
0x7fc85c7dc000
mmap(NULL, 4096, PROT_READ|PROT_WRITE, MAP_PRIVATE|MAP_ANONYMOUS, -1, 0) =
0x7fc85c7db000
mmap(NULL, 4096, PROT_READ|PROT_WRITE, MAP_PRIVATE|MAP_ANONYMOUS, -1, 0) =
0x7fc85c7da000
arch_prctl(ARCH_SET_FS, 0x7fc85c7db700) = 0
mprotect(0x3b0e38a000, 16384, PROT_READ) = 0
mprotect(0x3b0de1f000, 4096, PROT_READ) = 0
munmap(0x7fc85c7dd000, 95195)             = 0
brk(0)                                    = 0x9fc000
brk(0xa1d000)                             = 0xa1d000
fstat(1, {st_mode=S_IFCHR|0620, st_rdev=makedev(136, 11), ...}) = 0
mmap(NULL, 4096, PROT_READ|PROT_WRITE, MAP_PRIVATE|MAP_ANONYMOUS, -1, 0) =
0x7fc85c7f4000
```

```
write(1, "TMP: testing\n", 13)          = 13
exit_group(0)                            = ?
+++ exited with 0 +++
```

How it works...

The first lines are standard start up commands for any application. The execve call is the system call to initialize a new executable. The brk call returns the current memory address, and the mmap call allocates 4,096 bytes of memory for dynamic libraries and other applications that load housekeeping.

The attempt to access ld.so.preload fails because ld.so.preload is a hook to preload the libraries. It is not required on most production systems.

The ld.so.cache file is the memory-resident copy of /etc/ld.so,conf.d, which contains the paths for loading dynamic libraries. These values are kept in memory to reduce the overhead in starting programs.

The next lines with mmap, mprotect, arch_prctl, and munmap calls continue to load the libraries and mapping devices to memory.

The two calls to brk are invoked by the program's malloc call. This allocates 100 bytes from the heap.

The strcat call is a user-space function that doesn't generate any system calls.

The printf call doesn't generate a system call to format the data, but it makes calls to send the formatted string to stdout.

The fstat and mmap calls load and initialize the stdout device. These calls occur only once in a program that generates output to stdout.

The write system call sends the string to stdout.

Finally, the exit_group call exits the program, frees resources, and terminates all the threads associated with the executable.

Note that there is no `brk` call associated with freeing memory. The `malloc` and `free` functions are user-space functions that manage a task's memory. They only invoke the `brk` function if the program's overall memory footprint changes. When your program allocates *N* bites, it needs to add that many bytes to its available memory. When it frees that block, the memory is marked available, but it remains a part of this program's memory pool. The next `malloc` uses memory from the pool of available memory space until it's exhausted. At this point, another `brk` call adds more memory to the program's memory pool.

Tracing dynamic library functions with ltrace

Knowing the user-space library functions being called is as useful as knowing the system functions being invoked. The `ltrace` command provides a similar function to `strace`; however, it tracks user-space library calls instead of system calls.

Getting ready

Have the `ltrace` command installed using the Developer tools.

How to do it...

To trace user-space dynamic library calls, invoke the `strace` command, followed by the command you want to trace:

```
$ ltrace myApplication
```

The next example is a program with a subroutine:

```
$ cat test.c
#include <stdio.h>
#include <stdlib.h>
#include <string.h>

int print (char *str) {
  printf("%s\n", str);
}
main () {
  char *tmp;
  tmp=malloc(100);
  strcat(tmp, "testing");
  print(tmp);
  free(tmp);
```

```
    exit(0);
}
$ gcc test.c
$ ltrace ./a.out
(0, 0, 603904, -1, 0x1f25bc2)                                        = 0x3b0de21160
__libc_start_main(0x4005fe, 1, 0x7ffd334a95f8, 0x400660, 0x400650
<unfinished ...>
malloc(100)                                                          = 0x137b010
strcat("", "testing")                                               = "testing"
puts("testing")                                                     = 8
free(0x137b010)                                                     = <void>
exit(0 <unfinished ...>
+++ exited (status 0) +++
```

In the ltrace output, we see the call to the dynamically linked strcat; however, we do not see the statically linked local function, namely print. The call to printf was simplified to a call to puts. The calls to malloc and free are shown since they are user-space function calls.

How it works...

The ltrace and strace utilities use the ptrace function to rewrite the **Procedure Linkage Table (PLT)** which maps between dynamic library calls and the actual memory address of the called function. This means that ltrace can trap any dynamically linked function call but not a statically linked function.

There's more...

The ltrace and strace commands are useful, but it would be really nice to trace both user-space and system-space function calls. The -S option to ltrace will do this. The next example shows the ltrace -S output from the previous executable:

```
$> ltrace -S ./a.out
SYS_brk(NULL)                                                       = 0xa9f000
SYS_mmap(0, 4096, 3, 34, 0xffffffff)                               = 0x7fcdce4ce000
SYS_access(0x3b0dc1d380, 4, 0x3b0dc00158, 0, 0)                    = -2
SYS_open("/etc/ld.so.cache", 0, 01)                               = 4
SYS_fstat(4, 0x7ffd70342bc0, 0x7ffd70342bc0, 0, 0xfefefefefefefeff) = 0
SYS_mmap(0, 95195, 1, 2, 4)                                        = 0x7fcdce4b6000
SYS_close(4)                                                       = 0
SYS_open("/lib64/libc.so.6", 0, 00)                               = 4
SYS_read(4, "\177ELF\002\001\001\003", 832)                       = 832
SYS_fstat(4, 0x7ffd70342c20, 0x7ffd70342c20, 4, 0x7fcdce4ce640) = 0
```

```
SYS_mmap(0x3b0e000000, 0x393928, 5, 2050, 4)                    = 0x3b0e000000
SYS_mprotect(0x3b0e18a000, 0x200000, 0, 1, 4)                   = 0
SYS_mmap(0x3b0e38a000, 24576, 3, 2066, 4)                       = 0x3b0e38a000
SYS_mmap(0x3b0e390000, 14632, 3, 50, 0xffffffff)               = 0x3b0e390000
SYS_close(4)                                                    = 0
SYS_mmap(0, 4096, 3, 34, 0xffffffff)                            = 0x7fcdce4b5000
SYS_mmap(0, 4096, 3, 34, 0xffffffff)                            = 0x7fcdce4b4000
SYS_mmap(0, 4096, 3, 34, 0xffffffff)                            = 0x7fcdce4b3000
SYS_arch_prctl(4098, 0x7fcdce4b4700, 0x7fcdce4b3000, 34, 0xffffffff) = 0
SYS_mprotect(0x3b0e38a000, 16384, 1, 0x3b0de20fd8, 0x1f25bc2) = 0
SYS_mprotect(0x3b0de1f000, 4096, 1, 0x4003e0, 0x1f25bc2) = 0
(0, 0, 987392, -1, 0x1f25bc2)                                   = 0x3b0de21160
SYS_munmap(0x7fcdce4b6000, 95195)                               = 0
__libc_start_main(0x4005fe, 1, 0x7ffd703435c8, 0x400660, 0x400650
<unfinished ...>
malloc(100 <unfinished ...>
SYS_brk(NULL)                                                   = 0xa9f000
SYS_brk(0xac0000)                                               = 0xac0000
<... malloc resumed> )                                          = 0xa9f010
strcat("", "testing")                                           = "testing"
puts("testing" <unfinished ...>
SYS_fstat(1, 0x7ffd70343370, 0x7ffd70343370, 0x7ffd70343230, 0x3b0e38f040)
= 0
SYS_mmap(0, 4096, 3, 34, 0xffffffff)                            = 0x7fcdce4cd000
SYS_write(1, "testing\n", 8)                                    = 8
<... puts resumed> )                                            = 8
free(0xa9f010)                                                  = <void>
exit(0 <unfinished ...>
SYS_exit_group(0 <no return ...>
+++ exited (status 0) +++
```

This shows the same type of startup call (sbrk, mmap, and so on) as the strace example.

When a user-space function invokes a system-space function (as with the malloc and puts calls), the display shows that the user-space function was interrupted (malloc(100 <unfinished...>) and then resumed (<... malloc resumed>) after the system call was completed.

Note that the malloc call needed to pass control to sbrk to allocate more memory for the application. However, the free call does not shrink the application; it just frees the memory for future use by this application.

12

Tuning a Linux System

In this chapter, we will cover the following recipes:

- Identifying services
- Gathering socket data with `ss`
- Gathering system I/O usage with `dstat`
- Identifying a resource hog with `pidstat`
- Tuning the Linux kernel with `sysctl`
- Tuning a Linux system with config files
- Changing scheduler priority using the `nice` command

Introduction

No system runs as fast as we need it to run, and any computer's performance can be improved.

We can improve the performance of a system by turning off unused services, by tuning the kernel parameters, or by adding new hardware.

The first step in tuning a system is understanding what the demands are and whether they are being met. Different types of applications have different critical needs. The questions to ask yourself include the following:

- Is the CPU the critical resource for this system? A system doing engineering simulations requires CPU cycles more than other resources.
- Is network bandwidth critical for this system? A file server does little computation, but can saturate its network capacity.

- Is disk access speed critical for this system? A file server or database server will put more demand on the disks than a calculation engine does.
- Is RAM the critical resource for this system? All systems need RAM, but a database server commonly builds large in-memory tables to perform queries, and file servers are more efficient with larger RAM for disk caches.
- Has your system been hacked? A system can suddenly become unresponsive because it's running unexpected malware. This is not common on Linux machines, but a system with many users (like a college or business network) is vulnerable to a brute-force password attack.

The next question to ask is: How do I measure usage? Knowing how a system is being used will lead you to the questions, but may not lead you to the answer. A fileserver will cache commonly accessed files in the memory, so one with too little memory may be disk/RAM limited rather than network limited.

Linux has tools for analyzing a system. Many have been discussed in `Chapter 8`, *The Old-Boy Network*, `Chapter 9`, *Put on The Monitor's Cap*, and `Chapter 11`, *Tracing The Clues*. This chapter will introduce more monitoring tools.

Here is a list of subsystems and tools to examine them. Many (but not all) of these tools have been discussed in this book.

- CPU: `top`, `dstat`, `perf`, `ps`, `mpstat`, `strace`, `ltrace`
- Network: `netstat`, `ss`, `iotop`, `ip`, `iptraf`, `nicstat`, `ethtool`, `lsof`
- Disk: `ftrace`, `iostat`, `dstat`, `blktrace`
- RAM: `top`, `dstat`, `perf`, `vmstat`, `swapon`

Many of these tools are part of a standard Linux distribution. The others can be loaded with your package manager.

Identifying services

A Linux system can run hundreds of tasks at a time. Most of these are part of the operating system environment, but you might discover you're running a daemon or two you don't need.

Linux distributions support one of the three utilities that start daemons and services. The traditional `SysV` system uses scripts in `/etc/init.d`. The newer `systemd` daemon uses the same `/etc/init.d` scripts and also uses a `systemctl` call. Some distributions use Upstart, which stores configuration scripts in `/etc/init`.

The SysV init system is being phased out in favor of the systemd suite. The upstart utility was developed and used by Ubuntu, but discarded in favor of systemd with the 14.04 release. This chapter will focus on systemd, since that's the system used by most distributions.

Getting ready

The first step is to determine whether your system is using the SysV init calls, systemd, or upstart.

Linux/Unix systems must have an initialization process running as PID 1. This process executes a fork and exec to start every other process. The ps command may tell you which initialization process is running:

```
$ ps -p 1 -o cmd
/lib/system/systemd
```

In the previous example, the system is definitely running systemd. However, on some distributions, the SysV init program is sym-linked to the actual init process, and ps will always show /sbin/init, whether it's SysV init, upstart, or systemd that's actually being used:

```
$ ps -p 1 -o cmd
/sbin/init
```

The ps and grep commands give more clues:

```
$ ps -eaf | grep upstart
```

Alternatively, they can be used like this:

```
ps -eaf | grep systemd
```

If either of these commands return tasks such as upstart-udev-bridge or systemd/systemd, the system is running upstart or systemd, respectively. If there are no matches, then your system is probably running the SysV init utility.

How to do it...

The service command is supported on most distributions. The -status-all option will report the current status of all services defined in /etc/init.d.

The output format varies between distributions:

```
$> service -status-all
```

Debian:

```
[ + ]   acpid
[ - ]   alsa-utils
[ - ]   anacron
[ + ]   atd
[ + ]   avahi-daemon
[ - ]   bootlogs
[ - ]   bootmisc.sh
. . .
```

CentOS:

```
abrt-ccpp hook is installed
abrtd (pid  4009) is running...
abrt-dump-oops is stopped
acpid (pid  3674) is running...
atd (pid  4056) is running...
auditd (pid  3029) is running...
. . .
```

The `grep` command will reduce the output to only running tasks:

Debian:

```
$ service -status-all | grep +
```

CentOS:

```
$ service -status-all | grep running
```

You should disable any unnecessary services. This reduces the load on the system and improves the system security.

Services to check for include the following:

- `smbd`, nmbd: These are the Samba daemons used to share resources between Linux and Windows systems.
- `telnet`: This is the old, insecure login program. Unless there is an overwhelming need for this, use SSH.
- `ftp`: This is the old, insecure File Transfer Protocol. Use SSH and scp instead.
- `rlogin`: This is remote login. SSH is more secure.

- `rexec`: This is remote exec. SSH is more secure.
- `automount`: If you are not using NFS or Samba you probably don't need this.
- `named`: This daemon provides **Domain Name Service (DNS)**. It's only necessary if the system is defining the local names and IP addresses. You don't need it to resolve names and access the net.
- `lpd`: The **Line Printer Daemon** lets other systems use this system's printer. If this is not a print server, you don't need this service.
- `nfsd`: This is the **Network File System** daemon. It lets remote machines mount this computer's disk partitions. If this is not a file server, you probably don't need this service.
- `portmap`: This is part of the NFS support. If the system is not using NFS, you don't need this.
- `mysql`: The **mysql** application is a database server. It may be used by your webserver.
- `httpd`: This is the HTTP daemon. It sometimes gets installed as part of a **Server System** set of packages.

There are several potential ways to disable an unnecessary service depending on whether your system is Redhat or Debian derived, and whether it's running `systemd`, SysV, or Upstart. All of these commands must be run with root privileges.

systemd-based computers

The `systemctl` command enables and disables services. The syntax is as follows:

```
systemctl enable SERVICENAME
```

Alternatively, it can also be as follows:

```
systemctl disable SERVICENAME
```

To disable an FTP server, use the following command:

```
# systemctl disable ftp
```

RedHat-based computers

The `chkconfig` utility provides a frontend for working with SysV style initialization scripts in `/etc/rc#.d`. The `-del` option disables a service, while the `-add` option enables a service. Note that an initialization file must already exist to add a service.

The syntax is as follows:

```
# chkconfig -del SERVICENAME
# chkconfig -add SERVICENAME
```

To disable the HTTPD daemon, use the following command:

```
# chkconfig -del httpd
```

Debian-based computers

Debian-based systems provide the `update-rc.d` utility to control SysV style initialization scripts. The `update-rc.d` command supports `enable` and `disable` as subcommands:

To disable the telnet daemon, use the following command:

```
# update-rc.d disable telnetd
```

There's more

These techniques will find services that have been started at root with the SysV or systemd initialization scripts. However, services may be started manually, or in a boot script, or with `xinetd`.

The `xinetd` daemon functions in a similar way to init: it starts services. Unlike init, the `xinitd` daemon only starts a service when it's requested. For services such as SSH, which are required infrequently and run for a long time once started, this reduces the system load. Services such as `httpd` that perform small actions (serve a web page) frequently are more efficient to start once and keep running.

The configuration file for **xinet** is `/etc/xinetd.conf`. The individual service files are commonly stored in `/etc/xinetd.d`.

The individual service files resemble this:

```
# cat /etc/xinetd.d/talk
# description: The talk server accepts talk requests for chatting \
# with users on other systems.
service talk
{
 flags      = IPv4
 disable    = no
 socket_type = dgram
 wait     = yes
```

```
user    = nobody
group   = tty
server  = /usr/sbin/in.talkd
}
```

A service can be enabled or disabled by changing the value of the `disable` field. If `disable` is `no`, the service is enabled. If disable is `yes`, the service is disabled.

After editing a service file, you must restart `xinetd`:

```
# cd /etc/init.d
# ./inetd restart
```

Gathering socket data with ss

The daemons started by `init` and `xinetd` may not be the only services running on a system. Daemons can be started by commands in an `init` local file (`/etc/rc.d/rc.local`), a `crontab` entry, or even by a user with privileges.

The `ss` command returns socket statistics, including services using sockets, and current socket status.

Getting ready

The `ss` utility is included in the `iproute2` package that is already installed on most modern distributions.

How to do it...

The `ss` command displays more information than the `netstat` command. These recipes will introduce a few of its features.

Displaying the status of tcp sockets

A tcp socket connection is opened for every HTTP access, every SSH session, and so on. The -t option reports the status of TCP connections:

```
$ ss -t
ESTAB       0       0    192.168.1.44:740       192.168.1.2:nfs
ESTAB       0       0    192.168.1.44:35484     192.168.1.4:ssh

CLOSE-WAIT  0       0    192.168.1.44:47135      23.217.139.9:http
```

This example shows an NFS server connected at IP address 192.168.1.2 and an SSH connection to 192.168.1.4.

The CLOSE-WAIT socket status means that the FIN signal has been sent, but the socket has not been fully closed. A socket can remain in this state forever (or until you reboot). Terminating the process that owns the socket may free the socket, but that's not guaranteed.

Tracing applications listening on ports

A service on your system will open a socket in the listen mode to accept network connections from a remote site. The SSHD application does this to listen for SSH connections, http servers do this to accept HTTP requests, and so on.

If your system has been hacked, it might have a new application listening for instructions from its master.

The -l option to ss will list sockets that are open in the listen mode. The -u option specifies to report UDP sockets. A -t option reports TCP sockets.

This command shows a subset of the listening UDP sockets on a Linux workstation:

```
$ ss -ul
State         Recv-Q  Send-Q   Local Address:Port     Peer
Address:Port
UNCONN        0       0        *:sunrpc               *:*
UNCONN        0       0        *:ipp                  *:*
UNCONN        0       0        *:ntp                  *:*
UNCONN        0       0        127.0.0.1:766          *:*
UNCONN        0       0        *:898                  *:*
```

This output shows that this system will accept **Remote Procedure Calls (sunrpc)**. This port is used by the `portmap` program. The `portmap` program controls access to the RPC services and is used by the `nfs` client and server.

The `ipp` and `ntp` ports are used for **Internet Printing Protocol** and **Network Time Protocol**. Both are useful tools, but may not be required on a given system.

Ports `766` and `898` are not listed in `/etc/services`. The `-I` option of the `lsof` command will display the task that has a port open. You may need to have root access to view this:

```
# lsof -I :898
```

Or:

```
# lsof -n -I :898
COMMAND   PID USER     FD    TYPE DEVICE SIZE/OFF NODE NAME
rpcbind 3267 rpc      7u    IPv4 16584       0t0  UDP *:898
rpcbind 3267 rpc     10u    IPv6 16589       0t0  UDP *:898
```

This command shows that the tasks listening on port `898` are part of the RPC system, not a hacker.

How it works

The `ss` command uses system calls to extract information from the internal kernel tables. The known services and ports on your system are defined in `/etc/services`.

Gathering system I/O usage with dstat

Knowing what services are running may not tell you which services are slowing down your system. The top command (discussed in Chapter 9, *Put on the Monitor's Cap*) will tell you about CPU usage and how much time is spent waiting for IO, but it might not tell you enough to track down a task that's overloading the system.

Tracking I/O and context switches can help trace a problem to its source.

The `dstat` utility can point you to a potential bottleneck.

Getting ready

The **dstat** application is not commonly installed. It will need to be installed with your package manager. It requires Python 2.2, which is installed by default on modern Linux systems:

```
# apt-get install dstat
# yum install dstat
```

How to do it...

The dstat application displays disk, network, memory usage, and running task information at regular intervals. The default output gives you an overview of the system activity. By default, this report is updated every second on a new line, allowing easy comparison with previous values.

The default output lets you track overall system activity. The application supports more options to track top resource users.

Viewing system activity

Invoking dstat with no arguments will show CPU activity, disk I/O, network I/O, paging, interrupts, and context switches at one second intervals.

The following example shows the default `dstat` output:

```
$ dstat
----total-cpu-usage---- -dsk/total- -net/total- ---paging-- ---system--
usr sys idl wai hiq siq| read  writ| recv  send|  in   out | int   csw
  1   2  97   0   0   0|5457B   55k|   0     0 |   0     0 |1702  3177
  1   2  97   0   0   0|   0     0 |  15k 2580B|   0     0 |2166  4830
  1   2  96   0   0   0|   0    36k|1970B 1015B|   0     0 |2122  4794
```

You can ignore the first line. Those values are the initial contents of the tables dstat mines. The subsequent lines show the activity during a time slice.

In this sample, the CPU is mostly idle, and there is little disk activity. The system is generating network traffic, but only a few packets a second.

There is no paging on this system. Linux only pages out memory to disk when the main memory is exhausted. Paging lets a system run more applications than it could run without paging, but disk access is thousands of times slower than memory access, so a computer will slow to a crawl if it needs to page.

If your system sees consistent paging activity, it needs more RAM or fewer applications.

A database application can cause intermittent paging when queries that require building large in-memory arrays are evaluated. It may be possible to rewrite these queries using the IN operation instead of a JOIN to reduce the memory requirement. (This is a more advanced SQL than what is covered in this book.)

Context switches (csw) happen with every system call (refer to the strace and ltrace discussion in `Chapter 11`, *Tracing the Clues*) and when a timeslice expires and another application is given access to the CPU. A system call happens whenever I/O is performed or a program resizes itself.

If the system is performing tens of thousands of context switches per second, it's a symptom of a potential problem.

How it works

The `dstat` utility is a Python script that collects and analyzes data from the `/proc` filesystem described in `Chapter 10`, *Administration Calls*.

There's more...

The `dstat` utility can identify the top resource user in a category:

- **-top-bio Disk Usage**: This reports the process performing the most block I/O
- **-top-cpu CPU Usage**: This reports the process using the most CPU resources
- **-top-io I/O usage**: This reports the process performing the most I/O (usually network I/O)
- **-top-latency System Load**: This shows the process with the highest latency
- **-top-mem Memory Usage**: This shows the process using the most memory

The following example displays the CPU and Network usage and the top users in each category:

```
$ dstat -c -top-cpu -n -top-io
----total-cpu-usage---- -most-expensive- -net/total- ----most-expensive----
usr sys idl wai hiq siq|  cpu process   | recv  send|    i/o process
  1   2  97   0   0   0|vmware-vmx   1.0|   0     0 |bash          26k    2B
  2   1  97   0   0   0|vmware-vmx   1.7| 18k 3346B|xterm        235B 1064B
  2   2  97   0   0   0|vmware-vmx   1.9|700B 1015B|firefox       82B   32k
```

On a system running an active virtual machine, the VM uses the most CPU time, but not the bulk of the IO. The CPU is spending most of its time in the idle state.

The -c and -n options specify showing the CPU usage and Network usage, respectively.

Identifying a resource hog with pidstat

The -top-io and -top-cpu flags will identify a top resource user, but might not provide enough information to identify the problem if there are multiple instances of a resource hog.

The pidstat program will report per-process statistics, which can be sorted to provide more insight.

Getting ready

The pidstat application may not be installed by default. It can be installed with this command:

```
# apt-get install sysstat
```

How to do it...

The pidstat application has several options for generating different reports:

- -d: This reports IO statistics
- -r: This reports page faults and memory utilization
- -u: This reports CPU utilization
- -w: This reports task switches

Report Context Switch activity:

```
$ pidstat -w | head -5
Linux 2.6.32-642.11.1.el6.x86_64 (rtdaserver.cflynt.com)
02/15/2017  _x86_64_  (12 CPU)

11:18:35 AM      PID    cswch/s  nvcswch/s  Command
11:18:35 AM        1       0.00       0.00  init
11:18:35 AM        2       0.00       0.00  kthreadd
```

The pidstat application sorts its report by the PID number. The data can be re-organized with the sort utility. The following command displays the five applications that generate the most context switches per second (*Field 4* in the -w output):

```
$ pidstat -w | sort -nr -k 4 | head -5
11:13:55 AM     13054      351.49      9.12  vmware-vmx
11:13:55 AM      5763       37.57      1.10  vmware-vmx
11:13:55 AM      3157       27.79      0.00  kondemand/0
11:13:55 AM      3167       21.18      0.00  kondemand/10
11:13:55 AM      3158       21.17      0.00  kondemand/1
```

How it works

The pidstat application queries the kernel to get task information. The sort and head utilities reduce the data to pinpoint the program hogging a resource.

Tuning the Linux kernel with sysctl

The Linux kernel has about 1,000 tunable parameters. These default to reasonable values for common usage, which means they are not perfect for anyone.

Getting started

The sysctl command is available on all Linux systems. You must be root to modify kernel parameters.

The sysctl command will change the parameter value immediately, but the value will revert to the original value upon reboot unless you add a line to define the parameter to /etc/sysctl.conf.

It's a good policy to change a value manually and test it before modifying `sysctl.conf`. You can make a system unbootable by applying bad values to `/etc/sysctl.conf`.

How to do it...

The `sysctl` command supports several options:

- `-a`: This reports all available parameters
- `-p FILENAME`: This reads values from `FILENAME`. By default from `/etc/sysctl.conf`
- `PARAM`: This reports the current value of `PARAM`
- `PARAM=NEWVAL`: This sets the value of `PARAM`

Tuning the task scheduler

The task scheduler is optimized for a desktop environment, where a fast response to a user is more important than overall efficiency. Increasing the time a task stays resident improves the performance of server systems. The following example examines the value of `kernel.sched_migration_cost_ns`:

```
$ sysctl.kernel.shed_migration_cost_ns
kernel.sched_migration_cost_ns = 500000
```

The `kernel_sched_migration_cost_ns` (and `kernel.sched_migration_cost` in older kernels) controls how long a task will remain active before being exchanged for another task. On systems with many tasks or many threads, this can result in too much overhead being used for context switching. The default value of `500000` ns is too small for systems running Postgres or Apache servers. It's recommended that you change the value to 5 ms:

```
# sysctl kernel.sched_migration_cost_ns=5000000
```

On some systems (postgres servers in particular), unsetting the `sched_autogroup_enabled` parameter improves performance.

Tuning a network

The default values for network buffers may be too small on a system performing many network operations (NFS client, NFS server, and so on).

Examine the values for maximum read buffer memory:

```
$ sysctl net.core.rmem_max
net.core.rmem_max = 124928
```

Increase values for network servers:

```
# sysctl net.core.rmem_max=16777216
# sysctl net.core.wmem_max=16777216
# sysctl net.ipv4.tcp_rmem="4096 87380 16777216"
# sysctl net.ipv4.tcp_wmem="4096 65536 16777216"
# sysctl net.ipv4.tcp_max_syn_backlog=4096
```

How it works

The `sysctl` command lets you directly access kernel parameters. By default, most distributions optimize these parameters for a normal workstation.

If your system has lots of memory, you can improve performance by increasing the amount of memory devoted to buffers. If it's short on memory, you may want to shrink these. If the system is a server, you may want to keep tasks resident longer than you would for a single-user workstation.

There's more...

The `/proc` filesystem is available on all Linux distributions. It includes a folder for every running task and folders for all the major kernel subsystems. The files within these folders can be viewed and updated with `cat`.

The parameters supported by sysctl are commonly supported by the `/proc` filesystem as well.

Thus, `net.core.rmem_max` can also be accessed as `/proc/sys/net/core/rmem_max`.

Tuning a Linux system with config files

The Linux system includes several files to define how disks are mounted, and so on. Some parameters can be set in these files instead of using /proc or sysctl.

Getting ready

There are several files in /etc that control how a system is configured. These can be edited with a standard text editor such as vi or emacs. The changes may not take effect until the system is rebooted.

How to do it...

The /etc/fstab file defines how disks are to be mounted and what options are supported.

The Linux system records when a file is created, modified, and read. There is little value in knowing that a file has been read, and updating the Acessed timestamp every time a common utility like cat is accessed gets expensive.

The noatime and relatime mount options will reduce disk thrashing:

```
$ cat /dev/fstab
/dev/mapper/vg_example_root   /     ext4 defaults,noatime  1 1
/dev/mapper/gb_example_spool /var ext4 defaults,relatime 1 1
```

How it works

The preceding example mounts the / partition (which includes /bin and /usr/bin) with the usual default options, plus the noatime parameter to disable updating the disk every time a file is accessed. The /var partition (which includes the mail spool folder) has the realtime option set, which will update time at least once every day, but not every time a file is accessed.

Changing scheduler priority using the nice command

Every task on a Linux system has a priority. The priority values range from -20 to 19. The lower the priority (**-20**), the more CPU time a task will be allocated. The default priority is **0**.

Not all tasks need the same priority. An interactive application needs to respond quickly or it becomes difficult to use. A background task run via `crontab` only needs to finish before it is scheduled to run again.

The `nice` command will modify a task's priority. It can be used to invoke a task with modified priority. Raising a task's priority value will free resources for other tasks.

How to do it...

Invoking the `nice` command with no arguments will report a task's current priority:

```
$ cat nicetest.sh
echo "my nice is `nice`"
$ sh nicetest.sh
my nice is 0
```

Invoking the `nice` command followed by another command name will run the second command with a *niceness* of 10–it will add 10 to the task's default priority:

```
$ nice sh nicetest.sh
my nice is 10
```

Invoking the `nice` command with a value before the command will run the command with a defined *niceness*:

```
$ nice -15 sh nicetest.sh
my nice is 15
```

Only a superuser can give a task a higher priority (lower priority number), by assigning a negative niceness value:

```
# nice -adjustment=-15 nicetest.sh
my nice is -15
```

How it works

The `nice` command modifies the kernel's scheduling table to run a task with a greater or lesser priority. The lower the priority value, the more time the scheduler will give to this task.

There's more

The `renice` command modifies the priority of a running task. Tasks that use a lot of resources, but are not time-critical, can be made *nicer* with this command. The `top` command is useful to find tasks that are utilizing the CPU the most.

The `renice` command is invoked with a new priority value and the program ID (PID):

```
$ renice 10 12345
12345: old priority 0, new priority 10
```

13

Containers, Virtual Machines, and the Cloud

In this chapter, we will cover the following topics:

- Using Linux Containers
- Using Docker
- Using Virtual Machines in Linux
- Linux in the cloud

Introduction

Modern Linux applications can be deployed on dedicated hardware, containers, Virtual Machines (VMs), or the cloud. Each solution has strengths and weaknesses, and each of them can be configured and maintained with scripts as well as GUIs.

A container is ideal if you want to deploy many copies of a single application where each instance needs its own copy of data. For example, containers work well with database-driven web servers where each server needs the same web infrastructure but has private data.

However, the downside of a container is that it relies on the host system's kernel. You can run multiple Linux distributions on a Linux host, but you can't run Windows in a container.

Using a VM is your best bet if you need a complete environment that is not the same for all instances. With VMs, you can run Windows and Linux on a single host. This is ideal for validation testing when you don't want a dozen boxes in your office but need to test against different distributions and operating systems.

The downside of VMs is that they are huge. Each VM implements an entire computer-operating system, device drivers, all the applications and utilities, and so on. Each Linux VM needs at least one core and 1 GB RAM. A Windows VM may need two cores and 4 GB RAM. If you wish to run multiple VMs simultaneously, you need enough RAM to support each one of the VMs; otherwise, the host will start swapping and performance will suffer.

The cloud is like having many computers and lots of bandwidth at your fingertips. You may actually be running on a VM or container in the cloud, or you might have your own dedicated system.

The biggest advantage of the cloud is that it can scale. If you think your application might go viral or your usage is cyclic, the ability to scale up and down quickly without needing to buy or lease new hardware new connectivity is necessary. For example, if your system processes college registrations, it will be overworked for about two weeks, twice a year, and almost dormant for the rest of the time. You may need a dozen sets of hardware for those two weeks, but you don't want to have them sitting idle for the rest of the year.

The downside of the cloud is that it's not something you can see. All of the maintenance and configuration has to be done remotely.

Using Linux containers

Linux Container (lxc) packages provide the basic container functionality used by Docker and LXD container deployment systems.

A Linux container uses kernel level support for **Control Groups (cgroups)** and the `systemd` tools described in `Chapter 12`, *Tuning a Linux System*. The cgroups support provides tools to control the resources available to a group of programs. This informs kernel control about the resources that are available to the processes running in a container. A container may have limited access to devices, network connectivity, memory, and so on. This control keeps the containers from interfering with each other or potentially damaging the host system.

Getting ready

Container support is not provided in stock distributions. You'll need to install it separately. The level of support across distributions is inconsistent. The **lxc** container system was developed by Canonical, so Ubuntu distributions have complete container support. Debian 9 (Stretch) is better than Debian 8 (Jessie) in this regard.

Fedora has limited support for lxc containers. It is easy to create privileged containers and a bridged Ethernet connection, but as of Fedora 25, the cgmanager service required for unprivileged containers is unavailable.

SuSE supports limited use of lxc. SuSE's libvirt-lxc package is similar but not identical to lxc. SuSE's libvirt-lxc package is not covered in this chapter. A privileged container with no Ethernet is easy to create under SuSE, but it does not support unprivileged containers and bridged Ethernet.

Here's how to install lxc support on major distributions.

For Ubuntu, use the following code:

```
# apt-get install lxc1
```

Next we have Debian. Debian distributions may only include the security repositories in /etc/apt/sources.list. If so, you'll need to add deb http://ftp.us.debian.org/debian stretch main contrib to /etc/apt/sources.list and then perform apt-get update before, loading the lxc package:

```
# apt-get install lxc
```

For OpenSuSE, use the following code:

```
# zypper install lxc
RedHat, Fedora:
```

For Red Hat/Fedora-based systems, add the following Epel repository:

```
# yum install epel-release
```

Once you've done this, install the following packages before you install lxc support:

```
# yum install perl libvirt debootstrap
```

The `libvirt` package provides networking support, and `debootstrap` is required to run Debian-based containers:

```
# yum install lxc lxc-templates tunctl bridge-utils
```

How to do it...

The `lxc` package adds several commands to your system. These include:

- `lxc-create`: This is to create an lxc container
- `lxc-ls`: This is a list of the available containers
- `lxc-start`: This is to start a container
- `lxc-stop`: This is to stop a container
- `lxc-attach`: This is to connect to the root shell of a container
- `lxc-console`: This is to connect to a login session in a container

On Red Hat-based systems, you may need to disable SELinux while testing. On OpenSuSE systems, you may need to disable **AppArmor**. You'll need to reboot after disabling AppArmor via `yast2`.

Linux containers come in two basic flavors: privileged and unprivileged. Privileged containers are created by the root and the underlying system has root privileges. An unprivileged container is created by a user and only has user privileges.

Privileged containers are easier to create and more widely supported since they don't require `uid` and `gid` mapping, device permissions, and so on. However, if a user or application manages to escape from the container, they'll have full privileges on the host.

Creating a privileged container is a good way to confirm that all the required packages are installed on your system. After you create a privileged container, use unprivileged containers for your applications.

Creating a privileged container

The easiest way to get started with Linux containers is to download a prebuilt distribution in a privileged container. The `lxc-create` command creates a base container structure and can populate it with a predefined Linux distribution.

The syntax of the `lxc-create` command is as follows:

```
lxc-create -n NAME -t TYPE
```

The `-n` option defines a name for this container. This name will be used to identify this container when it is started, stopped, or reconfigured.

The `-t` option defines the template to be used to create this container. The type `download` connects your system to a repository of prebuilt containers and prompts you for the container to download.

This is an easy way to experiment with other distributions or create an application that needs a distribution other than the host's Linux distribution:

```
$ sudo lxc-create -t download -n ContainerName
```

The download template retrieves a list of the available predefined containers from the Internet and populates the container from the network archive. The create command provides a list of the available containers and then prompts for the **Distribution**, **Release**, and Architecture. You can only run a container if your hardware supports this Architecture. You cannot run an Arm container if your system has an Intel CPU, but you can run a 32-bit i386 container on a system with a 64-bit Intel CPU:

```
$ sudo lxc-create -t download -n ubuntuContainer
...
ubuntu   zesty    armhf    default 20170225_03:49
ubuntu   zesty    i386     default 20170225_03:49
ubuntu   zesty    powerpc  default 20170225_03:49
ubuntu   zesty    ppc64el  default 20170225_03:49
ubuntu   zesty    s390x    default 20170225_03:49
---

Distribution: ubuntu
Release: trusty
Architecture: i386

Downloading the image index
Downloading the rootfs
Downloading the metadata
The image cache is now ready
Unpacking the rootfs

---

You just created an Ubuntu container (release=trusty, arch=i386,
variant=default)
To enable sshd, run: apt-get install openssh-server
For security reason, container images ship without user accounts and
```

```
without a root password.
Use lxc-attach or chroot directly into the rootfs to set a root password or
create user accounts.
```

You can create a container based on your current distribution by selecting a template that matches the current installation. The templates are defined in `/usr/share/lxc/templates`:

```
# ls /usr/share/lxc/templates
lxc-busybox    lxc-debian    lxc-download ...
```

To create a container for your current distribution, select the appropriate template and run the `lxc-create` command. The download process and installation takes several minutes. The following example skips most of the installation and configuration messages:

```
$ cat /etc/issue
Debian GNU/Linux 8
$ sudo lxc-create -t debian -n debianContainer
debootstrap is /usr/sbin/debootstrap
Checking cache download in /var/cache/lxc/debian/rootfs-jessie-i386 ...
Downloading debian minimal ...
I: Retrieving Release
I: Retrieving Release.gpg
I: Checking Release signature
I: Valid Release signature (key id
75DDC3C4A499F1A18CB5F3C8CBF8D6FD518E17E1)
...
I: Retrieving Packages
I: Validating Packages
I: Checking component main on http://http.debian.net/debian...
I: Retrieving acl 2.2.52-2
I: Validating acl 2.2.52-2
I: Retrieving libacl1 2.2.52-2
I: Validating libacl1 2.2.52-2

I: Configuring libc-bin...
I: Configuring systemd...
I: Base system installed successfully.
Current default time zone: 'America/New_York'
Local time is now:      Sun Feb 26 11:38:38 EST 2017.
Universal Time is now:  Sun Feb 26 16:38:38 UTC 2017.

Root password is 'W+IkcKkk', please change !
```

The preceding command populates the new container from the repositories defined in your package manager. Before you can use a container, you must start it.

Starting a container

The `lxc-start` command starts a container. As with other lxc commands, you must provide the name of the container to start:

```
# lxc-start -n ubuntuContainer
```

The boot sequence may hang and you may see errors similar to the following one. These are caused by the container's boot sequence trying to perform graphics operations, such as displaying a splash screen without graphics support in the client:

```
<4>init: plymouth-upstart-bridge main process (5) terminated with
status 1
...
```

You can wait for these errors to time out and ignore them, or you can disable the splash screen. Disabling the splash screen varies between distributions and releases. The files may be in /etc/init, but that's not guaranteed.

There are two ways to work within a container:

- `lxc-attach`: This attaches directly to a root account on a running container
- `lxc-console`: This opens a console for a login session on a running container

The first use of a container is to attach directly to create user accounts:

```
# lxc-attach -n containerName
root@containerName:/#
root@containerName:/# useradd -d /home/USERNAME -m  USERNAME
root@containerName:/# passwd USERNAME
Enter new UNIX password:
Retype new UNIX password:
```

After you've created a user account, log in as an unprivileged user or root with the `lxc-console` application:

```
$ lxc-console -n containerName
Connected to tty 1
Type <Ctrl+a q> to exit the console,
<Ctrl+a Ctrl+a> to enter Ctrl+a itself
Login:
```

Stopping a container

The `lxc-stop` command stops a container:

```
# lxc-stop -n containerName
```

Listing known containers

The `lxc-ls` command lists the container names that are available for the current user. This does not list all the containers in a system, only those that the current user owns:

```
$ lxc-ls
container1Name container2Name...
```

Displaying container information

The `lxc-info` command displays information about a container:

```
$ lxc-info -n containerName
Name:    testContainer
State:    STOPPED
```

This command will only display information about a single container, though. Using a shell loop, as described in `Chapter` 1, *Shell Something Out*, we can display information about all the containers:

```
$ for c in `lxc-ls`
do
lxc-info -n $c
echo
done
Name:   name1
State:  STOPPED

Name:   name2
State:  RUNNING
PID:   1234
IP   10.0.3.225
CPU use:   4.48 seconds
BlkIO use:   728.00 KiB
Memory use:   15.07 MiB
KMem use:   2.40 MiB
Link:   vethMU5I00
 TX bytes:   20.48 KiB
 RX bytes:   30.01 KiB
```

```
Total bytes:   50.49 KiB
```

If the container is stopped, there is no status information available. Running containers record their CPU, memory, disk (block), I/O, and network usage. This tool lets you monitor your containers to see which ones are most active.

Creating an unprivileged container

Unprivileged containers are recommended for normal use. There is potential for a badly configured container or badly configured application to allow control to escape from the container. Since containers invoke system calls in the host kernel, if the container is running as the root, the system calls will also run as the root. However, unprivileged containers run with normal user privileges and are thus safer.

To create unprivileged containers, the host must support Linux Control Groups and uid mapping. This support is included in basic Ubuntu distributions, but it needs to be added to other distributions. The cgmanager package is not available in all distributions. You cannot start an unprivileged container without this package:

```
# apt-get install cgmanager uidmap systemd-services
```

Start cgmanager:

```
$ sudo service cgmanager start
```

Debian systems may require that clone support be enabled. If you receive a chown error when creating a container, these lines will fix it:

```
# echo 1 > /sys/fs/cgroup/cpuset/cgroup.clone_children
# echo 1 > /proc/sys/kernel/unprivileged_userns_clone
```

The username of an account that's allowed to create containers must be included in the etc mapping tables:

```
$ sudo usermod --add-subuids 100000-165536 $USER
$ sudo usermod --add-subgids 100000-165536 $USER
$ sudo chmod +x $HOME
```

These commands add the user to the User ID and Group ID mapping tables (/etc/subuid and /etc/subgid) and assign UIDs from 100000 -> 165536 to the user.

Next, set up the configuration file for your containers:

```
$ mkdir ~/.config/lxc
$ cp /etc/lxc/default.conf ~/.config/lxc
```

Add the following lines to `~/.config/lxc/default.conf`:

```
lxc.id_map = u 0 100000 65536
lxc.id_map = g 0 100000 65536
```

If the containers support network access, add a line to `/etc/lxc/lxc-usernet` to define the users who will have access to the network bridge:

```
USERNAME veth BRIDGENAME COUNT
```

Here, `USERNAME` is the name of the user who owns the container. `veth` is the usual name for the virtual Ethernet device. `BRIDGENAME` is the name that's displayed by `ifconfig`. It is usually either `br0` or `lxcbro`. `COUNT` is the number of simultaneous connections that will be allowed:

```
$ cat /etc/lxc/lxc-usernet
clif veth lxcbr0 10
```

Creating an Ethernet bridge

A container cannot access your Ethernet adapter directly. It requires a bridge between the Virtual Ethernet and the actual Ethernet. Recent Ubuntu distributions create an Ethernet bridge automatically when you install the lxc package. Debian and Fedora may require that you manually create the bridge. To create a bridge on Fedora, use the `libvirt` package to create a virtual bridge first:

```
# systemctl start libvirtd
```

Then, edit `/etc/lxc/default.conf` to reference `virbr0` instead of `lxcbr0`:

```
lxc.network_link = virbr0
```

If you've already created a container, edit the config file for that container as well.

To create a bridge on Debian systems, you must edit the network configuration and the container configuration files.

Edit `/etc/lxc/default.conf`. Comment out the default empty network and add a definition for the lxc bridge:

```
# lxc.network.type = empty
lxc.network.type = veth
lxc.network.link = lxcbr0
lxc.network.flage = up`
```

Next, create the networking bridge:

```
# systemctl enable lxc-net
# systemctl start lxc-net
```

Containers created after these steps are performed will have networking enabled. Network support can be added to the existing containers by adding the lxc.network lines to the container's config file.

How it works...

The container created by the lxc-create command is a directory tree that includes the configuration options and root filesystem for the container. Privileged containers are constructed under /var/lib/lxc. Nonprivileged containers are stored under $HOME/.local/lxc:

```
$ ls /var/lib/lxc/CONTAINERNAME
config rootfs
```

You can examine or modify a container's configuration by editing the config file in the container's top directory:

```
# vim /var/lib/lxc/CONTAINERNAME/config
```

The rootfs folder contains a root filesystem for the container. This is the root (/) folder of a running container:

```
# ls /var/lib/lxc/CONTAINERNAME/rootfs
bin    boot cdrom dev   etc   home lib    media mnt   proc
root   run  sbin  sys   tmp   usr  var
```

You can populate a container by adding, deleting, or modifying files in the rootfs folder. For instance, to run web services, a container might have basic web services installed via the package manager and the actual data of each service installed by copying files to the rootfs.

Using Docker

The lxc containers are complex and can be difficult to work with. These issues led to the Docker package. Docker uses the same underlying Linux functionalities of namespaces and cgroups to create lightweight containers.

Docker is only officially supported on 64-bit systems, making `lxc` the better choice for legacy systems.

The major difference between a Docker container and an lxc container is that a Docker container commonly runs one process, while an lxc container runs many. To deploy a database-backed web server, you need at least two Docker containers–one for the web server and one for the database server–but only one lxc container.

The Docker philosophy makes it easy to construct systems from smaller building blocks, but it can make it harder to develop blocks since so many Linux utilities are expected to run inside a full Linux system with `crontab` entries to carry out operations such as cleanup, log rotation, and so on.

Once a Docker container is created, it will run exactly as expected on other Docker servers. This makes it very easy to deploy Docker containers on cloud clusters or remote sites.

Getting ready

Docker is not installed with most distributions. It is distributed via Docker's repositories. Using these requires adding new repositories to your package manager with new checksums.

Docker has instructions for each distribution and different releases on their main page, which is available at `http://docs.docker.com`.

How to do it...

When Docker is first installed, it is not running. You must start the server with a command such as the following:

```
# service docker start
```

The Docker command has many subcommands that provide functionality. These commands will find a Docker container and download and run it. Here's a bit about the subcommands:

- `# docker search`: This searches Docker archives for containers with names that match a key
- `# docker pull`: This pulls the named container to your system
- `# docker run`: This runs an application in a container
- `# docker ps`: This lists the running Docker containers

- # `docker attach`: This attaches to a running container
- # `docker stop`: This stops a container
- # `docker rm`: This removes a container

The default Docker installation requires that the `docker` command be run either as a `root` or using `sudo`.

Each of these commands have a `man` page. This page is named by combining the command and subcommand with a dash. To view the `docker search` man page, use `man docker-search`.

The next recipe demonstrates how to download a Docker container and run it.

Finding a container

The `docker search` command returns a list of Docker containers that match a search term:

```
docker search TERM
```

Here TERM is an alphanumeric string (no wild cards). The search command will return up to 25 containers that include the string in their name:

```
# docker search apache
NAME                 DESCRIPTION                 STARS OFFICIAL   AUTOMATED
eboraas/apache       Apache (with SSL support)   70                  [OK]
bitnami/apache       Bitnami Apache Docker       25                  [OK]
apache/nutch         Apache Nutch                12                  [OK]
apache/marmotta      Apache Marmotta             4                   [OK]
lephare/apache       Apache container            3                   [OK]
```

Here STARS represent a rating for the container. The containers are ordered with the highest rating first.

Downloading a container

The `docker pull` command downloads a container from the Docker registry. By default, it pulls data from Docker's public registry at `registry-1.docker.io`. The downloaded container is added to your system. The containers are commonly stored under `/var/lib/docker`:

```
# docker pull lephare/apache
latest: Pulling from lephare/apache
425e28bb756f: Pull complete
```

```
ce4a2c3907b1: Extracting [======================>  ] 2.522 MB/2.522 MB
40e152766c6c: Downloading [==================>     ] 2.333 MB/5.416 MB
db2f8d577dce: Download complete
Digest:
sha256:e11a0f7e53b34584f6a714cc4dfa383cbd6aef1f542bacf69f5fccefa0108ff8
Status: Image is up to date for lephare/apache:latest
```

Starting a Docker container

The `docker run` command starts a process in a container. Commonly, the process is a `bash` shell that allows you to attach to the container and start other processes. This command returns a hash value that defines this session.

When a Docker container starts, a network connection is created for it automatically.

The syntax for the run command is as follows:

```
docker run [OPTIONS] CONTAINER COMMAND
```

The `docker run` command supports many options, including:

- `-t`: Allocate a pseudo tty (by default, false)
- `-i`: Keep an interactive session open while unattached
- `-d`: Start the container detached (running in the background)
- `--name`: The name to assign to this instance

This example starts the bash shell in the container that was previously pulled:

```
# docker run -t -i -d --name leph1 lephare/apache  /bin/bash
1d862d7552bcaadf5311c96d439378617d85593843131ad499...
```

Listing the Docker sessions

The `docker ps` command lists the currently running Docker sessions:

```
# docker ps
CONTAINER ID    IMAGE           COMMAND    CREATED   STATUS   PORTS    NAMES
123456abc       lephare/apache  /bin/bash  10:05     up       80/tcp   leph1
```

The `-a` option will list all the Docker containers on your system, whether they are running or not.

Attaching your display to a running Docker container

The `docker attach` command attaches your display to the `tty` session in a running container. You need to run as the root within this container.

To exit an attached session, type `^P^Q`.

This example creates an HTML page and starts the Apache web server in the container:

```
$ docker attach leph1
root@131aaaeeac79:/# cd /var/www
root@131aaaeeac79:/var/www# mkdir symfony
root@131aaaeeac79:/var/www# mkdir symfony/web
root@131aaaeeac79:/var/www# cd  symfony/web
root@131aaaeeac79:/var/www/symfony/web# echo "<html><body><h1>It's
Alive</h1></body></html>"
    >index.html
root@131aaaeeac79:/# cd /etc/init.d
root@131aaaeeac79:/etc/init.d# ./apache2 start
[....] Starting web server: apache2/usr/sbin/apache2ctl: 87: ulimit: error
setting limit (Operation
    not permitted)
Setting ulimit failed. See README.Debian for more information.
AH00558: apache2: Could not reliably determine the server's fully qualified
domain name, using
    172.17.0.5. Set the 'ServerName' directive globally to suppress this
message
. ok
```

Browsing to `172.17.0.5` will show the `It's Alive` page.

Stopping a Docker session

The `docker stop` command terminates a running Docker session:

```
# docker stop leph1
```

Removing a Docker instance

The `docker rm` command removes a container. The container must be stopped before removing it. A container can be removed either by name or identifier:

```
# docker rm leph1
```

Alternatively, you can use this:

```
# docker rm 131aaaeeac79
```

How it works

The Docker containers use the same `namespace` and `cgroup` kernel support as that of the `lxc` containers. Initially, Docker was a layer over `lxc`, but it has since evolved into a unique system.

The main configuration files for the server are stored at `/var/lib/docker` and `/etc/docker`.

Using Virtual Machines in Linux

There are four options for using VMs in Linux. The three open source options are KVM, XEN, and VirtualBox. Commercially, VMware supplies a virtual engine that can be hosted in Linux and an executive that can run VMs.

VMware has been supporting VMs longer than anyone else. They support Unix, Linux, Mac OS X, and Windows as hosts and Unix, Linux, and Windows as guest systems. For commercial use, VMware Player or VMWare Workstation are the two best choices you have.

KVM and VirtualBox are the two most popular VM engines for Linux. KVM delivers better performance, but it requires a CPU that supports virtualization (Intel VT-x). Most modern Intel and AMD CPUs support these features. VirtualBox has the advantage of being ported to Windows and Mac OS X, allowing you to move a virtual machine to another platform easily. VirtualBox does not require VT-x support, making it suitable for legacy systems as well as modern systems.

Getting ready

VirtualBox is supported by most distributions, but it may not be part of these distributions' default package repositories.

To install VirtualBox on Debian 9, you need to add the virtualbox.org repository to the sites that apt-get will accept packages from:

```
# vi /etc/apt/sources.list
## ADD:
deb http://download.virtualbox.org/virtualbox/debian stretch contrib
```

The `curl` package is required to install the proper keys. If this is not already present, install it before adding the key and updating the repository information:

```
# apt-get install curl
# curl -O https://www.virtualbox.org/download/oracle_vbox_2016.asc
# apt-key add oracle_vbox_2016.asc
# apt-get update
```

Once the repository is updated, you can install VirtualBox with `apt-get`:

```
# apt-get install virtualbox-5.1

OpenSuSE
# zypper install gcc make kernel-devel
Open yast2, select Software Management, search for virtualbox.
Select virtualbox, virtualbox-host-kmp-default, and virtualbox-qt.
```

How to do it...

When VirtualBox is installed, it creates an item in the start menu. It may be under System or Applications/System Tools. The GUI can be started from a terminal session as `virtualbox` or as `VirtualBox`.

The VirtualBox GUI makes it easy to create and run VMs. The GUI has a button named New in the upper-left corner; this is used to create a new, empty VM. The wizard prompts you for information such as memory and disk limits for the new VM.

Once the VM is created, the Start button is activated. The default settings connect the virtual machine's CD-ROM to the host's CD-ROM. You can put an installation disk in the CD-ROM and click on Start to install the operating system on a new VM.

Linux in the cloud

There are two primary reasons to use a cloud server. Service providers use a commercial cloud service, such as Amazon's AWS, because it lets them easily ramp up their resources when demand is higher and ramp down their costs when demand is lower. Cloud storage providers, such as Google Docs, allow users to access their data from any device and share data with others.

The OwnCloud package transforms your Linux server into a private cloud storage system. You can use an OwnCloud server as a private corporate file sharing system to share files with friends or as a remote backup for your phone or tablet.

The OwnCloud project forked in 2016. The NextCloud server and applications are expected to use the same protocol as that of OwnCloud and to be interchangeable.

Getting ready

Running the OwnCloud package requires a **LAMP (Linux, Apache, MySQL, PHP)** installation. These packages are supported by all Linux distributions, though they may not be installed by default. Administering and installing MySQL is discussed in Chapter 10, *Administration Calls*.

Most distributions do not include the OwnCloud server in their repositories. Instead, the OwnCloud project maintains repositories to support the distributions. You'll need to attach OwnCloud to your RPM or apt repository before you download.

Ubuntu 16.10

The following steps will install the LAMP stack on a Ubuntu 16.10 system. Similar commands will work for any Debian-based system. Unfortunately, package names sometimes vary between releases:

```
apt-get install apache2
apt-get install mysql-server php-mysql
```

OwnCloud requires security beyond default settings. The mysql_secure_installation script will configure MySQL properly:

```
/usr/bin/mysql_secure_installation
```

Configure the `OwnCloud` repository:

```
curl \ https://download.owncloud.org/download/repositories/stable/ \
Ubuntu_16.10/Release.key/'| sudo tee \
/etc/apt/sources.list.d/owncloud.list

apt-get update
```

Once the repository is in place, apt will install and start the server:

```
apt-get install owncloud
```

OpenSuSE Tumbleweed

Install the **LAMP** stack with **Yast2**. Open `yast2`, select **Software Management**, and install `apache2`, `mysql`, and `owncloud-client`.

Next, select the `System` tab, and from this tab, select the `Services Manager` tab. Confirm that the `mysql` and `apache2` services are enabled and active.

These steps install the OwnCloud client that will let you synchronize your workspace to an OwnCloud server and the system requirements for a server.

OwnCloud requires security beyond default settings. The `mysql_secure_installation` script will configure MySQL properly:

```
/usr/bin/mysql_secure_installation
```

The following commands will install and start the OwnCloud server. The first three commands configure `zypper` to include the OwnCloud repository. Once these repositories are added, the Owncloud package is installed like any other package:

```
rpm --import
https://download.owncloud.org/download/repositories/stable/openSUSE_Leap_42
.2/repodata/repomd.xml.key

zypper addrepo
http://download.owncloud.org/download/repositories/stable/openSUSE_Leap_42.
2/ce:stable.repo

zypper refresh

zypper install owncloud
```

How to do it...

Once OwnCloud is installed, you can configure an admin account, and from there, add user accounts. The NextCloud Android app will communicate with the OwnCloud server as well as the NextCloud server.

Configuring OwnCloud

Once `owncloud` is installed, you can configure it by browsing to your local address:

```
$ konqueror http://127.0.0.1/owncloud
```

The initial screen will prompt you for an admin username and password. You can log in as the user to create backups and copy files between phones, tablets, and computers.

There's more...

The bare installation process we just discussed is suitable for testing. OwnCloud and NextCloud will use HTTPS sessions if HTTPS support is available. Enabling HTTPS support requires an X.509 security certificate.

You can purchase a security certificate from one of the dozens of commercial providers, self-sign a certificate for your own use, or create a free certificate with **Let's Encrypt** (http://letsencrypt.org).

A self-signed certificate is adequate for testing, but most browsers and phone apps will flag this as an untrusted site. Let's Encrypt is a service of the Internet Security Research Group (ISRG). The certificates they generate are fully registered and all applications can accept them.

The first step in acquiring a certificate is verifying that your site is what you claim it is. Let's Encrypt certificates are validated using a system called Automated Certificate Management Environment (ACME). The ACME system creates a hidden file on your web server, tells the **Certificate Authority** (**CA**) where that file is, and the CA confirms that the expected file is there. This proves that you have access to the web server and that DNS records point to the proper hardware.

If you are using a common web server, such as Nginx or Apache, the simplest way to set up your certificates is with the `certbot` created by EFF:

```
# wget https://dl.eff.org/certbot-auto
# chmod a+x certbot-auto
# ./certbot-auto
```

This robot will add new packages and install your new certificate in the proper place.

If you are using a less common server or have a non-standard installation, the `getssl` package is more configurable. The `getssl` package is a bash script that reads two configuration files to automate the creation of the certificate. Download the package from here and unzip from `https://github.com/srvrco/getssl`.

Unzipping `getssl.zip` creates a folder named `getssl_master`.

Generating and installing the certificates requires three steps:

1. Create the default configuration files with `getssl -c DOMAIN.com`.
2. Edit the configuration files.
3. Create the certificates.

Start by `cd-ing` to the `getssl_master` folder and creating the configuration files:

```
# cd getssl_master
# getssl -c DOMAIN.com
```

Replace `DOMAIN` with the name of your domain.

This step creates the `$HOME/.getssl` and `$HOME/.getssl/DOMAIN.com` folders and creates a file named `getssl.cfg` in both of these. Each of these files must be edited.

Edit `~/.getssl/getssl.cfg` and add your email address:

```
ACCOUNT_EMAIL='myName@mySite.com'
```

The default values in the rest of the fields are suitable for most sites.

Next, edit `~/.getssl/DOMAIN.com/getssl.cfg`. There are several fields to modify in this file.

The main change is to set the Acme Challenge Location (ACL) field. The ACME protocol will try to find a file in `http://www.DOMAIN.com/.well-known/acme-challenge`. The ACL value is the physical location of that folder on your system. You must create the `.well-known` and `.well-known/acme-challenge` folders and set ownership if they don't exist.

If your web pages are kept in `/var/web/DOMAIN`, you could create new folders as follows:

```
# mkdir /var/web/DOMAIN/.well-known
# mkdir /var/web/DOMAIN/.well-known/acme-challenge
# chown webUser.webGroup /var/web/DOMAIN/.well-known
# chown webUser.webGroup /var/web/DOMAIN/.well-known/acme-challenge
```

The ACL lines would resemble the following:

```
ACL="/var/web/DOMAIN/.well-known/acme-challenge"
USE_SINGLE_ACL="true"
```

You must also define where the certificates are to be placed. This location must match the configuration option in your web server. For instance, if certificates are kept in `/var/web/certs`, the definitions will resemble this:

```
DOMAIN_CERT_LOCATION="/var/web/certs/DOMAIN.crt"
DOMAIN_KEY_LOCATION="/var/web/certs/DOMAIN.key"
CA_CERT_LOCATION="/var/web/certs/DOMAIN.com.bundle"
```

You must set the type of test that the ACME protocol will use. These are commented out at the bottom of the configuration file. Using the default values are usually best:

```
SERVER_TYPE="https"
CHECK_REMOTE="true"
```

After these edits are complete, test them by running this:

```
./getssl DOMAIN.com
```

This command resembles the first one, but it does not include the `-c` (create) option. You can repeat this command until you've corrected any errors and are happy with the results.

The default behavior of the `getssl` script is to generate a test certificate that's not really valid. This is done because Let's Encrypt limits the number of actual certificates it will generate for a site to avoid abuse.

Once the configuration files are correct, edit them again and change the server–from the Staging server to the actual Let's Encrypt server:

```
CA="https://acme-v01.api.letsencrypt.org"
```

Then, rerun the `getssl` script one last time with the `-f` option to force it to rebuild and replace the previous files:

```
./getssl -f DOMAIN.com
```

You may need to restart your web server or reboot your system before the new files are recognized.

Index

CPSIA information can be obtained
at www.ICGtesting.com
Printed in the USA
LVOW04s1915050717
540360LV00005B/428/P

9 781785 881985